# Hard Coal and Coal Cars

# Hard Coal and Coal Cars

## Hauling Anthracite on the New York, Ontario & Western Railway

by

## Martin Robert Karig III

SCRANTON: UNIVERSITY OF SCRANTON PRESS

**Library of Congress Cataloging-in-Publication Data**

Karig, Martin Robert, III, 1946-
    Hard Coal and Coal Cars: Hauling Anthracite on the New York, Ontario &
Western Railway / Martin Robert Karig, III.
     p. cm.
    Includes bibliographical references and index.
    ISBN 1-58966-120-6
    1. Railroads—United States—Freight-cars. 2. New York, Ontario, and
Western Railway Co. I. Title.

TF479.K37 2005
385.3′4—dc22                                      2005055970

Distribution:

University of Scranton Press
Chicago Distribution Center
11030 S. Langley
Chicago, IL 60628

Printed in China
by Sun Fung Offset Binding Co., Ltd.

*for Grandpa*

**New York, Ontario & Western Railway Train #1 heads north out of North Bergen on December 25, 1940, with Engineer Henry P. Kortright at the throttle of Class Y-2 #453.** *[O&WRHS Archives]*

ABOUT THE COVER:
The cover is an original water color done by famed railroad artist Carl A. Ohlson based upon this black and white photograph taken at the Waddell Coal Company breaker in the late 1930's. The picture shows a blend of O&W steel hopper cars loaded with various sizes of anthracite. In the foreground, P-Class consolidation #202 labors, just as it has since it was first introduced into service in 1900. In 1947, it will be one of the last of these reliable workhorses retired by the railroad. [*Thomas B. Walsh, III Collection*]

# Table of Contents

This book began as a pamphlet about the steel hopper cars of the New York, Ontario & Western Railway, but it's long since become more than that. The first problem that I encountered was finding a logical stopping point. I thought that that would be an easy task, but I quickly discovered that there was no logical stopping point until I got all the way back to 1880 and the O&W's first wooden coal cars. As I was researching those cars, I began to wonder what choices were available to the O&W, how it stacked up against other railroads, and why it made the choices it did. Thus, this became more than a book about hoppers or coal cars; it became a book about the world in which they operated, too.

In 1902, C.A. Seley, one of the most noted car designers of the period remarked that the "money represented in freight car equipment of the average railroad is probably close to three times the amount invested in freight locomotives." At one point in the O&W's history, coal cars outnumbered locomotives by over 30 to 1, and yet there's nary a mention of its coal cars while there are all sorts of books and magazine articles devoted to its locomotives. We know every rivet on every locomotive, and yet we can barely tell one coal car from another. This book attempts to remedy that.

I was amazed when I learned how little we actually know about the O&W's bread and butter fleet. After all, it was the coal car that made the O&W its money. All those locomotives did was haul these valuable cash cows to market. Then I was more amazed, and a little disappointed, at how little the industry knows about hopper cars in general. It seemed that every author of every book I read assumed some level of knowledge on the part of the reader or dismissed significant details or was just plain ignorant of them. I often suspected the last. Except for comprehensive books like John White's *The American Railroad Freight Car*, most are little more than picture books with very little attention paid to detail. In order to present a true history of the O&W's coal cars, I needed to go back and examine the history of coal cars in general. I've included that history in this volume so that you too can appreciate the choices that were available to the O&W at the time it was making them.

Just as I needed to understand the history of coal cars to understand the O&W's actions, I needed to understand the business conditions in which it was operating. Consequently, I spent some time learning about the anthracite industry in the United States and the O&W's role in it, and I've included that history in this book, also. While it's certainly not a comprehensive examination of those topics — that will have to wait for my next book — I think that there's enough information for you to understand the context in which the O&W was operating and making its decisions.

Unfortunately, most modern sources evaluate the history of railroading through the polished lens of hindsight. In most cases, I've gone back to the original sources, and what I found was an entirely different picture of events of the time. Although it didn't start out that way, this book became an examination of the decisions made by the railroad based upon contemporary accounts. I was not surprised that some of these historical accounts did not agree, so I spent quite a bit of time trying to sort those accounts out. What I'm presenting to you is, what I believe to be, the true account of those histories. It is almost certain that you will find accounts that differ from what I'm presenting to you. Therefore, I've been careful to document and footnote these facts to provide you the opportunity to go back and evaluate them for yourself.

My goal is that you learn something new on every page of this book. No, actually, it's more than that. I'd like you to say, "Wow, I didn't know that!" at least once on every page of this book. Now, I confess that you're going to find some redundancy in these pages, but I hope you'll forgive that transgression. One of the most annoying things for me in reading a book is having to flip back and forth between pages trying to find a related fact. Therefore, I've tried to group all the facts bearing on a particular topic together, even if that sometimes means saying something more than once.

This book is not intended to be a book that you read once and put back on the shelf. It's intended to be a book that's a constant reference, not only about the O&W's coal cars but about coal cars and anthracite operations in general. I've carefully documented each of the facts in the book with references, so that you can go back and check my facts or read more on each subject. I've tried to make this the best book ever written on coal cars.

I need to take a moment to talk with you about the figures in this book. My research has taken me into some musty archives from which I was able to retrieve some wonderful old drawings and engravings. Unfortunately, time is not always the best friend of these works of art, and some, through the effects of age or multiple reproductions, are not as clear as they once were. Now, to the purist, these images should never be tampered with. However, my goal in this book is to present information to the reader, and therefore I've spent a great deal of effort cleaning and restoring these old prints. My goal in each case was to make these old images clearly legible for the reader while at the same time trying to preserve the original character of some of these original prints and engravings. I apologize if I've offended any sensibilities in doing so.

Before I finish, I want to share some conclusions that I've drawn in the course of my research. We've all heard that the O&W should never have been built. "The line that began nowhere, went nowhere, and stopped nowhere in between." "The line built at right angles to the mountains." "The railroad that should never have been built." "The railroad built on a shoestring." If you've ever read anything about the O&W, you've heard these disparaging remarks and more. In fact, you can read an article to this effect on the front page of the *Middletown Times Herald* in Chapter 2. During my research, I came to a different conclusion—while all of these assertions have some basis in fact, they are grossly unfair.

In fact, the O&W was a railroad that not only should have been built, it needed to be built. Yes, it was built at right angles to the mountains, but if you want to go from Cornwall to Oswego via Middletown, Cadosia, and the other cities in between, you're pretty much constrained to doing that. In terms of shoddy construction, what I've found is that the Midland and then the O&W followed the prevailing practice of the day, and that is to get the line up and running as quickly and cheaply as possible, and then improve the line using surplus revenue. It's wrong to say that the O&W should never have been built. That would be like saying that the D&H Canal, which had about the same life span, should never have been built. Each served a valuable role during its lifetime but ulti-

mately fell prey to progress. The O&W provided an important link for the citizens of New York who would otherwise have had to wait for the development of motor cars and highways to reach the outside world.

To say that it bypassed some cities with which it should have been connected, and connected with others simply because they were willing to issue bonds to support the construction of the railroad, seems somewhat arrogant to me. The fact is that without those cities' assistance, the railroad would never have been built, and there would be no story to tell. The fact is that the fate of the O&W would have been the same even if the O&W had connected to Syracuse or Buffalo or any of a number of other cities often cited by the "should-haves."

The O&W was a regional railroad, and that's what its managers chose it to be. Who could have predicted the advent of the automobile and airplane when the Midland was built? After all, the introduction of railroads connecting cities and regions was a revolution beyond the imagination of most people of that period. To be able to travel across the county and even the state in less than a day was unimaginable to most 19th century Americans. Most people in the United States never ventured outside of a twenty mile radius of their birthplaces during their entire lives. It was only the Civil War that caused many Americans to travel beyond their birthplaces to see what lay beyond their homes. It was only with the introduction of steam power, first with the steam boat and then with the steam railroad, that people began traveling in a way any different than the Romans had traveled 2000 years earlier. In other words, the railroads were breaking a tradition of millennia as they were being built. Who could have considered that their importance in connecting the towns and villages of America would have been so short-lived?

The O&W was a railroad that should have been built. For a brief moment in history, it was a vital link from Oswego to New York and Scranton to Cadosia, and at least four generations of New Yorkers and Pennsylvanians can trace their prosperity to that railroad. Who would have denied them that opportunity?

This book would not have been written without the enthusiastic support of Walter Kierzkowski, whose vast photographic collection convinced me that a book about O&W coal cars was within the art of the doable. I also owe a debt to Allan F. Seebach,

Jr., who has kept the spirit of the O&W alive in words and deeds, and to Ron Stanulevich who encouraged me to step back a few more years to include the O&W's woodies in this book so that it truly was a history of the O&W's coal cars, from beginning to end.

There are many other people without whose help this book could not have been written. The archivists for the Railroad Museum of Pennsylvania and the New York, Ontario & Western Railway Historical Society (O&WRHS), Mr. Kurt Bell and Mr. Arthur Robb have gone out of their way to help me locate critical pieces of information for this book. Mr. Bill Scott, also of the O&WRHS, has been enormously helpful in finding those little details that make a difference between a good story and a great story.

I am indebted to several other people for their invaluable assistance—Greg Ames, J.W. Barriger III National RR Library; Constance Carter, Library of Congress; Michael Hardy, Smithsonian Institute; Jim Hart, Johnstown America Corporation; Thomas Melvin, University of Delaware Library; Robert Powell, Carbondale Historical Society; and Richard Stanislaus, Pennsylvania Anthracite Heritage Museum. I am also grateful to Ian Fischer, Walter Keeley, Park Ritter, David Thompson, and John White for pointing me in the right direction on several important topics. The O&WRHS's Ed Crist, Malcolm Houck, Robert E. Mohowski, Jeff Otto, Bill Schneider and George Shammas were also very helpful in getting this project over the finish line.

The following people contributed photographs and drawings that make this book complete— Richard Burg, John Forni, Carl Ohlson, Al Patterson, J. R. Quinn, Keith Retterer, Sharon Sergeant, Keith Sirmas, Thomas B. Walsh, III, and Ron Ziel. Special thanks goes to the many organizations for their assistance and permissions—the American Association of Railroads, Bob's Photo, Commonwealth Business Media, Inc., Education Direct, the Hagley Museum and Library, Johnstown America Corporation, the Library of Congress, Middletown Times Herald-Record, National Archives of Canada, National Archives of the United States, Pennsylvania State Archives, Railroad Museum of Pennsylvania, Simmons-Boardman Publications, the Smithsonian Institution Library, and the St. Louis Merchantile Library.

I want to thank Jeff Gainey and Patricia A. Mecadon at the University of Scranton Press for their enthusiastic support in publishing this book and Trinka Ravaioli Pettinato of Grapevine Design for her cover design. I also want to acknowledge the contributions that Forman Applegate, Hillary Gourlay, Alana Price, Robert W. Rose, and Pamela D. Worden have made to this effort and my life.

I especially want to thank Carl Ohlson for his original water color used for the front cover.

I hope you enjoy the book.

Bob Karig

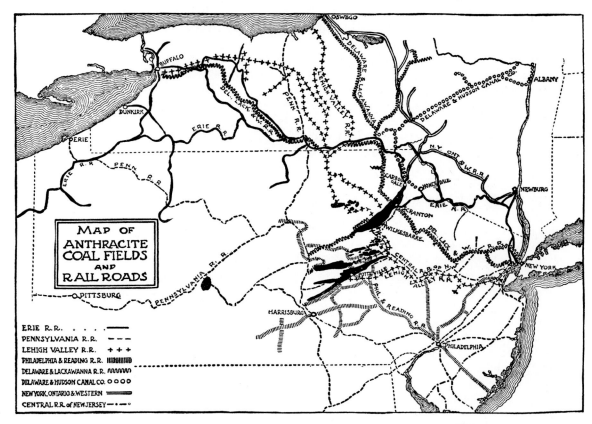

This map, prepared by the United States Industrial Commission, shows the anthracite regions of Pennsylvania and the major anthracite railroads which served them. The map was published in an article entitled "The Anthracite-Carrying Railways," by H. T. Newcomb in 1902. Note that four of the eight railroads depicted make connections to Lake Ontario. [*The American Monthly Review of Reviews, July 1902*]

# Chapter 1       The Anthracite Region and the Development of the Railroad

Anthracite is a hard coal noted for its high carbon content and clean burning qualities, and the Allegheny region in Pennsylvania is home to some of the richest deposits of anthracite in the world. Those deposits served not only as a major source of fuel for the economic development of that region, but also as the catalyst for the development of some of the first transportation networks in the nation. Moving anthracite to market inspired the development of some of the first railroads in the United States, the trial of the first commercial steam locomotive in the United States, and ultimately the development of nine class-one railroads, all of which depended upon moving these "burning rocks" for a large share of their profits.

## DEVELOPING A TRANSPORTATION SYSTEM

There are conflicting claims as to who first discovered anthracite, just as there are conflicting claims as to who first recognized its potential as a fuel. However, there is little controversy over the fact that its value was slow to be recognized. At the turn of the 19th century, wood was still abundant and cheap, and anthracite was hard to ignite and harder to keep burning.[1] It was only through the marketing efforts of several entrepreneurs, combined with the growing scarcity and cost of wood, that the use of anthracite ultimately succeeded. In 1807, Abijah and John Smith began floating anthracite down the Susquehanna River to interior markets in Pennsylvania, and by 1812 they were floating it all the way to Havre-de-Grace, Maryland, where it was loaded onto schooners for shipment to New York.[2] In 1817, Joshua White and Erskine Hazard leased the Lehigh Coal Company, which had been largely unsuccessful in marketing the anthracite it mined, and succeeded in shipping large quantities of anthracite down the Lehigh and Delaware Rivers for sale in Philadelphia.[3]

These first attempts at moving anthracite to market used existing, natural waterways—the Susquehanna River from the northern and western fields and the Lehigh and Delaware Rivers from the southern. These rivers, however, were not always navigable, and it soon became apparent that a more reliable method of moving coal to market was required. The marketers naturally turned to the centuries' proven method of moving bulk items, the canal, and coal miners joined the rest of the nation in a frenzy of canal building. In 1824, the first shipments of coal were made down the Schuylkill Canal connecting Pottsville and Philadelphia.[4] In 1828, the Delaware & Hudson Canal opened connecting the northern fields to the Hudson River at Rondout (Kingston).[5] In 1829, the Lehigh Canal was opened from Mauch Chunk to Easton, thus eliminating the series of "bear-trap locks" the Lehigh Coal and Navigation Company had been using to send its coal arks down the Lehigh River,[6] and in 1828, ground was broken for the North Branch canal running 67 miles from Northumberland to Nanticoke paralleling the Susquehanna River.[8]

THE "STOURBRIDGE LION."

FIGURE 1.1

**The first commercial steam engine operated in the United States, the Stourbridge Lion, was intended to haul anthracite cars between the planes on the D&H's gravity railroad. Unfortunately, the locomotive was heavier than expected and proved to be too much for the railroad's wrought-iron-strapped 6" x 12" hemlock rails, and the locomotive was retired from service, never having pulled a coal train.[7]** [*The Railroad Gazette, August 4, 1876*]

The task remaining for operators was moving the coal to these waterways. In 1826, Abraham Pott paved the way for future railroad development when he built a tramway using horse-drawn, wooden cars to transport anthracite from his mine near Pottsville to the Schuylkill Canal, a distance of ½ mile.[9] Two years later and two years before the Lehigh Canal opened, the Lehigh Coal and Navigation System completed a gravity railroad to transport anthracite from its mines at Summit Hill to the Lehigh River at Mauch Chunk, ultimately saving 64½¢ per ton in shipping costs over the cost of the turnpike road that it replaced.[10] Even as the Mauch Chunk Railway was being built, plans were underway to connect the northern anthracite fields near Scranton to the Delaware & Hudson canal terminus at Honesdale using a railroad that used stationary steam engines to pull the loaded coal cars up inclined planes over the Moosic Mountains and gravity for them to descend down similar planes to the canal. The actual opening of that railroad was preceded by the test of the first commercial steam locomotive operated in the United States, the Stourbridge Lion, on August 8, 1829. The D&H planned to use the "Lion" to pull the coal cars between the inclined planes.[11] Unfortunately, that experiment proved unsuccessful because the wooden rails could not support the weight of the locomotive, and the railroad was forced to begin operation on October 9 of that year using horses to pull the loaded coal cars from the top of one plane to the bottom of the next.[12]

These railroads operated by canal companies were soon joined by other independent operators attempting to link their mines to various waterways, the Mill Creek Railroad, the Norwegian and Mount Carbon Railroad, the Schuylkill Valley Railroad, and the Mine Hill and Schuylkill Haven Railroad, to name a few.[13] The largest of these independent lines was the Pennsylvania Coal Company's gravity railroad, which opened in 1850. It ran 46 miles from Pittston to Hawley, just south of and parallel to the D&H's Carbondale Railroad, where its coal was loaded onto canal boats for shipment down the Delaware & Hudson Canal.[14]

The real revolution in moving anthracite to market, however, was taking place in the southern fields. Even as a vast network of canals was being built in Pennsylvania, experiments in England were showing the viability of pulling loaded coal cars behind steam locomotives, and in 1842, the Philadelphia and Reading Railroad opened a rail link between the anthracite fields in Pottsville to the

markets in Philadelphia.[15] The success of the Reading, as shown in Table 1.1, immediately led the way for more steam railroads connecting the anthracite fields of Pennsylvania with the markets in the north and east.

TABLE 1.1
**Anthracite Tonnage carried by Schuylkill Navigation & Philadelphia & Reading Railroad 1841-1849**[16]

| Year | Schuylkill Navigation | Philadelphia & Reading RR |
|---|---|---|
| 1841 | 584,692 | 850 |
| 1842 | 491,602 | 49,902 |
| 1843 | 447,058 | 230,254 |
| 1844 | 398,887 | 441,491 |
| 1845 | 263,587 | 820,237 |
| 1846* | 3,440 | 1,233,142 |
| 1847 | 222,693 | 1,360,681 |
| 1848 | 436,60 | 1,216,233 |
| 1849 | 489,208 | 1,115,918 |

**\*Canal in course of reconstruction**

The next major railroad development was to the north, and it was constructed by a pair of brothers connected with neither railroads nor coal. George and Seldon Scranton operated the Lackawanna Iron Works in what is now Scranton, Pennsylvania, and they had prospered by making iron rails for the Erie Railroad as it pushed west along the southern boundary of New York.[17] In 1847, the Scrantons purchased the charter for the Ligett's Gap Railroad, which ran north from Scranton to a connection with the Erie at Great Bend, and in 1851 they purchased the charter for the Delaware & Cobb's Gap Railroad, which ran southeast to the Delaware Water Gap, ultimately connecting with the Central of New Jersey near New Hampton, New Jersey, via the Warren Railroad. The northern extension was completed in 1851, and the southern extension was completed in 1856. Together these two railroads became the Delaware, Lackawanna, and Western Railroad, and in 1869, it purchased the Oswego and Syracuse Railroad and became known as the "Atlantic and Lake Ontario Line."[18] Ultimately, it would extend its lines to Lake Erie, becoming the third railroad after the New York Central & Hudson River and the New York, Lake Erie & Western Railroads to make the connection between New York and Buffalo.

Close on the heels of the Lackawanna, the Lehigh Valley Railroad opened a rail connection from the Lehigh fields at Mauch Chunk to Easton,

**Hard Coal and Coal Cars**

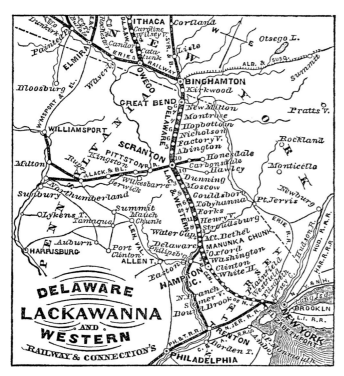

FIGURE 1.2
The Delaware, Lackawanna & Western was formed from the Ligett's Gap Railroad running north from Scranton to Great Bend, where it connected to the Erie Railroad, and the Delaware & Cobb's Gap Railroad running southeast to the Delaware Water Gap. There it met the Warren Railroad, which connected with the Central of New Jersey near New Hampton to provide the Lackawanna access to tidewater. [*Appletons' Railway and Steam Navigation Guide, May 1866*]

FIGURE 1.3
The Central of New Jersey became a major anthracite carrier when both the Lehigh Valley and the Delaware, Lackawanna & Western connected to it in 1856 to transport their coal to tidewater. The Lehigh Valley connected to the CNJ at Easton and the DL&W connected to the CNJ via the Warren Railroad near New Hampton. [*Appletons' Railway and Steam Navigation Guide, July 1864*]

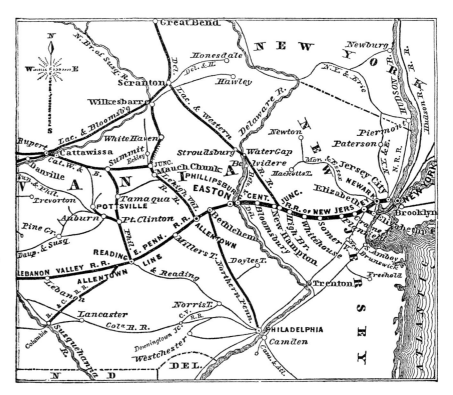

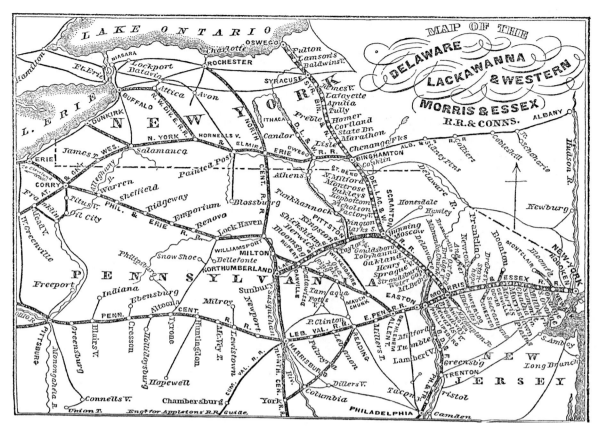

FIGURE 1.4

**In 1868, the DL&W secured its own access to tidewater by leasing the Morris & Essex railroad and in 1869, it leased the Oswego & Syracuse Railroad to complete its route from Oswego to New York City, gaining it the title, "The Atlantic and Lake Ontario Line." To replace the loss of the DL&W's anthracite traffic, the Central of New Jersey leased the Lehigh & Susquehanna Railroad to extend its own line into the anthracite fields. This action by its former partner caused the Lehigh Valley to withdraw its shipments from the CNJ and seek its own route to tidewater.** *[Appletons' Railway and Steam Navigation Guide, July 1871]*

also connecting to the Central of New Jersey. The Lehigh Valley would ultimately extend its reach up into the northern fields at Wilkes-Barre and by 1869, it had made a connection with the Erie at Waverly, New York following the path of the North Branch Canal.[19]

     With the Lackawanna and the Lehigh Valley both feeding it coal, the Central of New Jersey became a major anthracite carrier in its own right. However, when the Lackawanna procured its own link to tidewater in 1868 by leasing the Morris & Essex Railroad,[20] the Central of New Jersey saw its anthracite revenue plummet. To alleviate this shortfall, the CNJ extended its own line into the anthracite region in 1871 by leasing the Lehigh & Susquehanna Railroad and buying up coal land in the northern fields.[21] With its former partner now becoming a competitor, the Lehigh Valley now sought its own outlet to tidewater. It obtained con-

trol of the Perth Amboy & Bound Brook Railroad and chartered the Bound Brook & Easton Railroad and consolidated the two into the Easton & Amboy Railway Company. The Lehigh Valley completed this connection to tidewater in 1875.[22]

     In 1857, a rate dispute broke out between the Pennsylvania Coal Company and the Delaware & Hudson Coal Company, and as a result, the PCC sought another outlet for its anthracite. In 1860, it obtained a charter to build a railroad from its gravity railroad's terminus at Hawley to a connection with the Erie at Lackawaxen.[23] This 16 mile connection was completed in 1863, and in 1865, the PCC withdrew all of its business from the D&H Canal.[24] In 1882, in collaboration with the Erie, the PCC began building the Erie & Wyoming Valley Railroad to replace its gravity system. When the Erie & Wyoming Valley Railroad opened in 1885, the PCC ceased its gravity operations.

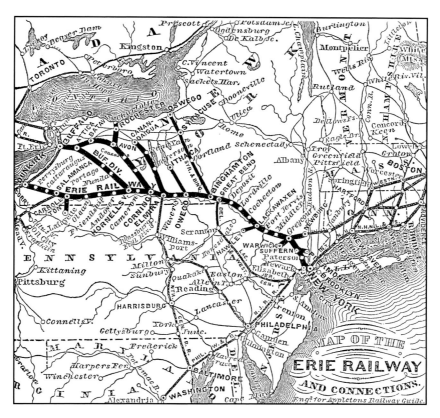

FIGURE 1.5
The Erie was the key to early efforts to move anthracite out of the northern fields by rail. This 1869 engraving shows the DL&W's connection to the Erie at Great Bend and the beginnings of the Erie & Wyoming Valley railroad running from Lackawaxen to connect with the Pennsylvania Coal Company's gravity railroad at Hawley. The Erie & Wyoming Valley would reach the coal fields in 1885 enabling the PCC to close its gravity railroad. In 1868, the D&H would contract with the Erie to build a line from Carbondale to connect with the Erie at Jefferson Junction, and by 1869, the Lehigh Valley had also connected with the Erie by following the route of the North Branch Canal from Wilkes-Barre to Waverly. [*Appletons' Railway and Steam Navigation Guide, April 1869*]

Even as the D&H was making major improvements on its gravity railroad in the mid-1860's, it was beginning to recognize the ascendancy of steam railroads around it. It also recognized another problem. With its canal system, it was constrained to tidewater markets where competition was fiercest and margins were slimmest. The use of steam railroads would enable it to reach interior markets where profits were higher.

The D&H had been using steam locomotives to feed its gravity system since it had opened its 4' 3" gauge extension from Olyphant to Providence (outside Scranton) in 1860.[27] However, in 1868, it began to secure its own rail connection to the Erie by contracting to build the Jefferson Railroad from Carbondale to Jefferson Junction (Lanesboro). In 1870, it leased in perpetuity the recently completed six foot gauge Albany & Susquehanna Railroad, and it also contracted to build the Lackawanna & Susquehanna Railroad to complete the connection

from Lanesboro to the Albany & Susquehanna at Ninevah. This ultimately became the D&H's Ninevah Division.[28] It then leased the Renssalear & Saratoga Railroad to extend to the north on the way to becoming the "Bridge Route to Canada."[29]

The D&H had one more major connection to make. The Albany & Susquehanna connected with the newly completed New York & Oswego Midland Railroad at Sidney Plains, New York, and as the result of that connection, it could reach the port of Oswego on Lake Ontario as well as additional interior markets served by the Rome & Clinton and the Utica, Clinton & Binghamton railroads, which it controlled. In 1872, the D&H leased these two railroads to the Midland with accompanying revenue guarantees, and in 1873, the D&H loaned the Midland $200,000 to enable the latter to continue its operations. Despite this loan and the D&H's traffic guarantees, the Midland entered bankruptcy following the Panic of 1873. This would force the D&H

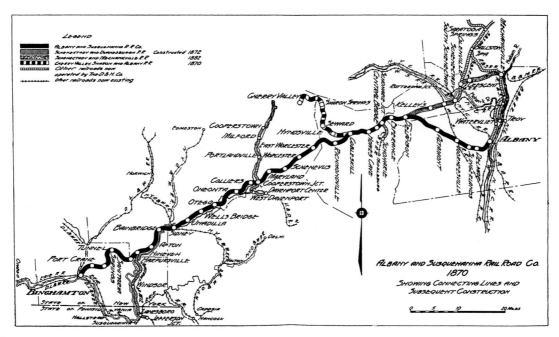

FIGURE 1.6

**In 1870, the Delaware & Hudson Canal Company sought its own rail connection to interior markets as an alternative to shipment by its canal. In 1868 it contracted to build the Jefferson Railroad from Carbondale to Lanesboro and in 1870 it leased in perpetuity the Albany & Susquehanna Railroad running from Binghamton to Albany. The Albany & Susquehanna made an important connection with the newly completed New York & Oswego Midland at Sidney Plains, which enabled the D&H to reach additional interior markets and Lake Ontario with its coal.** [*A Century of Progress, History of the Delaware & Hudson Company, 1823-1923*]

to turn the operations of the Rome & Clinton and the Utica, Clinton & Binghamton Railroads over to the Delaware, Lackawanna & Western.[30]

The Midland's bankruptcy notwithstanding, Sidney remained a prized connection for the D&H, and it would bind these two railroads, and the Midland's successor, the New York, Ontario & Western Railway, until the "commodities clause" of the Hepburn Act would force the D&H to withdraw

from its marketing agreements with the O&W in 1908.[31] Although the D&H would continue its canal operation until 1898, with the opening of its rail link, the D&H foresaw the closing of its canal and began making announcements to that effect as early as 1881.[32] In 1889, the youngest of the coal carriers, the New York, Ontario & Western Railway, its appetite for coal whetted by its relationship with the D&H, decided to enter the anthracite fields for itself.

## THE BUSINESS OF ANTHRACITE

However lucrative the transportation of anthracite might have seemed, it was an industry with significant problems and uncertainties that the anthracite carriers struggled throughout their histories to get under control. In order to appreciate the problems faced by the anthracite carriers, it's important to understand some of the peculiarities of the anthracite business. Anthracite is not simply a bulk commodity. After it's mined, it must be separated from any impurities and then broken into marketable sizes. This work was done in "coal break-

ers," which dominated the landscape throughout the anthracite region. Once it's broken and sorted, the anthracite is loaded into coal cars by sizes, and shipped to the appropriate market. The Anthracite Coal Strike Commission provided some insight into the business in its 1902 report to the President (see inset on page 9).

The sizes of anthracite, as described in the commission's report, determine its value, that is, the larger or domestic sizes of anthracite command a higher value than the lower sizes as shown in Table 1.2. During the early years, prior to 1900, the only

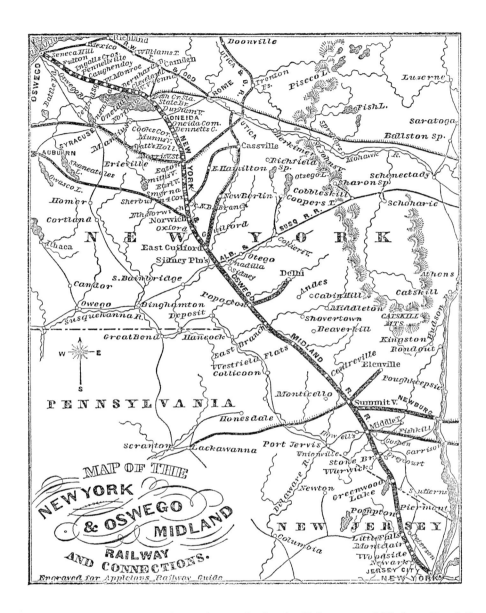

FIGURE 1.7

The New York & Oswego Midland provided a perfect outlet for the Delaware and Hudson Canal Company in 1872. With its connection with the D&H at Sidney, the Midland could transport D&H coal to the port of Oswego for transportation across the Great Lakes. It could also transport D&H anthracite to Randallsville where it could make connections with the Utica, Clinton & Binghamton and Rome & Clinton Railroads, which the D&H leased to the Midland in 1872, as well as to other interior markets served by the Midland. Coal distribution agreements continued between the D&H and the Midland and later, the O&W until 1908 when the D&H had to separate its railroad and anthracite operations because of the Hepburn Act. The proposed rail link from Summitville to Lackawanna shown on this map indicates that Midland management already had its eyes cast on the anthracite fields of Pennsylvania, even at this early date. [Appletons' Railway and Steam Navigation Guide, July 1871]

**The Anthracite Region and the Development of the Railroad**

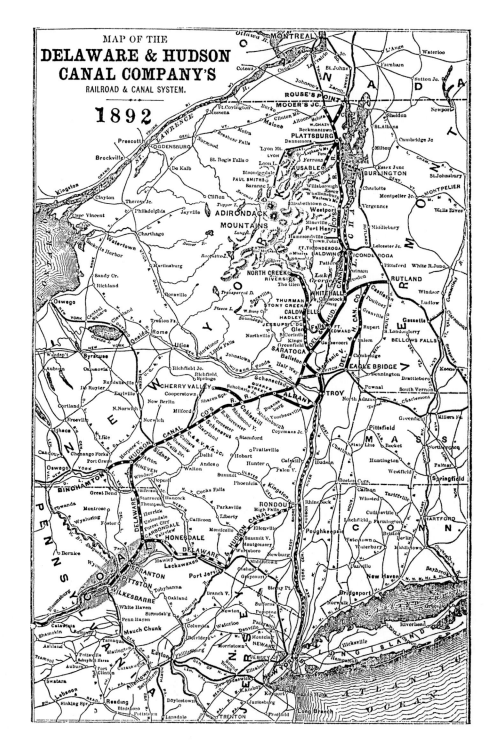

FIGURE 1.8

Although the Delaware & Hudson had the distinction of operating the first commercial steam engine in the United States, it was primarily a canal company until 1868 when it contracted to build the Jefferson Railroad to connect with the Erie at Lanesboro. In 1870, it leased the Albany & Susquehanna Railroad, and contracted to build the Lackawanna & Susquehanna Railroad to link the Jefferson Railroad with the Albany & Susquehanna at Ninevah. The D&H ceased its canal operations in 1898. After a brief battle during which the O&W combined forces with the Erie against the Pennsylvania Coal Company, the O&W gained the right to build its Ellenville & Kingston Branch along the old canal route. *[New York Legislative Manual of 1892, Sharon Sergeant Collection]*

Hard Coal and Coal Cars

sizes marketed were the domestic sizes—broken, egg, stove and chestnut. Anything sized pea or smaller was considered culm and discarded onto culm banks.[34] After the turn of the century, uses were found for these "steam sizes" and new markets developed for them, which enabled miners not only to sell these smaller sizes as they were mined, but also to recover those sizes from culm banks by building washeries for that purpose.

There is another important aspect regarding the shipment of anthracite—anthracite is a fragile commodity. With every handling, the larger sizes are subject to breakage into smaller sizes with a concomitant loss of value.

"...For example, when a hundred tons of Stove size are shipped to storage from a colliery, some breakage will occur in handling so that when the time arrives to reload the coal for shipment to market, perhaps only 95 tons will retain the original size, the other five tons having broken into Chestnut, Pea and Buckwheat sizes. These smaller sizes are removed by the screens in the reloading tower and the coal shipped from storage is every bit as good as the freshly mined product....The only effect which long storage has upon anthracite is a diminution of its naturally glossy appearance...the burning qualities of anthracite are not in the least affected by long storage."[35]

Monitoring the transportation of various grades and sizes of anthracite was only the beginning of the railroads' problems. As demand for anthracite grew, more mines were opened and more railroads were built into the fields to deliver that commodity to market. Thus, while the first fifty years of anthracite production were marked by high profits, during the latter half of the 19th century, the industry was marked by overproduction and fierce competition.

FIGURE 1.9
**Hopper cars are being loaded with anthracite in this 1927 promotional movie on Philadelphia & Reading anthracite. Note that the cars are being loaded by size—nut, stove, and egg. The railroads would be required to manage each coal car by the size of the anthracite with which it was loaded.** *[Author's Collection]*

TABLE 1.2
Tons of Anthracite Shipped and Prices, All Sources (1901)[36]

| Grade | Approximate Size | Long Tons Shipped | Per Cent of Total | FOB Price Per Ton |
|---|---|---|---|---|
| Lump | > 4 3/8" | 2,187,553 | 4.1% | NA |
| Grate | 3 1/4" - 4 3/8" | 4,423,584 | 8.3% | $3.4472 |
| Egg | 2 7/16" - 3 1/4" | 6,989,330 | 13.1% | $3.9778 |
| Stove | 1 5/8" - 2 7/16" | 10,561,957 | 19.7% | $4.3211 |
| Chestnut | 13/16" - 1 5/8" | 10,250,550 | 19.1% | $4.3230 |
| Pea | 9/16" - 13/16" | 7,555,948 | 14.1% | $2.5769 |
| Buckwheat No. 1 | 5/16" - 9/16" | 7,894,613 | 14.7% | $2.1020 |
| Buckwheat No. 2 (Rice) | 3/16" - 5/16" | 3,705,066 | 6.9% | $1.4383 |
| Buckwheat No. 3 (Barley) | 3/32" - 3/16" | Incl w/Bckwht2 | Incl w/Bckwht2 | $1.1575 |
| Total | | 53,568,601 | 100.0% | |

Railroads tried desperately to gain control of the situation. Those railroads, such as the Philadelphia & Reading, which did not own their own coal supply, found themselves at a competitive disadvantage to those railroads that had become vertically integrated, and there was a rush by the railroads to purchase their coal lands outright.[37] Thus, by 1899, it was estimated that the railroads and their affiliated coal companies produced 62 percent of the total output of the mines and controlled a vast share of the remainder through contractual agreements with independent producers.[38]

Burdened with the cost of these coal land purchases, mining improvements, railroad operations and interest charges, and faced with declining profit margins because of increasing competition, many railroads teetered on the brink of insolvency.[39] Indeed, the Philadelphia & Reading entered bankruptcy proceedings three times during the latter half of the 19th century.[40] As a result, railroads desperately sought ways to limit the competition and bring prices and margins under control. The first effort to emerge was pooling, that is, dividing a market up among competitors and setting prices to ensure that each had a profitable share. In 1872, the anthracite

railroads established the first railroad pool. This agreement remained in effect until 1876, when some railroads' cheating forced it to fall apart. A second pool was established in 1878. This one lasted only a year. Its arrangement is shown in Table 1.3.

TABLE 1.4
Anthracite Agreement of 1896[42]

| | Percent |
|---|---|
| Central of New Jersey | 11.70 |
| Delaware & Hudson | 9.00 |
| Delaware, Lackawanna & Western | 13.35 |
| Delaware, Susquehanna & Schuylkill | 3.50 |
| Erie Railroad | 4.00 |
| Lehigh Valley | 15.65 |
| New York, Ontario & Western | 3.10 |
| New York, Susquehanna & Western | 3.20 |
| Pennsylvania Railroad | 11.40 |
| Pennsylvania Coal Company | 4.00 |
| Philadelphia & Reading | 20.50 |

The initial anthracite pools were destined to fail because the market had not yet stabilized, specifically because railroads, such as the New York, Susquehanna & Western and the New York, Ontario & Western were continuing to enter the marketplace. However, by the end of the century market conditions has stabilized to the point that the railroads were able to establish the sharing agreement shown in Table 1.4. Table 1.5 shows the shares of the anthracite trade as they existed during the first 25 years of the 20th century.

One of the ways in which the railroads were able to create this stability was through the introduction of "interlocking directorates," that is, members of the board of one railroad served concurrently on

TABLE 1.3
Anthracite pool of 1878[41]

| | Percent |
|---|---|
| Central of New Jersey | 12.905 |
| Delaware & Hudson | 12.480 |
| Delaware, Lackawanna & Western | 12.750 |
| Lehigh Valley | 19.750 |
| Pennsylvania Railroad | 7.625 |
| Pennsylvania Coal Company | 5.865 |
| Philadelphia & Reading | 28.625 |
| Total | 100.000 |

the boards of other railroads. However, just as the railroads were beginning to stabilize their markets, two outside forces intervened to destabilize the situation—government and labor.

Beginning in 1887 with the passage of the Interstate Commerce Act, a series of legislative actions were taken to exercise control over the business practices of the railroads. Many of these legislative actions, starting with the Interstate Commerce Act, were generated in specific response to the actions of the anthracite railroads. In 1893, the Sherman Anti-Trust Act was passed limiting combinations in restraint of trade, and in 1906, the Hepburn Act became the strictest legislation to date affecting the anthracite roads. In particular, it forbade the practice of interlocking directorates, and its commodities clause prohibited railroads from shipping coal which they owned at the time of shipment.[43] These laws were followed by the Mann-Elkins Act of 1910, which further strengthened the power of the ICC to establish rates, the Clayton Act of 1914, which further restricted the practice of members serving on the boards of competing organizations, and the Adamson Act of 1916, which established the 8-hour day for railroad workers.

TABLE 1.5
**Percentages of Anthracite Traffic Hauled by Major Railroads, 1912-1925**[44]

| | 1912 | 1916 | 1920 | 1925 |
|---|---|---|---|---|
| Central of New Jersey | 13.1* | 11.4 | 8.2 | 7.8 |
| Delaware & Hudson | 10.0 | 11.1 | 15.6 | 15.3 |
| Delaware, Lackawanna & Western | 14.3 | 14.7 | 14.0 | 14.5 |
| Erie** | 11.7 | 11.7 | 9.4 | 11.7 |
| Lehigh & New England | .. | 3.0 | 4.9 | 4.8 |
| Lehigh Valley | 18.5 | 18.5 | 17.4 | 15.5 |
| New York, Ontario & Western | 3.5 | 3.0 | 3.6 | 3.3 |
| Pennsylvania | 8.7 | 9.0 | 7.5 | 8.5 |
| Philadelphia & Reading | 20.2 | 17.6 | 19.4 | 18.6 |
| Total | 100.0 | 100.0 | 100.0 | 100.0 |

*Includes Lehigh & New England
**Includes New York, Susquehanna & Western

The anthracite carriers were being squeezed from both sides. During this same period, the United Mine Workers were entering the anthracite region and beginning to agitate for recognition and reform. From the turn of the century forward, the anthracite region was plagued by labor unrest and a series of costly strikes. Work stoppages in 1902, 1906, 1912, 1922, 1923, and 1925-26 cost a total of 607 days lost. The results of these strikes were increasing prices for anthracite and growing customer concern over the reliability of obtaining anthracite as a heating fuel. Anthracite production would peak in 1917. Although the O&W's shipments would not peak until fifteen years later, the period of anthracite dominance was over.

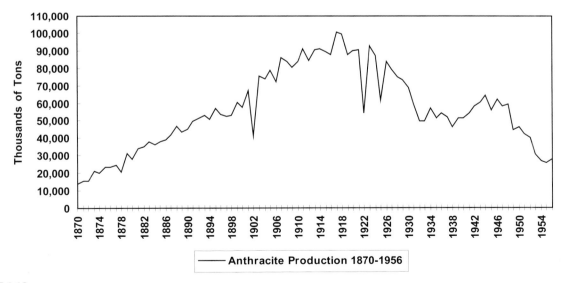

— Anthracite Production 1870-1956

FIGURE 1.10
**This graph shows anthracite production from 1870 through1956 in thousands of tons. The major strikes in the anthracite fields are clearly marked by the deep troughs in production in 1902, 1906, 1922, and 1925-26.** [*Annual Report on Mining Activities, 2000, Commonwealth of Pennsylvania*]

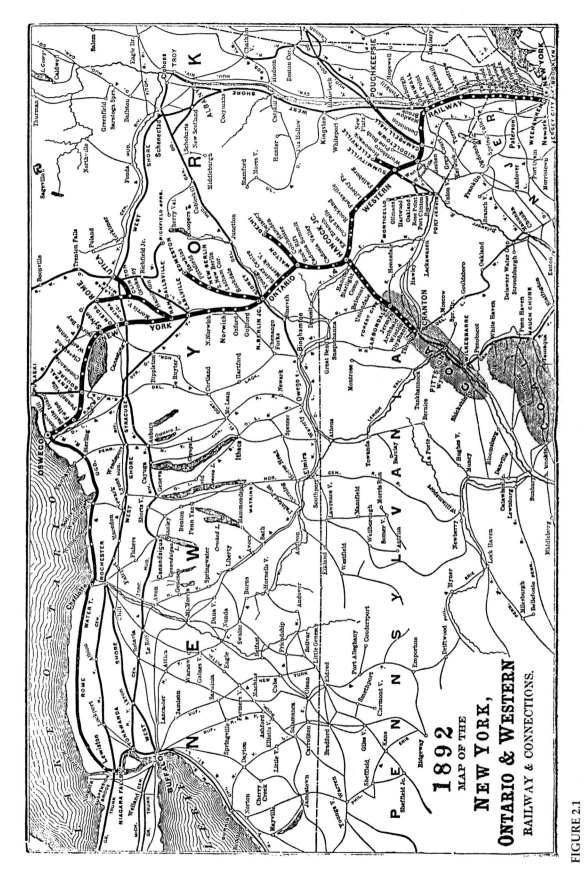

FIGURE 2.1
This 1892 map lays out the O&W's route structure two years after the Scranton Extension was opened and shows the extent to which the Scranton Extension actually penetrated the northern anthracite field. In 1898, the D&H will cease its canal operations, and in December 1902, the O&W will open its Ellenville & Kingston (E & K) Branch along the old canal route, which, combined with the trackage of the Port Jervis, Monticello & Summitville (PJ, M & S) line, would complete its route from Port Jervis to Kingston. [New York Legislative Manual of 1892, Sharon Sergeant Collection]

# Chapter 2    The Anthracite Operations of the New York, Ontario & Western Ry.

The history of coal on the O&W can be traced back to 1870 when the Delaware and Hudson Canal Company acquired control of the Albany and Susquehanna Railroad that ran from Binghamton to Albany, New York. This route connected with the New York and Oswego Midland at Sidney Plains, providing it a rail connection to the Great Lakes and the Midland's interior markets. However, since the Albany & Susquehanna was built as a six foot railroad to match the gauge of the Erie, any shipments of coal up the Midland to Oswego would have required transloading the anthracite into the Midland's standard gauge cars at Sidney Plains.[1] By December 1871, the D&H had converted to standard gauge, and the following year, it sub-leased the Rome & Clinton and the Utica, Clinton, & Binghamton Railroads to the Midland with guarantees of coal revenue for the new railroad.[2] Thus began the NY&OM's history as a coal carrier, and it was this connection that allowed the New York, Ontario & Western Railway to begin its life as an anthracite railroad when it was chartered from the remains of the NY&OM in 1880.

## THE EARLY YEARS (1880-1888)

In October 1881, the O&W signed a five year contract with the D&H to transport coal from their connection at Sidney Plains to the port at Oswego. That agreement provided that:

• The O&W would have exclusive right to transport D&H Canal Company Coal to points reached by the O&W.
• The O&W would maintain terminal facilities and pockets at Oswego for loading vessels.
• Both companies would contribute coal cars in proportion to the respective mileage served by each over this route. In the event that one company contributed more than its share, that company would be reimbursed at a rate of $3/8$'s of one cent per mile for four wheel cars and $3/4$'s of one cent per mile for eight wheel cars.
• One half of the selling cost of the coal would be attributed for the cost of transporting the coal. This would be apportioned based upon the mileage served by the two railroads between the coal mines

FIGURE 2.2
**Johnson #1 was one of the many coal breakers serving the O&W. Here the freshly mined coal was separated from impurities, broken into marketable sizes, graded, and loaded into coal cars.** *[Walter Kierzkowski Collection]*

and the port at Oswego—113 miles by the D&H and 124 miles by the O&W. The agreement also contained payment provisions for the delivery of D&H coal to other points served by the O&W.

• The O&W would be able to sell D&H coal through its own agents along its route structure.

• Facilities would be maintained by both railroads for the transfer of coal cars at Sidney Plains.

• The agreement established 2240 pounds as a ton of coal.[3]

In May 1886, the O&W extended its relationship with the D&H by leasing the Utica, Clinton & Binghamton Railroad and the Rome & Clinton Railroads from the canal company. Under that agreement, the O&W received exclusive rights to transport D&H coal over those extensions, with a guaranteed minimum of 150,000 tons annually. The D&H would pay the O&W "one (1) cent per ton per mile for each mile the same shall be transported...

through to Utica and Rome; to points beyond Oriskany Falls and south of Utica and Rome, two (2) cents per ton per mile; to all other stations on said roads, local rates to be established from time to time by the [O&W]."[4]

In order to handle this tonnage and live up to its agreements with the D&H, the O&W built 300 hopper bottom gondolas in its Middletown shops in 1882 and it purchased another 150 gondolas from the Terre Haute Car Company in 1887.

Before the Rome & Clinton agreement, coal had already become 32% of the O&W's total tonnage.[5] One year after that agreement, coal had climbed to 42.07% of the total tonnage carried by the O&W.[6] By 1888, it would be hard to argue that the O&W hadn't become a coal road. The only thing that the O&W lacked was direct access to the coal fields of northern Pennsylvania.

## BRANCHING OUT (1889-1898)

In 1889, the O&W remedied its lack of access to the anthracite region by acquiring the stock of the Ontario, Carbondale & Scranton Railway, which had been formed by consolidating the Hancock & Pennsylvania, Forest City & State Line, and the Scranton & Forest City Railroad Companies.[7] Thus the Scranton Extension, which ran from Hancock to Scranton and later became known as the Scranton Division, was born.

In addition to having a rail connection, the railroad needed two other elements to become a full-fledged coal road—sources and outlets. At first, there was some doubt as to whether the O&W could gain access to anthracite output given its late entry into the coal fields. However, by offering loans and favorable terms to mine operators to help them develop their coal properties, the O&W was able to obtain guarantees of about one million tons per year by the time the Scranton Extension was opened in 1890.[8] The O&W also sponsored the formation of the New York & Ontario Land Company to acquire land in the anthracite region for lease to the New York & Scranton Coal Company, which then would construct collieries on those sites and deliver their anthracite under an exclusive transportation contract to the O&W.[9]

The O&W then needed outlets for its anthracite, and its experience with the D&H proved favorable in this regard. In 1889, it purchased land in Oswego,

Cornwall, and Weehawken to erect coal trestles to load ships,[10] and in 1890, as rails were being laid from Hancock to Scranton, the O&W built coal trestles at Oswego, Rome, and Weehawken.[11] This gave the O&W marketing outlets to the Great Lakes, the Erie and Black River Canals, and tidewater, in addition to the retail outlets throughout its route structure. The use of a transfer station at Oneida enabled the O&W to load anthracite on New York Central box cars for shipment west. In the end, the O&W had developed a secure and well-balanced distribution system. To handle the sales of anthracite throughout this system, the railway enlisted the firm of Dickson and Eddy as General Sales Agents for O&W anthracite.[12]

In 1892, the O&W added another element to its distribution system, a coal trestle at Cornwall on the Hudson River. Cornwall provided several elements that were otherwise missing. It provided access to markets along the Hudson River and across the Hudson to New England via the New York & New England railroad. Furthermore, it provided a seasonal outlet to tidewater, enabling the O&W to avoid the additional tariffs associated with transporting the coal by rail down the West Shore to Weehawken.[13]

By 1894, the O&W was shipping coal from twelve breakers.[14] In order to handle the large volume of coal coming out of the Lackawanna region, the O&W purchased 3,850 hopper-bottom gondolas, and as new contracts were signed, the

Hard Coal and Coal Cars

## FIGURE 2.3

The agreement with the Delaware & Hudson of 1881 required that the O&W maintain a coal trestle in Oswego for D&H coal. After the O&W entered the coal fields, it built a second trestle for its own use. The D&H trestle was removed in 1918. The O&W stopped using its trestle in 1936 and used the DL&W's trestle for what coal it did ship through Oswego. By 1938, the O&W's trestle had also been razed.[15] This 1907 photo shows a line of 6600 series hopper-bottom gondolas sagging under their loads of anthracite while they wait to be unloaded. *[Photo by Herman Ferguson; George Slawson Collection, O&WRHS Archives]*

## FIGURE 2.4

The first coal trestle at Weehawken was completed in January 1891. This is how the docks looked in 1910 after Pier #2 was rebuilt. *[O&WRHS Archives]*

FIGURE 2.5
**The trestle at Cornwall was built in 1892 to give the O&W access to the river and avoid the cost of moving coal trains down the New York & West Shore to Weehawken.** *[John Stellwagen Collection; O&WRHS Archives]*

FIGURE 2.6
**The O&W maintained a large fleet of river barges to transport its anthracite from Cornwall to New York and in and around the harbor. Here we see one of the O&W's fleet of river barges being loaded at Cornwall. Anthracite needed to be loaded carefully to avoid breakage, which could reduce the value of the coal.** *[Dennis Carpunter Collection; O&WRHS Archives]*

O&W continued to purchase and/or build additional coal cars to meet the demand. By 1898, the O&W had purchased 4,120 new, hopper-bottom gondolas, and it had rebuilt many of its older coal cars with higher capacities to meet the demand.

In addition to making these investments in its coal car fleet, the O&W invested in its distribution system. At Weehawken, it added an additional coal trestle and expanded its yard facilities to facilitate the handling of the large volume of coal cars. These improvements increased the capacity of those facilities by 50 percent while at the same time reducing the handling costs per ton.[16] It also improved the coal trestle at Oswego to increase its capacity for shipments to Canada, which was becoming an important market for O&W anthracite.[17] Then, in 1894, the O&W began assembling its own flotilla to transport coal from Cornwall to New York City and to points within New York Harbor. Two years later, it expanded its capability by adding larger vessels to ship anthracite along Long Island Sound and to the ports of Providence and Boston.[18] At its peak, the O&W owned 42 pieces of water-line equipment.

The O&W was also making improvements to its rail system. Foremost among these, of course, was the Scranton Extension itself, which opened on July 1, 1890. The extension was built with 67-pound

FIGURE 2.7
**The O&W ordered 42 of these S-Class "Dickson Hogs" to handle the additional coal traffic generated by the opening of the Scranton Extension. Each of these Consolidations weighed 136,000 pounds and had a tractive effort of 26,100 pounds.** *[Karl Schlachter photo; J.R. Quinn Collection]*

rail. The masonry was described as "first-class," and the truss bridges were constructed of iron and sufficiently strong "to carry a continuous train of the heaviest consolidation engines in use."[19] The pride in this accomplishment would be short-lived. Within a decade, track and trestles designed to carry 70-ton locomotives and 30-ton coal cars would need to be upgraded to handle 100-ton locomotives and 40-ton coal cars, and a decade later to handle 170-ton locomotives and 55-ton coal cars. Within just seven years of its construction, the Scranton Division was already inadequate for the tonnage being handled by the O&W.

Other changes were taking place along the main line to accommodate the coal traffic. Notable among these were the completions of the "Zig Zag" tunnel in 1891, the new iron Lyon Brook trestle in 1894, and the Pecksport Loop in 1896. As these improvements were being made, the railroad was busily replacing old ties and upgrading the main line to 76-pound rail. By the end of the decade, the future looked bright. In his report to the stockholders in 1897, President Fowler reported that "over half of the freight revenues come from coal. Forecasts indicate that the coal will last another 26 years. With additions under consideration, this could be extended to 30-40 years."[20] Little did he realize how prophetic those words were.

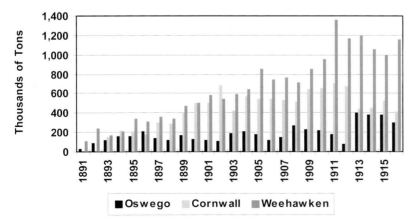

FIGURE 2.8
**Tonnage of anthracite shipped by the O&W to Oswego, Cornwall and Weehawken (1891-1916)** *[Source: O&W Annual Reports]*

## CONSOLIDATION AND GROWTH (1899-1917)

In just ten years, the O&W had transformed itself, according to President Fowler in his 1901 report to the stockholders, "from a condition which, by many competent persons, was considered almost hopeless a decade ago, to the present time, when the amount of the annual net earnings fully equals the sum of the gross revenue at the time."[21]   It was now time to consolidate those gains and plan for future growth.  The first opportunity to do that occurred in 1899.

In January 1899, the O&W was approached by the Lackawanna Iron and Steel Company to determine if it was interested in buying its anthracite operations.  As a result of that meeting, the Scranton Coal Company was formed to purchase the Lackawanna's properties, which consisted of the Pine Brook and Capouse breakers.  To procure these properties, the coal company borrowed $3,875,000 from the railroad secured by a first and second mortgage on the coal properties.  In exchange, the coal company agreed to ship 250,000 tons per breaker per year over the railroad.  The board viewed this step as imperative in order to secure coal for shipment over the railroad.[22]  A year later, a similar situation presented itself.  The Elk Hill Coal and Iron Company sought to acquire additional properties, and the railroad loaned it $3,500,000 to purchase a total of seven collieries.[23]  By 1905, these

two coal companies would operate a total of 10 collieries and 3 washeries, the entire output of which was committed to the O&W.[24]

From 1891 to 1898, the tonnage of anthracite shipped on the O&W nearly doubled from 811,485 tons to 1,605,508 tons.  From 1898 to 1905, it would nearly double again to 3,141,260 tons.  The flood of coal coming out of the Scranton Extension was creating problems of its own.

Several significant changes were taking place in the anthracite business at the turn of the century.  For the preceding ten years, the industry had been plagued by over-production, and indeed the railroads, which controlled the majority of anthracite output, had begun limiting production as a way of supporting the price structure of the commodity.[25]  However, by the beginning of 20th century, diminishing supplies and increased demand seemed to have eliminated this concern over pricing.[26]

The second major change in the business occurred when new markets were developed for the smaller sizes of anthracite.[27]  In the early days of anthracite mining, there were few markets for the smaller sizes, and they were simply discarded in culm piles.  These new markets meant that a greater percentage of the coal brought up from the mines could actually be marketed.  It also meant that much of that coal that had been discarded could now be recovered through washeries erected near the existing culm piles.  Although these sizes might still be sold below the average cost of production, they provided income where heretofore there had been none, thus increasing the demand for coal cars to transport this commodity to tidewater.

Since 1890, the railroad's management had identified the need to build storage facilities to hold the anthracite when it came out of the mines until it was needed during the winter months.[28]  There were two alternatives to building storage facilities—selling the anthracite at lower prices during the off-season or storing the coal in its coal cars until it was needed.  Despite the identified need, no action was taken by the railroad until the sit-

FIGURE 2.9
**The collapse of the bridge at Fish's Eddy under the weight of a coal train in 1897 is evidence that the O&W didn't always keep up with the demands of heavier trains and equipment.  Barely discernible on car number 12682 in the foreground is "Built by Peninsular Car Company."** [*DeForest Douglas Diver Railroad Photographs, ca. 1870-1950. Collection 1948.  Courtesy of the Division of Rare and Manuscript Collections, Cornell University Library*]

Hard Coal and Coal Cars

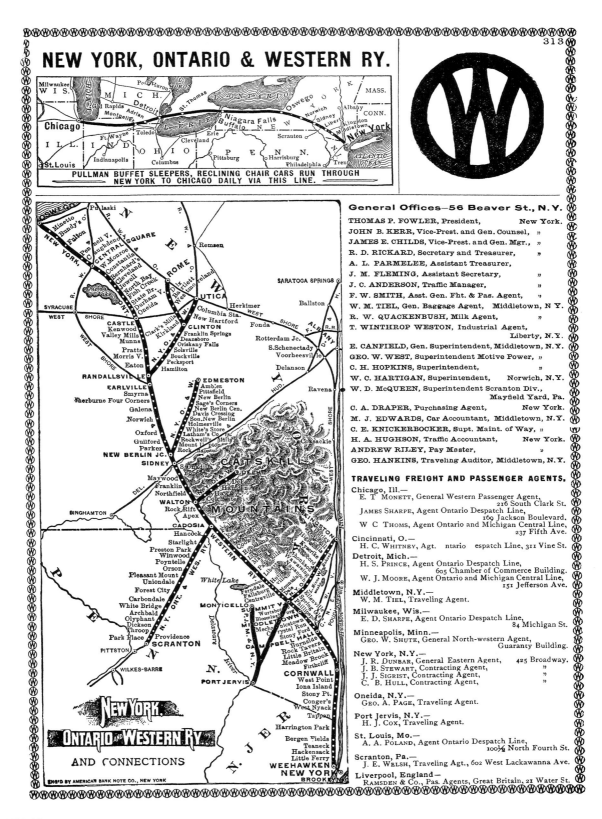

FIGURE 2.10

This 1905 O&W advertisement shows the O&W route structure at its peak. Note how the O&W has portrayed its route as skirting the southern edge of the Catskills. *[Official Guide of the Railways and Steam Navigation Lines of the United States, November 1905]*

uation became desperate at the turn of the century, when "from twenty-five hundred to three thousand cars [would be] loaded up with sizes for which there [was] no immediate demand, causing scarcity of cars at the mines and enforcing a restriction on output."[29]  To alleviate this problem, the railroad contracted with the Dodge Coal Storage Company to erect a coal storage plant at Middletown with a capacity of four piles of thirty thousand tons each.[30]  By 1908, the O&W had increased the capacity of those facilities by another 50% to 180,000 tons, and in 1911 it would complete another Dodge storage facility at Cadosia.[31]

FIGURE 2. 11

**The O&W built this Dodge Storage Facility in 1901 to hold anthracite during summer months in anticipation of winter demand.  It originally erected four plants capable of storing 30,000 tons each.  In 1908, it increased the capacity by 50% to 180,000 tons.  The O&W erected a similar facility at Cadosia in 1911..  [DeForest Douglas Diver collection, O&WRHS Archives]**

Increased tonnages meant increased train weights.  Increased train weights meant the need for more motive power, which could be satisfied by either adding more pushers or purchasing heavier locomotives to pull these trains over the O&W's tortuous grades.  The railroad chose the latter, and in 1900 it purchased the first of its 200,000 pound P-Class Consolidations, which had 67% more tractive power than the 136,000 pound S-Class Consolidations purchased a decade earlier.[32]  Heavier motive power, however, meant the need to rebuild existing bridges to accommodate the increased loads, and it meant increasing the weight of the rails.  Increased train lengths meant delays on the railroad's single track main line and Scranton Extension.  Therefore, over the next dozen years, the O&W undertook a major rebuilding program, first replacing its 67-pound rail with 76-pound rail and then 85 and 90-pound rail.  Then, beginning in 1902, it began double tracking its main line from Cornwall to Cadosia,[33] an effort that was completed in October 1908.[34]  The double-tracking of the Scranton Division, which included the replacement of a number of large bridges and viaducts to accommodate the ever heavier motive power, was completed in December 1912.[35]

The railroad was also expanding during this period.  After a bitter fight which allied the O&W with the Erie against the Pennsylvania Coal Company, the O&W gained access to the route from Port Jervis through Summitville and Ellenville to Kingston with its leases of the Port Jervis & Monticello Railroad and Ellenville & Kingston Railroad.  This gave it direct rail access to the area formerly served by the Delaware & Hudson Canal,[36] which had been abandoned in 1899.[37]  Then, in 1910, it reached farther to the

FIGURE 2.12

**In 1900, the O&W began purchasing these P-Class Consolidations to handle the increasing tonnage coming out of the Scranton Division.  Each of these locomotives weighed a total of 200,000 pounds and had 67% greater tractive effort than the S-Class.  [O&WRHS Archives]**

Hard Coal and Coal Cars

FIGURE 2.13

In 1910, the O&W began ordering these all-purpose W-Class Consolidations, known affectionately as "Long Johns." Each weighed a total of 206,000 pounds and had a tractive effort of 45,400 pounds. O&W GLa #2632 is visible in the background. *[O&WRHS Archives]*

FIGURE 2.14

In order to keep up with the increasing tonnages coming out of the Scranton Division, the O&W began purchasing 12 of these 2-10-2 X-Class locomotives from Alco in 1915. The 352,000 pound total weight of these "Bullmooses" required the "rebuilding of two bridges, the strengthening of a few others, and the addition of 5 stalls to the Middletown round house."[38] Each had a tractive effort of 71,200 pounds. A Westmoreland Coal GLa, #1968, loaded with bituminous coal to feed these beasts, is visible in the background. In 1932, the O&W would purchase 220 of these GLa's from Westmoreland to augment its coal car fleet. *[O&WRHS Archives]*

FIGURE 2.15

**In 1908, the O&W purchased two harbor tugs, the "Ontario" and the "Western" to handle the river traffic in New York Harbor. Here the Ontario is tied up at Cornwall. The Western was sold in 1927; the Ontario, a year later.** *[John Stellwagen Collection; enhanced by Carl A. Ohlson; O&WRHS Archives]*

dolas in 1901, it remained commited to wood construction during the first decade of the twentieth century by building and purchasing over 1100 all-wood, 42½-ton hopper-bottom gondolas. By 1909, the toll that the heavier trains were taking on all-wood cars caused the O&W to rethink its position, and in 1910 it began to build and purchase a total of 1351 composite wood and steel hoppers and reinforce 1000 of those 42½-ton wood gondolas with steel underframes. In 1913, it purchased its first 500 all-steel hoppers, and in 1916, it purchased 400 more. This would be the O&W's last purchase of new hoppers. To pull these heavier trains, the railroad invested in even heavier motive power with the purchase of a dozen X-Class 2-10-2's from Alco in 1915.

south by extending its Capouse Branch down the Wyoming to connect with the Lehigh Valley Railroad.[39]

During the first twenty years of the 20th century, the O&W almost completely changed over its coal car fleet. The heavier load requirements meant that railroads were looking for ways to reduce the "dead weight" of their trains. This meant building cars with larger capacities constructed of lighter materials. The turn of the century saw the introduction of steel as a building material for railroad cars. However, although the O&W experimented with two different kinds of all-steel, hopper-bottom gon-

Thus, as the O&W completed this period of consolidation and growth, it had extended its reach as far as it would; it had rebuilt virtually its entire physical plant with heavier rail and bridges; double-tracked its heaviest traveled sections; invested in new motive power; and had an entire coal car fleet that was less than ten years old. However, storm clouds were forming on the horizon. Government imposed rules were increasing the cost of labor and the ICC was beginning to interfere in the rate structure of railroads. ...and there was trouble brewing in the mines.

## STORM CLOUDS FORMING (1918-1929)

Two significant events occurred in 1917. Scranton Coal Company and Elk Hill Coal & Iron began paying back interest that had been accumulating since June 30, 1912, and the United States Government took possession of the railroad on December 27, 1917, upon America's entry into World War I.[40] Of these two events, it is easily argued that the former was more telling. The United States Railway Administration relinquished control of the railroad in 1920, but the coal companies would continue to face the challenge of repaying their loans. In fact, they never would.

The O&W entered the 1920's looking for ways to achieve greater economy in its operation. In 1922, the ICC had ordered a 10% reduction in anthracite rates based upon a projected increase in volume that, in fact, was never realized. This alone resulted in a $900,000 decrease in revenues for that year.[41] The resulting reduction in revenue per ton, combined with wage rate increases, caused the O&W's operating margins to shrink dramatically. Aggravating this situation were two devastating coal strikes in 1922 and 1925-26, which severely cut anthracite shipments, and according to some, accelerated consumers' switch to other, more reliable sources of heat.[42]

As the result of these strikes and their outcomes, the coal companies faced further challenges in being able to market their coal profitably and repay their loans to the O&W. In 1923, the Scranton Coal Company and Elk Hill stopped paying against the principal of their mortgages held by the railroad, and in 1925, Scranton Coal Company, which was also managing the Elk Hill properties, notified the O&W that it was unable to meet its interest obligations either. In hopes of salvaging the situation, the O&W refinanced their mortgages by issuing a new, joint mortgage to the two coal companies at more favorable terms.

One of the ways in which the O&W sought to economize was to increase the size of its motive power. In 1921, the O&W purchased four Class Y "Mountain" locomotives from the American Locomotive Company.[43] Liking its experience with these locomotives, the O&W purchased six more in 1923,[44] and in 1924, it experimented with a booster on one of these locomotives to enable it to overcome short grades or dips without assistance.[45] Then, in 1929, the O&W purchased ten more, larger "Mountains," designated Class Y-2.

FIGURE 2.16
**In 1921, the O&W began the purchase of ten Y-Class light mountains from Alco. In 1924, they equipped one of these locomotives with a booster to help it surmount short grades without the assistance of a helper. The booster-equipped locomotive, which became Class Y-1, apparently did not live up to its expectations, because the O&W did not equip any other locomotives with this device.[46] Each of these Y's weighed 317,000 pounds and had a tractive effort of 50,300 pounds.** *[O&WRHS Archives]*

Despite the problems in the coal fields, the O&W's shipments of anthracite reached new highs during the 1920's as shipments peaked following each strike to catch up with pent-up demand. The O&W needed additional coal cars, not only to carry these higher shipments, but also to replace the wooden cars that remained in its inventory and were wearing out and becoming obsolete. Unfortunately, the cash-strapped railroad could no longer afford to buy new coal cars, so it resorted to buying second-hand cars to meet its needs. From 1926 to 1928, the O&W purchased 740 used hoppers as it retired the remainder of its wooden fleet.

In 1925, the O&W began selling off its harbor fleet. By 1927, the much photographed tug "Western" had been sold, and by 1928, even her sister, the "Ontario," was gone.[47] The one bright spot on the O&W's horizon as the decade closed and the nation entered the Great Depression was the fact the Federal Government had approved swego's request for building a new harbor.[48]

FIGURE 2.17
**Based upon its success with the Y-Class, the O&W purchased ten Y-2's in 1929. These acquisitions of heavier motive power were motivated by the railroad's need to reduce its operating costs. Each Y-2 weighed 360,000 pounds and had a tractive effort of 60,620 pounds.** *[O&WRHS Archives]*

## DESPERATE MEASURES (1930-1937)

There is an old expression to the effect that "If you loan a man $1000, you own him, but if you loan a man a $1,000,000, he owns you." Nothing could more accurately describe the situation in which the O&W found itself in 1930. By the end of 1929, the Scranton and Elk Hill Coal Companies were $610,000 in arrears on their joint mortgage issued in 1926 for $3,225,000.[49] The problem, as presented to the board, lay in the fact that the Elk Hill properties were losing money and their losses were devouring Scranton's profits. Their answer was to permit the two companies to restructure themselves.[50]

The Scranton Coal Company consisted of the Pine Brook, Capouse, and Riverside Collieries, and a 1/6 interest in the Johnson Colliery. Only Pine Brook was profitable. Elk Hill consisted of the Ontario, Raymond, West Ridge, Mt. Pleasant, and Richmond #3 collieries, and a 5/6 interest in Johnson. Of these, only Mt. Pleasant and Richmond #3 were making money. In exchange for releasing it from the joint mortgage, Elk Hill transferred its profitable operations to Scranton and received Scranton's unprofitable operations. Once this transfer had taken place, the coal companies were organized as shown in Table 2.1.

Following this reorganization, Elk Hill combined with the former South Penn Group, which owned the Legitt's Creek and Von Storch collieries, to form the Penn Anthracite Company. The investors believed that these formerly money-losing operations could be made profitable by processing the coal of the former Elk Hill collieries through the new Chance Cone system installed in the Van Storch

TABLE 2.1

**Alignment of Scranton Coal Company and Elk Hill Coal & Iron Company after the 1930 reorganization.**

| Scranton Coal | Elk Hill Coal | |
|---|---|---|
| Pine Brook | Ontario | Johnson |
| Mt. Pleasant | Raymond | Capouse |
| Richmond #3 | West Ridge | Riverside |

breaker.[51] In order to help the venture get underway and to secure transportation rights from the new company, the O&W would ultimately loan the Penn Anthracite Company $800,000 secured by mortgage bonds.[52]

With Penn Anthracite providing two more breakers and the commitment to transport the anthracite from them over the O&W, the railroad immediately began shopping for more second-hand hopper cars, which it obtained from Westmoreland Coal and Pennsylvania Coal and Coke Companies. These were the last large purchases of freight cars made by the O&W. It's uncertain whether the purchase of this second-hand equipment was more problematic than helpful given the condition of these cars at the time of the railroad's bankruptcy filing. (See Chapter 7) However, on the other hand, one could argue that they held out as long as the coal did.

These final, desperate measures proved futile. After having its debt restructured during the 1930 reorganization, Scranton Coal Company was already another $214,263.81 in arrears to the O&W by 1933.[53] At its April 1935 meeting, the O&W's Board of Directors was informed that the Scranton Coal Company's reserves would be depleted by 1942. In order for the coal company to obtain a loan from the Reconstruction Finance Corporation (RFC) to buy additional coal rights, the RFC required the railroad to subordinate its debt from the coal company.[54] However, by the time the coal company actually received the loan, it could do little more than pay current expenses. On May 28, 1937, Scranton filed for bankruptcy.[55] During that same month, Penn Anthracite defaulted on its loans.[56] Without the income from the coal companies' obligations, the O&W couldn't pay the interest on its own debt. In anticipation of their filings, it too filed for bankruptcy.[57] The O&W's days as an anthracite railroad were nearing an end.

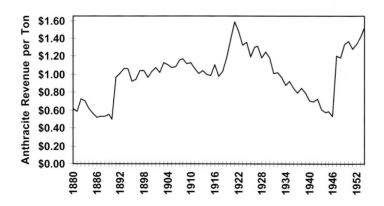

FIGURE 2.18
**The steep decline in anthracite revenue per ton after 1922 was a major factor in the O&W's declining profitability.** *[Multiple Sources]*

## DEATH THROES (1938-1947)

On May 14, 1937, the New York, Ontario & Western Railway filed a petition with the U.S. District Court at New York seeking reorganization under Section 77 of the Federal Bankruptcy Act.[58] At the time of the filing, it is uncertain whether the board realized that the reorganization would result in the railroad's transformation from what it had once claimed to be, an anthracite railroad. Both Scranton Coal and Penn Anthracite were in bankruptcy proceedings. Shortly thereafter, Monarch Coal Company, to which Scranton Coal was heavily indebted, also filed for bankruptcy. Together, these three coal companies accounted for 55% of the O&W's anthracite tonnage.[59] Only Penn Anthracite would survive into the next decade.

When Frederick Lyford assumed control as trustee, the situation was bleak. The total indebtedness of the bankrupt coal companies to the O&W exceeded $7.9 million. Revenue from the railroad's principal sources of income—coal, milk, and passengers—had fallen off sharply. If the railroad were to survive, it would indeed require a complete transformation. However, the new trustee's plans for reorganization were rejected by the ICC because "recent operations of the railway 'show that it cannot be expected to earn the expenses incurred in the operation of the property until there has been developed a solution for the difficulties of the coal companies supplying the debtor's traffic which will insure a continual supply of such traffic, or there has been discovered some other source of traffic, not now apparent.'"[60] It never would. The anthracite fields in northern Pennsylvania were being exhausted. The output of those collieries that were still mining was already spoken for. By the end of the next ten years, the O&W would be barely recognizable as the once proud anthracite carrier.

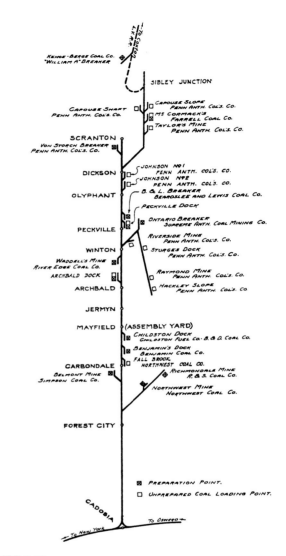

FIGURE 2.19

**This map, prepared for the Jeddo-Highland Anthracite Case in July 1941, shows the collieries still serving the O&W in the early 1940's.** [O&WRHS Archives]

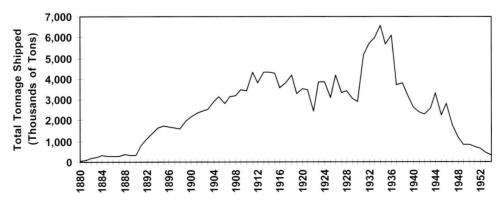

FIGURE 2.20

**The total tonnage of anthracite shipped by the O&W from all sources (1880-1954).** [Multiple Sources]

Lyford fixed what he could and got rid of what he couldn't. One of his first actions was to extend the capacity of 500 of the railroad's used hopper cars in an attempt to stem the abysmal balance of per diem payments to other railroads. Those cars that were obsolete or no longer needed were sold off. From 1937 to 1947, the O&W sent over 3400 coal cars to the scrappers. They didn't go alone. In 1941, the O&W purchased its first diesel-electrics, and the railroad was soon sending its labor-intensive steam fleet to join them. By 1947, only a few miles of double track remained between Cornwall and Cadosia, and the double track along the Scranton Division was being ripped up right behind it. The Dodge plants at Middletown and Cadosia were coming down, and the railroad was seeking a lessee for its coaling docks at Weehawken. The O&W was no longer an anthracite railroad. Unfortunately, it was no longer a milk carrier or passenger line, either.

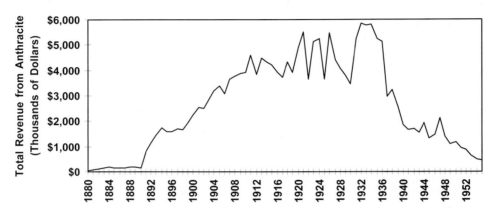

FIGURE 2.21
**The O&W's total revenue from anthracite traffic from 1880 through 1955. [Multiple Sources]**

**END OF THE LINE (1948-1957)**

The O&W completed its dieselization in 1948 and while the railroad still carried over one million tons of anthracite during that year, it was carrying less than a third of that amount six years later. On March 29, 1957, after almost 20 years in bankruptcy, the last regularly scheduled train on the railroad, No. 10 from Norwich, was brought in at 5:00 p.m. with Engineer Henry P. Kortright at the throttle.[61]

# Middletown Times Herald

LOCAL WEATHER FORECAST: Generally clear and moder ate tonight and tomorrow.



106th Year; 75th Issue; 10,225 Copies Printed Today. MIDDLETOWN, N. Y., SATURDAY, MARCH 30, 1957 FOURTEEN PAGES FINAL EDITION SINGLE COPY FIVE CENTS WEEKLY RATES THIRTY CENTS

## 80-Year Old Carrier Rolls Into Oblivion

# 'Old and Weary' Calls It Quits

**Driver Hurt:** Wreckage of a car in which Robert Thompson, 47, of 176 West Main street, was injured in Mt. Hope Road upset yesterday.—Photo by Milburn.

## Car Snaps Pole, Upsets; Driver Is Hospitalized

Robert Thompson, 47, of 176 West Main street, was in fair condition today in Horton Hospital with injuries suffered when the car he was driving went out of control, sheared off a light pole and overturned on the Mount Hope-Finchville road, about one mile west of the Otisville road, yesterday afternoon.

Thompson suffered a compound fracture of the right leg and cuts on the face and was taken to the hospital by the Otisville Volunteer Ambulance, according to Sgt. Arthur French of the Middletown State Police barracks.

Sgt. French said the accident was under investigation today.

In another local accident, a New Jersey motorist was given a summons for failure to keep his car under control, after the car ran into the back of a milk truck on Rte. 17 in Bloomingburg, State Police of the Wurtsboro barracks reported.

Emil Tabor, the ticketed driver, and his wife, Dorothea, of Fairlawn, N. J., received minor injuries and were treated by Dr. Paul Ellis of Bloomingburg, the troopers said. The summons was issued on complaint of Mark O'Brien of Highland Mills, driver of the truck, which was owned by Marcus Trucking Co. of Monroe, according to the police.

### Grantland Rice Estate Valued at $242,907

NEW YORK (AP)—Sports writer Grantland Rice left a net estate of $242,907 when he died July 13, 1954, it was disclosed yesterday.

An estate tax appraisal listed gross assets of $266,698.

Principal beneficiaries were his widow, Mrs. Katherine Hollis Rice of New York, and a daughter, Florence Rice Butler of Venice, Calif.

### Today's Times Herald

*Helpful Hints to Hurried Readers*

Today's Times Herald teems with stories and pictures of the demise of the O&W. The AP's Robert Farrington pens an interesting obituary on **Page 2**.

Transfer of New Hampton employes from New York City rolls to state service stirs a protest in today's Public Forum. Page 4. On the same page, "Another Polio Year" discusses the current shortage of Salk vaccine.

**Mildred Parker Seese** offers a brief account of an 1883 "milk war" on **Page 14.**

In the sports section: Another of staffer **Glenn Doty's** analyses of area high school baseball prospects. Spotlighted is Pine Bush Central School. **Page 9.**

Our **Beatrice G. Rosenblum's** column on today's Antiques Page—a new Times Herald feature—reports on "'Oscar' Originals in Circleville." Page 11.

**P.S.:** Hungry swains make things rough for Etta Kett. **On The Best Comic Page in New York State.** Page 10.

## Reserve Training Requirements Cut

WASHINGTON (AP) — The Army has cut by more than half the length of time youthful reservists must continue training after active duty. It also reduced the total service obligation of draftees and regular Army volunteers.

The changes in requirements for reservists and National Guardsmen were announced yesterday. They become effective next Monday.

Under the new program, below draft-age youths who volunteer for six months' active duty training will be required to serve three years instead of the present 7 in the ready reserve, subject to immediate call to active duty.

The ready reserve obligation for Army draftees was reduced from five years to four. Draftees spend two years on active duty, and the reduction means they now will stay in the ready reserve an additional two years instead of three.

Likewise, the total obligation for regular Army volunteers was reduced from five to four years. Men may volunteer for three, four or more years. A three-year volunteer henceforth will be required to spend only one additional year in the ready reserve.

The Army did not give reasons for the reserve modifications, but spokesmen said the changes obviously were designed to make the reserve program more attractive.

The changes embody the recent compromise over National Guard training which resulted from a feud between the Pentagon and the National Guard Assn.

## Two Ship Convoys Traversing Canal

PORT SAID, Egypt (AP) — Two ship convoys were moving through the Suez Canal today, marking a major step toward resumption of normal operations in the 103-mile waterway.

A five-nation, nine-ship convoy which entered the canal yesterday from Suez at the southern end resumed its voyage at dawn after being stalled by a severe sand storm.

Another five-ship convoy entered the canal today at Suez. They were the first to begin passage since the waterway was blocked during the October - November British, French and Israeli attacks on Egypt.

Some individual ships have transited the waterway since limited operation was resumed.

Both convoys entered the canal on strictly Egyptians terms, paying tolls to the nationalized Suez Canal Authority.

A U. N. salvage team, headed by U. S. Lt. Gen. Raymond A. Wheeler (Ret.), planned to remove the last major obstruction from the canal Monday or Tuesday. It is the 1,461-ton Egyptian frigate Abukir, sunk near the southern entrance. Egypt then is expected to proclaim the canal open to all normal shipping.

### Soothing the Beasts

MILWAUKEE (AP) — Music is going to the dogs — and the cats — and any other animal at the Wisconsin Humane Society Shelter.

A hi-fi system, paid for and installed by society people, has been put into operation "to help quiet the animals and give them a more relaxed, homey atmosphere."

"Of course," a spokesman added, "it also will help relax visitors and employes."

## Warren, Former School Head Here, Joins Architects

CARL V. WARREN

Carl V. Warren, superintendent of schools in Middletown from 1939 until 1949, has accepted a position as educational consultant with the architectural firm of Kelly and Gruzen, in New York City, it was learned today.

Mr. Warren, who helped in the planning and construction of Middletown High School, retired this year as superintendent of public schools at Huntington, L. I.

Mr. Warren, 57, succeeded Ernest H. Burdick as superintendent in Middletown. In 1949 Mr. Warren was succeeded by Ralph S. Shattuck, present superintendent. Mr. Warren was superintendent of schools at Massena, N. Y. from 1936 to 1939 and is a native of Oneida County. He graduated from Hamilton College in 1923 and received his Master of Arts degree from Columbia University in 1933.

He helped plan and construct

(Continued on Page 2 Col 2)

## Union Rumbles Threaten Beck 'Truth' Fund

### Top Leaders Deny Knowledge of Telephone Poll for Approval

WASHINGTON (AP) — Teamsters President Dave Beck's million dollar campaign to clear himself of charges of misusing union funds was threatened today by powerful rumblings from within his own union.

Beck, who wouldn't tell inquisitive senators anything about his own finances, insisted yesterday he has secured "overwhelming approval" for a million dollar "truth" fund.

The rotund Teamsters chief, bounced yesterday from his AFL-CIO executive council post pending a May 20 hearing, said the million dollar item was approved in a telephone poll of the Teamsters executive board.

**Treasurer Opposed**

But John English, the Teamsters secretary-treasurer, a board member and popular figure with the rank and file membership, said he had not been consulted about any such plan and was not in favor of it.

In St. Louis another Teamsters board member, Daniel J. Murphy, said no one polled him about it either.

Beck's troubles mounted on the heels of the AFL-CIO executive council's action yesterday suspending him as one of its members and as an AFL-CIO vice president.

The council—top command of the 15-million member AFL-CIO—ordered a full scale investigation by the federation's ethical practices committee into charges that Beck has brought "the labor movement into disrepute." This probe also would cover corruption allegations against several other high Teamsters officials, some of whom are under indictment on various charges.

Meanwhile Senate Rackets Committee sources said they are not "half through" investigating Beck's complex financial dealings, but may not call him back for quizzing unless he agrees to talk. They said other witnesses and documentary evidence could tell most of the story.

The AFL-CIO council's move against Beck came after he invoked his Fifth Amendment protection against possible self-incrimination in refusing to tell the rackets committee about his finances. The Senate investigators say he turned to his personal use more than $320,000 in Teamster funds.

If it follows past practice, the AFL-CIO council is likely to give the 1½ million member union an opportunity to oust certain of its officers. The penalty for not doing so would be suspension from the giant federation—and a possible later move to create a rival union in the same field.

**Beck Non-Commital**

Beck—who did not attend the council meeting—told a reporter in Seattle "I have nothing to say" about the action against him. Beck said he expects to call a special meeting soon of the Teamsters executive board. He didn't say where or when the board would meet.

AFL-CIO President George Meany said yesterday Beck has been summoned to a hearing here May 20 to answer "for his actions in bringing the labor movement into disrepute and his failing to explain many charges against him

(Continued on Page 2. Col 1)

**Deserted Yards:** A general view of the O&W's yards at Wisner avenue focuses attention on the stillness enveloping the rolling stock of the defunct railroad. Some 80 pieces of equipment, including 47 diesel electric locomotives lie idle in the yards following the shutdown of the road at midnight last night.

**Last Closing:** Yard Clerk Wilson Turner locks yard office of O&W Railroad for last time at 8:15 last night as Louis W. Cashon, left and Harry Thornton, center, look on. Mr. Wilson, 39, was with the railroad for 20 years; Mr. Cashon, 60, a car inspector, for 36 years, and Mr. Thornton, 61, a conductor, for 20 years.—Photos by Freilich.

## Milk Hearing Sessions End

NEW YORK (AP) — A marathon federal hearing into the New York-New Jersey milk industry ended yesterday.

The 9-month-old hearing ground through 102 sessions and 16,000 pages of testimony. The findings will soon go to Secretary of Agriculture Benson.

G. Osmond Hyde, hearing examiner, set April 15 for the filing of briefs prior to his forwarding the records to the Agriculture Department.

The inquiry into milk marketing practices began last June 18. The first sessions concerned proposals for separate marketing orders for New York and New Jersey.

Opposition to that proposal led

(Continued on Page 2 Col 1)

## Crew of 30-Year Veterans Bring In Last O&W Train; Torpedoes Sound Requiem

By ALAN KENNEDY

The last regularly scheduled train of the Ontario & Western Railroad, No. 10 from Norwick, was brought in at five p. m. yesterday by a

The five-man crew had an aggregate age of 329 years. Each was older in point of service than the rolling stock in the train.

"I'm just glad to be getting home safe and sound," said Conductor Leon Tompkins, 70, of 6 Harrison street, who is retiring after 49 years on the O & W.

Engineer Henry P. Kortright, 72, of 21 Myrtle avenue, also is retiring, as is Fred Shields, 65, of 116 Lake avenue, rear brakeman.

But the other two crew members, like many of the line's veteran railroaders, still have some time to go before they can get pensions, and hence must find other means. They are George Sayer, 60, of Watkins avenue extension, the head brakeman, and Fireman T. M. Carmody, 62, of 65 Wickham avenue.

"Retired? We're all going to be 'tired' after tonight," said Engineer Kortright to a reporter riding with him, Mr. Sayer and Mr. Carmody in the Diesel cab on the last run. All operating employes were laid off as of midnight.

"It's a very sad thing, and it's going to be hard for a lot of people," Mr. Kortright observed in between the long-long-short-long blasts of the Diesel's horn as the train lumbered past grade crossings and began to slow down for Middletown.

(Continued on Page 2 Col 5)

## Milk Guild Opens Conclave; Dorney Regains Office

Disclosure that the Rev. John W. Dorney, of Balesville, N. J., has been reinstated as executive director highlighted the opening of the Tri - State Master Dairy Farmers Guild, convention at Middletown High School this morning.

Mr. Dorney, who lost his position as executive director on the 19th of March, when the job was abolished, was re-appointed yesterday when the position was re-established at a closed meeting of the grand guild and guild delegates in Baleville, according to David Fortune, business manager for the guild.

Following a welcoming address to the guild by Mayor Raymond E. Swalm, Robert Easley, district president of the American Federation of Grain Millers, of the AFL-CIO, offered the Tri-State Master Dairy Farmers Guild an affiliation with his union. Since the dairy farmers and grain millers are closely related, Mr. Easley said both would benefit from the affiliation because it is impossible "to stand alone."

Mr. Easley stated that he considers the guild as a union, even

(Continued on Page 2. Col 4)

**OVERNIGHT LOW 32**

Middletown's overnight low, as recorded at the municipal ... Plant, was 32 degrees. Yesterday's high was 50 degrees. Precipitation yesterday was reported as .03 inches.

## O&W Founders Were Wrong

By EDWARD P. DOUGHERTY
Editor, Times Herald

Founders of the Ontario & Western Railway guessed wrong.

They mapped their line diagonally across the state from the Port of New York to Oswego on Lake Ontario and gambled that Oswego would someday become the state's major inland port — and direct water link to the west.

Oswego never attained that status. It was Buffalo, west of the obstacle of Niagara Falls, that became the major inland port.

Even though the founders' dreams were shattered, the railroad had its great days. Opened in 1870 — 87 years ago — the railroad prospered through good times and depression right up to 1935.

**The Golden Years**

The golden years were those between 1910 and 1935 when anthracite, mined in Scranton, Pa., and other sections of that state was shipped over the line. Anthracite was called "black gold" for the railway got its greatest income from this source for a long period. Tonnage shipped over the Scranton branch was sufficient to support the operation of the entire line at one time.

But times were to change. And the O & W was to become the victim of those changes as much as it was of the original wrong guess.

Coal strikes put emphasis on fuel heating. The more industries and homes that converted to oil, the less coal there was shipped over the Scranton branch. And the Scranton fields had no oil to take up the slack!

Long before the coal business began to taper off, the O & W had felt the advent of the car and truck. In its early days the railroad transported milk from Orange and Delaware Counties — still the rich dairyland of the state — to New York City.

Modern highways and milk tankers provided rapid transport for this perishable product and the railroad lost out.

The car dealt another serious blow on the road's economy. For years the O & W scheduled passenger train service to the vacationland of the Catskills and Middletowners will well remember the crowded trains that stopped at the Wickham avenue station to and from the resort land of Sullivan County.

Passengers would pour from the cars and into the spacious O & W restaurant, so immaculately kept by

(Continued on Page 2 Col 1)

## Closing Idles 450 Employes Along Line

By SAUL FREILICH

The jobs of 450 persons were wiped out at midnight last night when the 80-year old New York, Ontario and Western Railroad officially ceased operations. Sixty-six others will remain at their posts until they are dismissed.

The last scheduled train of the O&W arrived in Middletown at 5 p. m. yesterday though two other unscheduled trains followed. The last one came from Oswego and arrived at 3:15 a.m. today.

Following the shutdown, plans were underway to begin the final accounting and inventory of equipment owned by the defunct road. Robert H. McGraw, general manager said that he will remain at work until the O&W is completely liquidated to supervise the inventory and final disposal of property.

Harry Weeks, office manager, reported today that 30 persons would be retained in the accounting office in Middletown and six office employes in New York would remain. Other employes who will be retained on the payroll include watchmen along the line.

Thomas Gire, assistant to Mr. McGraw, said the 450 persons who lost jobs yesterday made the total number laid off since the railroad went into receivership on Feb.

Other story and photos on Page 2.

eighth 1,056. He said that 344 persons were previously dropped and the remainder were parttime employes who were laid off.

Efforts to aid some of the employes whose jobs were abolished will begin Monday morning. At 10 a.m., persons eligible for pensions will register with representatives of the Railroad Retirement Board.

Retirement Board agents will be in Middletown from Monday through Wednesday and will be at the O & W station from 10 a.m. to five p.m. each day.

A meeting has been arranged with Retirement Board on Thursday night at 7:15 in the Chamber of Commerce Assembly room for persons unemployed as a result of the shutdown, Arthur E. Calhoun, secretary of the general committee of the Brotherhood of Railroad Trainmen reported.

Mr. Calhoun said the Retirement Board agents will inform the people about the railroad retirement annuities and social security benefits. The meeting is open to employes of all crafts and to the members of interested families.

Mr. Calhoun also said that a telegram had been sent by the Brotherhood of Railroad Trainmen to Owen F. Clarke, chairman of the Interstate Commerce Committee formally requesting approval of agreements made with other railroads to service section of the O&W housing large industrial plants. He was asked also to protect the rights of those employed yesterday on the O&W to man trains and crews that

(Continued on Page 2 Col 2)

### INDEX TO FEATURES





FIGURE 2.22
*Middletown Times Herald,* March 30, 1957 *[Courtesy: Times Herald-Record]*

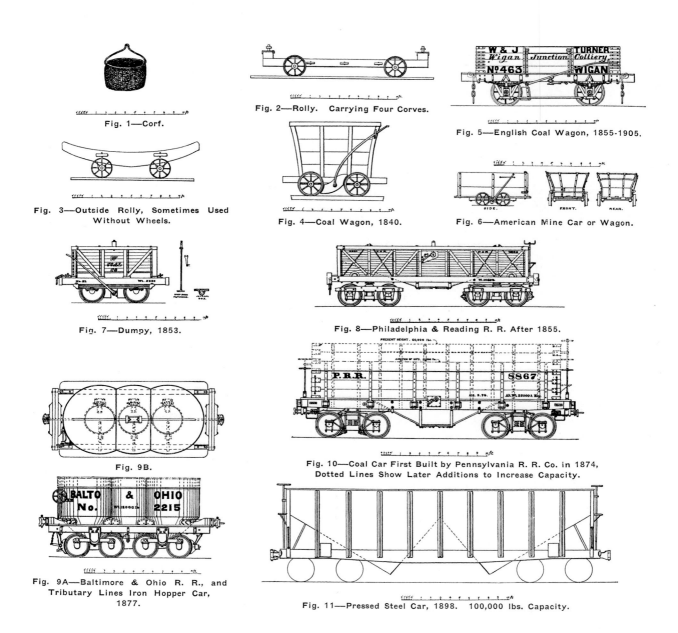

Fig. 1—Corf.

Fig. 2—Rolly.  Carrying Four Corves.

Fig. 5—English Coal Wagon, 1855-1905.

Fig. 3—Outside Rolly, Sometimes Used Without Wheels.

Fig. 4—Coal Wagon, 1840.

Fig. 6—American Mine Car or Wagon.

Fig. 7—Dumpy, 1853.

Fig. 8—Philadelphia & Reading R. R. After 1855.

Fig. 9B.

Fig. 10—Coal Car First Built by Pennsylvania R. R. Co. in 1874, Dotted Lines Show Later Additions to Increase Capacity.

Fig. 9A—Baltimore & Ohio R. R., and Tributary Lines Iron Hopper Car, 1877.

Fig. 11—Pressed Steel Car, 1898.  100,000 lbs. Capacity.

FIGURE 3.1

In October 1905, C.H. Caruthers traced "The Evolution of the Coal Car" in an article for *The Railroad Gazette*.  Figure 1 is a "corf" or basket that was used to haul coal from the mines in the early 15th and 16th centuries.  Figures 2 and 3 are wagons developed in the 1600's to carry the corfs.  These were ultimately replaced by the wagons shown in Figures 4, 5 & 6, which were used through the middle of the 19th century.  Figure 7 shows a "dumpy" (or "Jimmy") used during the mid to late 19th century.  Figure 8 is the all-wood, 10-ton hopper built by the Philadelphia & Reading Railroad in the mid-1850's.  Figure 9 A & B shows an iron hopper car built by the Baltimore & Ohio Railroad.  It had a weight of 17,300 pounds and was rated at a capacity of 40,000 pounds.[1]  Figure 10 is an all-wood, hopper-bottom gondola designed and built at the Pennsylvania Railroad's Altoona shops in the mid to late 1870's.  Dotted lines show how the capacity of the car was increased over time.  Figure 11 is the first all-steel production hopper car built for the Bessemer & Lake Erie Railroad by the Pressed Steel Car Company in 1898.[2]  *[The Railroad Gazette, October 1905]*

The history of railroads and the history of coal mining are inextricably linked. The first railroad cars were open-top cars run on rails to transport coal and iron ore out of the mines. Initially, the rails were nothing more than the trunks of small trees laid parallel to each other, and the coal cars were simple boxes riding on twin-flanged, wooden wheels shaped like pulleys. In 1676, Roger North described a railway in England this way: "The rails of timber were placed end to end and exactly straight, and in two lines parallel to each other. On these bulky cars were made to run on four rollers fitting these rails, whereby the carriage was made so easy that one horse would draw four or five chaldrons of coal at a load."[3]

FIGURE 3.2
**This 17th century engraving shows an early tramway. Note the twin-flanged rollers riding on the small saplings.** *[The Science of Railways, 1902]*

FIGURE 3.3
**Early engraving of first steam locomotive pulling ore cars. The locomotive was built by Richard Trevithick in 1804 and operated on flanged, cast iron rails at the Penydaren iron works in Wales. The locomotive proved too heavy for the rails and did not remain in service.** *[The Science of Railways, 1902]*

Over time, the rails were shaped with a flat running surface so that ordinary carts could run on the rails. To keep the carts on the track, iron flanges were added to the rails, first to the outside and then to the inside. As cars became heavier, iron straps were nailed to the running surface to reduce friction and extend the life of the rails. In this way, it was noted that "one horse could do the work of eight on a common road."[4]

It's difficult for us today to appreciate what a revolution Richard Trevithick's successful demonstration of the Penydaren steam locomotive began in 1804. Although the weight of his locomotive proved disastrous for the flanged iron railway over which it was run, the use of steam to pull a train

revolutionized the way people thought about moving products to market. For millennia, mankind had relied upon animal power to haul products overland to the nearest navigable waterway for shipment to faraway destinations. Now a single locomotive could do the work of several draft animals. At first, railroads were conceived as nothing more than replacements for the traditional means of moving products to the nearest waterway for shipment to the market. It would be many years before a railroad would be built to move the products all the way to their ultimate destination.

FIGURE 3.4
**The world's first coal train pulled by a steam locomotive ran from the Middletown Colliery in northeast England to the town of Leeds. The cogged locomotive could pull up to thirty loaded coal cars.** *[The Science of Railways, 1902]*

FIGURE 3.5
**Locomotive and coal car for the Stockton & Darlington Railway built by George Stephenson in 1825. The line carried coal mined near Darlington to the river at Stockton using a combination of steam locomotives to pull the cars over level planes and stationary steam engines to pull cars up inclined planes to surmount hills. The S&DR served as the model for the Carbondale Railroad built by the Delaware & Hudson Canal Company.** *[The American Railway, 1889]*

Eight years elapsed from the time of Trevithick's demonstration to the development of the first commercial railroad, and the first commercial railroad was a coal road. In 1812, Matthew Murray developed a cogged locomotive to haul coal from the Middletown Colliery Railway in northeast England to the town of Leeds. This locomotive was able to pull thirty loaded coal cars the three and one quarter mile distance in just one hour. The system was so successful that the colliery quickly built several more locomotives, which remained in service for several years thereafter.[5]

The forerunner of the modern steam locomotive was introduced by George Stephenson at the Killingworth Colliery near Newcastle-upon-Tyne in northwest England in 1814. While still somewhat crude, the Blucher could pull eight loaded wagons totaling thirty tons at four miles per hour up an ascending grade of one in four hundred and fifty feet (.2%), making it the strongest locomotive built up to that time.[6] One factor set the Blucher apart from all other locomotives—it had flanged wheels. Even though cast-iron "edge rail" and flanged wheels had been developed twenty five years earlier by William Jessop,[7] no locomotive had yet been built that combined those features and used simple adhesion for forward propulsion. Stephenson's Blucher was the first.

In 1825, Stephenson went on to build the Stockton & Darlington Railway, the first railroad opened for general traffic.[8] The Stockton &

Darlington was a coal road, and the first train pulled over the railway was a coal train. To celebrate the railway's opening, however, it was interspersed with sufficient special cars to carry 600 passengers, which also gave it the distinction of being the first railroad to carry passengers.[9] The railroad used a combination of steam locomotives, which pulled the cars along level planes, and stationary steam engines, which pulled the cars up inclined planes to surmount hills, to move the coal from the collieries near Darlington to the river at Stockton. It is certain that American engineers visited the S&DR to gain ideas on how to move coal over similar obstacles in the United States. Originally designed to move 10,000 tons per year, the S&DR would be hauling 500,000 tons per year within a few years of its inception.[10]

George Stephenson left many legacies to future railroaders. Out of his early experiments, he demonstrated the value of exhausting the steam up the smoke stack to increase the draft in locomotive fireboxes. In 1818, he conducted experiments with case-hardened, chilled cast-iron wheels, which would go on to become the industry standard for over one hundred years.[11] When he built the Stockton & Darlington Railway, he chose to set the width between the rails at 4' 8½", the same distance between the rails he used at Killingworth.[12] The "Stephenson gauge" has since become the standard gauge in England, the United States, and most of continental Europe. Stephenson continued to improve his locomotives and ultimately cemented his place in railroading history when his "Rocket" won the Rainhill trials sponsored by the Manchester & Liverpool Railway in 1829.

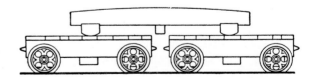

FIGURE 3.6
**This early drawing shows how the Quincy railroad used two cars to distribute the weight of the marble blocks it was transporting. The drawing was used by litigants against Ross Winans to prove that he did not invent the concept of the swiveling truck as he claimed in his patent of 1834.[13]** *[The American Railway, 1889]*

Hard Coal and Coal Cars

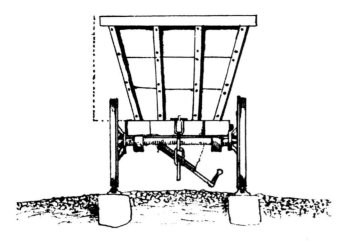

FIGURE 3.7
**19th century English engraving of early American coal car showing chain coupling, large wheels, and drop door.** [*Development of Transportation Systems in the United States, 1888*]

Entrepreneurs on the other side of the Atlantic were also experimenting with railroads. In 1826, a three mile railroad was constructed in Quincy, Massachusetts, to haul marble from quarries to a nearby river. This has often been identified as the first American railroad, but there is convincing evidence that it was actually predated by three or more other railroads or tramways throughout the United States.[14] However, it was the movement of coal that was to provide the first real impetus to railroad development in the United States. Indeed, in the same year that the Quincy tramway was built, Abraham Pott was building a half mile long railroad to transport coal from his anthracite mine near Pottsville, Pennsylvania to the Schuylkill Canal for shipment to Philadelphia. The rails were made of wood, and the cars, which were apparently self-clearing, could each carry 1½ tons of coal. It was noted that a single horse could pull thirteen of these loaded coal cars from the mines to the waterway along this road.[15]

Over the next decade, railroad development in the United States continued to follow the model of Potts' simple railroad and Stephenson's Stockton & Darlington Railway, that is, they were a means to move coal to a waterway for transport to market.

Railroads were still not considered to be a means of moving a product all the way to market. Indeed, a locomotive capable of reliably pulling a coal train over the distances required had not been demonstrated.

In 1827, the first "major" coal railroad was built by the Lehigh Coal & Navigation Company to connect its anthracite mines at Summit Hill to the Lehigh Canal at Mauch Chunk (now Jim Thorpe). The "Mauch Chunk Rail Way" was a gravity railroad, whose cars descended by gravity the nine miles from the mines to the canal. The 1½ ton cars were generally linked in groups of six to ten cars for the descent to the canal where the anthracite would be transloaded into arks for shipment to tidewater. Mules would ride in the last car on the downhill ride to pull the empties back up to the summit. The wooden rails were capped with strap iron measuring ¼ inch by ½ inches. Eventually, the railroad was extended farther back into the coal fields, using a series of "switchbacks" to traverse the mountainsides to the canal. Hence, the Mauch Chunk railroad eventually became known as the "Switchback Gravity Railroad."[16]

Two years later, in 1829, the northern coal fields were breached by the Carbondale Railroad, which was built by the Delaware and Hudson Canal Company to connect its coal fields in the Lackawanna Valley to the head of its canal at

FIGURE 3.8
**A string of empty coal cars is shown returning down the Delaware & Hudson Canal Company's gravity railroad. Note the crude four-wheel swiveling trucks under these cars. Heavier duty trucks would not have been required since these cars didn't venture off the gravity railroad and weren't subjected to the speeds or rigors of interchange service.** [*DeForest Douglas Diver Railroad Photographs, ca. 1870-1950. Collection 1948. Courtesy of the Division of Rare and Manuscript Collections, Cornell University Library*]

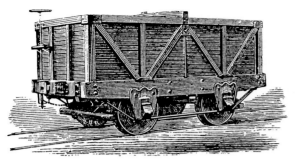

FIGURE 3.9
**Coal "Jimmy" used by the New York Central & Hudson River Railway. This car had a weight of 9500 pounds and a capacity of 16,000 pounds.[17]** [*The Car Builder's Dictionary, 1888*]

Honesdale on the other side of Moosic Mountain. John Jervis, who designed the railroad, was heavily influenced by the developments in England and in particular the Hetton Colliery and Stockton & Darlington Railways.[18] To ascend the mountain, the railroad employed a series of inclined planes up which the cars would be pulled by stationary steam engines. From the top of one plane to the bottom of the next, the "waggons" would descend by gravity or be pulled by a steam locomotive. Unfortunately, the wooden rails proved inadequate to support the weight of the steam locomotives that the canal company had purchased, and the railroad defaulted to using animal power and ultimately gravity to move the coal cars from plane to plane.

Based upon the success of these two railroads, various entrepreneurs began building independent railroads to haul anthracite from the mines to various waterways. The Mill Creek & Mine Hill Railroad, the Mine Hill & Schuylkill Haven Railroad, and the Little Schuylkill Railroad were constructed using animal power to haul the coal from the mines to the waterways. The Little Schuylkill used cars with a three ton capacity and wheels three feet in diameter.[19] In 1833, it became the first of these railroads to replace its animals with steam locomotives. However, all of these railroads were still just connections to waterways over which the coal would be shipped to market. Their importance, however, can not be understated. As John

White states in his comprehensive work on freight cars:

"...Coal indeed gave birth to the industry, whose origins can be found in horse-powered tramways established in northern England during the eighteenth century. Rail transport was introduced into this country about a century later on the gravity railways at Mauch Chunk and Honesdale, Pennsylvania, which were created to service the coal mines. The practical success of these two small lines in moving coal from the mountaintop to nearby canal landings demonstrated the general utility of railways for other transport purposes."[20]

It was not until 1842 that a railroad was built that actually connected the coal fields directly to the market. On January 10, 1842, the Philadelphia & Reading Railroad was completed from Pottsville to Philadelphia. Unlike other railroads of the time that were built on a shoe string, the P&R was solidly built with iron rails, minimal grades and moderate curves over which a single locomotive was capable of pulling 101 loaded cars at an average speed of 10 miles per hour.[21] The railroad was an immediate success, and it is from this point that the story of the modern railroad coal car begins.

The coal car that dominated the anthracite railroads, both gravity and steam, during their first fifty years, was the four wheel "jimmy" or "dumpy." In 1875, almost fifty years after the gravity railroads started operation and forty years after Ross Winans patented the four-wheeled bogey truck, there were still up to fifty-five thousand jimmies in service.[22] It seems difficult to believe that this diminutive vehicle could survive for so long. Some historians have suggested that the reason that the jimmy stayed in service was that it was easy for men to move without the

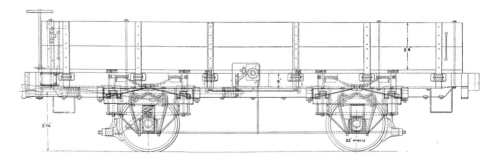

FIGURE 3.10
**It is very likely that these four-wheeled, drop-bottom gondolas used by the Delaware & Hudson to haul anthracite would have been seen on the O&W in interchange service.** [*Railroad Car Journal, November 1898*]

aid of a locomotive,[23] but period instructional manuals suggest that the heaviest cars that men could move easily were in the range of 2½ to 3 tons.[24] Therefore, there must have been other reasons why the jimmy stayed in service as long as it did.

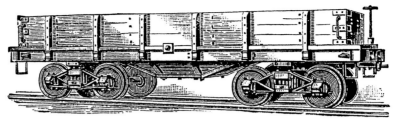

FIGURE 3.11
**Early hopper-bottom gondola circa late 1870's.** [*Car Builder's Dictionary, 1888*]

The fact is that the jimmy was well suited for the anthracite business. The first breaker did not begin operation until 1844,[25] and the output of these early breakers was in the neighborhood of only 200 tons of coal a day.[26] Because this limited output would need to be further segregated by size, and since the railroads would want to achieve continuous movement of filled coal cars throughout their systems, these smaller coal cars may have been exactly what the coal companies needed to provide a continuous flow of coal over their roads.

There is another factor to consider. The jimmy was actually more efficient than early cars with swiveling trucks. One of the truisms of railroad car building in the early 19th century was that it took one pound of freight car to carry one pound of freight in cars with swiveling trucks.[27] Dead weight yields no revenue, and railroad executives were anxious to find a way of increasing the "paying freight to total weight" ratio above this 1:2 ratio. One of the key factors limiting the capacity of these cars was the quality of the journals. When trains were short, loads light, and speeds low, journals were not much

of a factor. However, as these three factors increased, journal strength became a critical issue. A hot box or broken journal could derail a train and shut down a railroad's revenue stream. Journal size remains the governing factor in the load that a freight car can carry to this day.

An article in the May 1882 issue of *National Car Builder* addressed this issue. Railroads had the desire and the ability to build wooden cars with higher capacities, but they were constrained in the total weight of cars by journal technology. As shown in Table 3.1, the paying freight to total weight ratio was actually better in the jimmy than in the early 10-ton, two truck car.' It was not until the 1880's that journals were developed that permitted the two-truck car to exceed the paying weight to total weight ratio of the jimmy. However, given the huge capital investment that the railroads had made in these smaller cars, the jimmy would survive well into the 1890's. After that time, their inability to

TABLE 3.1
**Comparison of Paying Freight to Total Weight of Three Coal Cars — The lack of a journal capable of withstanding higher loads delayed the introduction of high capacity coal cars. Until that time, the 4-wheel jimmy was actually the more efficient coal car. In the early 1880's, higher capacity journals were introduced that enabled railroads to introduce higher efficiency, 2 truck coal cars as shown in the table below.[28]**

|  | 4-Wheel Jimmy* | 1870's 10-Ton 2-Truck Car** | 1880's 30-Ton 2-Truck Car** |
|---|---|---|---|
| Total Weight of Car | 7,900 | 20,000 | 24,238 |
| Less wheels and axles | 2,600*** | 5,200 | 5,400 |
| Weight on journals | 5,300 | 14,800 | 18,838 |
| Add load | 13,000 | 20,000 | 60,000 |
| Total weight on journals | 18,300 | 34,800 | 78,838 |
| Total weight on each journal | 4,575 | 4,350 | 9,855 |
| Weight per square inch on journal | 173 | 167 | 379 |
| *Ratio of paying freight to total weight* | 62.20% | 50.00% | 71.23% |

**Sources:** *Car Builder's Dictionary, 1888, **National Car Builder, May 1882; ***Estimated*

*The Delaware & Hudson Canal Company was actually running 2-truck cars weighing 5,500 pounds and having a 5-ton capacity over its gravity railroad in the 1860's. However, these cars did not have to stand up to the rigors of long distance hauls or interchange.

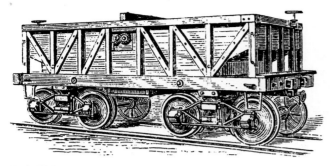

FIGURE 3.12
**The Philadelphia & Reading built a number of these wooden hoppers in the 1860's. Each had a capacity of 20,000 pounds.**[29] *[The Car Builder's Dictionary, 1888]*

stand up to handing with larger freight cars and the cost of bringing these lightweight cars into compliance with the National Railway Safety Act meant that they would not survive into the twentieth century.

A major change in the way that American railroads conducted their business occurred after the Civil War. Up through the 1850's, freight cars tended to stay on their own lines. When cargo was shipped beyond the limits of a particular railroad's line, it would be off-loaded from the one railroad's cars, carried by teamsters, often across town, and reloaded onto the next railroad line's cars. After the Civil War, railroads moved quickly to integrate their lines so that they could send freight through by exchanging freight cars rather than continuing to endure the time-consuming and labor intensive exchange of loads at terminals.[30]

The interchange of freight cars from one line to another created another world of problems, and in 1866, representatives from the car departments of

eleven railroads met in Adrian, Michigan, to address them. In order to facilitate repairs of foreign cars, they agreed to standardize axles, journals, and other running parts of freight cars, and they agreed to establish uniform rates for the repair of foreign cars. They also agreed to meet again, and in September 1867, they met in Altoona, Pennsylvania, to establish the Master Car Builders' Association to govern the interchange of freight and passenger cars.[32] Ultimately, the M.C.B.A. would publish a comprehensive *Code of Rules Governing the Condition of, and Repairs to, Freight Cars for the Interchange of Traffic,* and it would establish standards and recommended practices governing all aspects of interchange service from journal size and composition to the proper lettering of a freight car. Its success in reducing the number of component parts of freight cars to ease the logistical burden upon the railroads is shown in Table 3.2. Perhaps foremost among its accomplishments, however, were the selections of the automatic coupler and automatic brake discussed in Chapter 4.

TABLE 3.2
**Comparison of Component Items, 1882 & 1918. One of the goals of the Master Car Builders' Association was to rationalize the component parts of freight cars to ease the logistics burden upon the railroads' repair shops. Shown here is its success in reducing the types of several items from 1882 to 1918.**[33]

|  | Varieties of Items | |
|---|---|---|
| Item | 1882 | 1918 |
| Axles | 56 | 5 |
| Journal boxes | 58 | 5 |
| Couplers | 26 | 2 |
| Brake heads | 27 | 1 |
| Brake shoes | 20 | 1 |

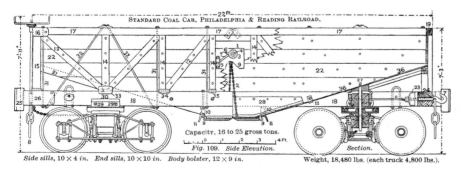

FIGURE 3.13
**Philadelphia & Reading wood hopper circa 1880's. This car had a weight of 18,480 pounds and was rated in trade literature as having a capacity of 40,000 pounds, or twice that of the 1860's vintage Reading hopper shown in Figure 3.12.**[31] *[Car Builder's Dictionary, 1888]*

Another factor that would affect the development of coal cars in the anthracite region would be the diminishing role that canals and the increasing role that railroads would play in moving coal to market. From the time it was opened in 1828, the Delaware and Hudson Canal Company enjoyed a virtual monopoly in moving anthracite from the northern fields to tidewater for delivery to New York and New England, and it had become one of the nation's largest corporations as a result. However, with the opening of the Philadelphia & Reading Railroad in 1842 and the subsequent encroachment of steam railroads into the northern fields, the ascendancy of steam railroads was clear.

The increasing number of railroads in the anthracite region meant that an ever-increasing quantity of coal went by rail. Coal cars were no longer limited to short trips over a railroad's own rails from the mines to the canal terminus. Now they had to be designed to travel long distances at greater speeds and withstand the rigors of interchange with other railroads. Furthermore, railroads were looking for ways to increase a car's efficiency as a way of reducing their operating costs. These demands, combined with government-imposed safety requirements, would provide car designers with significant challenges during the latter half of the 19th century.

With the need for capacity growing and the technology available to support the increased weight, car builders began constructing coal cars to meet this demand—first with a capacity of 24,000 pounds, then 28,000 pounds, and upwards to 40, 50, and 60,000 pounds by 1890. With the increasing size and weight, the paying weight to total weight ratios improved, which meant that railroads were not only hauling more coal, but they were hauling it more efficiently.

In 1884, the Philadelphia & Reading introduced a wood hopper, which was rated at a capacity of twenty tons.[34] This car was clearly designed to haul anthracite. The gently slanting slope sheets provided two economic advantages for this hopper. First, the lower slope increased the capacity of the hopper. Second, and perhaps more important, it allowed the load to be discharged slowly, thus minimizing breakage of the anthracite during unloading. This car required a full three minutes to discharge its load.[35] However, after having as many as 3,134 of these hoppers in service, the Reading reverted to the use of hopper bottom gondolas.[36]

One has to wonder why a railroad would abandon what appears to us to be a truly modern design for the labor-intensive gondola. The answer may be in the numbers and the technology of the times. By the end of the 19th century, car builders were reaching their limits with the building material at hand—wood.[37] A comparison of the geometries of a hopper and hopper-bottom gondola is instructive in this regard. The bulk of the load in a hopper is directly over that area that is weakest—the center of the car. Furthermore, the capacity of the car is decreased by the area beneath the slope sheets.

The hopper-bottom gondola, on the other hand, has the entire area above the side sills available for loading, and the load is evenly distributed throughout the car. In fact, the loaded ends serve somewhat like cantilevers reducing the strain on the center of the car. The primary disadvantage of the hopper-bottom gondola is the labor required to unload the car, but labor was cheap in the 19th century.

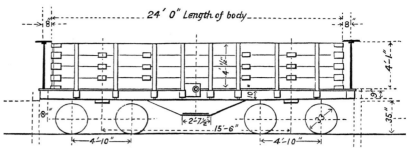

FIGURE 3.14

**Elevation drawing of wood hopper-bottom gondola with a weight of 19,800 pounds and a capacity of 50,000 pounds, circa 1880's. This car is similar in design to those purchased by the O&W in the early 1890's.** *[Car Builder's Dictionary, 1888]*

TABLE 3.3

**Comparison of Capacities of Wood Hopper-Bottom Gondola and Wood Hopper**

|  | Hopper-Bottom Gondola | Reading Wood Hopper |
|---|---|---|
| Total weight of car in pounds | 19,800 | 18,480 |
| Capacity in pounds | 50,000 | 40,000 |
| *Ratio of paying freight to total weight* | *71.63%* | *68.40%* |

**Sources:** *National Car Builder, March 1884; Car Builder's Dictionary, 1888*

Table 3.3 provides an insightful comparison between the Reading hopper and an equivalently-sized hopper-bottom gondola similar to those purchased by the O&W in the early 1890's. Note that the hopper-bottom gondola has a 25% greater capacity with a 5% better weight-carrying ratio. Fewer cars meant shorter trains and less cost-of-maintenance, no small considerations in an industry in which margins were measured in pennies.

The rising cost of labor ultimately intervened in car design. In 1907, the *American Engineer and Railroad Journal* reported that self-clearing cars could be unloaded for at least six cents a ton less than the cost of unloading flat bottom cars by hand. "Using 15 per cent per annum of the original cost as the cost of the plant," it stated, "an expense of $146 is justified to save handling one ton a day by hand."[38] Thus, the days of hopper-bottom gondolas were numbered.

The end of the 19th century would witness a complete change in the way that freight cars were constructed. High quality lumber was becoming scarce, and steel was becoming increasingly affordable. Furthermore, the increasing lengths and weights of trains were pushing wood freight cars to their limits, and railroads were having to spend increasing amounts of money on the repair and maintenance of their wooden fleets. One period estimate indicated that it cost $95.38 or 37.8% of the car's total value per year to maintain a wooden coal car. For what they were spending on maintaining their wooden fleets, a "company could buy 3,000 new steel cars having a total capacity 20 per cent greater than that of the 4,600 wooden cars, and out of the amount that it would cost to maintain the wooden cars for one year they could pay 6 per cent interest on the cost price of the new steel cars and have remaining over $215,000."[39]

Car builders began employing this new building material in three different ways. By 1900, they were already building steel-reinforced wood cars, composite wood and steel cars, and all-steel cars. Furthermore, there was a heated debate among car builders as to what kind of building components should be used in steel construction. The O&W participated in every aspect of this experiment.

Perhaps the most heated argument, other than whether steel should replace wood at all, was whether custom made, pressed-steel shapes or rolled, structural-steel shapes should be used in car construction. The pressed-steel components offered lighter weight but required the expense of specially designed presses to manufacture. The rolled-steel components offered less expense in fabrication, but at the cost of greater weight.[40] This argument extended to every aspect of freight car design, from body and truck bolsters, to truck side frames and brake beams, to the underframe of the freight car. As new freight cars were introduced, trade journals made a point of discussing whether the designer was using pressed-steel or structural-steel components.

The O&W bought two of what are perhaps the most extreme examples of each type of construction—the Sterlingworth rolled-steel hopper-bottom gondola and the Pressed Steel Car Company hopper-bottom gondola. These are discussed in further detail in chapters 7 and 8. It went on to produce and purchase just about every variant of coal car as they were developed.

The first all-steel freight cars were not sponsored by a railroad but by the Carnegie Steel Company, which had a vested interest in seeing steel replace wood as a building material. In 1894, it worked in partnership with the Fox Solid Pressed Steel Car Company to produce the first all-steel freight car in the United States, a flat car with a capacity of 80,000 pounds. Two years later, Carnegie contracted with the Keystone Bridge Works to produce the first, all-steel hopper car. These cars had a 100,000 pound capacity and were constructed of structural-steel components. Carnegie exhibited these cars at the Car Builders' convention in 1896 and then put them into service on the Pittsburgh, Bessemer & Lake Erie Railroad.[41] A picture of this car is shown in Figure 3.15.

These all-steel hoppers proved so successful that the Pittsburgh, Bessemer & Lake Erie Railroad signed the first production contract for all-steel hoppers the following year. Under that agreement, the Schoen Pressed Steel Car Company produced two variations of all-steel hopper cars for the railroad—400 based upon a design by Carnegie using structural-steel shapes and 600 based upon a Schoen design using pressed-steel shapes. Both cars were rated at 100,000 pounds capacity. The structural-steel design weighed 37,150 pounds whereas the pressed-steel design weighed only 34,350 pounds.[42] The drawings for these cars are shown in Figures 3.16 and 3.18. The builder's photo for the Pressed Steel car is seen in Figure 3.17.

FIGURE 3.15

**This real photo postcard from Atlantic City in 1937 shows the first all-steel hopper car built for an American railroad, Pittsburgh, Bessemer & Lake Erie #5700. It was built for the Carnegie Steel Company by the Keystone Bridge Works in 1896 from structural-steel components, and it is shown here still being supported on its Schoen pressed-steel trucks. The Keystone Bridge Works is the same company that the O&W employed in 1882 to provide reinforcing for the Lyon Brook trestle.**
*[Railroad Museum of Pennsylvania Archives]*

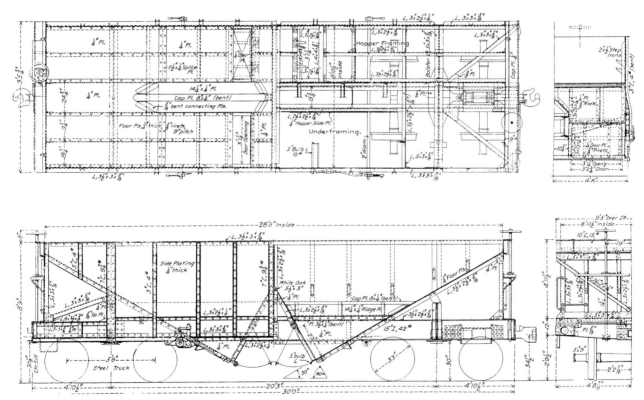

FIRST STRUCTURAL HOPPER CARS BUILT FOR THE PITTSBURG, BESSEMER & LAKE ERIE R. R. BY THE SCHOEN PRESSED STEEL CAR CO.,
CARNEGIE DESIGN—1897.

FIGURE 3.16

**Based upon its satisfaction with the Carnegie/Keystone prototype all-steel hopper, the Pittsburgh, Bessemer & Lake Erie ordered one thousand all-steel hoppers produced by the Schoen Pressed Steel Car Company. Four hundred of these cars were built using Carnegie's design with structural-steel components, and six hundred were built using Schoen's design with pressed-steel components. Shown here are drawings for the structural-steel version. Note how the sides have been opened up at the ends to save weight as compared to the prototype built by Keystone shown in Figure 3.15.**[41]    *[American Engineer & Railroad Journal, May 1903]*

FIGURE 3.17
This Pressed Steel Car Company builder's photo shows the first pressed-steel hopper built for the Pittsburgh, Bessemer & Lake Erie. The Pennsylvania Railroad purchased a number of similar cars beginning in 1898. These became its GL-Class, one of which is on display at the Railroad Museum of Pennsylvania. *[Pressed Steel Car Company Photo; D. K. Retterer Collection]*

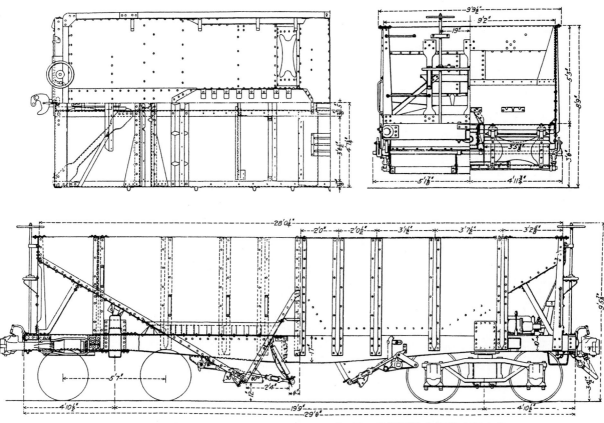

FIRST SCHOEN PRESSED STEEL HOPPER CARS FOR PITTSBURG, BESSEMER & LAKE ERIE R. R.

FIGURE 3.18
The Pittsburgh, Bessemer & Lake Erie's order for one thousand cars from the Schoen Pressed Steel Car Company in 1897 was the first production contract for all-steel hoppers in the United States. Shown here are the drawings for the six hundred cars that were built using pressed-steel components.[43] The builder's photo for this series is shown in Figure 3.17. *[American Engineer & Railroad Journal, May 1903]*

One of the key advantages of the use of steel in hopper construction was the ability of the sides to carry the load. In a wood car, "the carrying strength [is] provided in the underframing...The upper framing, therefore, is light and contributes little in carrying the load. Shrinkage and the working of the body loosens the structure generally and tightening of rods and renailing of sideing [sic] are considerable items in the expense of maintenance. It has been conclusively proved that by the use of steel in hoppers, gondolas and box cars the side framing will successfully carry that portion of the load coming to the sides."[45] What this meant, of course, was that larger capacity cars could be built with less understructure and hence, less weight. In its 1901 catalogue, the Pressed Steel Car Company boasted that from the moment the Pittsburg, Bessemer & Lake Erie Railroad put its 100,000 pound capacity, all-steel hopper cars into operation, "it showed a 73½ per cent paying load to train weight and showed train-mile earnings of $5.38 per mile."[46]

Railroads were not ready to abandon wood, though, especially in the coal trade. Impurities in coal, in particular sulfur, attack the unprotected surfaces of metal. Therefore, several car builders still preferred to use wood where contact was made with coal.[47] Thus, the composite freight car arose. The most frequently cited examples of this type of construction are the cars designed by C.A. Seley, the Mechanical Engineer for the Norfolk & Western Railroad. These cars had a steel underframe, steel truss framing, and a wood box. With the use of steel framing, Seley was able to take advantage of the use of the sides of the cars to carry a portion of the load, which significantly reduced the weight of the car.[48] Although these cars were applauded when introduced, some experts began to question why the railroad chose to use composite construction rather than all-steel.[49] This notwithstanding, the O&W would build and buy 1350 cars of this design in 1910 and 1911.

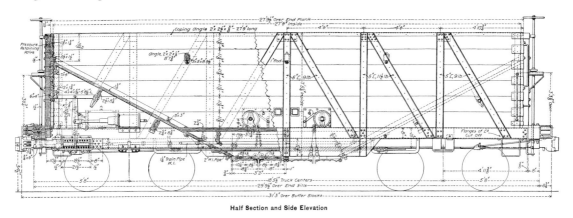

**Half Section and Side Elevation**

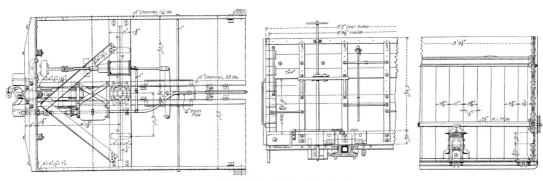

**Partial Frame Plan, End View and Section.**
**40 TON COMPOSITE HOPPER CAR—NORFOLK & WESTERN RAILWAY.**

FIGURE 3.19
**The "Seley" Hopper, developed by C.A. Seley for the Norfolk & Western Railroad, became a model for composite hoppers used on many American railroads, including the O&W. This design was first introduced as a 50-ton hopper in 1900. The trusswork on the sides of the car helped support the weight of the load, unlike all-wood cars in which the entire load was supported by the underframe. Shown here is the 40-ton version introduced in 1902, which served as the basis for the O&W's 15000 series.** [*American Engineer & Railroad Journal, May 1903*]

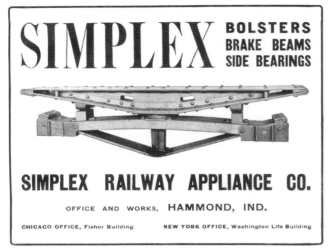

FIGURE 3.20
**This 1903 ad for the Simplex Railway Appliance Company shows the Simplex steel bolsters that the O&W favored when it was rebuilding its wooden cars in the early 1900's.** *[The Car Builders' Dictionary, 1903 Edition; Courtesy: Simmons-Boardman Publishing Corp.]*

The center sills of the Seley hopper were "15 in. 33-lb. channels; the side sills, 8 in., 11¼-pound channels, and the side posts and bracket, 5 in. channels, connected at their upper ends by gusset plates and also attaching to a heavy angle iron forming the top chord of the truss. This angle also serves as a coping

for the wooden lining."[50]   Clearly, the rolled-steel advocates won the debate in the construction of this car, and the selection of these materials provided a clear advantage for the railroads, such as the O&W, which wanted to manufacture and repair cars in their own shops out of common components.

The introduction of all-steel cars did not mean the end of the railroads' wooden fleets. Some railroads, including the O&W, continued to buy all-wood freight cars even as the merits of all-steel construction were being recognized. Nor could the railroads afford to abandon their existing wooden fleets even as they were being beaten up by heavier steel cars. To protect the railroads' investments, manufacturers began offering steel components with which railroaders could upgrade their wooden cars. Steel body bolsters and underframes were popularly offered and used by the O&W and others. Figure 3.20 shows a Simplex truck and body bolster, which was a favorite of the O&W when rebuilding its wooden fleet in the early 20th century, and Figure 3.21 shows a Martin steel underframe designed to reinforce the O&W's all-wood, 30-ton cars.

Which technology prevailed in the end? The Pressed Steel Car Company's production statistics provide the answer. In 1897 it built 501 all-steel cars; in 1898, 2931; in 1899, 9624, in 1900, 16,671; and

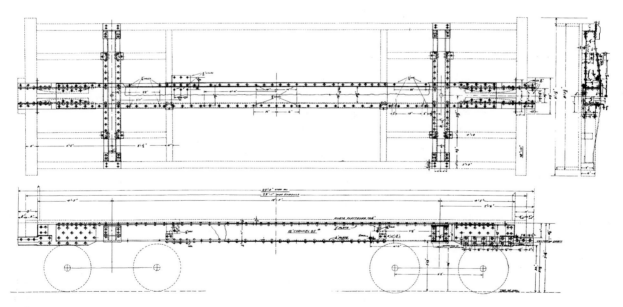

FIGURE 3.21
**In the early 1900's, manufacturers began offering railroads steel underframes to reinforce their all-wood cars. Shown here is a Martin rolled-steel underframe built by the Standard Steel Car Company in Pittsburg. The O&W rebuilt at least 265 of its all wood hopper-bottom gondolas in the 10000-14120 series with these steel underframes beginning in 1908 so that they could withstand the handling in trains intermixed with the larger, all-steel freight cars that were being introduced in that period.** *[O&WRHS Archives]*

TABLE 3.4

**Comparison of coal cars made of wood, composite wood and steel, and all-steel construction**

|  | O&W Wood Hopper-Bottom Gondola, 1901 | Seley Composite Hopper, 1902 | Pressed Steel All-Steel Hopper, 1897 |
|---|---|---|---|
| Total Weight of Car | 38,900 | 33,700 | 34,200 |
| Capacity in Pounds | 85,300 | 80,000 | 100,000 |
| *Ratio of paying freight to total weight* | 68.60% | 70.36% | 74.52% |

**Sources:** *O&WRHS Archives; Car Builders' Dictionary, 1903*

through November 1901, 23,381.[51]  With the exception of a short period during World War II when composite cars were produced due to steel shortages, the all-steel car has been the premier coal car for over 100 years.  The steel car won on several points.  A period report estimated that steel cars would last from 1½ to 2 times as long as wood cars and their lifetime maintenance costs would still be less than the wood cars.[52]  Steel also won the efficiency battle.  A comparison of three different types of car construction is shown in Table 3.4.

In terms of component parts, the results were mixed.  Cast-steel was the clear winner for truck side frames and specialized reinforcing pieces, and pressed-steel components saw continued use in such items as side and end stakes.  However, rolled-steel components prevailed for the major support structures such as sills, sides, and body bolsters.  The pressed-steel center sill in the Pennsylvania Railroad's GL cars proved troublesome,[53] and therefore, when Pennsy introduced its GLa car in 1904, it turned to rolled-steel channels for its longitudinal sills,[54] as did other manufacturers.

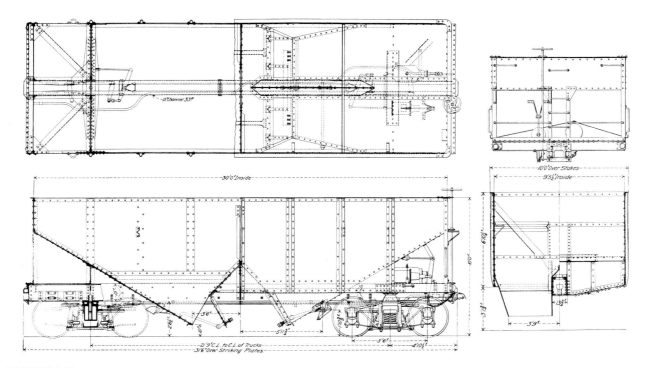

FIGURE 3.22

**These plans for an all-steel hopper car were featured in the 1906** *Car Builders' Dictionary.*  **The design is very similar to cars produced from 1911 through 1916 by Cambria Steel, American Car & Foundry and Standard Steel Car Company that ultimately became the O&W's 18000 and 19000 series.  The O&W referred to this as the "A.R.A. design."  It features triangular end post gussets and 7" platform end sills.**  [*The Car Builders' Dictionary, 1906; Courtesy: Simmons-Boardman Publishing Corp.*]

One more development impacted freight car construction during the life of the O&W— the push for standardization. Two factors drove this development, both were cost-related. The most pressing was the desire to reduce the cost of foreign car repairs, but an important second reason was the desire to reduce development and manufacturing costs. The American Railway Association approached this matter in two ways. The first, as previously discussed, was to develop standards for component parts, such as trucks, side frames, bolsters, and draft gear, and where specific standards could not be developed, to develop standard dimensions for those components to facilitate the interchange of parts.[55] The second effort was to develop a standard car design.

An early example of a "de facto" standard car design was the Pennsylvania Railroad's GLa hopper. Almost 30,000 cars of this design were built, not just for the railroad, but also for many of the coal companies that were served by the "Pennsy." By purchasing cars of the same design used by the railroad that served them, these coal companies sought to capitalize on the economies of scale in production and also

the economies of common repair items.[56] The O&W would ultimately purchase 720 of these GLa's in separate purchases from the Pennsylvania Coal and Coke Company and the Westmoreland Coal Company in the early 1930's.

In 1905, a design for all-steel hoppers was introduced that was widely adopted by a number of railroads. The hopper can be identified by a short platform end sill (7"), angle iron end posts, and triangular end post gussets. Thousands of these cars were produced by several different builders for dozens of railroads, including the New York, Ontario & Western Railway. Its 18000 and 19000 series, produced by Cambria Steel, American Car & Foundry and Standard Steel Car Company, were of this design. The O&W referred to these as "A.R.A. design," but these cars predated any attempts by the A.R.A. to develop a standard car design.

The first successful attempt to develop standardized car designs occurred in 1918 when the United States Railway Administration (USRA) developed standard designs for everything from locomotives to freight car trucks. Working in conjunction with the

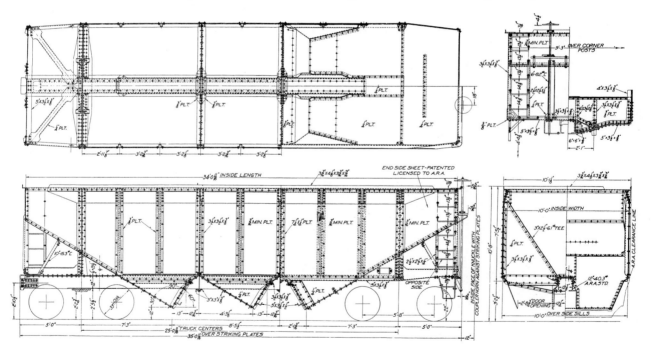

FIGURE 3.23
**In an effort to reduce construction and repair costs, the A.R.A.'s Committee on Car Construction proposed the standard self-clearing hopper car shown here. As depicted, the three-bay hopper car had a nominal capacity of 50 tons and a cubic capacity of 2500 cubic feet. By adding an additional 6' 6" hopper section the car became a four-bay hopper car with a nominal capacity of 70 tons and a cubic capacity of 3000 cubic feet. By using common components for both the 50-ton and 70-ton car, the committee hoped to significantly reduce the cost of production and repairs.[58]**
*[Railway Age, June 12, 1926]*

A.R.A.'s Committee on Car Construction, the USRA produced designs for several standard freight cars, including a 55-ton, all-steel hopper car. This experiment in standardization was both an effort to rationalize production to meet wartime needs and minimize repair and logistics costs.[57] The USRA built 22,000 of these hopper cars, and its design was sufficiently popular that it remained in production for at least ten years after the USRA returned control to the railroads. The O&W would ultimately purchase a total of 301 of these cars, and many would remain in service until 1957.

Based upon the success of the USRA designs and driven by the need to reduce repair costs, the A.R.A.'s Committee on Car Construction began an effort in the early 1920's to develop its own standard car designs. In 1926, it proposed standard 50-ton, three-bay and 70-ton, four-bay hoppers. The two cars were essentially identical, the difference being that the four-bay hopper was created by inserting a 6' 6" extension with hopper into the center of the three-bay hopper to create the larger capacity.[59] In 1928, the A.R.A. adopted this design as a recommended practice for nominal 50-ton and 70-ton hoppers.[60] With these three-and four-bay designs introduced, the USRA design remained the dominant twin hopper through end of the 1920's.

In 1932 the A.R.A. began exploring new hopper designs to take advantage of new, lightweight building techniques,[61] and in 1935, the now renamed American Association of Railroads (A.A.R.) adopted a two-bay hopper and a three-bay hopper as A.A.R. standard 50 ton and 70 ton hoppers respectively.[62] These cars can be identified by the absence of a platform end sill, pressed-steel end posts, the "offset sides," and the internally mounted side stakes, which allowed additional interior capacity. These cars remained the A.A.R. standard twin hopper throughout the remainder of the O&W's life, although the O&W never owned any of these cars itself.

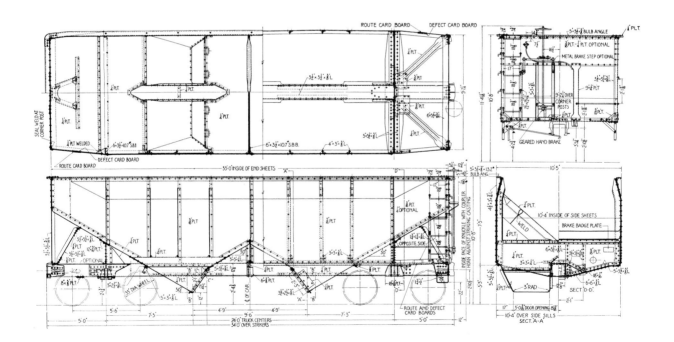

FIGURE 3.24

**The Association of American Railroads adopted this 50-ton, twin hopper design as A.A.R. Standard in 1935. This design used internal side posts, which permitted the sides to be offset to increase the car's cubic capacity.** *[Car Builders' Cyclopedia, 1946; Courtesy: Simmons-Boardman Publishing Corp.]*

**A Brief History of Coal Cars**

Braking in Hard Weather.

FIGURE 4.1
This 19th century engraving dramatized the hazards of braking in inclement
weather before the advent of the automatic brake.  The brakeman might also use a
hickory club to gain additional leverage in turning the brake wheel.  *[The
American Railway, 1889]*

A coal car is just an open box on wheels. It's not until you attach appliances such as couplers and doors and ladders that it becomes a railroad car. Just as there's a history to coal cars in general, there's a history to the appliances that make them what they are. In fact, in many cases, the history of those appliances is more celebrated than that of the cars themselves. The stories of couplers and automatic brakes are just such examples. However, the story doesn't end with those two items. There are grab irons, draft gear, and doors to consider as well.

## COUPLERS AND AUTOMATIC BRAKES

This history of automatic couplers and automatic brakes are interwoven, because, to a great degree, the selection of one depended upon the selection of the other. It is widely, though incorrectly, believed that the history of these two devices begins with the Railway Safety Appliance Act of 1893. It is also widely, though incorrectly, believed that the Safety Appliance Act mandated the Janney automatic coupler and the Westinghouse Air Brake. Neither was the case. What the act did require is shown in the inset below.

Coupling.

FIGURE 4.2
**This hazards of the link and pin coupler system are shown in this 19th century engraving. A man's hand could be caught between the drawheads as he was guiding the link, or he could be crushed between the two cars. [The American Railway, 1889]**

Every railroader "knows" that Eli Janney patented the automatic coupler in 1868, and George Westinghouse patented the air brake in 1869, yet it

---

*Provisions of the Railway Safety Appliance Act of 1893 as the apply to Coal Cars*

*Section 1. ...That from and after the first day of January, eighteen hundred and ninety-eight (subsequently extended), it shall be unlawful for any common carrier engaged in interstate commerce by railroad to use on its line any locomotive engine in moving interstate traffic not equipped with a power driving-wheel brake and appliances for operating the train-brake system, or to run any train in such traffic after said date that has not a sufficient number of cars in it so equipped with power or train brakes that the engineer on the locomotive drawing such train can control its speed without requiring brakemen to use the common hand brake for that purpose.*

*Section 2. That on and after the first day of January, eighteen hundred and ninety-eight (subsequently extended), it shall be unlawful for any such common carrier to haul or permit to be hauled or used on its line any car used in moving interstate traffic not equipped with couplers coupling automatically by impact, and which can be uncoupled without the necessity of men going between the ends of the cars.*

*Section 4. That from and after the first day of July, eighteen hundred and ninety-five (subsequently extended), until otherwise ordered by the Interstate Commerce Commission, it shall be unlawful for any railroad company to use any car in interstate commerce that is not provided with secure grab irons or handholds in the ends and sides of each car for greater security to men in coupling and uncoupling cars.*

*Section 5. That within ninety days from the passage of this act the American Railway Association is authorized hereby to designate to the Interstate Commerce Commission the standard height of drawbars for freight cars, measured perpendicular from the level of the tops of the rails to the centers of the drawbars....(subsequently set for standard gauge railroads at maximum 34 ½ inches; minimum 31½ inches)[1]*

---

FIGURE 4.3
**You can try your skill with a link and pin coupler at the Railroad Museum of Pennsylvania.** *[Author's Collection]*

took an act of Congress in 1893 to force the railroads to install these safety appliances in their fleets. The story isn't quite that simple. In fact, the literature of the period indicates that the railroads were as anxious to find a satisfactory automatic coupler and automatic brake as much as those who lobbied for them for reasons of safety. The difficulty, however, was summed up by this statement in the *National Car Builder* in 1882.

"With the exception of perpetual motion, there is no mechanical problem that has been belabored with such persevering diligence as that which relates to the coupling of railway cars."[2]

Indeed, the problem wasn't finding *an* automatic brake or *an* automatic coupler. The problem was in finding *the* automatic coupler and *the* automatic brake. In 1884, there were 800,000 freight cars equipped with link and pin couplers and manual brakes.[3] In order for a system to be effective, it would have to enable every one of those cars to interoperate with each of those other cars. This was a period of cut-throat competition in the railroad business, and the industry was marked by vicious price wars and frequent bankruptcies. Therefore, although many railroads were experimenting with a variety of different automatic brakes and automatic couplers, none could afford to equip its entire fleet with systems that either wouldn't interoper-

ate with the freight cars of every other railroad or was subject to becoming obsolete if another standard was established or imposed.

The fact is that there was no clearly superior brake or coupler at this point in history. This point is made clear by the actions of state railroad commissions. When the railroads and the federal government failed to mandate safety appliances on freight cars, several states, including Massachusetts, Michigan, and New York, passed laws requiring that automatic couplers be installed on all new or rebuilt cars. In each case, the commissions were able to select couplers that met minimum standards, but none was able to select a clear winner.[4] In the case of Massachusetts, the commission ultimately called for a national convention to select a coupler since it was a problem that "demands a national solution in the face of a vast network of interchanging traffic."[5]

Indeed, the railroads were anxious to find a solution because they were being driven by economics to do so. As early as 1884, Master Car Builders recognized that automatic brakes would permit longer trains to be operated faster and under greater control by the engineer.[6] One of the problems facing railroads was the increasing number of accidents caused by trains breaking in two. "The liability of the train to break apart is great for several reasons: Our trains are growing longer and heavier, and we have old cars mixed in with better ones, cars with weak draw-gear, which conduce to such accidents, and the liability of trains to break apart is greater

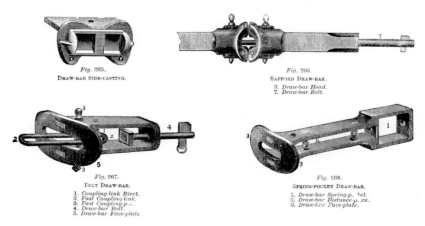

FIGURE 4.4
**A few of the dozens of different kinds of link and pin drawbars available in 1879. Note the concave face in the Safford Draw Bar, which was designed to protect a man's hand while guiding the link into position.** *[Car Builder's Dictionary, 1879]*

**Hard Coal and Coal Cars**

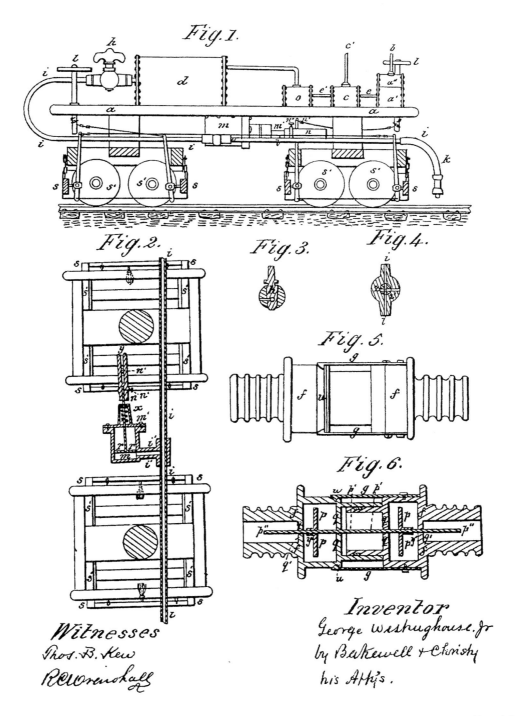

**FIGURE 4.5**

George Westinghouse received his first patent for an air brake in 1869. His initial design, however, suffered from a major shortcoming—it was a "straight air" brake, which meant that it used positive air pressure to apply the brakes. Thus, if the engineer lost air pressure or if the air hose ruptured, such as happened when a train broke in two, the entire train lost its brakes. It wasn't until 1873 when Westinghouse invented the triple valve, which permitted "fail-safe" operation, that this shortcoming was overcome. [*U.S. Patent and Trademark Office*]

Appliances and Accessories for Coal Cars

47

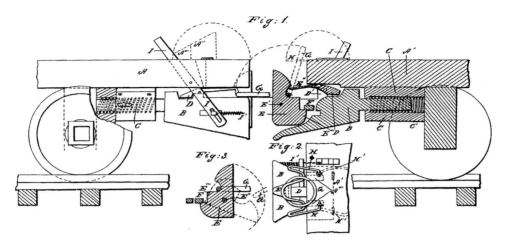

FIGURE 4.6

**Eli Janney's original coupler design patented in 1868 bore little resemblance to today's couplers. In 1873, he patented a revised design, the contour of which was adopted by the Master Car Builders' Association as its standard in 1888. That basic contour is still in use today, as can be seen in Figure 4.18. [U.S. Patent and Trademark Office]**

than ever before, and the best managed roads are not exempt from it."[7]

As a result, many railroads were experimenting with new couplers and automatic brakes on their own. The Atchison, Topeka & Santa Fe, the C, B. & Q., the Denver & Rio Grande, and the Pennsylvania Railroads were all evaluating the Westinghouse automatic brake for freight use. However, although that brake worked well on trains of 25-50 cars or less, it proved unsuitable on longer trains.[8] Until *the* solution came along, what many railroads did, including the O&W, was to fix the equipment that did not travel off their own lines, such as their passenger equipment, and wait for the solution to come along to fix their freight equipment that interchanged with other railroads. By the end of 1888 the Master Car Builders' Association had identified those solutions, and many railroads, including the O&W, were beginning to equip their freight cars according to these new standards almost five years before the passage of the National Railway Safety Appliance Act.

**Automatic Couplers**

Railroad historians trace the origin of the link and pin coupler to 1831.[9] The link and pin coupler was a vast improvement over its predecessor, the linked chain, but it still had numerous shortcomings. The safety problems with the link and pin are well documented and commonly understood. Having to guide the link into the drawbar left many brakemen without fingers and hands, and stepping between moving cars could result in a trainman's being

crushed to death. The risk associated with the link and pin coupler is seen in the O&W's Annual Reports to the Interstate Commerce Commission. In 1889, the year before the Scranton Extension was opened, twenty O&W trainmen were injured in coupling and uncoupling accidents. Three years later, even as the O&W was installing automatic couplers on all of its new cars, one man was killed and 29 were injured. A year later, four trainmen were killed and 37 injured in coupling and uncoupling accidents.[10] One is forced to wonder why brakemen didn't use a stick to guide the link into the drawhead

FIGURE 4.7

**1882 advertisement for the Perry Safety Coupler. The O&W had these couplers "at work" on 200 of its coal cars and 100 of its box cars in the early 1880's. [National Car Builder, October 1882]**

before dropping the pin. Indeed, some railroads did give their brakemen such devices, but most trainmen refused to use them because they were considered unmanly.[11]

The link and pin suffered from operational problems as well. There was no standard for either links or pins, which meant that links and pins from one railroad might not fit the drawheads of another. Because pins were often lost, trainmen had to carry a heavy assortment of extra pins to insure that they had pins that fit in the holes to link the cars together. To present some idea of the problem, it was reported that one railroad had to carry "for their supply 42 different patterns of 31 lengths."[12] In 1879, the Master Car Builders' Association attempted to rectify the problem by establishing a standard for draw-bars, but this still left the other shortcomings unresolved.[13]

One of the characteristics of the link and pin coupler was the amount of slack between the drawheads. "There are 8 inches of slack between the drawheads [with the link and pin]. In a 60 car train, the engine will move 40 feet before the rear of the train moves."[14] This much slack action could easily break a train in two as the slack ran out, or derail a train as the slack ran in. Both were a significant cause of railroad accidents. However, slack action was a two-edged sword. Many railroad professionals believed that this slack was necessary to permit locomotives to start long trains. By backing the locomotive up and taking in the train's slack, the engineer could start a train one car at a time rather than all at once.

It is widely believed that Eli Janney invented the first automatic coupler. This is not so. The patent office was issuing hundreds of patents on automatic couplers during this period. The first successful, widely used automatic coupler was the Miller Hook, which was patented in 1863, well before Janney patented the first, unsuccessful version of his coupler. While the Miller Hook had several shortcomings that made it unacceptable for freight use, many railroads had adopted it for passenger

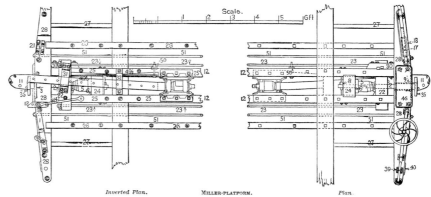

FIGURE 4.8

**The Miller Platform and Coupler. Also known as the "Miller Hook," this was the first automatic coupler widely used, primarily on passenger cars. The O&W had installed it on all of its passenger and milk cars by 1885. [*Car Builder's Dictionary, 1879*]**

service by the 1870's.[15] The O&W was among those railroads, and in 1885, it installed the Miller on its milk cars as well.[16]

In 1873, Eli Janney received a patent on the design that would ultimately evolve into today's automatic coupler. He revised that design in 1877, and by 1878, he was having it tested on passenger cars of the Pennsylvania Railroad, which had

Perry.—Adopted.

FIGURE 4.9

**The Perry Automatic Coupler received high marks during early testing by both governments and railroads. It was deemed an acceptable automatic coupler by the states of Michigan and New York, and it was a finalist in the M.C.B.A. trials for a standard automatic coupler. This engraving shows the coupler as it was tested by the M.C.B.A. in trials at Buffalo in 1885. [*The Railway Gazette, September 25, 1885*]**

Smillie.

FIGURE 4.10
**The Smillie automatic coupler was also deemed acceptable by the state of New York. The coupler is shown here as it was tested by the M.C.B.A. in 1885 with an attached link and drop pin. By the following year, it had been modified to use a vertical hook to catch the link as it was pushed into the throat of the drawbar, and the attached link had been replaced with a standard link. The O&W installed these couplers on the 150 hopper-bottom gondolas that it purchased from the Terre Haute Car Company in 1887. The Smillie was also used by the Delaware, Lackawanna & Western.** *[The Railway Gazette, September 25, 1885]*

refused to install the Miller coupler.[17] In 1879, the Pennsy began installing the Janney coupler in its entire fleet of passenger cars. This amounted to a considerable endorsement of the Janney coupler.[18]

However, while a railroad could easily adapt a coupler as standard on passenger cars, which rarely left their own lines, they couldn't do the same for their freight cars, which were widely interchanged. There was no shortage of options. Thousands of patents were being issued for automatic couplers. *The National Car Builder* lamented in 1883, "The more urgent the necessity for a standard car-coupling device, and the greater the number of such devices, the more difficult it is to make a choice."[19]

No less an authority than Matthias Forney had this to say, "One of the obstacles in the way of this has been the mechanical difficulty of finding a mechanism which will satisfactorily accomplish the purpose for which it was intended. After thirty or forty years of invention and experiment, no automatic coupler has been produced, which has been approved by competent judges with a sufficient degree of

unanimity to justify its general adoption."[20] The Interstate Commerce Commission agreed. In its third annual report, it lamented, "Although some thousands of couplers have been patented, the difficulty has not been to choose among good ones, but to find any good one."[21]

As obvious a choice as the Janney coupler seems today, it had a major drawback that precluded its being accepted as a standard for freight service at that time—it could not be coupled automatically to the thousands of link and pin coupler systems already in service. Therefore, when railroads experimented with automatic couplers for freight systems, they tended to use those automatic couplers that were compatible with their existing link and pin couplers.

For this reason, fully 90% of coupler inventions involved variants of the link and pin,[22] most of which used a catch or dog to hold the pin up. As the link entered the drawbar, it would throw the dog back and the pin would drop.[23] The Perry Safety Coupler was just such a coupler, and in 1885, the O&W reported that it had equipped three hundred of its freight cars, 200 coal cars and 100 freight cars, with this coupler.[24]

In 1884, the state of New York passed a law requiring that, "After July 1, 1886, no couplers shall be placed upon any new freight car to be built or purchased for use, in whole or in part, upon any steam railroad in this state, unless the same can be coupled and uncoupled automatically, without the

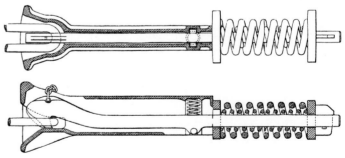

THE ARCHER CAR-COUPLER.

FIGURE 4.11
**The Archer Coupler fell into the same category as the improved Smillie Coupler, using a hook to catch the link as it entered the draw head. This cutaway engraving shows the way in which they operated. The Archer was used by the Delaware & Hudson.** *[The Railway Gazette, October 2, 1885]*

necessity of having a person guide the link, lift the pin by hand or go between the ends of the cars."[25] To this end, the New York State Railroad Commission conducted a series of tests to identify those couplers that met the state's criteria for safety. In its findings, the commission recommended, in priority, (1) link and pin couplers in which the pin was held up by a catch or dog such as the Perry Automatic Coupler and (2) couplers such as the Smillie and Archer in which the link was pushed onto a hook. Vertical plane couplers, such as the Janney, fell into a third category, having been downgraded because they could not couple automatically with existing link and pin couplers or with each other.

Following the state's guidance, the O&W installed the Smillie coupler on 150 new hopper-bottom gondolas that it ordered from the Terre Haute Car Company in 1887. It's unclear why the O&W chose to switch from Perry couplers to Smillie couplers on these new cars.

The fact that a link and pin coupler could now be operated safely, however, did not alleviate the operational problem of the amount of slack that the

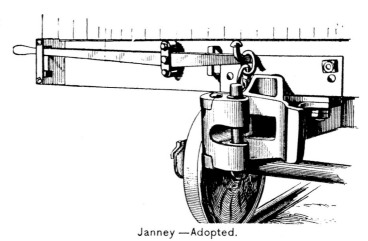

Janney —Adopted.

FIGURE 4.12
**The Janney Coupler as tested in Buffalo in 1885. Note the slot in the knuckle of the coupler, which was designed to accept a link and pin to accommodate those cars not yet equipped with automatic couplers.** *[The Railway Gazette, September 25, 1885]*

coupler allowed between cars. This situation was coming to a head because air brakes aggravated the slack action created by the loose link and pin couplers. Railroads looked to the Master Car Builders' Association for a solution.

In 1884, the M.C.B.A. established a committee to take up the issue of automatic couplers, and in September 1885, it conducted a series of tests involving 80 cars equipped with 42 different couplers in Buffalo, New York. Out of those tests, the committee selected twelve finalists, six of the "vertical plane" type and six of the link type. The Janney was among the finalists for the vertical plane type, and the Perry was among the finalists for the link type. Both had been selected in other trials as well.[26]

In April 1887, the committee conducted additional field tests of these couplers, but it may have been the trials of automatic brakes being conducted in Burlington, Iowa, that proved most decisive in the matter. Two facts emerged from those trials. First, the slack between cars was problematic in the application of automatic brakes, and second, the "vertical hook was no obstacle to starting heavy trains."[27] These conclusions virtually eliminated the link and pin from further consideration by the M.C.B.A.

In late 1887, after trials at Weehawken, New Jersey, the committee announced that "in view of the evident superiority of a close coupler of the vertical hook type, which will couple to and with others of the same class and type, this Committee will admit to further consideration only such couplers as are of

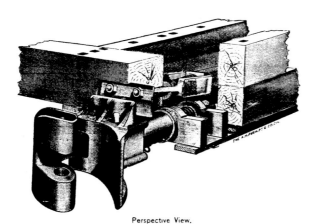

Perspective View.

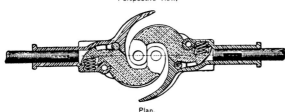

Plan.
THE DOWLING CAR COUPLER.

FIGURE 4.13
**The Janney was not the only "vertical-plane" coupler offered for consideration. Shown here is the Dowling coupler tested by the M.C.B.A. in 1885.** *[The Railway Gazette, October 2, 1885]*

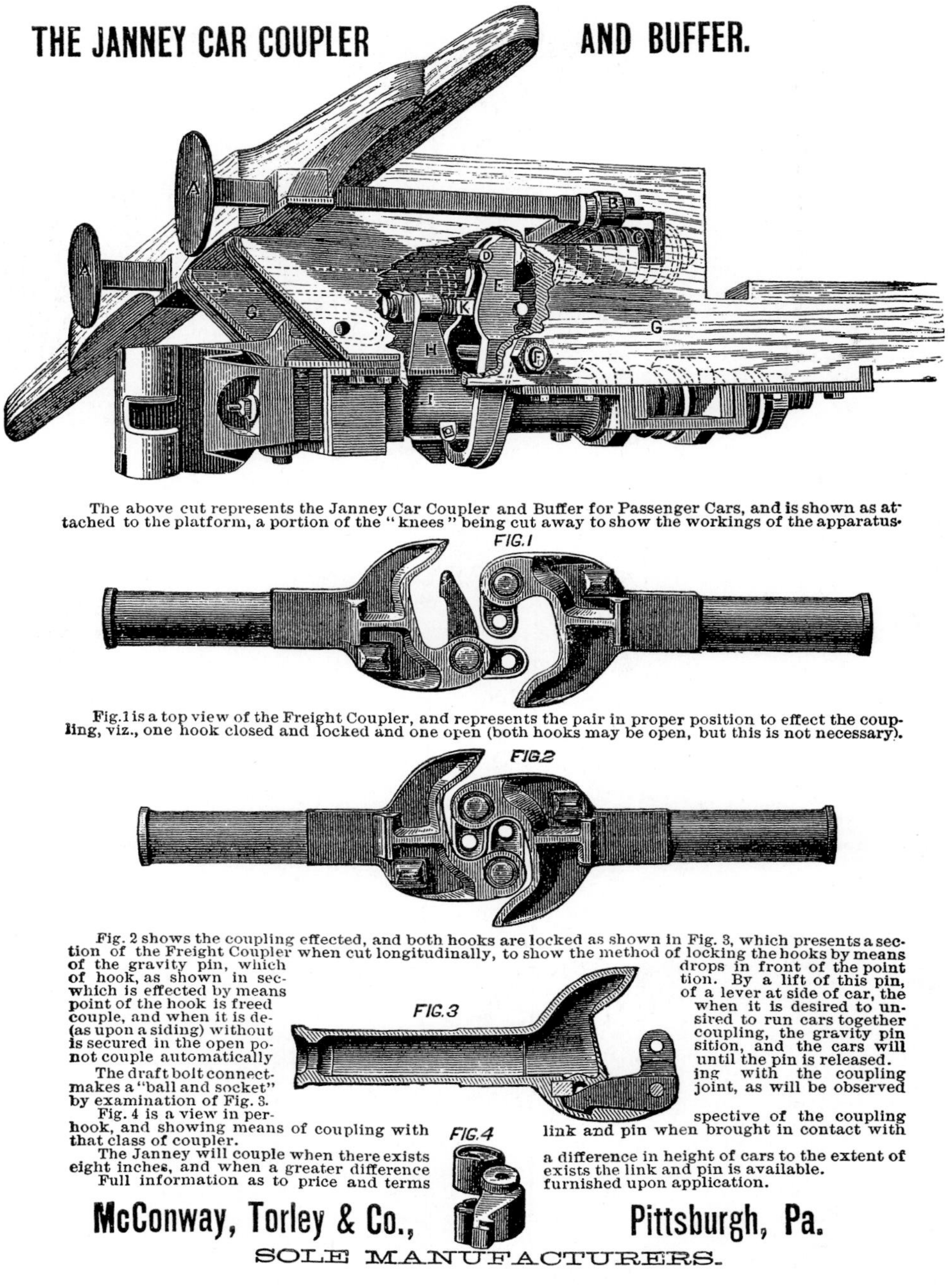

# THE JANNEY CAR COUPLER AND BUFFER.

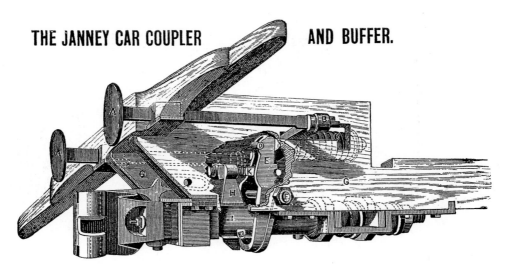

The above cut represents the Janney Car Coupler and Buffer for Passenger Cars, and is shown as attached to the platform, a portion of the "knees" being cut away to show the workings of the apparatus.

*FIG. 1*

Fig. 1 is a top view of the Freight Coupler, and represents the pair in proper position to effect the coupling, viz., one hook closed and locked and one open (both hooks may be open, but this is not necessary).

*FIG. 2*

Fig. 2 shows the coupling effected, and both hooks are locked as shown in Fig. 3, which presents a section of the Freight Coupler when cut longitudinally, to show the method of locking the hooks by means of the gravity pin, which drops in front of the point of hook, as shown in section. By a lift of this pin, which is effected by means of a lever at side of car, the point of the hook is freed when it is desired to uncouple, and when it is decoupled. The cars will couple automatically, the gravity pin is secured in the open position, and the cars will not couple automatically until the pin is released.

The draft bolt connecting with the coupling makes a "ball and socket" joint, as will be observed by examination of Fig. 3.

*FIG. 3*

Fig. 4 is a view in perspective of the coupling hook, and showing means of coupling with link and pin when brought in contact with that class of coupler.

The Janney will couple when there exists a difference in height of cars to the extent of eight inches, and when a greater difference exists the link and pin is available.

Full information as to price and terms furnished upon application.

*FIG. 4*

## McConway, Torley & Co.,      Pittsburgh, Pa.
### SOLE MANUFACTURERS.

FIGURE 4.14

**This 1882 advertisement for the Janney automatic coupler and buffer appeared in several trade magazines. The coupler was heavily promoted by its manufacturer, McConway, Torley & Company.** [*The Railroad Gazette, October 27, 1882*]

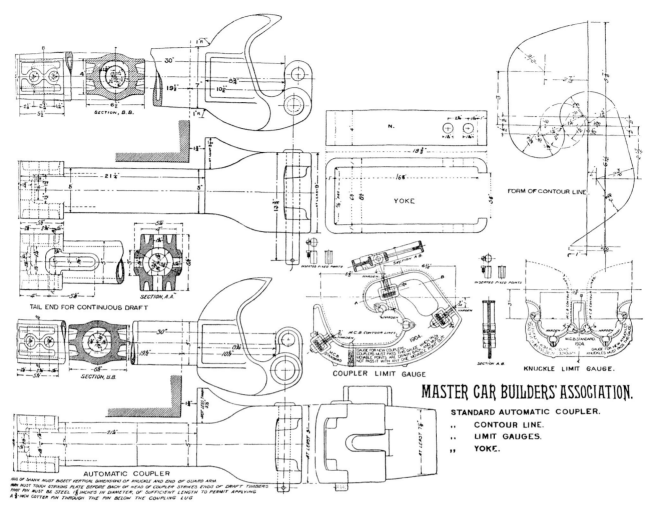

**FIGURE 4.15**

**M.C.B.A. Diagram showing Standard Automatic Coupler Contour Line, Limit Gauges and Yoke.  The contour line described in the upper right hand corner was based upon the Janney design and was adopted by the M.C.B.A. to allow couplers from different manufacturers to interoperate.** *[The Science of Railways, 1906]*

the type know as the Janney type of vertical hook couplers."[28]  Finally, in 1888, the M.C.B.A. obtained a release on the patent right to the contour lines for the Janney coupler and endorsed this contour as standard.  This opened up the market for other manufacturers to produce couplers that were acceptable as long as they mated to the Janney contour.[29]

Evidence of the wide variety of automatic couplers that were being manufactured can be seen in the New York, Ontario & Western Railway's 1904 Annual Report to the Interstate Commerce Commission, when it reported that 100% of its coal car fleet was equipped with automatic couplers. These are shown in Table 4.1.

The number of competing coupler designs created real problems for the railroads, not because

they didn't interoperate, but because they created a logistical nightmare.  Each railroad was required to

**TABLE 4.1**

**Automatic Couplers in use on the O&W's Coal Cars in 1904.** *[NYO&W Annual Report to the ICC, 1904]*

| Manufacturer | Quantity |
|---|---|
| Gould | 5240 |
| Thurman | 466 |
| Empire | 16 |
| Buckeye | 25 |
| American | 10 |
| Pasley | 2 |
| Janney | 5 |
| Drexel | 2 |
| Lone Star | 2 |
| Smith | 6 |

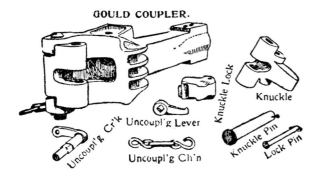

GOULD COUPLER.

FIGURE 4.16
**Components of the Gould Coupler, a favorite of the O&W.** *[The Science of Railways, 1906]*

repair those foreign cars that became damaged while on their lines. This meant that each railroad's repair shop would have to maintain repair parts for over a hundred different makes and models of couplers. By 1901, there was already a clamor for the M.C.B.A. to put an end to this diversity.[30] Finally, in 1911, the M.C.B.A. invited coupler manufacturers to develop a single design that might be used by all railroads. This led to the Type D coupler, which was made standard by the M.C.B.A. in 1916.[31] This coupler came in a variety of shank sizes, 5" x 5", 5" x 7", and 6" x 8". One of the first actions following the acceptance of the Type D coupler as standard was to require the largest shank size on all newly constructed cars in order to withstand the growing weight of trains. Thus, all cars built after November 1, 1920, were required to have a 6" x 8" shank or they would not be accepted in interchange service.[32]

As trains increased in length and weight, railroads were forced to develop a stronger coupler, too. In 1930, the Type E coupler was introduced and in 1932, the American Railway Association, the successor to the M.C.B.A., adopted it as standard, requiring that all cars built on or after August 1, 1933, be equipped with Type E couplers with 6¼" x 8" shanks and all cars rebuilt after August 1, 1937 be equipped with Type E couplers, with certain exceptions to this rule being granted for the inability of some older cars to accept the larger shank sizes. To further promote the changeover, the rules prohibited the use of any Type D couplers cast after August 1, 1936.[33]

The next step that the American Association of Railroads, which succeeded the A.R.A. in 1934, took was to begin prohibiting older couplers with smaller shank sizes from interchange service, because these smaller shank sizes didn't hold up in longer, heavier trains. In 1940, it prohibited all cars with 5"x 5" shanks from interchange service after January 1, 1941.[34] This included all of the O&W's coal cars built before 1912. After several extensions, this ban became effective in 1949. Then, beginning in 1944, the A.A.R. took aim at couplers with 5"x 7" shanks, which were installed on all the O&W's cars built between 1912 and 1920. This ban was to become effective in 1945,[35] but extensions were granted that allowed these cars to be used right up to the O&W's abandonment. These shank sizes were finally banned in 1970, although Type D couplers had been banned two years earlier.[36]

FIGURE 4.17
**Side view of an early Janney coupler mated to an A.A.R. Type E Coupler, which was made standard in 1932. Note the differences in the sizes of the couplers and coupler shanks.** *[Photographed at the Railroad Museum of Pennsylvania.]*

FIGURE 4.18
**Top view of the couplers seen in Figure 4.17. Note the similarity in coupler contour lines despite the nearly 100 year difference in age.** *[Photographed at the Railroad Museum of Pennsylvania.]*

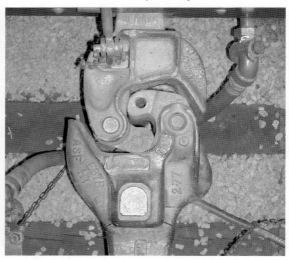

## Automatic Brakes

The power brake did not begin with George Westinghouse's patent in 1869. Robert Stephenson patented a steam powered brake for locomotives in 1833.[37] Indeed, George Westinghouse didn't even invent the air brake; it was patented by an Englishman named Crawford in 1845.[38] What set Westinghouse's invention apart was the continuous nature of his invention, that is, the ability to control the brakes throughout an entire train. Westinghouse's patent of 1869 was for a straight air brake, that is, as air was applied through the train lines to the brake cylinders under each car, the brakes were applied. This system worked reasonably well as long as air pressure could be supplied to the brake cylinders to apply the brakes. However, in the event that there was a loss of air pressure, for example if the train broke in two, the train was left without brakes.[39] Westinghouse solved this problem in 1872 with his invention of the triple valve, which made the automatic brake possible.[40]

"Westinghouse Air Brake engineers developed an automatic device called a 'triple valve' and they located one of these and an air reservoir on each car in addition to the main one on the locomotive. All the while a train was in motion, the pipe line and the car reservoirs were charged with compressed air. When the engineer wanted to stop the train, instead of letting air into the pipe line as before, he let the air out. The reduced pressure activated the triple valve which automatically turned the air from the car reservoir into the braking cylinder. The ingenious part of this arrangement was that, when a train broke in two, the automatic feature caused both parted sections to stop promptly. This safety feature is still acclaimed as one of the great inventions of all time."[41]

The improved comfort, reliability, and safety provided by the automatic brake gained it widespread acceptance for passenger service, and by the late 1870's, most passenger trains were equipped with Westinghouse brakes.[42] However, as effective as the air brake was on short passenger trains, it did not work well on long freight trains. The problem involved the time required for the "message" to be transmitted from the locomotive to the rear of the train. This was observed in the first Burlington trials conducted by the Master Car Builders' Association in 1886. On a fifty car train operating at twenty miles an hour, it took a full eighteen seconds for the brakes to be applied to the last car in the train. Considering that it only took fifteen seconds for the

FIGURE 4.19
**Lever brake as used on early gravity railroad coal cars.**
*[The Science of Railways, 1902]*

air brake to bring a twenty mile an hour locomotive to a complete stop, with eight inches of slack between every car with the link and pin coupler, it was possible that the front of the train could be stopped while the rear of the train was still moving at twenty miles an hour. The results were obvious and disastrous—a series of collisions between every car in the train.[43]

In the absence of a clear choice for an automatic brake, a number of alternatives, both credible and not-so-credible, emerged. The vacuum brake, which was widely used in Europe in passenger service, operated on the principle of using a vacuum to release the brakes. As air was let into the system, the brakes were applied. This offered the same failsafe properties as the Westinghouse brake, but it also suffered from the same shortcomings, as well as being too weak for freight use.[44] There were a variety of momentum brakes, which used the momentum of the train to apply the brakes to each car, and there were wind-up brakes, which applied the brakes by winding a chain around an axle.[45] There were also contenders that used electricity in combination with some of these other systems to solve the problem of the transmission time for the braking signal from the front to the rear of the train. Even though these fared well in the trials, the use of electricity was still in its infancy, and many were concerned about its reliability. However, if George Westinghouse had not acted quickly to fix the problems with his automatic brake after the Burlington trials, it's quite possible that railroads might be using an electro-pneumatic braking system today.

The growing desire by the railroads for an automatic braking system caused the M.C.B.A. to form a committee in 1885 to determine if any were capable of controlling a 50 car train.[46] This led to the Burlington trials conducted in July 1886 and May 1887. None of the contenders emerged a clear winner at either of these trials, but it began to appear as if the electric brake held the greatest promise for the future.

However, George Westinghouse attended the second of these trials, and after identifying the problems with his air brake in freight use, increased the diameter of his brake pipe from 1 inch to 1¼ inches and redesigned the triple valve to accelerate the communication between the cars.[47] Westinghouse returned to the trials with his new Quick-Action Brake in the summer of 1887 and demonstrated the ability to apply the brakes throughout the entire train in two seconds and stop the train in less than one-third its length.[48] Westinghouse immediately took the train on a tour throughout the country. Table 4.2 shows the average stopping distances demonstrated during this tour. Experts within the community termed the performance "remarkable" and estimated that automatic brakes, which cost no more than $55 per car to install, would pay for themselves in reduced accident costs.[49] In 1889, the Master Car Builders' Association adopted the quick action automatic brake as standard.[50]

The Quick Action Brake, which became the Type H series, came in several forms. The "HC" (Combined) arrangement had the triple valve and brake cylin-

JOHN C. THOMPSON, President.     JAS. H. SLADE, Vice-President and Sec'y.
GEORGE B. MASSEY, Treasurer.

# EAMES VACUUM BRAKE CO.,

### 123 Oliver Street, Boston, Mass.

### W. W. HOWSON, Supt.     A. P. MASSEY, Mechanical Eng'r.

### WORKS, WATERTOWN, N. Y.

The **EAMES AUTOMATIC VACUUM FREIGHT BRAKE** was the ONLY brake exhibited at the competitive brake trials at Burlington, Iowa, in May, 1887, which, without the aid of electricity, was able to handle fifty-car trains, light or loaded. The Carpenter brake was inoperative without electricity, and three stops which were made by the Westinghouse brake with fifty empty cars produced such excessive and dangerous shocks that all further attempts to operate it as an air brake were **ABANDONED**. The MAXIMUM shock in the emergency stops of the Eames Brake, with fifty cars, two-thirds loaded and one-third empty, was LESS THAN EIGHT INCHES. The MINIMUM shock with the Westinghouse brake with fifty cars, all empty, was OVER SEVENTY INCHES.

In the drifting tests, where trains were brought to the top of a grade at a speed of twenty miles an hour, which was to be reduced to fifteen miles an hour, and maintained at that rate to the foot of the grade, the maximum variation from fifteen miles with the Eames Brake was **ONLY TWO MILES**, while the Westinghouse speeds ranged from **NINE** to **THIRTY MILES**.

The superiority of the **EAMES DRIVER BRAKE** is shown by the following record of stops:

| *Engine and Dynamometer Car. Speed, forty miles an hour on down grade of fifty-three feet.* | | *Engine, Dynamometer Car, and fifty-one empty cars. Speed, twenty miles an hour, on level. Stops made with driver and tender brakes only.* | |
| --- | --- | --- | --- |
| | Speed. Length of Stop. | | Speed Length of Stop. |
| EAMES, . . . | 40 miles. 899 feet. | EAMES, . . . | 20 miles. 1,625 feet. |
| WESTINGHOUSE, | 40 " 1,016 " | WESTINGHOUSE, | 20 " 2,589 " |
| CARPENTER, . | 40 " 931 " | CARPENTER, . | 20 " 1,956 " |
| AMERICAN, . | 40 " 961 " | | |

FIGURE 4.20

**This 1887 advertisement for the Eames vacuum brake points out the shortcomings of the early Westinghouse brake and demonstrates that the acceptance of the Westinghouse brake was by no means a foregone conclusion.** *[Poor's Manual of Railroads, 1887]*

der mounted directly on the reservoir, as shown in Figure 4.25. This was the most common arrangement for freight cars. The "HD" (Detached) arrangement, shown in Figure 4.23, separated the brake cylinder from the triple valve and reservoir for those installations which would preclude the use of the "HC" arrangement. The only difference between the "HC" and "HD" arrangements was that the auxiliary reservoir and the brake cylinder were combined in the former and detached in the latter. Hopper cars commonly use the "HD" arrangement, because of the lack of contiguous space beneath the car.

TABLE 4.2

**Stopping distances for trains using hand-brakes and trains using Westinghouse Quick-Action Brake following the Burlington trials in 1887.[51]**

| | Feet |
| --- | --- |
| Hand-brakes, 50 cars, 20 miles an hour | 794 |
| Hand-brakes, 50 cars, 40 miles an hour | 2,500 |
| Air-brakes, 50 cars, 20 miles an hour | 166 |
| Air-brakes, 50 cars, 40 miles an hour | 581 |
| Air-brakes, 20 cars, 20 miles an hour | 99 |

Hard Coal and Coal Cars

*Geo. Westinghouse, Jr., President.* *John Caldwell, Treasurer.*
*T. W. Welsh, Superintendent.* *W. W. Card, Secretary.*
*H. H. Westinghouse, General Agent.*

# The Westinghouse Air Brake Co.,

## PITTSBURGH, PA., U. S. A.,

MANUFACTURERS OF THE

## WESTINGHOUSE AUTOMATIC BRAKE.

The WESTINGHOUSE AUTOMATIC BRAKE is now in use on 20,000 engines and 125,000 cars in all parts of the world. This includes 60,000 freight cars.

**The WESTINGHOUSE AUTOMATIC BRAKE is the only continuous brake that has been successfully used on freight trains.**

**THE AUTOMATIC BRAKE** will, in consequence of its quick application, stop a train in the least possible distance.

**THE AUTOMATIC BRAKE** on freight trains, as in passenger service, applies itself instantly to all parts of the train in the event of the train breaking into two or more parts, a feature of great importance in view of the statistics published in the *Railroad Gazette*, which show conclusively that a majority of the collisions are caused by the breaking in two of trains. (See *Railroad Gazette*, Feb. 12, 1886, page 113.)

**THE AUTOMATIC BRAKE** also applies itself to every car in the train, in the event of any accident to the brake apparatus of such a nature that it would render any non-automatic continuous brake inoperative.

**THE AUTOMATIC BRAKE** can be applied from the rear or from any portion of the train, if desired.

**THE AUTOMATIC BRAKE** will effect an increase of at least twenty-five per cent. in the efficient value of freight rolling stock, owing to the quicker time that can be made on the road, and the avoiding of delay at stations and sidings. Freight trains carrying perishable goods are being daily run on passenger schedules.

**THE AUTOMATIC BRAKE**, applied to freight cars, avoids the flattening of wheels and effects a yearly saving, in this item alone, nearly equal to the first cost of the apparatus.

**THE AUTOMATIC BRAKE** will prevent a greater part of the accidents to freight trains which form so large an item of expense in railway management.

**THE AUTOMATIC BRAKE** will save employes from the danger and exposure to which they are now subjected, having to ride on the tops of cars in cold and stormy weather, and often sacrificing their lives in the discharge of their duties.

**THE AUTOMATIC BRAKE** is simple in construction and operation, and cheaply maintained, the working parts being combined in one piece of mechanism.

**THE AUTOMATIC BRAKE** is not an experiment, but is the result of many years of practical experience, and its capabilities are well known to all railway managers.

FIGURE 4.21
**This advertisement for Westinghouse's Automatic Brake appeared opposite the Eames advertisement in Figure 4.20, showing two different interpretations of the same test results.** ***[Poor's Manual of Railroads, 1887]***

Diagrams from the period indicate that hopper-bottom and drop-bottom gondolas also used the "HD" arrangement. When detached, the distance between the brake cylinder and auxiliary reservoir could not exceed 8-10 feet without impairing the braking in the car. The triple valve also came in two configurations, H-1 and H-2. The H-1 configuration was used on 8" x 12" brake cylinders; the H-2, on 10" x 12" cylinders. The smaller brake cylinder was used on freight cars with a light weight greater than 22,000 pounds but less than 37,000 pounds; the larger cylinder was used on cars with a light weight greater than 37,000 pounds.[52]

The installation of air brakes by railroads was neither instant nor universal. The Railway Safety Appliance Act of 1893, as amended in 1896, only required that "a sufficient number of cars in it so equipped with power or train brakes that the engineer on the locomotive drawing such train can control its speed without requiring brakemen to use the common hand brake for that purpose." As a consequence, it remained a matter of judgment for the railroads as to how many cars in a train would be required to have air brakes for the engineer to control the train. It was common practice to group the cars with air brakes at the front of the train, and engineers developed the skill of controlling the slack in the entire train with the "braked" cars in the front of the train.[53] In fact, railroads even modified some of their cars with train lines running through them so that these non air braked cars could be placed between other cars with air brakes.[54]

In 1903, Congress again intervened and directed that "not less than fifty percentum of the cars in such train shall have their brakes used and operated by the engineer of the locomotive drawing such train..."[55] Then, in 1910, the Interstate Commerce Commission directed that "not less than 85 per cent of the cars of such train shall have their brakes used and operated by the engineer."[56] However, by this time, the railroads themselves, through the American Railway Association, had required that "quick-action" brakes be installed in all cars in interchange traffic. The O&W did not have 100% of its coal cars equipped with automatic brakes until 1913. A chart of the O&W's progress in this regard is shown in Chapter 7.

The Type H, quick-action brake was designed for trains of 50 cars or less. By the early 1900's, railroads were already running trains with more than 50 cars, and an improved system capable of handling trains of increased length was required. The Type H brake presented three problems with long trains—there was such a delay between the application of the brakes in the front and rear of the train that a buffeting action resulted which could damage the cars and break the train, there was such a delay

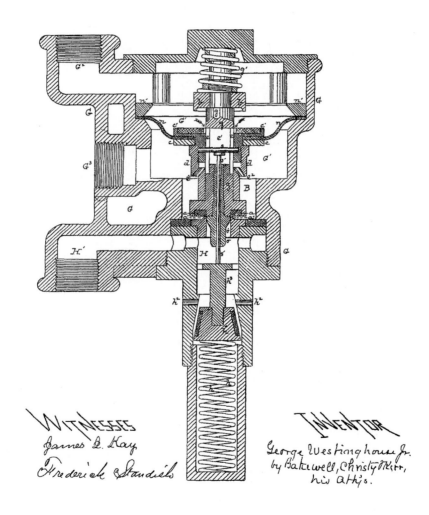

**G. WESTINGHOUSE, Jr.**

**Valve Devices for Fluid-Brakes.**

No. 141,685.

Patented August 12, 1873.

FIGURE 4.22

In 1873, Westinghouse improved his air brake system with the invention of the "triple valve." Rather than increase pressure in the train line to apply the train brakes, the engineer would reduce the train line brake pressure. As the train line brake pressure was reduced, the triple valve would cause air to flow from a reservoir under each car to apply the car's brakes. This invention provided a fail-safe system for the train, that is, if the train broke in two, all of the train's brakes would automatically be applied. *[U.S. Patent and Trademark Office]*

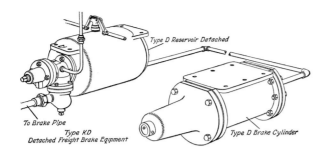

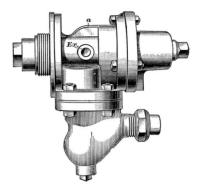

## FIGURE 4.23

**Components of KD (Brake Cylinder and Reservoir Detached) arrangement of quick-action brake for freight car use. Hoppers and hopper-bottom gondolas typically used this arrangement because they lacked the room beneath the car for the combined configuration.** [*Courtesy: Thomson Education Direct*]

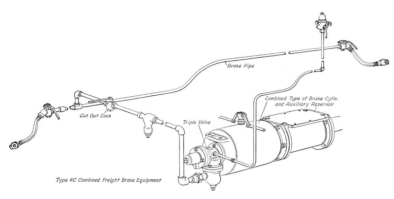

## FIGURE 4.24

**As freight cars increased in weight and trains increased in length, Westinghouse found it necessary to improve his original automatic braking system. Shown here is the K-2 Triple Valve, which was introduced in 1908. It was used with 10"x 12" brake cylinders for freight cars with light weights of 37,000 pounds or more.** [*Courtesy: Thomson Education Direct*]

## FIGURE 4.25

**Components of KC (Brake Cylinder and Reservoir Combined) arrangement of quick-action brake for freight car use.** [*Courtesy: Thomson Education Direct*]

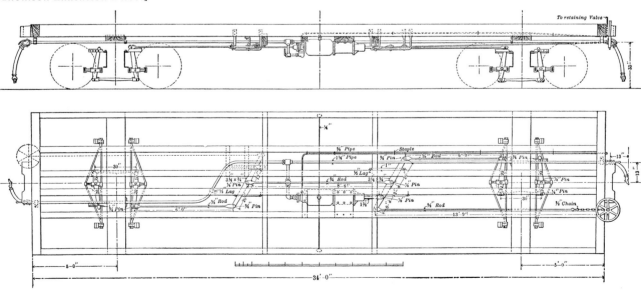

## FIGURE 4.26

**1892 drawing showing installation of Westinghouse Quick-Action Brake on an open-bottom freight car.** [*Railway Car Construction, 1892*]

FIGURE 4.27

**This 1898 all-steel hopper car shows the installation of the "HD" Series of the Westinghouse Quick-Action Air Brake. Note that the brake cylinder and brake wheel are located on the right side of the end of this early car.** *[Photographed at the Railroad Museum of Pennsylvania]*

between the release of the brakes in the front and rear of the train that the slack could run in or out without the engineer's ability to control it, and the difference in brake pipe pressures between the front and rear of the train could affect the ability of the auxiliary reservoirs to recharge. The Type K triple valve, introduced in 1908, solved these problems.[57] The Type K triple valve mounted on the existing brake cylinders and came in the same configurations as the Type H triple valve, that is, K-1, K-2, KC, and KD.

By the 1920's freight trains had grown even longer and heavier, and the demand for greater braking power increased. In response to this demand, the American Railway Association, in cooperation with the Interstate Commerce Commission, conducted a series of brake trials at Purdue University in 1926. The result of these tests was the development of a new brake system for freight car brakes, commonly referred to as the AB brake.

The AB brake was adopted as standard in 1933.[58] It was designed for trains of 120 or more cars,[59] providing improved quick service, improved release, and improved emergency application.[60] It replaced the triple valve with an AB valve and is easily distinguished from its predecessors by the two reservoirs bolted together. In 1933, the A.R.A. established rules that required that AB brakes be installed on all cars built new after September 1, 1933 or rebuilt after August 1, 1937. It also required that AB brakes be installed on all cars in interchange service after January 1, 1945. As with most of its other deadlines, the A.A.R. extended the deadline for having all cars in interchange service equipped with AB brakes several times, but the deadline became final on July 1, 1952.[61] Unfortunately, none of the O&W's hoppers were equipped with AB brakes on that date, and it was forced to buy 21 second-hand hoppers equipped with those brakes so that it continue to ship anthracite in interchange service.

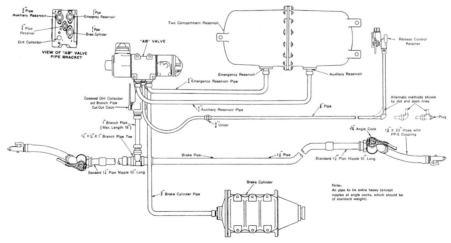

Piping Diagram of the Complete "AB" Freight Car Brake Equipment

FIGURE 4.28

**Diagram of "AB" Freight Car Brake Equipment. Note the distinguishing features: the two reservoirs bolted together and the larger "AB" valve, which replaced the standard triple valve.** *[Courtesy: Thomson Education Direct]*

Hard Coal and Coal Cars

## DRAFT GEAR

The draft gear is the component that connects the draw bar or coupler with the body of the car. The first draft gear was nothing more than a hook to which the chain connecting the cars was attached. With the introduction of link and pin couplers, railroads replaced their rigidly mounted hooks with spring draft gears, such as that shown in Figure 4.29, that absorbed the shock of compression and tension as the train's slack ran in and out.

In 1879, the Master Car Builders' Association recommended a draft spring with a 13,000 pound capacity. However, as the weights of freight cars grew and the lengths of trains grew, increasing demands were placed upon the draft gear, and within five years, the M.C.B.A. increased that capacity to 18,000 pounds. In 1893, after the automatic coupler had been adopted, they further increased the capacity to 22,000 pounds. They also set the travel limits at $2^1/8$ inches free motion.[62]

In 1887, the M.C.B.A.'s committee on draft gear recommended that two springs be used instead of one. Although this recommendation was not approved, many railroads adopted this two spring design.[63] The springs were mounted either concentrically, that is, one within the other, or in a tandem fashion, as shown in the Miner and Farlow draft gears pictured in Figures 4.29 and 4.33. The O&W used Miner draft gear on most of its early coal cars.

A freight car is like a system, and anyone who

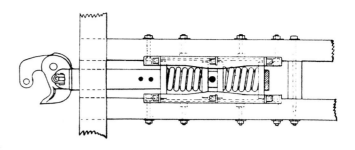

FIGURE 4.29

**This drawing of Miner Draft Gear for 60,000 and 80,000 pound cars with wooden sills appeared in the July 1901 edition of Railroad Digest. The O&W used this draft gear on the wood, hopper-bottom gondolas that it purchased in the 1890's and early 1900's. [*Railroad Digest, July 1901*]**

has worked with systems knows that if you tinker with one component of a system, it's certain to affect another. Such is the case with a car's draft gear. The key shortcoming of a sprung draft gear is that after it stretches or compresses, it springs back. This "ricochet effect" did not create much of a problem during the era of short trains and manual brakes. However, as trains became longer, the railroads experienced an increasing problem with trains breaking in two, with the culprit being the draft gear, which was acknowledged as being the weakest part of the freight car.[64]

One of the first to recognize this problem was George Westinghouse. The problem was this. Air brakes apply serially; that is, as the engineer makes a reduction, the brakes in the first car apply a split

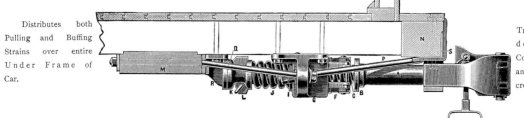

FIGURE 4.30

**Westinghouse developed his "Buffing Apparatus" in response to the extreme buffeting as the result of a train's slack action during the application of his air brakes. This 1889 advertisement describes the problem confronting the railroads with their draft mechanisms. [*National Car and Locomotive Builder, August 1889*]**

**Appliances and Accessories for Coal Cars**                                                                      **61**

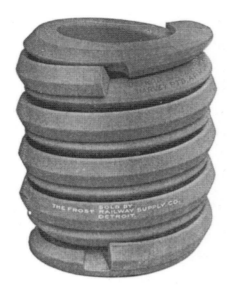

FIGURE 4.31

**The Harvey Friction Draft Spring was developed by the Frost Railway Supply Company to dampen spring motion in traditional spring draft gears. Rather than invest in friction draft gears, the O&W applied these springs to its cars in the early 20th century.** *[The Car Builders' Dictionary, 1912; Courtesy: Simmons-Boardman Publishing Corp.]*

second before the brakes in the next car, and so on throughout the train. The result is that the slack between the first and second car runs in, the second car bounces back and collides with the third car whose slack has just run in. The result is a series of minor collisions running the length of the train. These "collisions" are not only hard on the cars but their contents as well. Westinghouse first became aware of this problem when a train in England on which he was demonstrating his air brakes broke in

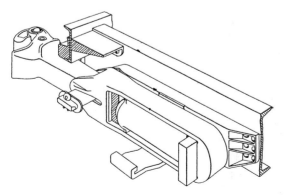

FIGURE 4.32

**The Miner A-24-A friction draft gear with cast steel yoke was specified by the O&W on its first all steel hoppers.** *[The Car Builders' Dictionary, 1912; Courtesy: Simmons-Boardman Publishing Corp.]*

two during a rapid brake application. It was reinforced during the Burlington trials when he observed the severe slack action throughout a train during another rapid brake application. This problem could have had severe consequences on the acceptance of his air brake, and therefore, Westinghouse developed and patented the first friction draft gear, which served to dampen the spring action much as a shock absorber dampens the spring action in a modern automobile. Although friction draft gears were slow to be accepted, they were fairly well established by the first decade of the 20th century.[65] The O&W wouldn't begin installing friction draft gears in its coal cars until it purchased its first all-steel hoppers in 1913. However, the O&W did install Harvey Friction Draft Springs in the spring draft gears of its composite cars to dampen the spring motion.

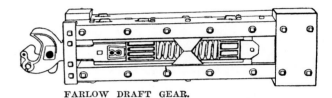

FARLOW DRAFT GEAR.

FIGURE 4.33

**The Farlow spring draft gear was used on the final series of composite hoppers that the O&W purchased from American Car and Foundry in 1911.** *[The Science of Railways, 1906]*

The railroad associations did not attempt to standardize draft gears until the late 1920's, but it did begin standardizing some of their components in 1905, including setting a standard distance between the draft sills of 12 7/8 inches. In the late 1920's, the American Railway Association conducted a series of trials on draft gears and developed specifications for such attributes as capacity, endurance, sturdiness, uniformity of action, freedom from sticking, dimensions, and travel. Using these specifications, the A.A.R. developed an approved list of draft gears for use in interchange service and required that all cars built after January 1, 1934, or rebuilt after August 1, 1937, be equipped with draft gears meeting those specifications.[66] At the time this rule was passed, very few of the O&W's fleet met the new requirements, but the O&W was granted a reprieve when the A.A.R. grandfathered existing draft gears, allowing them to be used until they wore out or became unserviceable.[67]

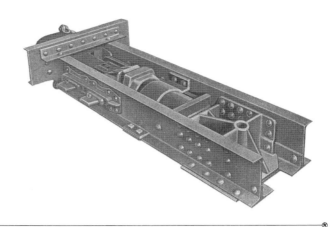

FIGURE 4.34
**Farlow developed a keyed draft attachment for friction draft gears. It is shown here with a Sessions draft gear as it was used on the O&W's second purchase of 18000 series hoppers and 6200 series gondolas in 1916.** [*The Car Builders' Dictionary and Cyclopedia, 1919; Courtesy: Simmons-Boardman Publishing Corp.*]

## DOOR OPERATING MECHANISMS

C.H. Caruthers relates an amusing story in his 1905 article, "The Evolution of the Coal Car."

"In this car, or 'dumpy,' as it was generally called, the bottom was of hopper form and the drop-doors were held shut by a simple device freer from trouble than some of the complicated schemes now used for the same purpose and which seldom come open in transit, although the writer once witnessed an amusing exception. While returning from school he was enjoying the breeze which swept through the train on a hot afternoon, when suddenly a freight train passed on the westbound line, and at the same instant a dense white cloud poured into the coaches through the open doors and windows and set everyone sneezing like a parcel of hay-fever patients. The train was promptly stopped and we dismounted to investigate. In the distance could be seen the rapidly vanishing freight train and extending back to and beyond us, was a narrow white line. One of these dumpies used by a lime company was attached to the rear of the train and its drop doors had become unfastened and were spreading its snowy load down its path."[68]

Despite the amusing nature of this story, an open drop door could prove catastrophic on a coal train. Therefore, a great deal of attention was paid to securing these doors. Figure 4.35 shows one of the earliest configurations of opening, closing, and latching the drop doors in a hopper bottom gondola using a wind-up chain. This type of mechanism can be clearly seen in the pictures of early O&W hoppers. As coal cars entered the all-steel era, new varieties of door mechanisms were introduced, most using lever and scissors type mechanisms, which were typically installed on the left side of the car. Varieties common to the O&W are shown in Figures 4.36-4.41.

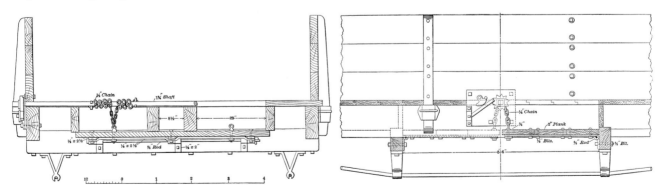

FIGURE 4.35
**The earliest hopper or drop doors were operated by a wind-up chain that was held closed by a ratcheting mechanism as shown in this 1892 drawing. A close examination of this popular drawing, however, indicates that the doors will not operate as drawn. The chain from both doors should wrap around the shaft in the same direction, in this case clockwise, so that the doors can be lowered.** [*Railway Car Construction, 1892*]

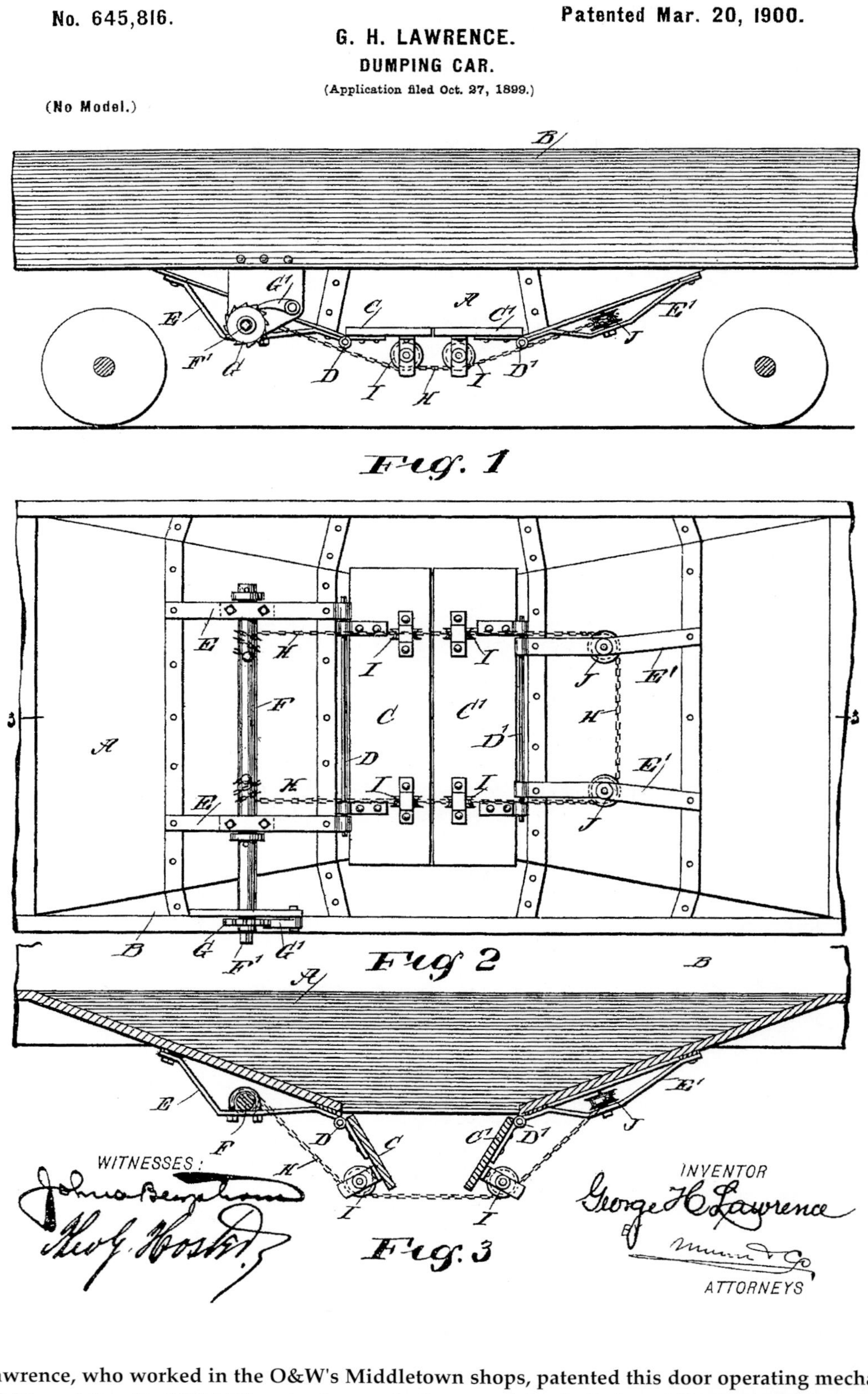

No. 645,816.

**G. H. LAWRENCE.**
**DUMPING CAR.**
(Application filed Oct. 27, 1899.)

Patented Mar. 20, 1900.

(No Model.)

*Fig. 1*

*Fig 2*

WITNESSES:

INVENTOR
George H. Lawrence

ATTORNEYS

*Fig. 3*

Figure 4.36
George H. Lawrence, who worked in the O&W's Middletown shops, patented this door operating mechanism in 1900. The O&W used it in its 6600-7700 series hopper bottom gondolas built from 1900 through 1902. According to the *Orange County Times* in November 1900, the O&W paid Mr. Lawrence $1800 for the use of his patent.[69] *[U.S. Patent and Trademark Office]*

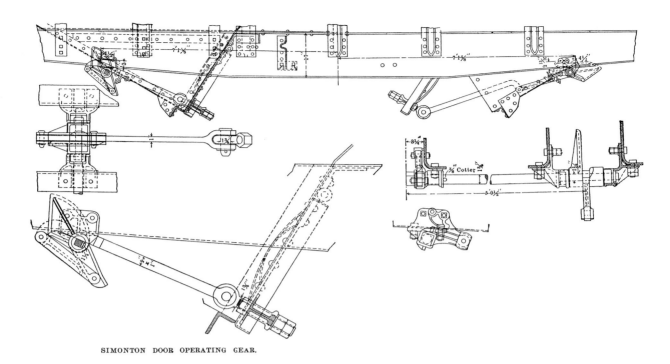

SIMONTON DOOR OPERATING GEAR.

FIGURE 4.37
Jackson Simonton of Altoona, Pennsylvania received a patent for his Operating Gear for Doors of Hopper-Bottom Cars in January 1901. This drawing shows how it was installed and operated. The Simonton Door Operating Mechanism was used on the O&W GLa-type hoppers, the cars in the 19000 series produced by Standard Steel, and the cars in the 12500 series. *[American Engineer and Railroad Journal, May 1905]*

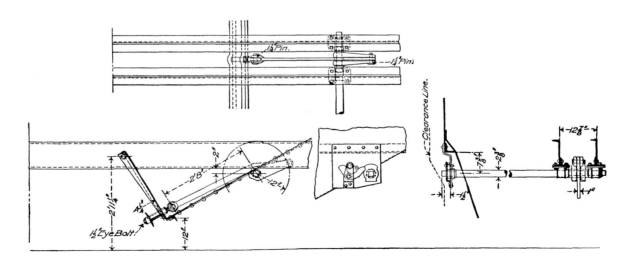

FIGURE 4.38
Dunham Door Operating Mechanism. Dunham door mechanisms were installed on O&W hoppers in the 11000, 17000, and 18000 series. *[Car Builders' Cyclopedia, 1922; Courtesy: Simmons-Boardman Publishing Corp.]*

**Appliances and Accessories for Coal Cars**

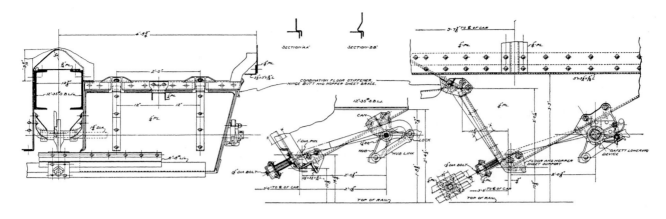

FIGURE 4.39
**Enterprise Door Operating Mechanism, Type C. This hopper door operating mechanism was used on the O&W's USRA-type hoppers in the 303-899 series.** *[Car Builders' Cyclopedia, 1922; Courtesy: Simmons-Boardman Publishing Corp.]*

FIGURE 4.40
**American Car & Foundry Door Operating Mechanism. The 55-ton cars in the 19000 series, built by AC&F had this type of mechanism.** *[American Car & Foundry photo; from the John W. Barriger III National Railroad Library at the University of Missouri-St. Louis]*

FIGURE 4.41
**Wine door Locks. The 21 hoppers that the O&W bought from the New Haven in 1953 came equipped with these door locks. The O&W also modified some of its hoppers in the late 1930's and early 1940's with these locks, including cars in the 11000, 12500 and 18000 series. These were indeed door locks and not door operating mechanisms. Unlike the operating mechanisms, door locks were located on both sides of the car.** *[Courtesy: Bob's Photo]*

## HAND HOLDS, GRAB IRONS AND OTHER SAFETY APPLIANCES

As early as 1879, a committee of the M.C.B.A. had made recommendations for the installation of standard hand holds and grab irons on freight cars, but these recommendations were not approved or implemented by the entire association.[70] Section 4 of the 1893 Safety Appliance Act required the installation of secure grab irons or handholds in the ends and sides of each car. Acting upon that legislation, the M.C.B.A. established a recommended practice for the installation of safety appliances, which generally followed the 1879 recommendations. After being revised slightly in 1896, these provisions were made standard in 1902 and then rewritten in 1908 to make their meaning and intent clearer.[71] These are shown graphically in Figure 4.41, and the complete standards, as they pertain to open top cars, are laid out in Appendix C.

The M.C.B.A. safety appliance standards had several shortcomings, and Congress was not satisfied with the M.C.B.A.'s progress in correcting them. For example, a review of the M.C.B.A.'s standards for ladders and grabirons indicates that it was permissible to place a single ladder at each end of the car and place it in such a position so that the only access to that ladder was by passing between the cars. Therefore, in 1910, Congress supplemented the Railway Safety Appliance Act with the following provision:

*Section 2. ...All cars must be equipped with secure sill steps and efficient hand brakes; all cars requiring secure ladders and secure running boards shall be equipped with such ladders and running boards, and all cars having ladders shall also be equipped with secure handholds or grab irons on their roofs at the tops of such ladders....*[72]

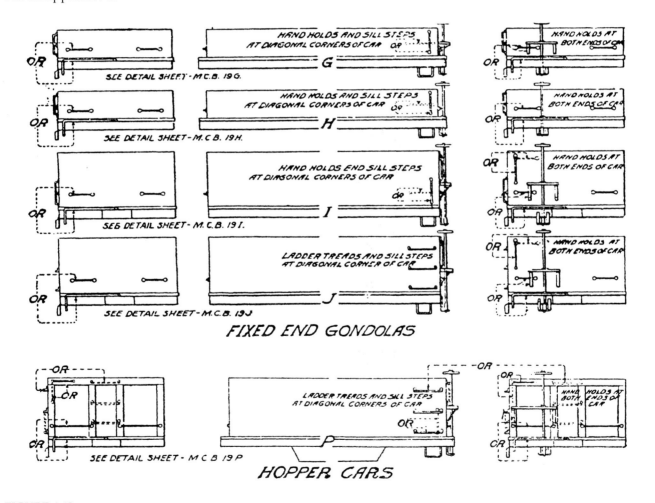

FIGURE 4.42
**M.C.B.A. Standards for Safety Appliances (1893-1911)** *[The Car Builders' Dictionary, 1909; Courtesy: Simmons-Boardman Publishing Corp.]*

**Appliances and Accessories for Coal Cars**

To implement this law, on March 13, 1911, the Interstate Commerce Commission issued an order, "In the Matter of Designating the Number, Dimensions, Location, and Manner of Application of Certain Safety Appliances," which established standards for items such as hand brakes, uncoupling levers, handholds, and ladders. Plate F, which shows the placement of safety appliances for hopper cars and high-side gondolas with fixed ends and platform end sills, is shown below in Figure 4.42. A synopsis of the standards for all hoppers and gondolas is presented in Appendix D.

In 1932, the ICC amended these standards to include provisions for a second grab iron on the left side of the car as shown in Figure 4.43.

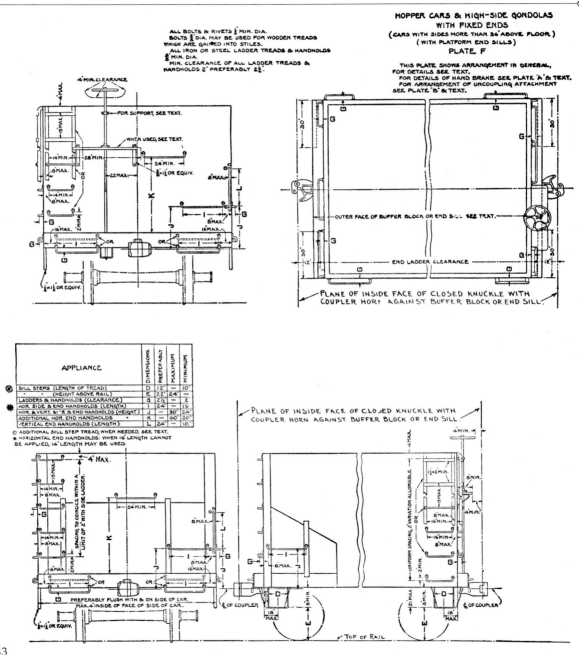

FIGURE 4.43
United States Safety Appliances, Plate F, shows the placement of safety items front and side view for hoppers and high-side gondolas with platform end sills. Most of the O&W's all-steel hoppers, with the exception of its USRA hoppers, fit this configuration. The remaining plates for hoppers and gondolas are shown in Appendix D.
*[Courtesy: American Association of Railroads]*

Hard Coal and Coal Cars

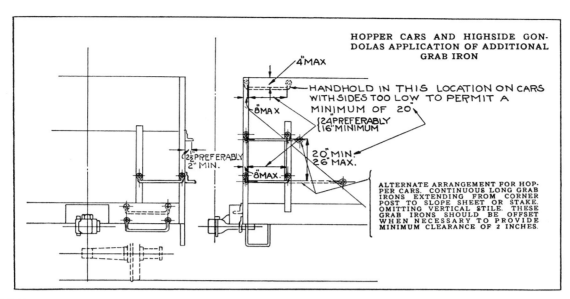

**FIGURE 4.44**

United States Safety Appliances; Application of Additional Grab Irons on Hopper Cars and High Side Gondolas, American Railway Association (1932). The A.R.A.'s successor, the American Association of Railroads, required that all "house cars, hopper cars and high side gondola cars built new or rebuilt on or after August 1, 1933" be equipped with this additional grab iron. Additionally, the A.A.R. recommended that all other such cars be so equipped when undergoing general maintenance.[73] This modification can be seen in the 18000 series hopper in Figure 4.49. *[Courtesy: American Association of Railroads]*

**FIGURE 4.45**

These two hoppers built by the Standard Steel Car Company in the early 20th century show the differences between the M.C.B.A. and the United States Safety Appliance standards. The Union hopper on the left, built in 1909 to the M.C.B.A. standards, has the ladder in the center of the end, which means that the trainmen would have to move between the cars to access it. The Central of New Jersey hopper on the right was built in 1915 to United States Safety Appliance standards. Note that the ladder grab irons have been moved to the side and the left side of the end of the car. The uncoupling lever has also been modified to comply with the new standards. *[Standard Steel Car Company photos; D.K. Retterer Collection]*

Appliances and Accessories for Coal Cars

## Hand Brakes

United States Safety Appliance Standards only specify that cars have an "efficient" hand-brake which operates in harmony with the power brake and complies with specified minimum standards. Those standards are displayed in Plate A in Appendix D. In 1924, the American Railway Association adopted minimum standards for the force required to set the hand brakes on freight cars.[74] In 1936, the American Association of Railroads established requirements for geared handbrakes and required that all cars built new or rebuilt on or after January 1, 1937, be so equipped.[75] In 1942, the A.A.R. revised its specifications for geared hand brakes and required that all cars built new or rebuilt after January 1, 1946, comply with this new standard.[76]

In 1939, the O&W received permission from the bankruptcy court to install power hand brakes on 500 hopper cars that it was modifying to increase their capacity. There are no records indicating that the O&W sought permission to install power hand brakes on any other cars, but power hand brakes soon begin appearing on other cars, as well. It's possible that the O&W was removing the hand brakes from the larger cars as they were being scrapped, and installing them on other cars as that needed them. An example of such a case is the 18000 series car in Figure 4.49.

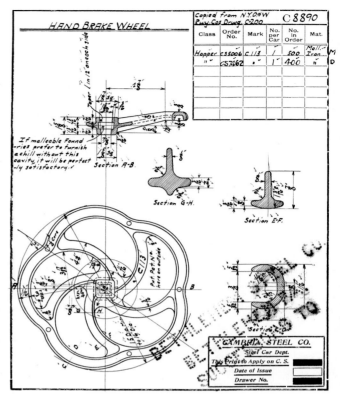

FIGURE 4.46
**The O&W went so far as to specify the brake wheel on the cars that it bought new. Shown above is the brake wheel it specified to Cambria Steel for the 18000 series.** [Courtesy: Johnstown American Corporation]

FIGURE 4.47
**The United States Safety Appliance standards also specified how uncoupling levers should be installed on freight cars. Shown here on the right are drawings for the uncoupling levers on the O&W's 18000 series hoppers, which were built to comply with those standards.** [Courtesy: Johnstown America Corporation]

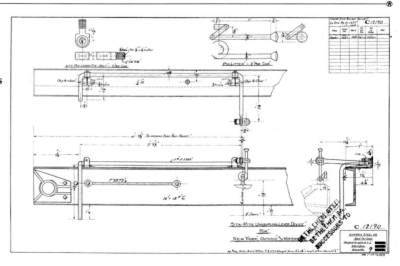

FIGURE 4.48
**The Carmer uncoupling mechanism was installed on a number of the O&W's hopper cars, including those in the 303-899 series, the 17000 series, and the 55-ton cars in the 19000 series.** [The Car Builders' Dictionary and Cyclopedia, 1919; Courtesy: Simmons-Boardman Publishing Corp.]

Hard Coal and Coal Cars

FIGURE 4.49
A railfan examines the power brake system on O&W hopper 18315 at Summitville in June 1947. The O&W received permission from the court in 1939 to install power hand brakes on 500 hoppers that it was modifying. Since the O&W had not received permission from the court to install power hand brakes on these older cars, it's possible the O&W removed them from other cars as they were scrapped and installed them on these older cars. This car is also equipped with the second grab iron on the left end of the car as required in the 1932 amendment to the United States Safety Appliance standards. *[O&WRHS Archives]*

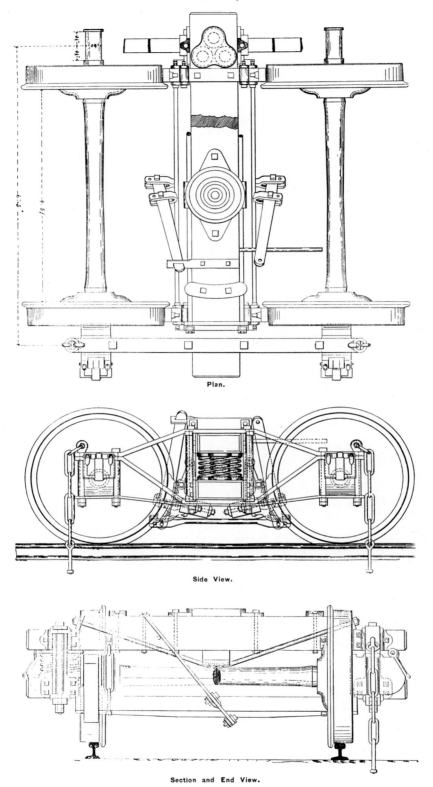

STANDARD FREIGHT CAR TRUCK—NEW YORK, ONTARIO & WESTERN RAILROAD.

Plan.

Side View.

Section and End View.

FIGURE 5.1
Early in its history, the O&W developed a standard truck for use on its freight cars. The railroad installed these trucks on the 300 hopper-bottom gondolas that it built in its Middletown shops in 1882. [*National Car-Builder, December 1882*]

From their introduction in the early 1600's and for over two hundred years, coal cars rode on four wheels. In 1834 Ross Winans was granted a patent for the swiveling truck. The four-wheel, swiveling truck was a major innovation for American railroads. They not only tracked well and provided a more stable ride on rough American tracks, they permitted railroads to operate longer and heavier freight cars by distributing the weight more evenly over the tracks. Unfortunately for Mr. Winans, the Supreme Court ultimately threw out his patent,[1] because the four-wheel, swiveling truck went on to serve under virtually every American freight car to this day.

The first freight trucks were of wood construction with rigidly mounted axles. These solid trucks quickly gave way, though, to pedestal trucks with spring suspension as shown in Figure 5.2.

The freight car truck that came to dominate the 19th century and served well into the 20th century was the Arch Bar or Diamond Arch Bar truck. Introduced in about 1865,[2] the arch bar truck was an elegantly simple design that performed well and was easy to manufacture out of common components.

In the mid to late 19th century the arch bars would have been constructed of wrought iron bar stock with wood bolsters and transoms. A common size for the upper arch bar to support a 40,000 pound capacity hopper would be 1" x 3½", and the lower arch bar would have been 1½" x 3½", slightly larger than the upper because of the increased load it carried. The two arch bars were held apart in the center by the two column castings, from which the arch bars were bent into the familiar diamond pattern that gave the truck its name. The journal box on each side was clamped in place between the arch bars and the tie-strap (½" x 3½") with journal box bolts. The two arch bars and the tie-strap were held in place at the column castings by the column casting bolts. The hardwood (usually oak) transom, a 5" x 12" timber, extended across the truck to give it its stiff-

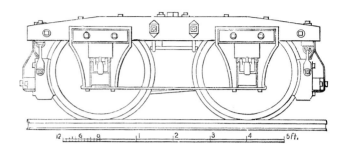

FIGURE 5.2

**Early Pedestal Freight Car Truck, New York & Harlem Railroad** *[Car Builder's Dictionary, 1879]*

ness, was bolted on top of the lower arch bar between the two column casting. The bolster, an 8" x 12" hardwood timber (usually oak), sat on top of the truck spring and rode vertically between the two column castings, guided by the column guides. Two spring plates, one on each end of the spring, protected the wooden bolster and transom. The truck center plate was mounted in the center of the bolster. It mated to the body center plate as shown in Figure 5.6. Note that the center pin serves only as a guide. The entire weight of the car is carried through the center plate and onto the truck bolster. At the edges of the bolster, there are two side bearings which ride against two similar bearings on the body bolster. These bearings are designed to limit the car body's

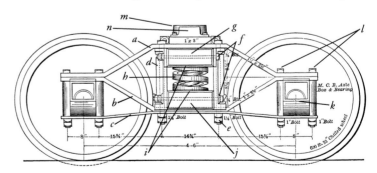

FIGURE 5.3

**Diamond Arch Bar Truck, side view, circa 1892:** *a*-upper arch bar; *b*-lower arch bar; *c*-tie-strap or tie bar; *d*-column castings; *e*-column casting bolts; *f*-column guides; *g*-truck bolster; *h*-truck spring; *i*-spring plates; *j*-spring plank; *k*-journal box; *l*-journal box bolts; *m*-truck center plate; *n*-side bearing *[Railway Car Construction, 1892]*

swaying and relieve some of the weight of the car from the center plate.[3]

The ease of construction also proved to be the arch bar's major shortcoming. The fact that it was bolted together meant that motion in the trucks tended to work the bolts loose and elongate the bolt holes. This would cause the truck to get out of alignment and track poorly as a result. In addition, the bottom arch bar, which bore the greatest load, was prone to breaks at the bends around the column castings and journal boxes. Thus, if not properly inspected and maintained, the arch bar truck could suffer catastrophic failure.

As freight cars became heavier, it became necessary to increase the strength of the arch bar truck. Table 5.1 shows how the size of the arch bars grew over time to accommodate heavier cars.

One of the most critical parts of any freight car truck is the journal because it supports the entire weight of the freight car. As the load-bearing part of the entire truck, the size of the journal ultimately determines the capacity of the car. The journal rides in the journal bearing or car brass, which is housed inside the journal box.

A journal box showing the component journal and journal bearing is shown in Figure 5.7. The journal bearing is generally bronze or brass with a Babbitt Metal lining. It's held in place by the key (also known as the wedge or slide), which presses the bearing squarely against the journal. The back of the journal box is protected from the elements by a collar or dust guard, generally made of wood. The collar also keeps the journal box oil from leaking out of the journal box. The journal box is packed with waste saturated with oil. As the journal turns, it picks up oil from the waste packing, and this oil forms a thin film between the journal and the bearing to lubricate the assembly.[4] This type of bearing, which is often referred to as a "friction bearing," was to remain the industry standard for over 100 years.

Perhaps the single greatest problem with this type of bearing was the infamous "hot box," which occurred when the journal became starved for lubrication, causing excess friction and heat to develop between the journal and bearing. Hot boxes were not a problem in the early days of railroading when cars were light, and trains and

distances were short, but they became increasingly problematic as cars became heavier, trains faster, and distances greater. The most common condition causing the bearing failure was the waste packing being picked up in the bearing, usually due to a sudden shock, such as hard braking.[5] One of the first acts of the Master Car Builders Association after it was formed in 1867 was to develop a standard journal bearing to facilitate repairs on foreign roads.

In 1914, the M.C.B.A. adopted rules stating that all cars built after October 1, 1915 (subsequently extended to October 1, 1920) would be required to have M.C.B. Standard journals and journal bearings, and in 1915, it required that all cars be equipped with MCB Standard axles after October 1, 1919 (subsequently extended to January 1, 1926).[6] Continuing their effort toward standardization, in 1920, the M.C.B.A. adopted as standard practice the labeling of journal sizes by a letter code to establish the maximum permissible weight allowed on the rails for cars with that journal size. This marked the end of a transition in the way that railroads accounted for the capacity of freight cars. Prior to 1916, railroads were required to match the journal sizes of their trucks to the marked weight limit or capacity of their cars, that is, a car with less than the required journal size for the marked weight or capacity would not be accepted in interchange.[7] Railroads, however, were allowed to exceed the marked capacity by up to ten percent.[8] This ten percent allowance was to create confusion after the rule change because the new rules established absolute limits for maximum weight on rail.

TABLE 5.1

**The size of the arch bars grew as car capacities increased. The M.C.B.A. did not establish standards for 40,000 or 60,000 pound trucks. In 1897, it recommended a standard for 80,000 pound cars. By 1912, it had also established a standard for 100,000 pound cars. In 1927, noting the increase in car weights, the A.R.A. increased the minimum size of the arch bars for 80,000 and 100,000 pound capacity cars. By 1931, the A.R.A. was taking action to eliminate these trucks from interchange service altogether.**

| Capacity | Upper Arch Bar | Lower Arch Bar | Tie Bar |
|---|---|---|---|
| 40,000 Pound (1892) | 1" x 3 ½" | 1 ½" x 3 ½" | ½" x 3 ½" |
| 60,000 Pound (1892) | 1 ¼" x 4" | 1 1/8" x 4" | ¾" x 4" |
| 80,000 Pound (1898) | 1 ½" x 4 ½" | 1 ½" x 4 ½" | 5/8" x 4 ½" |
| 80,000 Pound (1928) | 1 ¾" x 4 ½" | 1 ¾" x 4 ½" | 5/8" x 4 ½" |
| 100,000 Pound (1912) | 1 ½" x 5" | 1 ½" x 5" | 5/8" x 5" |
| 100,000 Pound (1928) | 1 ¾" x 5" | 1 ¾" x 5" | 5/8" x 5" |

Hard Coal and Coal Cars

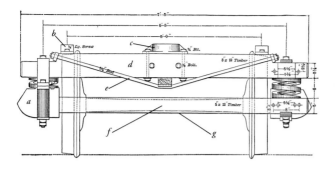

FIGURE 5.4
**Diamond Arch Bar Truck, end view, circa 1892:** *a*-journal box; *b*-side bearings; *c*-center plate; *d*-truck bolster; *e*-bolster truss rod; *f*-axle; *g*-spring plank *[Railway Car Construction, 1892]*

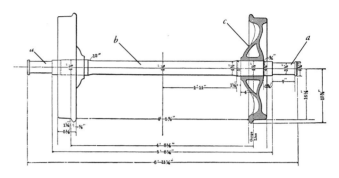

FIGURE 5.5
**Freight Car Axle:** *a*-journal; *b*-axle; *c*-cast iron wheel *[Railway Car Construction, 1892]*

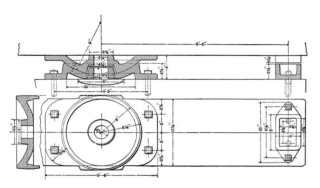

FIGURE 5.6
**Truck Center Plate and Side Bearing showing how body bolster mates to truck bolster.** The center bearing supports the full weight of the car. The side bearing is designed to prevent excess rocking, but may support some of the car weight when the car is leaning, such as on curves. One of the problems facing railroads as they began repairing foreign cars was that each railroad had its own proprietary center plate. Consequently, the trucks from one railroad would not fit under the cars of another. By the early 20th century, the M.C.B.A. rectified the situation by establishing a standard for center plates. *[Railway Car Construction, 1892]*

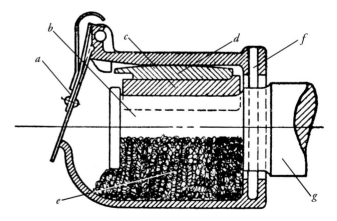

FIGURE 5.7
**Journal Box:** *a*-journal box lid; *b*-journal; *c*-journal bearing; *d*-key or wedge or slide; *e*-waste or packing; *f*-collar or dust guard; *g*-axle *[Courtesy: American Association of Railroads]*

TABLE 5.2
**1900 M.C.B.A. Interchange Rule 3 indicating the required axle and journal size given the marked capacity of a freight car.**[9]

| Capacity of Car | Journal | Wheel Seat | Center |
|---|---|---|---|
| 100,000 | 5″ | 6¾″ | 5⅞″ |
| 80,000 | 4½″ | 6¼″ | 5⁵⁄₁₆″ |
| 70,000 | 4″ | 5⅝″ | 4⅞″ |
| 60,000 | 3¾″ | 5″ | 4⅜″ |
| 50,000 | 3½″ | 4¾″ | 4⅛″ |
| 40,000 | 3¼″ | 4⅝″ | 3⅞″ |
| 30,000 | 3″ | 4¼″ | 3½″ |
| 20,000 | 2¾″ | 4¼″ | 3½″ |

With the A.R.A.'s adoption of the letter standard for labeling journal sizes in 1920, the philosophy shifted from one of matching the axle to the capacity of the car to one of using the journal size to determine the car's capacity. Thus, the maximum weight allowed on the rails was based upon the journal size (width times length) of the axle, a standard which remains in effect to today. As shown in the table below, a hopper with 5½" x 10" journals would have an axle designation of "D" and a maximum permissible weight on the rails of 169,000 pounds. (Compare the journal sizes from Table 5.2 from 1900 with those in Table 5.3 twenty years later.)

The maximum permissible weight on the rails is used to determine the capacity and load limit stenciled on the side of the hopper. Continuing the example above, if a hopper with an axle designation of "D" had a light weight of 36,000 pounds, it would have a load limit of 133,000 pounds. Note that two hoppers, one with a marked capacity of 100,000 pounds and the other with a marked capacity of 110,000 pounds, but both having an axle designation of "D," would both have a total allowable weight on the rails of 169,000 pounds.

As car weights increased, timber bolsters were no longer able to support the weight of the car. The first innovation to improve the timber bolster was to reinforce it with truss rods as shown in Figure 5.4. A photograph of the truss rods anchored into the bolster can be seen in Figure 5.8.

Advances in metallurgy made the next advancements in bolsters possible.[11] Wood bolsters, even those reinforced with truss rods, reached their practical limit, and by 1897, wood transoms and bolsters had almost entirely disappeared except on those few railroads with "benighted superintendents."[12] Wood bolsters and spring planks were replaced with steel, and the ongoing debate between rolled and pressed-steel components continued into the manufacturing of trucks. However, there was a third competitor in this field, cast-steel, which was the ultimate victor. The first steel bolsters were little more than twin I-beams that had been riveted together.[13] Next came the development of pressed-steel and cast-steel truck and body bolsters as shown in Figure 5.10.

In 1896, the O&W began replacing some of its older wood freight car trucks with standard freight car trucks with steel components. From 1896 through 1907, it replaced 2205 sets of trucks. In 1902, the railroad began replacing all of the wood truck bolsters in its remaining sets of freight car trucks. In that year, it installed 1046 new steel truck bolsters, and over the next nine years, it installed another 5376. Figure 5.9 shows an arch bar truck with steel truck bolster and spring plank.

On a traditional freight truck, the center plate supports the entire weight of the car, and the side bearings act merely to stabilize the car. However, these side bearings do come in contact during turning, and there can be considerable friction exerted between the truck and body bolsters when this occurs. As cars became heavier, this problem grew proportionately. To eliminate this friction, designers

TABLE 5.3
**Standard Journal Sizes, Nominal Car Capacity, & Total Allowable Weight on Rail, adopted by the A.R.A. in 1920.**[10]

| Axle Designation Letter | Journal Size | Nominal Capacity Pounds | Total Weight on Rail 4-Wheel Trucks | Total Weight on Rail 6-Wheel Trucks |
|---|---|---|---|---|
| A | 3¾″ x 7″ | 40,000 | 66,000 | 99,000 |
| B | 4½″ x 8″ | 60,000 | 103,000 | 154,500 |
| C | 5″ x 9″ | 80,000 | 136,000 | 204,000 |
| D | 5½″ x 10″ | 100,000 | 169,000 | 253,000 |
| E | 6″ x 11″ | 140,000 | 210,000 | 315,000 |
| F | 6½″ x 12″ | 200,000 | 251,000 | 376,500 |

FIGURE 5.8
This photo shows the wood bolster of an arch bar truck reinforced with truss rods. The nuts securing the truss rods are visible at the end of the wood bolster. *[Photographed at the Railroad Museum of Pennsylvania]*

FIGURE 5.9
As car weights increased, wood truck bolsters were first reinforced, as seen in Figure 5.8, and then replaced with steel, as seen here. *[Photographed at the Railroad Museum of Pennsylvania]*

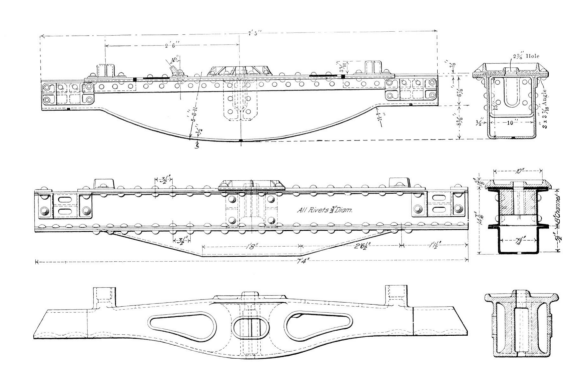

FIGURE 5.10
At the beginning of the 20th century, it was uncertain what type of steel fabrication would prevail in the construction of railroad cars. Shown here are three truck bolsters for 100,000 pound capacity cars using different types of fabrication. From top to bottom, pressed-steel bolster from Standard Steel Car Company, rolled-steel bolsters from Chicago Railway Equipment Company, and cast-steel truck bolster from Benjamin Atha & Co. *[The Car Builders' Dictionary, 1906; Courtesy: Simmons-Boardman Publishing Corp.]*

introduced "frictionless" or "anti-friction" truck side bearings, typically composed of roller or ball bearings such as the one depicted in Figure 5.11. The O&W would start adding roller side bearings to its coal cars in 1910.

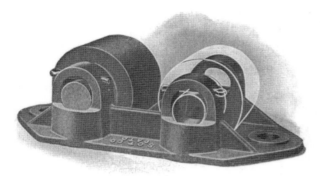

FIGURE 5.11
**Roller side bearings such as the one made by Barber shown here were used to reduce friction between the truck and body bolster during turns.** *[The Car Builders' Dictionary, 1916; Courtesy: Simmons-Boardman Publishing Corp.]*

The next change in truck design was the use of pressed-steel components in the side frames. As early as 1889, Samson Fox of Yorkshire, England, had introduced the pressed-steel truck that bore his name, the Fox truck. This truck used a pressed-steel side frame with pedestal jaws, which contained the springs and journal boxes. Its pressed-steel frame eliminated the problem of trucks becoming misaligned over time like the arch bar truck, but it was significantly more expensive. The design gained a brief period of favor and was imitated by several major American manufacturers, including Schoen's Pressed Steel Car Company, but it never gained widespread popularity.[14]

In 1899, the O&W experimented with Fox trucks by putting them under its milk cars,[15] but there is no evidence that the O&W ever put Fox trucks under any of its coal cars. A picture of one of the O&W's Fox trucks is shown in Figure 5.12.

Manufacturers also began using pressed-steel components to replace the bar stock components of the arch bar truck, and the literature of the period shows that a number of manufacturers followed this practice.

In 1901, the O&W purchased two different kinds of all-steel, hopper-bottom gondolas, one set from the Pressed Steel Car Company and the second set from the Sterlingworth Car Company. Each set represented a different philosophy of manufacturing. The Pressed Steel car used pressed-steel components, and the Sterlingworth car used rolled steel components. This difference extended all the way to the freight trucks.

The Pressed Steel cars were equipped with pressed-steel arch bar trucks. The Pressed Steel Car Company developed these trucks in cooperation with Axel S. Vogt of the Pennsylvania Railroad[16] and were often referred to as "Vogt trucks" or "Diamond Pattern Pressed Steel Trucks." A picture taken in Middletown in 1911 show the pressed-steel cars equipped with these trucks. A close-up view of these trucks is shown in Figure 5.13.

The Sterlingworth cars came equipped with trucks manufactured with rolled steel components by the Sterlingworth Car Company. A unique feature of this truck is the hinged pedestal shown in Figures 5.14 and 5.15 that allowed the journal bearing to be replaced without removing the truck. The Sterlingworth truck was based upon a design by Mr. G. R. Joughins of the Norfolk and Southern Railroad.[17] These trucks were short lived, as indicated by their disappearance from trade publications after 1903.

Cast steel side frames were introduced around the turn of the 20th century, and it appears that the O&W experimented with that style of side frame as well. The builder's photo for car number 7000, which was built in the Middletown shops, shows it equipped with an early, cast-steel side frame. These trucks look similar to the pressed-steel arch bar trucks installed on the pressed-steel gondolas, and they share the feature of removable journal boxes, which remained the O&W's preference throughout its life. The O&W must not have been impressed with these trucks, because it went on to equip the remainder of the 7000 series with arch bar trucks.

Two types of cast-steel side frames populated the early market, those with replaceable journal boxes and those with journal boxes cast into the side frame. The Bettendorf truck, which was first produced in 1903, had the journal boxes cast into the side frames. The most enduring truck with separable journal boxes was the Andrews truck introduced a year later by American Steel Foundries. Trucks with separable journal boxes were the preference of the O&W, but the Bettendorf style truck with cast journal boxes ultimately prevailed in the railroad industry.

**Hard Coal and Coal Cars**

FIGURE 5.12
This set of Fox trucks is seen in front of the new round-house being constructed in Middletown in 1906-07. The O&W used Fox trucks on its milk cars. There is no evidence that it ever used them on any of its coal cars. [O&WRHS Archives]

FIGURE 5.13
These Vogt-style, pressed-steel, arch bar trucks are similar to those manufactured by the Schoen Pressed Steel Car Company and installed on the pressed steel cars that the O&W bought from that company in 1901. [Photographed at the Strasburg Railroad]

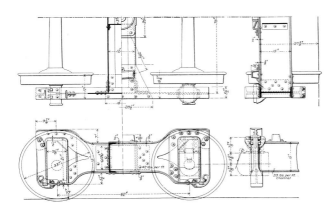

FIGURE 5.14
Mr. G. R. Joughins of the Norfolk & Southern Railroad developed this truck in 1898 using rolled-steel components. The Sterlingworth Steel Car Company of Easton, Pennsylvania, manufactured them. [The Car Builders' Dictionary, 1903; Courtesy: Simmons-Boardman Publishing Corp.]

FIGURE 5.15
The hopper-bottom gondolas that the O&W bought from the Sterlingworth Steel Car Company came equipped with these Joughins-style, all-steel trucks. Note the hinged pedestal leg to facilitate journal box replacement. [O&WRHS Archives]

FIGURE 5.16
This unidentified cast-steel side frame was installed on the all-wood, hopper-bottom gondola number 7000 built in the Middletown shops in 1900. [O&WRHS Archives]

FIGURE 5.17
There are not records to indicate that the O&W ever purchased any of these early "T-Section" Bettendorf freight trucks. [Photographed at the Strasburg Railroad]

One of the stated advantages of the Bettendorf truck was that the journal boxes were cast into the side frame and couldn't become misaligned, whereas the advantage of trucks with separable journal boxes was that the journal boxes were replaceable, and railroads could use their large stock of journal boxes from their arch bar days. The O&W showed a great preference for truck side frames with separable journal boxes. Its first, large purchase of cast-steel side frames was for Wolff trucks with separable journal boxes used in the retrofit of its thirty-ton hopper-bottom gondolas, as shown in Figure 5.18.

In 1906, the O&W reported that it installed "Lindenthal trucks" on 24 freight cars.[18] This indicates two important features of the period—first, the fact that even Gustav Lindenthal, the noted bridge designer, was designing equipment for railroads, and second, that the O&W continually experimented with new products. There is no evidence that the O&W purchased any more than 24 of these trucks.

In 1910, the O&W began its single largest purchase and construction of coal cars since 1890-93. The O&W equipped these Seley hoppers with cast-steel side frames from two different manufacturers whose trucks were remarkably similar in design. The cars built in the Middletown shops were equipped with "L-Section" Andrews cast side frames, which are shown in Figure 5.19. Those cars manufactured by American Car and Foundry were equipped with Gould cast side frames as shown in Figure 5.20.

Three years later, the O&W began purchasing its first all-steel hoppers, and it outfitted these with "T-Section" Andrews trucks. Although no records have been found to indicate how many Andrews trucks were actually purchased by the O&W, this was the truck that would dominate the O&W's freight car inventory until its final years. The trucks are shown in Figure 5.21, and original drawings of those side frames can be seen in Figure 5.25. Unfortunately, although these trucks survived until the final days of the railroad, they did not stand up well. After many extensions, the A.A.R. finally prohibited "L-Section" and "T-Section" trucks from use under all cars in interchange after January 1, 1957.[19]

The Andrews style truck had many champions. In 1917, the United States Government took over the railroads in a wartime emergency and turned over their management to the United States Railway Administration (USRA). One of the first actions of the USRA was to adopt standard designs for loco-motives, freight cars, and equipment, including specifying the "U-Section" or "Channel-Section" Andrews style sideframe as USRA standard. The USRA equipped over 100,000 freight cars with this truck, and railroads continued to produce it into the 1920's.[20] Photos show some of the O&W's second-hand hoppers equipped with these sideframes.

Based upon their wartime experience with USRA standard trucks, railroads began searching for a standard truck that could meet their future needs. In 1920, the American Railway Association established a committee to conduct this search.

By this time, evidence was growing that the "L-Section" and "T-Section" trucks had structural weaknesses that precluded their being viable candidates. Therefore, the committee settled on the "U-Section" truck as being the choice for the future. The committee provided two choices, one with replaceable journal boxes based upon the Vulcan truck and one with cast-in journal boxes based upon the Bettendorf design. The committee's recommendations were made standard in 1926.

The railroads clearly favored the design with the cast-in journal boxes, which are often mistakenly referred to as "Bettendorf trucks." Very few of the "Vulcan" design were ever produced.[21] In order to accommodate as many manufacturers as possible, the A.R.A. laid out its specifications in such a way that each could produce variants while still meeting A.R.A. specifications.

From 1926 onward, the A.R.A., and then its successor, the American Association of Railroads, steadfastly promoted trucks that conformed to its specifications. It first required trucks that met its design on all new cars, and then, on all rebuilt cars. Then it prohibited arch bar trucks, and finally it prohibited "L-Section" and "T-Section" trucks from interchange service. Five snapshots of those interchange rules are shown at the inset of page 84.

The 1930's welcomed the introduction of two additional innovations in freight truck design, the "spring plankless" or "self-aligning" truck and roller bearing journals. Although these two innovations were beyond the means of the bankrupt O&W, their introduction merits at least a footnote in this discussion.

From the introduction of the arch bar truck in the mid-19th century, most freight car trucks employed a spring plank, which supported the truck

FIGURE 5.18
Early Wolff cast-steel side frames installed on thirty-ton wood hopper-bottom gondola. Note the journal box retainer bar, reminiscent of the arch bar tie-strap, holding the journal boxes in place. This bar was common on side frames with separable journal boxes and is seen in the Gould and Andrews trucks below. [O&WRHS Archives]

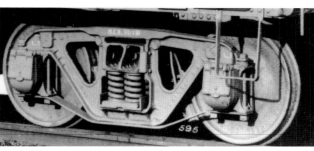

FIGURE 5.19
The O&W equipped the 15000 series composite hoppers that it built in its own shops with the Andrews "L-Section" cast-steel side frame. Note the similarity between this truck and the Gould truck in Figure 5.20. The Andrews truck can be identified by the "knee" in the casting next to the springs. [Standard Steel Car Company Photo; D. K. Retterer Collection]

FIGURE 5.20
Gould cast-steel side frame trucks were installed on the 15000 series composite hoppers and the 6200 series drop bottom gondolas built by American Car & Foundry in 1911. [American Car & Foundry photo; from the John W. Barriger, III National Railroad Library at the University of Missouri-St. Louis]

FIGURE 5.21
The O&W equipped its 18000 series all-steel hoppers and its second purchase of composite gondolas in the 6200 series with Andrews "T-Section" cast-steel side frame trucks. This style of truck would dominate the O&W's freight car inventory from 1915 through 1957. [American Car & Foundry photo; from the John W.

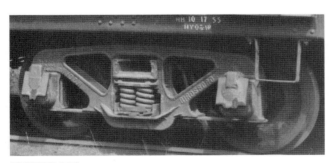

FIGURE 5.22
By 1917, the Andrews "U-Section" or "Channel-Section" truck had replaced the "T-Section" truck shown in Figure 5.21, and in 1918, the USRA adopted it as standard. These Andrews-style, "U-Section" trucks with 5" x 9" journals were photographed under an O&W box car in July 1957. The side frames indicate that they were cast for the O&W in 1928. [Courtesy: Bob's Photo]

FIGURE 5.23
In 1926, the A.R.A. adopted a design for a standard truck. The design ultimately called for "U-Section" construction with journal boxes cast into the side frame as shown here. [Photographed at the Railroad Museum of Pennsylvania]

No. 799,606.
PATENTED SEPT. 12, 1905.

G. LINDENTHAL.
CAR TRUCK.
APPLICATION FILED OCT. 23, 1903.

7 SHEETS—SHEET 1.

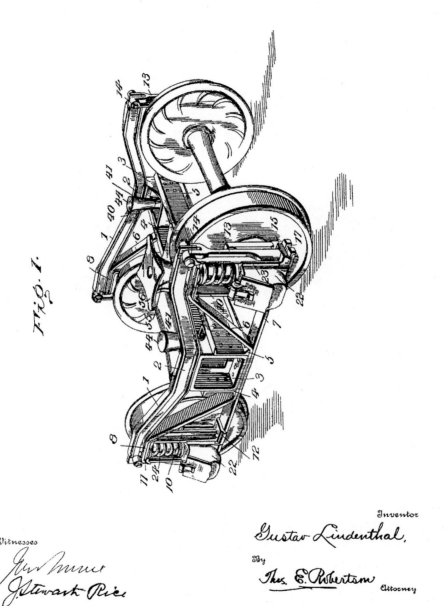

Witnesses

J. Stewart Rice

Inventor

Gustav Lindenthal,

By

Thos. E. Robertson

Attorney

FIGURE 5.24

Even noted bridge designer Gustav Lindenthal entered the freight truck design business at the beginning of the twentieth century. The distinguishing feature of Lindenthal trucks was that the whole weight of the car was borne on the side bearing. The center plate carried none of the weight of the car and was used simply as a pivot point for the swiveling truck. Lindenthal believed that placing the weight of the car directly over the frame would add stability to the load and increase the truck's ability to support the heavier weight of modern freight cars. He made several improvements in his design in subsequent years, but the design never caught on. The O&W tested these trucks on 24 of its freight cars beginning in 1906. [U.S. Patent and Trademark Office]

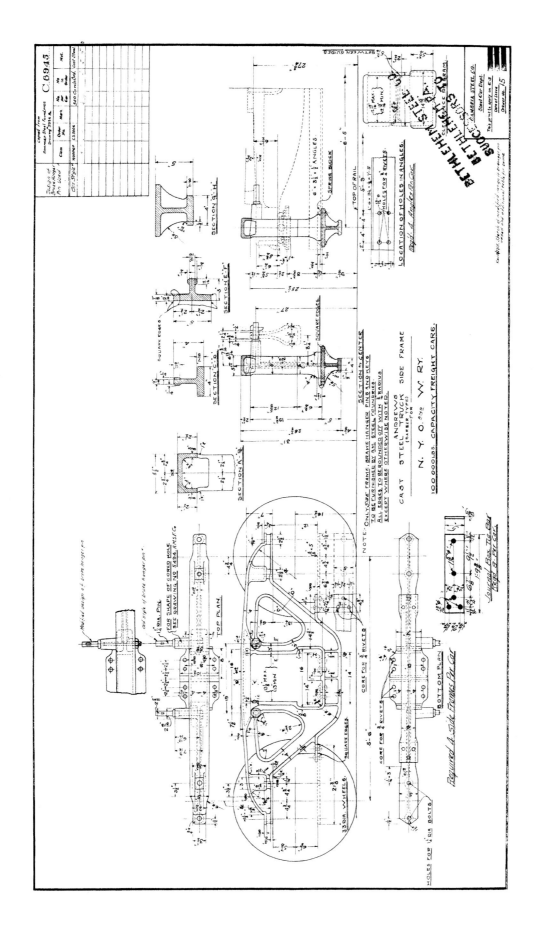

FIGURE 5.25

The Andrews "T-Section" cast-steel side frame became the O&W's preferred side frame beginning with the freight cars it procured in 1913. The O&W installed these on its 18000 series hoppers that it bought from Cambria Steel in 1913 and 1916, and its 6300 series gondolas that it bought from American Car & Foundry in 1916. They are also seen on several other series of O&W coal cars that it bought second-hand. A photo of this truck is seen in Figure 5.21. [Courtesy: Johnstown America Corporatoin]

springs and held the two side frames rigidly in place to keep the axles parallel with each other and square with the side frames. This design worked very well on straight track, but as the truck entered curves, the action of the wheels imposed a twisting stress upon the truck.[29] This twisting stress could both weaken the spring plank, causing truck failure, or pull the journals out of alignment, causing hot boxes.[30]

As its name implies, the "spring-plankless" truck eliminated the spring plank and used the truck bolster to keep the axles aligned, much as a sprung, scale model freight truck is kept aligned. Using the truck bolster for alignment permitted the trucks to flex and become "self-aligning" as they entered a curve, greatly reducing the stresses upon the truck assembly and journal boxes. These new designs could be manufactured in such a way that they complied with A.A.R. specifications, and, with fewer components, they produced the added advantage of

significantly reducing overall car weight.

Even though they had been introduced in the 1930's, roller bearing trucks were not in wide use before 1957. The roller bearing truck provided three significant advantages over the plain bearing. First, they virtually eliminated the problem of hot boxes. Since the wheel bearing was packed, there wasn't the same danger of the rotating journal becoming dry. This fact led to the second advantage, reduced maintenance. Third, the roller bearing greatly reduced the power required to start a train. In tests conducted on the Pennsylvania Railroad, it was shown that a 2-10-0 could start a 65 car train equipped with roller bearings that was stretched out, but it could only start a 37 car train with standard bearings that was stretched out.[31]

These advantages were mitigated by several factors. First, improvements in the design of the journal bearing and bearing lubrication was reducing the number of hot boxes.[32]  Secondly, as long as friction bearings were allowed in interchange service, railroads would still have to maintain their facilities to service them.  Thirdly, engineers could overcome the problems with starting a long train by increasing the slack in the train and then starting it one car at a time.  By doing so in the previously mentioned tests, the Pennsylvania Railroad showed that the 2-10-0 could start a 76 car train regardless of which bearing was used.  Furthermore, this big difference between the bearings only applied when the plain journal bearing was dry.  Once the train was underway and the bearings were being lubricated, there less than a ten percent difference in resistance between the two bearings.[33]

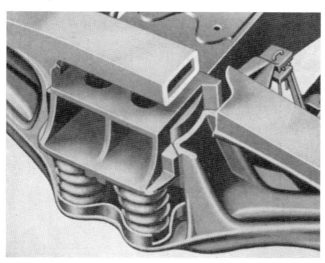

FIGURE 5.26
Cutaway view of "Spring-Plankless" truck showing how a "Spring-Plankless" or "Self-Aligning" truck is held in alignment by the interaction of the side frames and bolster. [Courtesy: Thomson Education Direct]

This difference in operating performance was not sufficient for the railroads to make the large investment to convert their trucks to roller bearings, especially since the operational savings accrue to the railroad that's pulling the car, which is not necessarily the railroad that's making the investment.  Thus, by 1957, less than 12% of the freight car fleet had been equipped with roller bearing trucks.[34]  In 1956, the Timken Roller Bearing Company released an economic study that stated that railroads could save $113.62 per car per year if they converted from friction bearings to roller bearings.[35]  However, in order to realize these savings, the study assumed that all freight cars were equipped with roller bearings.

FIGURE 5.27
This photo shows a set of A.A.R. Standard trucks with 5½" by 10" journal boxes that's been modified to accept roller bearings. [Photographed at the Railroad Museum of Pennsylvania]

Perhaps in response to this study, the A.A.R. made roller bearings standard on all new or rebuilt cars of 100 tons capacity or larger after 1966.  By 1968, they had made roller bearings standard on all new cars and by 1970, they required them on all rebuilt cars,[36] well after the O&W was just a fond memory.

In 1953, the O&W was forced to buy 21 secondhand hoppers from the New Haven railroad because none of its coal cars were suitable for interchange service.  Those 21 cars came equipped with Dalman A.R.A. Standard trucks.  The Dalman truck was a variation of the A.R.A. Standard design developed to improve the riding qualities of the car and to overcome harmonic vibrations created by the thirty-nine foot spacing of rail joints.  It accomplished these objectives by increasing the width of the bolster and adding more and softer springs.  These were the last cars and last freight car trucks purchased by the O&W.

FIGURE 5.28
The 21 hoppers that the O&W bought from the New Haven Railroad in 1953 came equipped with cast-steel Dalman trucks manufactured for the New Haven in 1928. [Courtesy: Bob's Photo]

FIGURE 6.1
The length of this "coal train" may help account for the O&W's declining anthracite revenue per mile in its later years. The hopper in the photo has one of the O&W's more unusual lettering schemes. It's a former Westmoreland Coal Company GLa that the O&W purchased second-hand from that coal company in 1933. Rather than repaint the entire car, the railroad simply painted over Westmoreland's reporting marks and inserted its own and reused the coal company's car number. The Westmoreland logo is still visible on the side of the car. *[Courtesy: J. R. Quinn]*

## Chapter 6

One of the first issues with which railroads had to contend when it began interchanging freight cars was identifying the cars of foreign roads; however, it was not until 1884 that the M.C.B.A. made any recommendations to the railroads to standardize their markings to facilitate that task. Unfortunately, those recommendations were rejected, and it was not until 1896 that any standards for labeling were adopted by the railroads.

The first requirements for labeling freight cars were established as a way of determining a car's compliance with safety standards being established both by the Master Car Builders' Association and the Federal Government as part of the Railroad Safety Appliance Act of 1893. In 1896, the Master Car Builders' Association adopted the following Recommended Practice pertaining to open-top cars:

*That all classes of cars have style of coupler and rear attachments, and style of brake beams stenciled in not less than 1½-inch letters near one end of car on each side, on each end of car directly above the buffer blocks where design of car permits it.*

*That where the construction of the truck permits, trucks shall be stenciled on each side, giving the size of journal and the letters "M.C.B." if the axle is M.C.B. standard axle. If the axle is not M.C.B. standard, use dimensions from center to center of journal in place of M.C.B. This stenciling to be in 1¼-inch letters, and to be put on end or side of bolster in Diamond trucks, and on side-truck frame in center on pedestal type of trucks.*

*That on all cars equipped with air brakes, the words "Air Brake," in letters not less than 3 inches high, be stenciled on the sides or ends of the cars, and that the make of air-brake equipment be stenciled (in smaller letters if desired) over or just preceding these words, to enable inspectors to detect repairs made with wrong material. Initials of the road should also appear in letters not less than 2 inches high on one side of bolster or transom of each truck.[1]*

In 1901, the foregoing was made Standard Practice by the M.C.B.A. In 1902, the M.C.B.A. made the following additions to its Standard to prevent errors in identifying modifications made to freight cars.[2]

*All freight equipment cars used in interchange shall be stenciled with a letter "B" on the end of car upon which the brake shaft is located and with the letter "A" on the opposite end. On cars having brake shafts on both ends, the end toward which the brake cylinder push rod travels should be stenciled "B" and the opposite end "A." The stenciling shall be in plain, block letters, not less than 1½ inches high, enclosed in a circle not less than 2¾ inches in diameter.*

*The location of the lettering to be as near the center line of end of car as convenient, and where possible be not less than ten inches, nor more than fourteen inches, above the buffer block, on box, stock and other classes of cars having stationary ends, and to be located on the end sill near the buffer block, or on the face of the buffer block, near the top, on other classes of cars.[3]*

At the turn of the 19th century, the light weighing of cars, which is covered in more detail later in this chapter, was becoming an increasingly important issue both for the management of trains and the collection of revenue. Thus, in 1898, the executive committee of the M.C.B.A. requested that all owners stencil the light weight on their cars.[4] By 1901, the

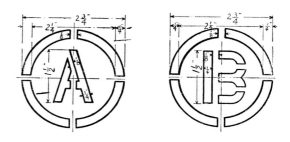

FREIGHT CAR STENCILING.

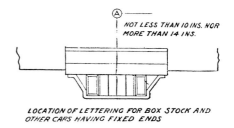

LOCATION OF LETTERING FOR BOX STOCK AND OTHER CARS HAVING FIXED ENDS

FIGURE 6.2

**Marking Freight Car's A & B Ends, circa 1902.** *[The Science of Railways, 1906]*

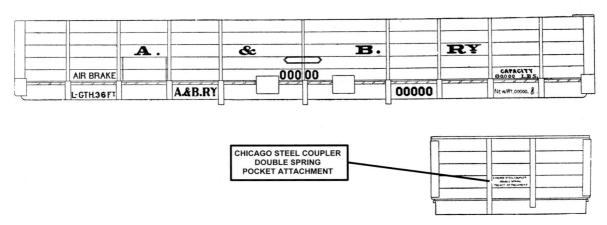

FIGURE 6.3
**Common practice among railroads for the stenciling of open top cars circa 1906.** *[The Science of Railways, 1906]*

Association of American Railway Accountants had gone a step further by requiring that the light weight be stenciled on all cars.[5]

Neither the M.C.B.A. nor the A.A.R.A. specified where or how the weight or any of the reporting marks should be displayed. In fact, they specifically declined to do so when requested, stating that "it will be particularly noted that the committee does not recommend the location on the car for the various marking, believing that each road desires more or less discretion in this respect, and also for the reason that this would be a very difficult matter at this time, on account of the various new types of steel-car equipment being introduced, which will not permit the same location for similar markings as on the old wooden equipment they are superseding."[6] However, a sort of de-facto standard had emerged for the lettering of open top freight cars as shown in Figure 6.3.

In 1905, the M.C.B.A.'s Committee on Stenciling Cars reported that "very little uniformity exists in regard to the size and design of letters and figures of different sizes on any railroad..., and it is with the object of having some uniformity that your committee submits this report..."[7] It's recommendations, which are shown in the inset below, became Recommended Practice in 1906 and Standard in 1911 and remained in practice throughout the remaining history of the O&W.[8]

At the time of its report, the committee did not make specific recommendations regarding the placement of various markings. However, in 1909, the M.C.B.A. established a Standard Practice for the placement of information regarding appliances on a freight car and for the placement of road name, car number, capacity, and empty weight. At the same time, it dropped the requirements to label the A and B ends of the car, and it also dropped the require-

---

### M.C.B.A. Standards for Lettering Freight Cars (1905)

*First. It is recommended that the Roman letters and figures of the designs shown in the attached drawings be adopted for uniform stenciling of freight cars.*

*Second. It is recommended that the sizes of these letters and figures shall be confined to the following heights: 1 inch, 2 inches, 3 inches, 4 inches, 7 inches and 9 inches.*

*Third. It is recommended that 7-inch and 9-inch letters or figures be adopted for the initials or name and numbers for the sides of cars, and 4-inch letters or figures for the same markings on the doors and ends.*

*Fourth. It is recommended that for other car-body markings on sides and ends, such as capacity, couplers, brake beams, class of car, date built, outside dimensions, inside dimensions and markings inside of car, 2-inch or 3-inch letters and figures should be used with the following exceptions:*

*1. All weight marks should be 3-inch or 4-inch letters or figures.*

*2. Trust marks, patent marks, and other private marks, should be 1-inch letters and figures.*

*Fifth. It is recommended that all marks on trucks should be confined to 1-inch and 2-inch letters or figures.*

*Sixth. It is recommended that stenciling on air-brake cylinders or reservoirs should be 1-inch letters or figures.[9]*

---

**Hard Coal and Coal Cars**

ment to label cars as having air brakes, because, by that time, all cars in interchange service were required to have air brakes.[10]  The revised standards stated:

*Freight Equipment Cars that have a superstructure which will permit should be stenciled with markings on sides of car, in the following order:*
  *Lettering (Initials or name of Road)*
  *Number*
  *Capacity*
  *Light Weight*
*This marking is to be located as nearly over the truck as the lettering will permit, preferably to the left of center line of side of car...The distance from the center line of coupler to the bottom of car number to be normally two feet four and one-half inches, with a minimum dimension*

*of one foot ten and one-half inches, and a maximum of two feet ten and one-half inches.  The spacing of the remaining marking to be shown on diagram.  The ends to show the initials or name of road and car number, in the upper half of end of car...*
  *...The 'date weighed' shall include the symbol of station where weighed...[This requirement was added in 1911.]*
  *...Wooden and steel underframe cars should be reweighed and remarked at least once every twelve months during the first two years the car is in service, and thereafter once every twenty-four months.  All-steel cars should be reweighed and restenciled at least once every thirty six months...[11]*

These requirements are shown below in Figures 6.4 and 6.5.

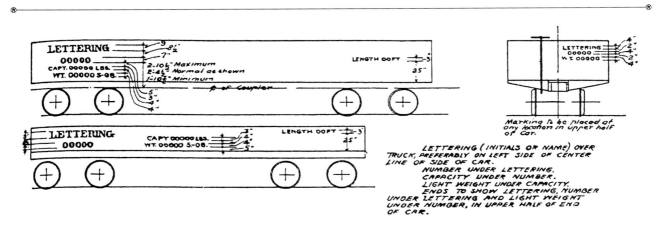

FIGURE 6.4
**Master Car Builders Association Standard for Marking of Open Top Freight Cars with Road Name, Car Number, and Capacities (circa 1909-1916).  Note that the size of lettering in Figures 6.3 and 6.4 corresponds to the 1905 recommendations of the M.C.B.A. Committee on Stenciling.** [*Car Builders' Dictionary, 1909; Courtesy:  Simmons-Boardman Publishing Corp.*]

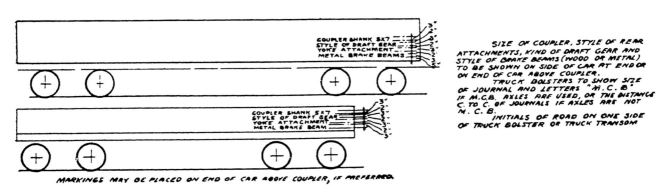

FIGURE 6.5
**Master Car Builders Association Standard for Marking of Open Top Freight Cars (circa 1909-1916).  An O&W gondola stenciled in the manner shown in Figures 6.3 and 6.4 can be seen on page 147.** [*Car Builders' Dictionary, 1909; Courtesy:  Simmons-Boardman Publishing Corp.*]

**Lettering and Marking of Coal Cars**

At this same time, the M.C.B.A. was linking an increasing number of its rules to the date that a car was built, that is, all cars built after a certain date would have to meet certain requirements; those built before that date would be grandfathered or would have a period of time to comply. To enforce this rule, the M.C.B.A. required that the date built be stenciled on all cars after July 1, 1916 (subsequently extended to January 1, 1923). For cars built before 1895, it would suffice to have the cars stenciled "Built prior to 1895."[13]

The Safety Appliance Act, as implemented by the Interstate Commerce Commission in 1910, made provisions for two cases, cars built prior to July 1,

1911, and those built after that date. It also prescribed that freight cars meeting those provisions be marked accordingly. To comply with that requirement, the Master Car Builders' Association issued M.C.B. Circular No. 25-1913-1914, which contained the provisions shown in the inset above.

In 1916, reporting marks were assigned to each railroad by the Association of Transportation and Car Accounting Officers to facilitate the identification of freight cars on foreign roads. The history of the O&W's reporting marks, as reported in the Official Railway Equipment Register, is shown in Table 6.1.

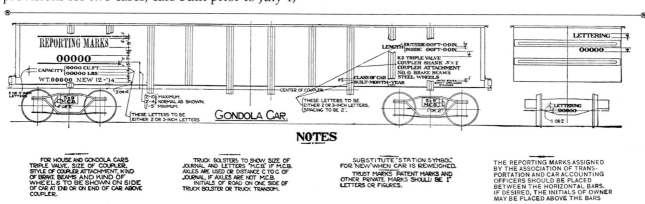

FIGURE 6.6
**Master Car Builders Association Standard Practice for Lettering for Open Top Freight Cars (circa 1916-1926). Note that the lettering diagram now includes the term "Reporting Marks" to implement the newly adopted rule from the Association of Transportation and Car Accounting Officers. Also note that the empty weight is no longer shown on the end of the car. An O&W gondola stenciled in this manner can be seen in the figure on page 147.** *[Car Builders' Dictionary, 1916; Courtesy: Simmons-Boardman Publishing Corp.]*

TABLE 6.1
**Labeling of New York, Ontario & Western Railway Freight Cars as reported in the** *Official Railway Equipment Register*

| Period From | Period To | Reporting Marks* | Marked |
|---|---|---|---|
| 1880 | ~1888 | | "N.Y. & O. M. RR"; "N.Y. & O. Midland RR"; "N.Y. Midland RR"; "N.Y. O. & W. Ry. Co." |
| ~1889 | 1904 | | "N.Y. O. & W. Ry. Co".; "Ontario Despatch" |
| 1904 | 1905 | | "N.Y. O. & W."; "Ontario Despatch"; "P.J.M. & S." |
| 1906 | 1915 | | "N.Y. O. & W."; "Ontario Despatch"; "P.J.M. & S." |
| 1916 | 1919 | O & W | "N.Y. O. & W."; "Ontario Despatch"; "P.J.M. & S." |
| 1920 | 1933 | O & W | "N.Y. O. & W." |
| 1934 | 1937 | O & W | "N.Y. O. & W."; "O. & W." |
| 1938 | 1942 | O W | "N.Y. O. & W."; "O. & W." |
| 1943 | 1957 | O W | "O. & W."; "O. W." |

**\*Reporting marks introduced in 1916 by the Association of Transportation and Car Accounting Officers**

Also in 1916, the M.C.B.A. revised its lettering and stenciling requirements to accommodate the new reporting marks and incorporate the requirement for the safety appliance markings. These changes are shown in Figure 6.6. Note that the empty weight is no longer shown on the end of the car. The M.C.B.A. recommended that the practice of marking the empty weight on the end of the car be discontinued "because of the liability of making errors in the stenciling of weights, the increase in the amount of work involved thereby, and the danger to employees...."[14]

After September 1, 1919, no cars would be accepted in interchange unless equipped with United States Safety Appliances or United States Safety Appliances, Standard,[15] and by the mid-1920's, M.C.B.A. standards for the equipping of freight cars in interchange had been widely implemented. Therefore, the need to identify these appliances on

---

### What do all those markings mean?

CU FT: The capacity, in cubic feet, of the hopper, level full, which includes all available space below the top ledge and sides. This is stenciled on the car by the car owner.

CAPY: The nominal capacity as provided in Rule 86 Association of American Railroads Rules of Interchange, which is generally known as "Marked Capacity" or an arbitrary capacity (in pounds) selected from a safety standpoint within reasonable physical limits of the vehicle. The nominal capacity must not exceed the stenciled load limit. Prior to 1920, the capacity represented the maximum capacity of the car, although a ten percent excess was permitted.

LT WT: The empty weight of the car. Most freight rates were determined by weight, and therefore, it was important to know the light weight of the freight car. A.A.R. rules required that the car be weighed when new and periodically thereafter as discussed on page 96.

LD LMT: The load limit is the maximum load permissible for the car, including lading, blocking, bracing racks, etc. It is determined by subtracting the light weight of the car from the total weight allowable on the rails. The stenciled load limit must not be less than the nominal capacity. Load limit markings were to be completed on all cars within three years of May 1, 1925.[16] (Subsequently extended to January 1, 1934.) When the car owner has marked the load limit down on account of structural limitations or other reasons, a star symbol (*) shall be placed to the immediate left of the words LD LMT.[17]

---

the car body was no longer required and, after 1925, those requirements were dropped from the M.C.B.A. Standard Practice. This led to the adoption of the lettering scheme shown in Figures 6.9 and 6.10 in 1926. This new scheme included the addition of LDLMT, which was the maximum permissible load for the car based upon the maximum permissible weight on the rails governed by the standard journal sizes adopted in 1920 and discussed in further detail in Chapter 5.

It should be noted that the periods for the application of these lettering schemes varies, and there was considerable overlap in their use. For example, the lettering scheme shown in Figure 6.6 was introduced in 1916 but not finally required in interchange service until after January 1, 1923.[18] The lettering scheme that followed, seen in Figures 6.9 and 6.10, was introduced in 1926 but not finally required on all cars in interchange service until after January 1, 1933.[19] Therefore, cars with the lettering scheme in Figure 6.6 might be seen anytime from the late teens to early thirties. The lettering scheme seen in Figures 6.9 and 6.10 was to remain virtually unchanged from its introduction through the O&W's abandonment in 1957.

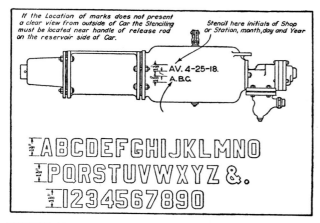

FIGURE 6.7

**Standard practice for marking K-Series air brakes from 1920 through 1957. Although it was not called for, railroads commonly used the one inch air brake stencil to mark their journal repacking information on the car side.** [Courtesy: Association of American Railroads]

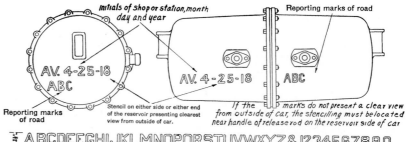

FIGURE 6.8

**Standard practice for marking AB-Series air brakes from 1935 through the remainder of the O&W's life. The only coal cars that the O&W had equipped with AB-series brakes were the 21 USRA hoppers that it bought from the New Haven Railroad in 1953.** [Courtesy: Association of American Railroads]

Hard Coal and Coal Cars

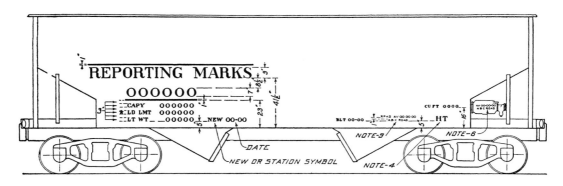

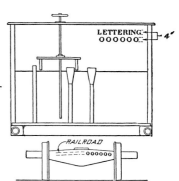

NOTE-1: SIZES AND SPACING OF LETTERS AND FIGURES: 7"LETTERS MAY BE USED FOR REPORTING MARKS. ALL LETTERING AND SPACING 2"UNLESS OTHERWISE SPECIFIED.

NOTE-2: THE REPORTING MARKS ASSIGNED BY THE ASSOCIATION OF TRANSPORTATION AND CAR ACCOUNTING OFFICERS SHOULD BE PLACED BETWEEN THE HORIZONTAL BARS. IF DESIRED THE NAME OR INITIALS OF OWNER MAY BE PLACED ABOVE THE BARS.

NOTE-3: ARRANGEMENT OF REPORTING MARKS, CAPACITY, LOAD LIMIT, LIGHT WEIGHT AND DATE SHOULD BE MAINTAINED AS SHOWN EXCEPT THAT THE ENTIRE ARRANGEMENT MAY BE MOVED SLIGHTLY IF NECESSARY TO SUIT CONSTRUCTION OF CAR.

NOTE-4: SYMBOL FOR CLASSIFICATION OF CAR IF USED SHALL BE APPLIED UNDER DIMENSION MARKING IN 4"LETTERS AND FIGURES AT RIGHT ON THE SIDE OF CAR ON A LINE WITH DATE BUILT.

NOTE-5: CAR NUMBER AND INITIALS TO BE STAMPED OR PAINTED ON INTERMEDIATE OR CENTER SILLS AT OPTION OF OWNER.

NOTE-6: STENCILING TO CONFORM TO INSTRUCTIONS SHOWN IN INTERCHANGE RULE NO 60

NOTE-7: IT IS RECOMMENDED THAT WHEN OWNER DESIRES INFORMATION REGARDING TRIPLE VALVE, COUPLERS, COUPLER ATTACHMENTS, BRAKE BEAMS, STEEL WHEELS, CENTRIFUGAL DIRT COLLECTOR, ETC., SHOWN ON CARS, SUCH INFORMATION BE STENCILED ON THE ENDS OF CARS IF POSSIBLE.

NOTE-8: A STAR MUST BE MAINTAINED CLOSE TO LEFT END OF LOAD LIMIT MARKING ON ALL CARS THAT ARE NOT CAPABLE OF CARRYING THE MAXIMUM LOAD LIMIT PERMITTED BY INTERCHANGE RULE NO. 66. THE STAR INDICATES THAT LOAD LIMIT SO MARKED MUST NOT BE CHANGED EXCEPT BY OWNER.

NOTE-9: STENCILING TO CONFORM TO INSTRUCTIONS SHOWN IN INTERCHANGE RULE NO. 66.

FIGURE 6.9

**American Association of Railroads Standard for Lettering and Marking Hopper Cars (circa 1926-1969)**[20]  *[Car Builders' Cyclopedia, 1940; Courtesy: Simmons-Boardman Publishing Corp.]*

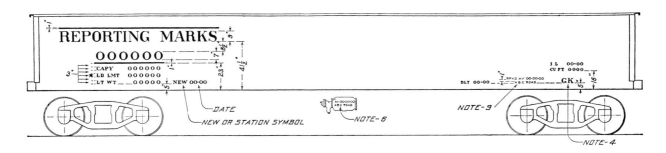

FIGURE 6.10

**American Association of Railroads Standard for Lettering and Marking Gondolas (circa 1926-1969)**  *[Car Builders' Cyclopedia, 1940; Courtesy: Simmons-Boardman Publishing Corp.]*

**Lettering and Marking of Coal Cars**

## Light Weighing of Freight Cars

In addition to the Master Car Builders' concern about the compatibility of equipment in interchange, the Association of American Railway Accountants was concerned about collecting appropriate freight charges for shipments. Since most freight charges were based upon weight, it was imperative that each freight car be easily identified and its weight known. Thus, in guidance that would ultimately become the A.A.R.'s Rule Number 30 in its Rules of Interchange, the A.A.R. established the following guidelines in 1901 regarding the light weight of freight cars.

*1. The correct light weighing and stenciling of freight cars is a matter of very great importance, and it would pay the railroads of this country to go to considerable expense to have it done periodically and systematically by competent men.*

*2. Freight cars, both home and foreign, irrespective of where they may be found should be weighed and stenciled once a year. Any car without stenciling should be immediately weighed and stenciled.*

*3. New cars should be weighed and stenciled with the actual weight immediately before being put into service, and again when the stenciling is more than six months old.*

*4. Cars which have received general repairs should be weighed and stenciled, with the actual weight, immediately before being put back into service.*

*5. A reasonable and uniform charge should be made on the owning road for the weighing and stenciling of foreign cars.*[21]

In 1911, the M.C.B.A. published the following procedure for the light weighing of cars in Rule 30 of its interchange rules:

*(a) The date (month and year), also weight and capacity, should be stenciled on each new car as it comes from the car works, under the supervision of the owner's inspector...*

*(b) Wooden and steel underframe cars one year old should be reweighed and restenciled, the weight to be followed by one star; cars two years old should be again weighed and stenciled, the weight to be followed by two stars; cars three or more years old should be again weighed and stenciled, the weight to be followed by three stars, which will be the final weight.*

*(c) Steel cars would be reweighed and restenciled after they have been in service twelve months, the weight to be followed by three stars, indicating the final weight.*

*(d) If cars are materially changed by reason of new appliances or general repairs, they should be reweighed and restenciled without change in the number of stars.*

*(e) Unless the owner instructs otherwise, any car without stenciling, or with a variation of 500 pounds, should be immediately reweighed and restenciled...*

*(f) The date (month and year) of each reweighing should be stenciled the same as provided for new cars.*[22]

The system of using stars to denote the time since the car was reweighed didn't last long. By 1914, the M.C.B.A. had simplified its reweighing schedule, wooden and steel underframe cars were to be reweighed every twelve months for the first two years and every twenty-four months thereafter; all-steel cars were to be reweighed and remarked every thirty-six months.[23]

In 1929, the intervals between reweighing were changed again. A synopsis of the revised rules is shown in Table 6.2.

TABLE 6.2
**Light Reweighing Schedule (1929)**[24]

| Type of Car | First Reweighing at Expiration of | Subsequent Reweighing at Expiration of | Subsequent Reweighing Permissible After |
|---|---|---|---|
| Wood | 12 months | 24 months | 18 months |
| Composite wood and steel underframe | 12 months | 24 months | 18 months |
| Steel underframe, with wood, steel or composite superstructure frame | 12 months | 24 months | 18 months |
| All-steel cars | 36 months | 36 months | 30 months |

TABLE 6.3
Light Reweighing Schedule (1935)[25]

| Type of Car<br>Wood | First Reweighing<br>at Expiration of | Subsequent Reweighing<br>at Expiration of | Subsequent Reweighing<br>Permissible After |
|---|---|---|---|
| | 15 months | 30 months | 24 months. |
| Composite wood and<br>steel underframe | 15 months | 30 months | 24 months |
| Steel underframe, with<br>wood, steel or composite<br>superstructure frame | 15 months | 30 months | 24 months |
| All-steel open-top cars,<br>including all-steel flat cars | 30 months | 30 months | 24 months |

Beginning in 1932, the A.R.A. established a separate category for all-steel, open-top cars. While the interval between reweighings for all-steel house cars remained at 36 months, the interval for all-steel, open-top cars was reduced to 24 months.[26] By 1935, however, the A.A. R. had standardized the interval between reweighings for open-top and house cars to that shown in the schedule in Table 6.3.

In 1940, the A.R.A. dropped the "Subsequent Reweighing Permissible After" column, and in 1950, the reweigh rules were changed for the final time during the O&W's lifetime by extending the subsequent reweighing of composite cars to 48 months. By this time, of course, wood cars were banned from interchange service, and their requirements had been deleted.[27]

TABLE 6.4

**Classification of Coal Cars. In 1912, the Master Car Builders' Association adopted standard designations for freight cars to facilitate reporting between railroads. These classifications changed very little over the years. One change was made in 1923. The classification "HE" was added to clarify the difference between hopper-bottom gondolas and true hopper cars. In 1928, the increasing size of hopper cars required a further change in classifications. The term "HM" was narrowed to just twin hoppers, and "HT" was revised to indicate only those self-clearing cars with three or more hoppers. As straight forward as these classifications seem to be, the O&W did not always follow these rules in reporting its coal cars. For example, from 1912 through 1918, the O&W reported its all-steel hoppers as "GA," while it carried its composite hoppers and new hopper-bottom gondolas as "HT" and its ancient hopper-bottom gondolas as "HM." From 1919 through 1922, it listed its composite and all steel hoppers as "HM." After 1922, it continued to carry its all-steel hoppers as "HM," but it began reporting both its newer hopper-bottom gondolas and its composite hoppers as "HT." In 1927, it began reporting all of its hopper-bottom gondolas as "HE," and in late 1928, it came into fully compliance with the reporting system by listing its composite hoppers as "HM." [Source: Official Railway Equipment Registers (1912-1957)]**

| | 1912 | 1923 | 1928 | 1957 |
|---|---|---|---|---|
| **Drop Bottom Gondola.** Fixed sides and ends. Drop bottom | GA | GA | GA | GA |
| **Gondola.** Fixed sides and ends. Solid bottom | GB | GB | GB | GB |
| **Drop Bottom, Drop End Gondola.** Fixed sides, drop bottom and ends | GE | GE | GE | GE |
| **Drop End Gondola.** Fixed sides, solid bottom, drop ends | GM | GM | GB | GB |
| **Hopper-Bottom Gondola.** Fixed sides and ends and bottom consisting of hoppers and self clearing | | HE | HE | HE |
| **Hopper.** Fixed sides and ends, open at top, hopper bottom and self clearing | HM | HM | | |
| **Twin Hopper.** Fixed sides and ends, open at top, equipped with two or more hopper doors instead of one | HT | HT | HM | HM |
| **Multiple Hopper Car.** Fixed sides and ends, open at top, equippped with three or more hoppers and self clearing. | | | HT | HT |

*Lettering and Marking an O&W Hopper (1926-1957)*

*a.* Upper Horizontal Line—One inch in height, positioned two inches above top of reporting marks.

*b.* Reporting Marks—Nine inches in height, although seven inches in height was permissible. Bottom of reporting marks is located 41½ inches above the bottom of the side sill. Even though A.R.A. Standards called for the railroad to letter the car with the reporting marks assigned by the Association of Transportation and Car Accounting Office, the O&W was not consistent in what it used. From 1916 through 1937, its reporting marks were "O & W," but the following variations were seen on its hoppers during that period, "N.Y.O. & W.," "O. & W.," "O & W," Likewise, from 1938 through 1957, its reporting marks were "O W," but both "O. W." and "O W" were used, the former during the late 30's and early 40's and the latter during the late 40's and 50's. Naturally, some of the cars lettered in the late 30's with the earlier lettering scheme would have been seen through the early 1940's. For a further discussion of the O&W's reporting marks, see Table 6.1. The O&W most commonly positioned the first part of the reporting marks in the second panel abutting the left side of the second side post and the "W" in the third panel abutting the right side of the second side post, although there are photographs of cars with all of the reporting marks in the second panel.

*c.* Car Number—Seven inches in height, positioned 8½ inches below the bottom of Reporting Marks. No car number on the O&W was longer than five digits. Typically, the O&W displayed the first set of digits in the second panel below the "O" and the last two digits in the third panel beneath the "W." However, there is at least one sighting in which the first two digits are positioned beneath the "O" and the last digit is positioned beneath the "W."

*d.* Lower Horizontal Line—One inch in height, positioned two inches below the bottom of the car number and three inches above the top of "CAPY."

*e.* CAPY, LD LMT, LT WT—Three inches in height, three inches apart with the bottom of LT WT positioned five inches above the bottom of the side sill. The O&W commonly displayed these data all together in the third panel from the left. However, in some photographs, they are shown displayed all together in the second panel and in some photographs, they are split between the second and third panels. For a further discussion of these data, see "What do all those markings mean?" on page 91.

*f.* Light-Weighing Data—Three inches in height, located five inches above bottom of side sill on a line to the right of and even with the LT WT of the car, generally in the hopper's fourth panel. Three common station symbols for re-weighing of cars were AV-Middletown, SD-Mayfield, and NH-Norwich. If the car was weighed new, then "NEW" could be substituted for the station symbol. However, the last new hopper that the O&W bought was in 1917, so this is an unlikely combination on an O&W car. For a further discussion of light weighing and the appropriate time intervals between those weighings, see "Light Weighing of Freight Cars" on page 94.

*g.* Built Date—Two inches in height, located five inches above the bottom of the side sill, generally in the sixth panel. Some railroads abbreviated the word built to "BLT," but the O&W typically spelled out the word "BUILT." If the car had been rebuilt,

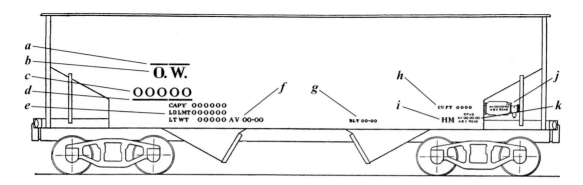

FIGURE 6.11
**Lettering and Marking Guide for O&W Hoppers-Side (Late 1920's through 1957)** *[Author's modification of drawing from the Car Builders' Cyclopedia, 1940; Courtesy: Simmons-Boardman Publishing Corp.]*

**Hard Coal and Coal Cars**

the rebuilt data will be posted in this position, with the built date stenciled above it. The O&W also spelled out the word "REBUILT."

h. Cubic Capacity—Two inches in height, located sixteen inches above the bottom of the side sill.

i. Classification—Four inches in height, located five inches above the bottom of the side sill on a line even with the built date, generally in the sixth panel. The standards show the classification as being centered in the sixth panel; however, the O&W sometimes placed the classification on the left side of the sixth panel, just to the right of the sixth side post. One variation seen on O&W cars is the word "Class" in three inch letters preceding the actual classification. The standard does not call for this. During the 1950's, the O&W would often display the classification as "HM2," but there was no need for the "2" since "HM" is a twin hopper.

j. Journal Repacking Data—Over time, Rule 66 regarding the repacking of the journals changed. Prior to March 1, 1929, the rule stated that journals "should be repacked when necessary, using properly prepared packing (new or renovated) in accordance with Recommended Practice, at which time all packing should be removed from the boxes and boxes cleaned; dust guards to be renewed (if necessary) or replaced when wheels are changed."[28] From March 1, 1929 through 1932, Rule 66 stated journal boxes should be repacked "after the expiration of twelve

months,"[29] and from 1933 through 1955, the interval was fifteen months.[30] In 1956, the interval was extended to eighteen months.[31] The standard calls for letters and figures not less than one inch in height, located just to the left of the body bolster, as close to 5 inches above the bottom of the side sill "as practical," although it is often seen on the O&W much lower than that. This information is generally presented in three lines. The first line is "RPKD." The second line is the station symbol and date of repacking, and the third line is the railroad performing the repacking.

k. Air Brake Cleaning Data—Rule 60 states that the air brakes must be cleaned at least once per year, and that the performing railroad place stencil the place, date, and performing railroad in one inch block letters in a conspicuous location, usually the auxiliary reservoir. See Figures 6.7 and 6.8.

l. End of Car Data (Figure 6.12)—Four inches in height, located in the upper right hand corner of each end.

m. Truck Data (Figure 6.12)—When the construction of the trucks permits, trucks shall be stenciled on each side, giving the size of journal and the letters "A.A.R." in one or two inch letters. The stenciling should be placed on the end of the bolster on arch bar trucks and on the side frame in pedestal or cast side frame trucks. Initials of the road should also appear in letters one or two inches high on one side of the bolster or transom of each truck.

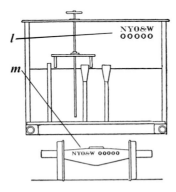

Figure 6.12
**Lettering and Marking Guide for O&W Hoppers-End (Late 1920's through 1957)** [*Author's modification of drawing from theCar Builders' Cyclopedia, 1940; Courtesy: Simmons-Boardman Publishing Corp.*]

FIGURE 7.1

The picture of Middletown Yard in 1911 is bustling with energy and optimism. The yard is filled with loaded wood and composite wood and steel coal cars waiting to discharge their cargo. The four Dodge storage plants in the background, each pile holding thirty tons of anthracite, are full, and two more plants behind them are waiting to be filled. *[O&WRHS Archives]*

FIGURE 7.2

Middletown Yard thirty years later paints a significantly different picture. The Dodge storage plants are empty and will be torn down soon. The wood and composite coal cars have been replaced by a thinning fleet of all-steel, second-hand hoppers, some of which have been modified to handle larger volumes of anthracite. *[Deforest Douglas Diver photo; Walter Kierzkowski Collection]*

## Chapter 7

The O&W's first coal cars were those it inherited from the New York & Ontario Midland in 1880. In 1870, the Midland connected with the Delaware & Hudson Canal Company's railroad at Sidney Plains, and in 1872, the Midland leased the Utica, Clinton & Binghamton Railroad and the Rome & Clinton Railroad from the D&H. Along with these agreements, the D&H provided the Midland with guarantees of minimum anthracite shipments over these lines.[1] By 1873, the Midland had 400 gondolas and 196 four-wheeled coal cars (jimmies) on its roster.[2] Seven years later, when the O&W inherited the Midland's equipment, the number of eight-wheeled gondolas on the roster had grown to 436 but the jimmies had been retired.

The coal cars inherited from the Midland were typical of the period. They were drop-bottom gondolas with a 24,000 to 28,000 pound capacity, and interior dimensions that yielded a capacity of 332 cubic feet. They were long and shallow, that is, they had an interior length of 26' 7" but a depth of only 1' 7". While specific details of their construction are not available, we can assume that they followed the generally accepted practice of the time, that is, wood construction with manual brakes and link and pin couplers.

In 1881, the O&W signed a five-year contract with the Delaware & Hudson Canal Company to haul its anthracite from Sidney Plains to Oswego and to connections with the Utica, Clinton & Binghamton and the Rome & Clinton Railroads. Under this agreement, the O&W agreed to provide coal cars to assist in the transportation of that coal, and to that end, it built 300 all-wood, 40,000 pound capacity, hopper-bottom gondolas in its Middletown shops.[3] These cars, which became the 5101-5400 series, were of wood construction with an interior capacity 75% greater than the original Midland cars. Although they were slightly shorter than the Midland cars, these new gondolas

were twice as deep. Plans for these cars are shown in Chapter 8. What is remarkable about these cars is that the O&W installed Perry Safety Couplers on 200 of them before there was a mandate for automatic couplers,[4] thus belying the notion that railroads were dragging their feet on providing such safety devices. After receiving these newer cars, the O&W retired 80 cars from the old Midland fleet.

When the O&W leased the Utica, Clinton & Binghamton and the Rome & Clinton Railroads from the Delaware & Hudson in 1886, the D&H guaranteed that it would ship at least 150,000 tons of coal per year over these lines.[5] This increased the O&W's need for coal cars, and in 1887, the O&W contracted with the Terre Haute Car and Manufacturing Company for 150 all-wood, 40,000 pound capacity, hopper-bottom gondolas for $385.00 per car. As was the practice of the period, the O&W provided its own draft springs and draw bars, which brought the total cost per car to $411.72.[6] In order to comply with an 1884 New York state law requiring them, the O&W installed automatic couplers on these cars as

FIGURE 7.3
One of the few remaining photos showing a 5101-5399 series hopper-bottom gondola. These cars were built in the Middletown shops in 1882 to meet its obligations under an agreement with the Delaware & Hudson Canal Company to haul coal to Oswego. *[Walter Kierzkowski Collection]*

# Terre Haute Car and Mfg. Co.,

Manufacturers of

ALL KINDS OF

## Freight, Coal, Dump and Hand Cars,

### RAILROAD CASTINGS

### and MACHINERY,

**TERRE HAUTE, IND.**

FIGURE 7.4

**Terre Haute provided the O&W its first "store bought" coal cars in 1887. In 1899, Terre Haute and the successors of the Michigan and Peninsular Car Companies combined with 11 other companies to form American Car and Foundry.** [*Poor's Manual of Railroads, 1883*]

well. However, instead of continuing to use the Perry couplers, the O&W experimented with couplers of a different design, the Smillie automatic coupler. These have been discussed in greater detail in Chapter 3.

This series, numbered 5401-5500 appears very similar to the cars that the O&W produced in its own shops in 1882, but these newer cars had a 25% greater capacity, because their sides had been raised nine inches, from 3'3" to 4'. Raising the sides of its coal cars would eventually create problems for the O&W because the sides would begin to bulge under heavy loads. The O&W would solve this problem at the beginning of the 20th century by installing side trusses in its entire fleet of wood gondolas.

The selection of the number of coal cars that the O&W purchased was not an arbitrary affair. The railroad had a formula to

determine the number of cars that would be needed, based upon the quantity of anthracite to be moved, the distance it was to be hauled, the time that it would take to off load the car and return it to service, and seasonal fluctuations in demand. As the railroad obtained more business, it used this formula to determine how many additional cars would be needed.

This calculus provides some insight into the operations of the railroad during this period. It took coal cars 15 days to make the round trip from the mines to Weehawken or Oswego, while cars sent to Canada, Buffalo or other points in New York state took 20 days to return. Cars sent to New England required a full month to make the round trip.[7] Knowing these round trip times, the output of the mines, and its commitment to provide cars under the D&H agreement, the railroad could easily calculate its need for coal cars.

With the opening of the Scranton Division in July 1890, this formula showed that the O&W's need for more coal cars was both dramatic and immediate. In 1889, Mr. Childs solicited bids from all of the major car manufacturers for coal cars, and in August

FIGURE 7.5

**Cars in the series 10001 to 10500 were originally lettered for the Ontario, Carbondale & Scranton Railway, but they were gradually restenciled into O&W livery after 1891. Car number 10500 was the last in the series of 500 25-ton, hopper-bottom gondolas that the O&W purchased from the Michigan Car Company in 1889 for $378.08 each. These cars had Gould automatic couplers matching the M.C.B.A. Vertical Plane (Janney) profile, but they did not have air brakes. Note the difference in the size of the anthracite in car number 10500 and the car directly behind it.** [*Walter Kierzkowski Collection*]

1889, the board of directors authorized the first in a series of purchases that was to become the O&W's largest purchase of coal cars—the 10001-14120 series.

The railroad purchased the first 500 cars in this series from the Michigan Car Company for $378.08 each. These all-wood, hopper-bottom gondolas had a 50,000 pound capacity, and the price included the cost of draft springs and couplers, which cost $35.58 per car and were furnished by the O&W. This was the O&W's first purchase of freight cars since the M.C.B.A. adopted the Janney vertical-plane profile in 1888, and these cars were equipped with Gould Automatic Couplers that met that standard. Six months later, the O&W contracted with the Lafayette Car Works for an additional 1,000 cars of the same dimensions for $394.00 each. The Gould automatic couplers and draft springs added another $25.00 to the price of each car.[8] The terms of the contract provided that the companies be paid as the cars were delivered in lots of 50, and on December 3, 1889, *The Middletown Daily Press*, reported that cars labeled Ontario, Carbondale & Scranton were already appearing on the D&H and Erie Railroads.[9]

FIGURE 7.6
**Car number 11026 was one of one thousand, 25-ton, hopper-bottom gondolas purchased by the O&W from the Lafayette Car Works in 1890. These cars were purchased to satisfy the demand for coal cars from the newly opened Scranton Division. They came equipped with automatic couplers but without air brakes. It is shown here in 1910 equipped with K-series air brakes. [O&WRHS Archives]**

The 500 cars from the Michigan Car Company, and 400 of the cars from the Lafayette Car Works were delivered during fiscal year 1890. Consequently, the O&W's *Eleventh Annual Report* shows the purchase of 900 cars during that year. The following year, the remaining 600 cars from the Lafayette Car Works were delivered and were accounted for in that fiscal year. The sharp increase in price between the two purchases did not go unnoticed by the board of directors and served as the cause of much discussion during its meeting in February 1890.[10] The steep increase in unit cost notwithstanding, *The Middletown Daily Press* reported on July 9, 1890 that the brake staffs on the 1000 cars delivered by Lafayette were too short and had to be replaced.[11]

The 1,500 cars in this series represented an additional 20% increase in volume and 25% increase in tonnage per car over the cars purchased from Terre Haute. They were equipped with wood-bolstered, arch bar trucks and automatic couplers, but they did not have air brakes.

FIGURE 7.7
**The O&W ordered 850 of these larger capacity 30-ton, hopper-bottom gondolas from the Lafayette Car Works in 1890. This photo of car number 1164x, taken at Mayfield in 1911, shows how the interior of these cars were laid out. [Carl A. Ohlson Collection]**

FIGURE 7.8
**Trust plate from British Wagon & Carriage Works Company, Ltd. This plate would have been attached to the car covered by this trust, Series, C.B.1, in this case one of the thirty-ton cars from Lafayette Car Works numbered from 11751-12000.** *[George Shammas Collection]*

comprised a large portion of the O&W's stockholders. The terms of those agreements are shown in the inset below.

In June 1892, the board authorized the purchase of an additional 500 of these 30-ton cars, to be numbered 12351-12850, from the Peninsular Car Company for $402.00, and in March 1893, the board approved the purchase of 500 more, numbered 12851-13350, from the Michigan Peninsular Car Company, for $405.75. With draft springs and couplers, the total for the first lot per car was $431.50, and the total for the second was $436.25.

By October 1890, the O&W had solicited and received bids from 16 car manufacturers for another 500 hopper-bottom gondolas. To reduce the number of cars it needed, the O&W increased the capacity of these cars from 867 to 973 cubic feet and from 50,000 to 60,000 pounds. The low bidder for these cars was the Lafayette Car Works with an offer of $415.00 each. Draft springs and automatic couplers brought the total to $440.00 per car. The board then directed that a "Car Trust" plan be developed to secure these and an additional 500 cars for the railroad.[12] In the end, however, the railroad only purchased an additional 350 gondolas, bringing this total buy from Lafayette Car Works to 850 gondolas. The railroad negotiated "Car Trust" agreements with two British firms: the British Wagon Company, Ltd. and the British Wagon & Carriage Works Company, Ltd. It is probably no coincidence that these trusts were awarded to two British firms, since the British

In December 1893, the president of Michigan Peninsular Car Company approached the president of the O&W, Thomas Fowler, with an "extremely low price" for 500 more cars in this series. These cars included a modification of the side bearings from the Hubbard anti-friction to cast-iron side bearings. With the Gould automatic couplers and the Oswego Spring Company's draft springs provided by the O&W, the total cost for this lot was $207,500 or $415.00 per car.[13] To finance this purchase, the O&W paid $20,000 down and secured a lease/trust agreement from the New York Guaranty and Indemnity Company to be repaid in twenty quarterly payments of $10,000 each.[15] These cars were numbered 13351-13850.

The final procurement in this series was approved by the board in November 1895. This lot consisted of 250 cars to handle the additional traffic

---

*Car Trust Agreements for 11501-12250 Series*

*October 25, 1890—British Wagon Company, Limited. for 250 cars (numbers 11501-11750) at $440.00 each payable 10% in cash and the balance in 84 monthly installments represented by notes for $1514.70 each.*

*October 25, 1890—British Wagon & Carriage Works Company, Limited for 250 cars (numbers 11751-12000) at the same rates and terms of payment. Trust CB1*

*January 15, 1891—British Wagon Company, Limited for 250 cars (numbers 12001-12250) at $440.00 each payable 10% in cash and balance in 84 monthly installments represented by notes of $1534.50 each.*

*January 15, 1891—British Wagon & Carriage Works Company, Limited for 100 cars (numbers 12251-12350) at $440.00 each and upon the same terms represented by notes of $513.80 each. Trust DB1[14]*

---

FIGURE 7.9
**Car number 12445 is one of a series of 500 hopper-bottom gondolas ordered from Peninsular Car Company in 1892. [Walter Kierzkowski Collection]**

FIGURE 7.10
**This real picture post card shows car number 13690 and a Pennsylvania Railroad GLa hopper waiting to be unloaded in South Unadilla in the mid-1910's. Car number 13690 was one of 1275 cars purchased from Michigan-Peninsular Car Company in three separate orders dating from 1892 to 1895.** *[O&WRHS Archives]*

generated by a new agreement with the Johnson Coal Company and included 25 cars to replace other cars that had been damaged or destroyed. These 275 cars, produced by Michigan-Peninsular Car Company and numbered 13851-14120, were the first coal cars to come equipped with Westinghouse air brakes. They were priced at $450 per car.[16]

With the completion of this buy, the O&W began replacing its twenty year old Midland drop-bottom gondolas on a two-for-one basis with larger cars in the same number series. The Midland cars were not holding up under their heavy use, and their minimal capacity of 12-14 tons was no longer adequate for the increased demands being placed upon the railroad. Furthermore, it was not worth upgrading these cars with air brakes and automatic couplers.

Therefore, the O&W scrapped 150 of these in 1895 and replaced them with larger, drop-bottom gondolas that it build in its Middletown shops.[17]

The first ten cars in this series, numbered 4400-4409, were built with a capacity of 660 cubic feet and 40,000 pounds. They had automatic couplers but not air brakes, though they were later retrofitted with them. Beginning with car number 4410, the O&W increased the weight capacity of this series to 60,000 pounds, probably by adding trucks with larger journals.* However, they reduced the cubic capacity of these gondolas to 510 cubic feet by limiting the height of the sides to two feet, which would have made these cars easier to unload manually. These heavier cars were equipped with both air brakes and automatic couplers. Over the next six

**The History of O&W Coal Cars**

FIGURE 7.11

**Car number 4473 was one of 152 drop-bottom gondolas built in the Middletown shops between 1895 and 1900 to replace the aging Midland cars. It is seen here at Mayfield in December 1910.** *[O&WRHS Archives]*

portion of the fleet that required retrofit. Also, those few cars that lacked automatic couplers still needed to have them installed. By 1904, the O&W could finally report to the ICC that 100% of its coal car fleet was equipped with automatic couplers,[19] but it was not until 1913 that it could say that its entire coal car fleet was equipped with air brakes.[20]

In 1899, the O&W began building another series of all-wood, drop-bottom gondolas in its Middletown shops, continuing its policy of replacing older cars with larger cars within the same number series. These cars, however, were larger than the previous replacements that it had built. With an additional two feet in length and 18 inches in height, these cars had almost twice the cubic capacity of the 4410-4563 series. These cars, which had also had a weight capacity of 60,000 pounds, were numbered 4600 to 4700. Again, because these were "replacements" for earlier cars, the O&W was able to charge the cost of their construction off as an operating expense.[21] A picture of one of these cars is shown in Figure 7.13.

years, the company built 152 of these all-wood, drop-bottom gondolas, no doubt reusing whatever metal components it could from the retired Midland cars. Because the O&W was assigning these cars previously used numbers, they were considered replacements for existing cars, and hence the O&W was able to charge the costs off as operating expenses in the years in which they were built. One of these cars is shown in Figure 7.11.

The decade before the turn of the century and the years just afterward were a period of great activity in the O&W's car shops. Increasingly heavy traffic on the Scranton Division was taking its toll on the O&W coal car fleet. In addition, the railroad was being pushed to comply with the provisions of the Railroad Safety Appliance Act. Although it had gotten a head start by putting automatic couplers on all its car purchases after 1889, it had not begun installing air brakes until 1896. While the railroad could boast in 1894 that 4705 of its freight cars or almost 75% of its entire fleet was equipped with automatic couplers, it could only take credit for a small portion of its fleet having air brakes.[18] Consequently, even as the car shops were having to cope with strengthening the O&W's wood car fleet to withstand the rigors of hauling anthracite, they were having to deal with modernizing that same car fleet to comply with federal law.

All cars built or bought by the O&W after 1895 were equipped with air brakes, but that still left a large

At a time when other railroads were converting to all-steel hoppers, the O&W remained committed to the wood, hopper-bottom gondola. In 1900, the O&W built its first 40-ton coal car in its Middletown shops, an all-wood, hopper-bottom gondola, car

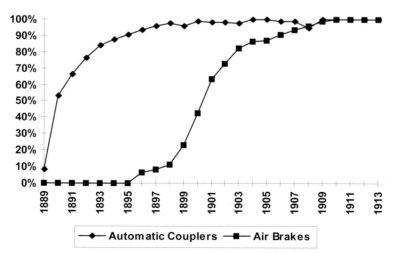

FIGURE 7.12

**Percentage of O&W Coal Cars with Automatic Couplers and Air Brakes.** *[Source: NYO&W Annual Reports to the ICC]*

*With the exception of car number 4414, which had the same dimensions as 4400-4409.

number 7000. Later that year, the shops built another one of these cars with an increased nominal capacity of 42.5 tons. Apparently, the O&W liked what it built, because it placed a series of orders with American Car & Foundry for a total of 1075 of these cars, while building 36 more in its company shops. The first 575 cars procured from AC&F were ordered in December 1900 for $462,500[22] and were numbered 7101-7675. The second 500 cars were purchased from AC&F in February 1902 for $397,500[23] and were numbered 6601-7100. The O&W built a total of 39 of these cars in its own shops from 1900 through 1906. Fourteen of them were new and numbered 7675-7689. The rest were replacements for cars that were destroyed in wrecks. Because of numbering conflicts with the AC&F orders, it appears that car number 7000, which is shown in Figure 7.14, was renumbered to 7688 and the second car produced in 1900 was renumbered to 7689. The 6600-7700 series was equipped with arch bar trucks with standard 5" x 9" journals and quick-action ("H") air brakes.

The O&W made several other equipment purchases in 1901, including seven locomotives, six vestibuled coaches, and its first all-steel coal cars. All of these items, including the 575 AC&F cars, were rolled into one equipment trust totaling $675,000. The following year, the O&W obtained another equipment trust totaling $463,500, for the second group of wood hopper-bottom gondolas

FIGURE 7.13
**This picture of car number 4678 taken at Mayfield in 1910 is interesting in a number of respects. Car number 4678 was one of 104 all-wood, drop-bottom gondolas built by the O&W in its Middletown shops in 1900 and 1908 to replace cars it inherited from the New York and Oswego Midland. It's coupled to car number 7171, showing the difference in size between the 4600 series and the 6600-7700 series. In addition to the difference in size, the 4600 series can be identified by the difference in spacing of the side stakes. Note the O&W's lettering scheme for the first decade of the 20th century.** *[O&WRHS Archives]*

produced by AC&F.

Along with the 575 all-wood, hopper-bottom gondolas, the O&W tip-toed into the steel car age with the purchase of 50 all-steel, hopper-bottom gondolas—25 rolled-steel cars from Sterlingworth Railway Supply Company and 25 pressed-steel cars from the Pressed Steel Car Company. It is probable that the O&W was experimenting with these cars just as it had experimented with car number 7000.

With the purchase of these two designs, the O&W entered the debate between structural-steel and pressed-steel construction. Virtually every component of these cars, including brake beams, center sills, truck and body bolsters, and truck side frames were consistently either pressed or rolled-steel. In the latter case, the Pressed Steel car came equipped with trucks that were essentially arch bar trucks made of pressed-steel components.[24] The Sterlingworth cars came equipped with Joughins style trucks that were manufactured out of rolled-steel by Sterlingworth. Both were equipped with 5" x 9" standard journals and Westinghouse quick-action ("H") air brakes.

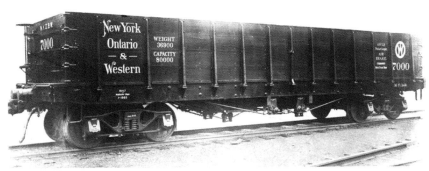

FIGURE 7.14
**Car number 7000 was built in the Middletown shops in 1900. The O&W liked the design and ultimately built 39 more in their company shops and ordered 1075 more from American Car & Foundry. These cars were equipped with a door operating mechanism patented by George H. Lawrence, an O&W employee who worked in the Middletown shops.** *[O&WRHS Archives]*

FIGURE 7.15
**This 1909 photo taken at Middletown shows a collection of the early, all-steel hopper-bottom gondolas purchased by the O&W in 1901. In the foreground is the Sterlingworth rolled beam gondola composed of structural steel components. Directly behind it are two of the Pressed Steel Car Company cars.** *[John Stellwagen Collection; Courtesy: Walter Kierzkowski]*

History offers no explanation as to why the O&W purchased these cars nor any explanation why it never purchased any more. For cars of all-steel construction, their lives on the O&W were relatively short. Both sets of cars were retired from interchange service in August 1916, although they remained in maintenance-of-way service into the mid 1930's.[25] Photos of the cars in service show them relatively beaten up. Perhaps they didn't stand up well in interchange traffic. Perhaps the car shops, accustomed to all-wood construction, were simply not prepared to maintain them. Perhaps it was their lack of capacity, since the all-wood cars were a couple of hundred cubic feet larger than the steel cars. Whatever the reason or reasons, the all-wood cars, subsequently modified with steel underframes, outlived these all-steel cars by over thirty years on the O&W.

While it was building and purchasing new coal cars, the O&W was also strengthening its old car fleet. In 1895, the O&W began adding subsills to its 30-ton cars to strengthen their undercarriages, and in 1898, the car shops began adding side trusses to keep their sides from bulging. Examining the numbers of cars that underwent these modifications provides some insights into the durability of the railroad's wooden fleet. From 1898 through 1907, the car shops added side trusses to a total of 10,607

cars, or approximately twice the total number of coal cars it had on its roster. This leads one to conclude that their initial efforts at reinforcing these car sides were unsuccessful, or that each of those wooden cars was repaired or rebuilt at least once during that ten year period after having its sides reinforced initially.

The second stage of improvements to its wooden fleet involved the use of steel. The car shops began modernizing their freight trucks in 1896, first by converting their coal cars to the M.C.B.A. standard [arch bar] truck and journal design and then by adding steel truck bolsters beginning in 1902. The old, wood bolstered trucks, even when reinforced with truss rods, were just not capable of withstanding the loads being imposed upon them. In 1907, during an extensive rebuilding program, the railroad began adding steel body bolsters to a large number of its 30-ton cars in the 10000-14120 series. The railroad continued

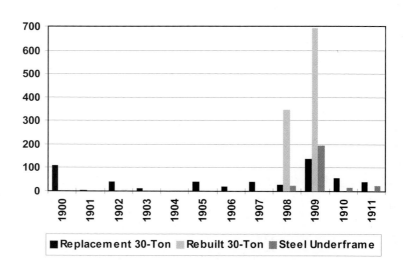

FIGURE 7.16
**During the first decade of the 20th century, the O&W began a series of improvements of its 10001-14120 series. The railroad categorized these improvements two ways— cars rebuilt and cars built new as replacements for cars damaged or destroyed. In reality, there was probably little difference between these two categories. Beginning in 1907, the O&W began using steel body bolsters as it built and rebuilt these cars, and in 1908, it experimented with steel underframes. Based upon the O&W's 1916 report to the ICC, it appears that all cars built or rebuilt after 1908 had steel underframes. Differences in quantities per year in the chart above are due to differences in fiscal and calendar reporting years in the reports from which the information was obtained.**

Hard Coal and Coal Cars

building and rebuilding these 30-ton cars through 1911.

From 1900 through 1911, the O&W built and/or rebuilt 1,568 of these wooden coal cars. In 1908, the O&W began rebuilding some of these cars with steel underframes along with steel body and truck (Simplex) bolsters, steel striking plates, Miner tandem draft gear, Martin steel underframes, and Westinghouse air brakes.[26] The photo in Figure 7.17 shows one of these early cars after being rebuilt. These efforts amounted to a complete rebuilding of these cars at a cost ranging from $560 to $600 per car.[27] In 1916, the railroad reported that it had modified 246 of these old woodies with steel underframes.[28] A summary of the rate at which these cars were built or rebuilt is shown in Figure 7.16.

FIGURE 7.17
**Car number 12164 sets on the transfer table in Middletown after being rebuilt in the company shops in August 1908. Note that early Wolff cast side frame trucks and Simplex bolsters have been added along with Westinghouse air brakes. This was among the first O&W coal cars to receive a steel underframe. By 1916, the O&W reported that it had modernized 246 of these 30-ton cars with steel underframes and other improvements. The car pictured here was finally retired in October 1924. [O&WRHS Archives]**

In December 1910, General Manager Childs went to the board of directors to inform them that these smaller cars were not holding up anymore. In fact, he stated that they were hazardous in the longer trains made up of heavier cars being pushed up mountain grades with additional motive power. Consequently, it was time for the railroad to procure heavier cars that could stand up to this abuse. As a result, the railroad set out to purchase a fleet of newer cars and reinforce what it could of the older ones.

The O&W was still not ready to abandon wood. The railroad had a large investment in its car shops, which were expert in working with wood. Rather than convert to all-steel cars as a number of larger railroads were doing, the O&W turned to a composite design developed by C.A. Seley, the Mechanical Engineer for the Norfolk & Western Railroad.[29] The "Seley Hopper," as it came to be known, was the perfect hopper for the railroad's transition from wood to steel cars. The steel undercarriage enabled the car to withstand the rigors of being intermixed in trains with heavier, all-steel cars; the interior and exterior steel bracing held the sides in place during loading and movement; and the wood sides and flooring could be easily maintained by the railroad's car shops, which were well equipped to build and maintain wooden cars.

The Seley hopper had one other advantage. As the railroad's first hopper car, it was, by definition, self-clearing. After the turn of the century, increasing populist legislative

FIGURE 7.18
**In 1910, the O&W began building and purchasing a total of 1350 composite wood and steel, 80,000-pound hoppers that were based upon a design by C.A. Seley. Car number 15567, pictured here, was built by American Car & Foundry in 1910. Note the early Gould cast-steel truck side frames. [Walter Kierzkowski Collection]**

FIGURE 7.19

**Car number 15616 was also part of the first buy of 500 "Seley hoppers" from American Car & Foundry in 1910. The 15000 series was a stalwart performer for the O&W. Though relegated to cinder service, this car is still serving its owner after over 25 years of service. Some of these cars stayed in service through 1946. Its original Gould trucks have been replaced by Andrews L-Section side frames. This picture shows how these cars were lettered by the O&W in the late 1920's and 30's. [O&WRHS Archives]**

sentiment was causing labor rates to rise, and consequently, self-clearing became an attractive, cost-saving feature. This notwithstanding, men are frequently seen inside these cars assisting in the unloading. Apparently the wood floor created enough friction that the contents did not empty entirely on their own.

The O&W started building these cars in its Middletown shops in 1910, and the first 100 of these cars entered service during that same year. Ultimately, it built 500 cars in its own shops, numbered 15001-15500, and purchased 850 cars from American Car and Foundry in lots of 500 and 350, numbered 15501-16350.

The Seley hopper had a capacity of 1385 cubic feet, which was 5% less than the O&W's last hopper-bottom gondola, but it was still over 40% greater than the 30-ton cars they were replacing. Once these cars entered service, the O&W began a wholesale

retirement of its all-wood, 30-ton car fleet. From the end of 1910 through 1920, it scrapped over 2700 of the old "woodies." The only bright spot in this retirement was that the railroad was able to sell 260 of these coal cars in 1917 for $375 each,[30] undoubtedly to one of the coal companies it controlled.

The Seley hoppers built in Middletown were equipped with "L-Section" Andrews cast-steel side frames, but the hoppers purchased from AC&F came equipped with Gould cast side frames. Both had 5" x 9" standard journals and Barber roller side bearings. These trucks are clearly visible in photographs of the period. These were also the first of the O&W's coal cars to be equipped with the new K-2 triple valve, which had been introduced in 1908. Cars 15001 to 15900 were equipped with Miner spring draft gear and cars 15901 to 16350 were equipped with Farlow spring draft gear.[31] Although it had installed spring draft gears in both of these sets, the O&W installed Harvey Friction Springs to dampen the spring motion.

The cars manufactured in the company shops were paid for out of the Additions and Betterments account. Equipment trusts were used to purchase the cars from AC&F. In examining these costs, it's interesting to note the progress along the learning curve for the first three lots of 50 cars produced by the railroad. It's also interesting to note the significant difference in unit cost between the first 500 cars purchased from AC&F and the second lot of 350.

At the same time that it was adding its first hoppers, the O&W was also purchasing low sided coal cars. In 1911, it purchased 100 40-ton composite, drop-bottom gondolas, numbered 6201 to 6300, from American Car and Foundry. These cars were equipped with Gould cast-steel side frames, Farlow

| | 15000-16350 Composite Hopper Costs | | |
|---|---|---|---|
| **Car Numbers** | **Builder** | **Cost** | **Cost per Car** |
| 15001-15050 | Middletown Shops | $ 48,366.29 | 967.33 |
| 15051-15100 | Middletown Shops | 47,263.15 | 945.26 |
| 15101-15150 | Middletown Shops | 46,457.87 | 929.16 |
| 15151-15500 | Middletown Shops | 324,374.51 | 926.78 |
| 15501-16000 | AC&F, Equipment Trust A | 503,625.26 | 1007.25 |
| 16001-16350 | AC&F, Equipment Trust B | 316,750.00 | 905.00 |

Hard Coal and Coal Cars

FIGURE 7.20
The O&W purchased 100 composite-construction, low-side, drop-bottom gondolas from AC&F in 1911, and in 1916, it purchased 100 more. Car number 6325, seen here in Middletown in 1957, was part of the 1916 purchase. [Courtesy: Bob's Photo]

FIGURE 7.21
The 6200-6399 series gondolas proved to be real workhorses for the railroad. In this 1957 photo, we see one of these cars that's been transferred to company road service. The photo provides a good view of the details of the "B" end of the car. [Courtesy: Bob's Photo]

FIGURE 7.22
The date is November 1911. In the foreground, the Middletown car shops are visible. In the background, cars from the 6600-7700 series are being renovated, displaying the ease of repair that inspired the O&W's preference for wood construction. The Middletown shops would rebuild 1000 of the cars in this series with AC&F steel underframesfrom 1912 to 1915 to help them endure the rigors of the Scranton Division in trains with all-steel cars. [Julius H. Reinewald Collection, O&WRHS Archives]

spring draft gear, and Barber roller side bearings. In 1916, the O&W bought another 100 of these 818 cubic foot gondolas from AC&F for $1092.75 per car.[32] The second purchase would come equipped with Andrews "T-Section" side frames and Session friction draft gear with Farlow attachments provided by the railroad. These gondolas would enjoy great success, remaining on the road right up until its abandonment in 1957.

In addition to purchasing these new cars, from 1912 to 1915, the O&W modified 1000 of the American Car and Foundry all-wood gondolas with steel underframes, Simplex bolsters, and Miner draft gear. Some of these cars remained in service through 1946. The total cost for these modifications was $127.00 per car[33] plus the $145.25 cost for the steel underframe from American Car and Foundry.[34]

In 1913, the O&W entered the all-steel hopper era with the purchase of 500 50-ton hoppers from the Cambria Steel Car Company. These cars cost $1012 apiece,[35] had an empty weight of 36,000 pounds and had a capacity of 1670 cubic feet. In other words, for about 10% more in cost and at the same empty weight as a composite hopper, the O&W obtained a 20% increase in both volume and weight capacity over the Seley hopper. These cars came equipped with the newer "T-Section" Andrews cast truck with 5½" x 10" journals. They were also equipped with Miner friction draft gear. This made these cars the first of the O&W's coal car fleet to be equipped with modern, friction draft gear.

In December 1915, the O&W sought bids for 400 more all-steel hoppers. The responses it received provide a glimpse of the freight car industry during this period—Cambria Steel, $1155 per car, delivery in March; Standard Steel, $1190, May; American Car and Foundry, $1173, April and May; Pressed Steel, $1165, April; and Ralston Car Sales, $1156.75, April.[36] Ultimately, the O&W purchased the 400 cars from Cambria Steel—300 for $1150 per car and 100 for $1134.50 per car. The difference in price between the two lots is attributed the cars having two different kinds of draft gear.[37] The lower priced cars had Miner draft gear; the higher priced cars had Sessions draft gear with Farlow keyed attaching mechanism.[38] These cars were the last new, all-steel hoppers the O&W would ever buy. They proved to be a good investment, though, with some staying in service all the way through 1957.

As the O&W entered the 1920's, it began to encounter capacity problems with its coal car fleet. Despite major strikes by the United Mine Workers, the O&W's shipments of anthracite remained steady and even grew in several years. Its wood fleet, which had once numbered in the thousands, now dwindled to a few hundred due to the rigors of the Scranton Division. Even those that might have survived would become obsolete after January 1, 1931, because cars of all-wood construction were banned from interchange service after that date.[39] The 85,000-pound hopper-bottom gondolas, which had had steel underframes added in the early teens, were beginning to wear out as they reached the end of their life. Additionally, higher labor costs associated with manually unloading these cars made them increasingly undesirable. The O&W needed more coal cars.

In December 1926, the O&W began remedying

this situation by buying 40 second-hand, 55-ton, all-steel hoppers from the receiver for the Struthers Furnace Company.[40] These were relatively new cars, built by the Pressed Steel Company in 1920, generally conforming to the Pennsylvania Railroad's GLa design, except that they were eleven inches taller. This gave them a capacity of 1960 cubic feet versus the GLa's 1683 cubic feet. The records indicate that these cars, which became the railroad's 17000 series, had trucks with cast-steel side frames and pressed-steel bolsters, but it is uncertain exactly what trucks they had. The O&W paid $1000 each for these cars. With freight charges, inspection, and painting, that total rose to $1067.25 per car.

Following this purchase, the O&W bought 400 second-hand, 50-ton all-steel hoppers from the Bethlehem Steel Company for a total cost of $297,390.44, including freight.[41] The purchase of these cars, which became the O&W's 19000 to 19399 series, is instructive. *The Official Railway Equipment Register* in February 1928 shows Bethlehem Steel's hopper series 8000-9699, the series from which the O&W was buying its cars, as having a capacity of 1800 cubic feet. It's clear that the O&W expected to receive cars of that capacity. Its practice was to reserve a spot in *The Official Railway Equipment Register* for the cars it expected to procure, and the initial entry for the 19000-19399 series show that the series had a capacity of 1800 cubic foot. That's not what it received.

Instead it received a mix of cars, some with 1800 cubic feet capacity, but most with only 1670 cubic feet.* Earlier editions of *The Official Railway Equipment Register* reveal that Bethlehem Steel series 8000 to 9699 was made up of Lackawanna Steel's series 3000 to 5299, which consisted of 1000 cars of 1800 cubic foot capacity and 700 cars with 1730 cubic foot capacity. When Bethlehem Steel renumbered these cars, it apparently registered them in *The Official Railway Equipment Register* with the cubic capacity of the majority of the cars in that series. Consequently, and apparently much to the O&W's surprise, the railroad didn't receive 400 hoppers with an 1800 cubic foot capacity, but rather a mix of cars, the majority of which had the lower capacity. Therefore, in 1929, the O&W had to amend its entry in the December issue of *The Official Railway Equipment Register* to reflect the cubic capacity that the majority of these hoppers had—1670 cubic feet.

---

*Lackawanna Steel reported these cars as having a capacity of 1730 cubic feet, while the O&W shows them as having a capacity of 1670 cubic feet. An inspection of early drawings indicates that Lackawanna Steel may have miscalculated the interior capacity. The dimensions of these cars are very similar to the O&W's 18000 series.

**FIGURE 7.23**
This photo, dating to the late 1910's, gives us a glimpse of car number 18317, which has already been repainted to comply with the 1916 changes in lettering and stenciling requirements. *[Alan F. Seebach, Jr. Collection]*

**FIGURE 7.24**
Car number 18315 is seen here in Summitville in 1947. The car has been modified with power brake, wine door locks, and a second grab iron that's been added on the left side of the car to comply with the 1932 U.S. Safety Appliance change. *[Jeff Otto Collection]*

**FIGURE 7.25**
In 1928, the O&W purchased 400 second-hand hoppers from Bethlehem Steel that became the 19000-19399 series. Among them were these 50-ton hoppers built by Standard Steel Car Company for Lackawanna Steel in 1916. Lackawanna Steel reported these cars as having a capacity of 1730 cubic feet, but the O&W carried them at a capacity of 1670 cubic feet. *[Standard Steel Company photo; D.K. Retterer Collection]*

**FIGURE 7.26**
The first purchase of second-hand hoppers from Bethlehem Steel also included 167 of these larger, 1800 cubic feet cars built by American Car & Foundry in 1916 and 1917. At the end of 1928, the O&W purchased 300 more of these larger cars from Bethlehem Steel that had recently been rebuilt. This second purchase became the O&W's 19400-19699 series. *[American Car & Foundry photo; from the John W. Barriger III National Railroad Library at the University of Missouri-St. Louis]*

| 19000-19399 Hopper Costs | | | |
|---|---|---|---|
| Car Numbers | Builder | Cost | Cost per Car |
| 19000-19299 | AC&F and Std Steel | $ 225,000.00 | 750.00 |
| 19300-19374 | AC&F and Std Steel | 54,000.00 | 720.00 |
| 19375-19378 | AC&F and Std Steel | 17,654.40 | 735.60 |
| 19399-19399 | Std Steel | 736.04 | 736.04 |
| Total | | $ 297,390.44 | |

The smaller cars were built by Standard Steel Car Company in 1916. The larger cars were built by American Car & Foundry in 1916 and 1917. Some of these cars came with arch bar trucks, and some came with cast-steel side frames. Although it's uncertain, it appears that the cast side frames were Andrews T-sections. The Authorization for Expenditure to procure these cars confirms that there was a real mix of cars and conditions. Unfortunately, the car numbers shown above do not correlate to their manufacturer, or the type of trucks they had.

Of the 400 cars in this purchase, at least 167 of them were the cars built by AC&F with the higher capacity. Beginning in 1932, the O&W began identifying the higher capacity cars in this series as a separate line item in *The Official Railway Equipment Register*. In 1933, it reported 121 cars in the 19000-19399 series with 1800 cubic feet and an increased nominal weight capacity of 110,000 pounds. By 1939, it reported 167 cars in this category. This implies that the O&W was doing something to these cars during that period that allowed it to increase

their nominal weight capacity, but the records do not indicate what, if any, actions it was taking. These cars already had the higher cubic capacity, so the railroad wasn't enlarging them in any way.

There are several possible explanations as to why the O&W initially rated these cars at only 100,000 pounds and what it did to increase their nominal capacity to 110,000 pounds. The simplest explanation is that the only difference between the two was the difference between painting "100,000" and "110,000" on the car sides, since the load limit would have been identical regardless of the marked capacity. If this were the case, though, one has to wonder why it took the railroad ten years to complete this simple task. Another thought is that it was changing their trucks. Some of these cars were originally equipped with arch-bar trucks. Even though these trucks were equipped with 5½" x 10" journals, the O&W may have wanted to put different trucks under these cars to comply with the A.R.A.'s 1928 standards for 100,000 pound arch bar trucks before claiming a 110,000 pound weight capacity as being within the reasonable limits of safety.

FIGURE 7.27
**A freshly painted 19028 is at the end of a 95 car train being helped by Y-class #401 heading north near Stony Ford in March 1942. This is one of the cars built by AC&F in 1916-1917 with a capacity of 1800 cubic feet, but which the O&W initially rated at a nominal capacity of only 50 tons. In this picture it has been upgraded to a capacity of 110,000 pounds. The lack of rebuilt information, as seen on car 19553, indicates that the O&W was not rebuilding these cars in order to upgrade their capacity. Note the 1940's and 50's lettering scheme on this car versus the 1920's and 30's lettering scheme on the car in Figure 7.28. [O&WRHS Archives]**

There is also the possibility that there was some structural limitation that precluded their being labeled at higher nominal capacity. However, it is difficult to imagine something structural that would create the difference between a 100,000 pound car and 110,000 pound car. If this were indeed the case, then the O&W would have had to add a star (*) to the left of the LDLMT to indicate that these cars had been derated from their full capacity.

At the end of 1928, the O&W purchased 300 more second-hand cars from Bethlehem Steel. This time it got the cars that it is was expecting, though it paid about $75.00 more per car to do so. These cars had been recently rebuilt, came equipped with cast-steel side frames, and had a nominal capacity of 110,000 pounds. They immediately entered service rated at the higher capacity. The cars cost $827.75 apiece, for a total of $248,324.80.[42]

Although the hopper cars in the 18000 and 19000 series were produced by three different manufacturers—Cambria Steel, Standard Steel, and American Car & Foundry—they were all of similar design. They each had an interior length of 30' 0", a distance between striking plates of 31' 6", 7" platform end sills, angle iron end posts, and triangular end post gussets. The O&W characterized cars with these features as "A.R.A. design." However, these should not be confused with the A.R.A. and A.A.R. standard hoppers designed in the 1920's and 1930's.

The 1930's are a difficult period in O&W history. In 1930, the O&W sold its money-losing Elk Hill Coal and Iron Company along with the three Scranton Coal Company's collieries that were losing money. This left the O&W and Scranton Coal Company with only three operating coal mines.

As part of the sales agreement of those collieries, the O&W negotiated for the exclusive transportation rights for the Penn Anthracite Collieries,[43] which had purchased the Elk Hill properties. The following year, the O&W was able to boost its anthracite shipments by an incredible 79% from 2,897,742 tons to 5,188,668 tons, and the year after that, shipments increased another 10.6% to 5,741,341 tons. Even as the O&W's shipments were increasing, though, its

FIGURE 7.28

**Car number 19553 stands ready to be weighed after being shopped in 1934. This car was built by AC&F in 1916 and was rebuilt by Bethlehem Steel in 1926 before joining the railroad as part of the second purchase of hoppers from that steel company. It had a capacity of 1800 cubic feet and was immediately rated by the railroad at 110,000 pounds capacity.** *[Jeff Otto Collection]*

profit margins were slipping, and it still needed more coal cars to move this increased tonnage. Its response was to buy more second-hand cars.

In January 1933, the O&W obtained 500 used hoppers in a sub-lease agreement from the Pennsylvania Coal and Coke Company for what amounted to $625.00 per car. The railroad paid $47,500 in cash for these cars, and the balance was covered in an equipment trust expiring in 1937.[44] The PCC cars were 50-ton all-steel hoppers of the GLa design. They were relatively new, built by American Car & Foundry in 1923, and they came equipped with cast side frames, probably U-Section Andrews type as seen in Figure 7.29. They became the O&W's 20000 to 20499 series.[45]

Three months later, the O&W purchased 500 used hoppers that it had been leasing from the Westmoreland Coal Company for $5600 per month. It paid $550 apiece for these cars.[46] They were a mix of 228 ancient GLa all-steel hoppers built between 1906 and 1916, and 272 newer USRA type, all-steel hoppers built between 1920 and 1926. The GLa cars were built by Cambria Steel Car Company, the same company that manufactured the O&W's 18000 series, and the USRA hoppers were probably built by Bethlehem Steel, the successor to Cambria. These cars had a mix of freight trucks.[47] The GLa's had arch-bar trucks, and the USRA's had a combination of cast and pressed-steel side

FIGURE 7.29

**In 1933 the O&W purchased 500 GLa-type cars from Pennsylvania Coal and Coke. One of these cars is shown here in Mayfield in the late 1940s. The circled X indicates that the car has been removed from interchange service.** *[Walter Kierzkowski Collection]*

FIGURE 7.30
**This photo taken in the Middletown yard in August of 1937 provides a wealth of information about O&W coal cars of the period. In the foreground is composite gondola 6230 still wearing its early Andrews trucks. Behind it is recently painted GLa car 2583 showing the lettering scheme of the mid-30's. This car is particularly interesting in that it has side gussets, a feature not normally found on GLa cars. This car and the USRA hopper in the background were both purchased from Westmoreland Coal in 1933. Rather than repaint these cars, the O&W kept Westmoreland's car numbers and simply painted over the Westmoreland reporting marks and inserted its own. After four years, the O&W still has not repainted the USRA hopper. The "O. & W." can be seen in the fourth panel of the car. [Courtesy: Bob's Photo]**

ing major repairs in the Middletown shops in the 1930's.

There is an interesting side note to this purchase from Westmoreland Coal Company. The O&W kept all of the Westmoreland car numbers when it placed these cars in service, i.e., Westmoreland car number 303 became O&W car number 303, and so forth. This was a carry-over from these cars being leased from the coal company. There are several photos that show how the O&W painted over the Westmoreland reporting marks on these hoppers and replaced them with O&W reporting marks, while leaving all other markings, including the Westmoreland logo, unchanged.

The Westmoreland USRA hoppers were numbered 303 to 899. The GLa hoppers were marked in three separate series: 906-935, 1203-2647, and 3249 to 3466. Keeping the Westmoreland numbers in the 900 series did create some minor difficulties, because the O&W already had several flat cars numbered in that series. However, these were simply treated as exceptions in *The Official Railway Equipment Register*.

frames. It is uncertain what the pressed-steel side frames were, but the cast-steel side frames probably conformed to the USRA Andrews-type design.[48]

The GLa cars had a capacity of 1683 cubic feet, and the USRA hoppers had a capacity of 1880 cubic feet. The O&W marked the nominal weight capacity of all the GLa hoppers at 100,000 pounds, but it marked the USRA hoppers at two different nominal weight capacities. In 1933, their first year of operation, the O&W marked 156 of the USRA cars at 100,000 pounds and 124 at 110,000 pounds capacity. By 1939, it had labeled all of these hoppers at 110,000 pounds capacity. The same question regarding nominal capacity arises with these USRA hoppers as arose with the cars in the 19000-19399 series. There are two indications that the O&W believed that these cars needed to be modified before being rated at the higher nominal capacity. First, it took the railroad a total of seven year to report all of these cars at the higher nominal capacity. Second, Figure 7.31 shows a number of the Westmoreland USRA cars undergo-

FIGURE 7.31
**This scene from the Middletown car shops during the 1930's shows Westmoreland USRA hoppers being repaired. It's not clear whether the O&W considered this type of overhaul necessary to increase the nominal capacity of these cars to 110,000 pounds. Despite the extent of these repairs, the O&W did not identify these cars as being "rebuilt." If they had, the railroad would have been required to bring the cars up to the latest A.A.R. standards, including AB brakes and A.A.R. standard trucks. [O&WRHS Archives]**

Hard Coal and Coal Cars

## Memo on the Condition of O&W Coal Cars in 1937

In the consideration of our freight equipment, it should be borne in mind that the life of a steel coal car is generally accepted to be about twenty-five years. However, if at about twenty years the car receives a general heavy repair job, it will probably be good for a total life of thirty-five years. The greatest percentage of our serviceable freight equipment is open top coal cars, and these will be considered first.

Series 6200: There are two hundred - 38 foot, steel underframe, composite steel and wood superstructure, 40 ton, cars in this series. They are general service cars, and in addition to use in the coal trade, are in brisk demand for sand, gravel, stone and company material. One hundred of these cars were bought new in 1911, and one hundred in 1916. About one hundred and twenty of these cars need heavy general repairs. The general condition of the trucks and underframes warrant this work.

Series 15000: There are 1116, 33 foot, steel underframe, composite steel and wood superstructure, 40 ton, cars in this series. Originally build in 1910 and 1911, there were 1350 of these cars. They are now wearing out - 234 have been retired and 65 are assigned to company cinder service, due to general worn out condition. The steel underframes are worn out and weak, the draft gear is of an obsolete and now inadequate type, and the truck side frames are worn out and crystallized, due to length of service. These cars should be retired as soon as possible, on account of their general worn out condition.

Series 17,000, 18,000, 19,000, 20,000 and 303 to 3466 are generally 30 foot, 50 and 55 ton, all steel, self clearing coal cars.

Series 17000: There are thirty-nine of these cars, built in 1920, and bought second hand in 1926. These cars are fundamentally sound and should be kept in service. New truck side frames are required on thirty-seven cars, and about twenty are in need of heavy general repairs.

Series 18000: 500 were bought new in 1913, and 400 in 1916; 106 have been retired. Out of the total 794 cars now in service, it estimated that about 100 more should be retired on account of worn out and broken center sills, and general condition. The remaining cars are in such condition as to warrant their being kept in service. The retirement of 100 cars would give us some second hand Miner draft gears, 100 car sets of second hand cast steel truck side frames, and other repair parts, which could be utilized. 175 cars are being held for heavy repairs and 90 are in run-of-mine coal service.

Series 19000: There are 654 cars in this series. 700 were built in 1916 and 1917, and bought second hand in 1927 and 1928. 46 have since been retired; 130 are being held for heavy repairs. 40 remain to be equipt with cast steel side frames. About 300 of these cars should receive heavy repairs, and the rest, light repairs, and painting, with the exception of perhaps, 30, which should be retired.

Series 20000: 500 cars built in 1923 and bought second hand in 1933. This series should all receive new draft gears and door locks. About 200 are in immediate need of heavy general repairs.

Series 303 to 3466: 500 cars bought second hand in 1933, and built new as follows:

| | |
|---|---|
| 37 cars - | 1906 to 1913 |
| 183 cars - | 1913 to 1915 |
| 279 cars - | 1920 to 1926 |

350 of these cars require cast steel truck side frames, 220 need new draft gears and 250 need heavy general repairs.[49]

In 1937, the O&W filed for bankruptcy. By 1938, the O&W was in the hands of its trustee, Frederic E. Lyford, and he found himself in a difficult situation. Of the O&W's 3803 coal cars, 1216 or 32% needed to be retired as soon as possible. Of the remaining 2587 coal cars, 1070 or 41% were in need of heavy general repairs to continue service, and although the O&W's anthracite tonnage plummeted in the first year of its bankruptcy from 6,094,612 to 3,732,2022 tons, that rate was still relatively high by historic standards. Once again, the O&W found itself with a lack of capacity due to the condition of its coal car fleet. An internal memo, shown in the inset on page 115, describes the condition of the O&W's fleet at the time.

FIGURE 7.32
**The paint peeling off this 11000 series hopper reveals its 18000 series heritage before the sides were raised to achieve greater capacity.** *[John Forni photo; Alan F. Seebach Collection]*

The composite 15000 series, built almost thirty years earlier, had worn out. Trying to repair these low capacity, composite cars that were no longer suitable for interchange service made no sense, so between 1937 and 1939, the O&W retired over 700 of the cars in this series. With anthracite demand still relatively high by historic standards, Mr. Lyford searched for an inexpensive way to increase the capacity of the O&W's coal fleet. In April 1939, he petitioned the bankruptcy court to achieve this additional capacity by raising the sides of 500 of the

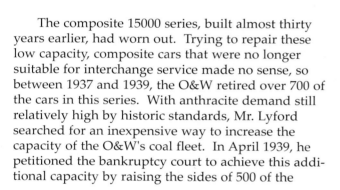

FIGURE 7.33
**This photo provides an interior view of the way in which the sides of these hoppers were raised to provide additional capacity. Note the two different sizes of anthracite in these two hoppers and the fact that neither hopper is filled to capacity.** *[Walter Kierzkowski Collection]*

O&W's hoppers by one foot. This would increase the capacity of each car by eight tons and reduce the per diem the railroad was paying to other railroads as a result. The O&W said that it could make these modifications for a total cost not to exceed $40,000.[50] The court approved this plan on May 1, 1939.[51]

It is fairly clear what the O&W's intentions were with regard to raising the sides of its hoppers. The O&W typically reserved a block of numbers with an associated car description in *The Official Railway Equipment Register* in advance of the cars actually coming into service. In early 1939 it reserved spaces for 300 cars in the series 10500 to 10799. The 10500 series can be described as GLa cars with their sides raised one foot. The use of GLa's appeared to be a good choice. The O&W had a large stock of them from which to choose, and, based upon the statements in the memo on page 115, the O&W was pleased with its 17000 series, which was essentially a taller GLa car. Furthermore, as noted in that same memo, 300 of the cars in the 20000 series were in good repair. The first car that the O&W modified with raised sides was one of its GLa cars, probably from its 3249 series. However, the O&W must not have liked the results, because car number 10500 was the only GLa so modified. Consequently, it had the distinction of becoming a series of one until it was retired in 1946.

The O&W went on to modify 500 hoppers to increase their capacity, though it had to substitute 399 hoppers from its 18000 series for the GLa cars. These modified 18000 series cars became the O&W's new 11000 series. Thus, the first all-steel hoppers

Hard Coal and Coal Cars

that the O&W had purchased had a new lease on life with a greater capacity of 1952 cubic feet, an increase of 282 cubic feet. The remaining 101 cars that were modified came from the 50-ton cars in the 19000-19399 series. These cars had the same dimensions as the 18000 series and produced the same results. The modified 19000 series cars became the 12500 series. Both were rated at 110,000 pounds.

The modifications to the cars were relatively straightforward. The car shops removed the side rail from the top of the hopper. They then prepared extension panels for the full perimeter of the car that were approximately 18" in height. They attached equivalent length side posts to these. The new side panel extensions slipped inside the old side panels and the side post extensions slipped outside the old side posts. The side posts and side panels were then riveted in place as shown in the accompanying photos. These modifications increased the empty weight of these cars by approximately 1000 pounds.

Before the O&W began the modifications, it returned to the court to request permission to equip these cars with power hand brakes and brake regulators, which Trustee Lyford claimed were needed because of the increased weight of the cars.[52] The court approved this request in August.[53] The esti-

FIGURE 7.34
**In 1953, the O&W purchased 21 second-hand USRA hoppers from the New Haven Railroad, because the rest of its hopper fleet was rendered obsolete for interchange service by changing regulations. This picture clearly shows the AB brake system, power hand brake, Wine door locks, and A.A.R. Standard trucks.** *[Walter Kierzkowski Collection]*

mated total cost for the power hand brakes and regulators was $17,500, bringing the total cost of these modifications to $57,500 or $115 per car. Despite all these efforts, these cars' lives were short. Half of these cars had been retired by the end of 1946 and only two would still be in O&W colors in 1957.

Anthracite shipments remained relatively stable during World War II, but the O&W coal car fleet did not. With the commitment of Trustee Lyford to transform the O&W into a "bridge route," and apparently deciding that it was cheaper to pay per diem than to perform the heavy general repairs required on its hopper fleet, the O&W scrapped or retired 1236 of its coal cars, or 49% of its entire fleet between 1941 and the end of 1945. Within another five years, the fleet had shrunk to 248 cars—less than 6% of its peak just 17 years earlier.

In 1953, almost as if to add insult to injury, after disposing of over 4000 coal cars in the preceding 20 years, the O&W had to return to the bankruptcy court to ask permission to buy 21 hoppers because none of its other coal cars were fit for interchange service due to their general condition and lack of AB brakes.[54] The court approved these requests for additional hoppers,[55] and they went on to become 21 of the most photographed hoppers in the history

FIGURE 7.35
**Five of the ten hoppers that the O&W sold to the Northwest Coal Company in 1951 were stranded at Eynon, Pennsylvania when the O&W was abandoned. These hoppers were ultimately buried in the culm pile visible in the background.** *[Walter Kierzkowski Collection]*

## What's a 110,000 pound capacity car?

The O&W marked its all-steel hoppers with either a 100,000 pound or 110,000 pound nominal capacity. As discussed Chapter 6, the marked capacity is an arbitrary number selected by the railroad to indicate the nominal capacity of the hopper within reasonable physical limits of the car. However, the marked capacity is not a governing number. The load limit governs the actual permissible loading of the car, and the load limit is determined by subtracting the light weight of the car from the maximum weight on rails permitted by the journal size of the freight trucks, regardless of the marked capacity. Since all of the O&W steel hoppers had 5½" x 10" journals, their load limits (total weight on rail) would have been the same regardless of their nominal or marked weight capacity. So, what's a 110,000 pound capacity car?

We do know that marking these cars at the higher nominal capacity created confusion even in the railroad community, because the question is raised specifically in the M.C.B. Code of Rules:

*Q. This rule [86] provides maximum loading for cars of 80,000 lb., 100,000 lb. and 140,000 lb. capacity, but no mention is made of cars stenciled 110,000 lb. capacity. Some roads are refusing to accept such cars if loaded beyond the nominal capacity stenciled thereon. What procedure should be followed?*

*A. If the car is equipped with 5½ by 10 in. A.R.A. Standard axle and the car is stenciled 110,000 lb., it can be loaded up to 169,000 lb., the total weight of car and lading for that capacity axle.[56]* [The same as if it had been stenciled 100,000 lb.]

So why did the O&W (and several other railroads) label some of its cars at the higher capacity? One explanation is that it may have just been a simplified way of accounting for train weights, since it correlated cubic capacity with a nominal loaded weight. The O&W followed the practice of labeling its hoppers with a cubic capacity less than 1700 cubic feet with a nominal weight capacity of 100,000 pounds and hoppers with a capacity greater than 1800 cubic feet with a nominal capacity of 110,000 pounds. Marketable sizes of bituminous coal weigh from 47 to 52 pounds per cubic foot, and anthracite weighs between 52 to 56 pounds per cubic foot,[57] and therefore the industry used 52 pounds per cubic foot to estimate the capacity of hopper cars. A 1700 cubic feet coal car with a 30 degree heap of coal, at 52 pounds per cubic foot, has a total capacity of about 2000 cubic feet, or 104,000 pounds. An 1800 cubic foot car with a 30 degree heap has a total capacity of about 2200 cubic feet or 114,400 pounds. Thus, the breaking point between 50 and 55 tons is between 1700 and 1800 cubic feet.

This only provides a partial explanation. The O&W purchased several second-hand cars with capacities greater than 1800 cubic feet, but rated them in *The Official Railway Equipment Register* at 100,000 pound capacity. Over time, the railroad increased the nominal capacities of these cars one-by-one to 110,000 pound capacity, as if they were modifying them in some way to handle the increased capacity. It is not clear whether the O&W believed that modifications were necessary to increase their nominal capacity, or if so, what those modifications might have been. However, Figure 7.31 does show the O&W making major repairs to some of the USRA-type hoppers that it purchased from Westmoreland coal. This may provide a possible explanation.

Neither is it clear if the O&W had placed any load restriction on these higher cubic capacity cars that had been rated at the lower nominal weight. If not, then their total load limit, as indicated above, would have been unaffected. If they did place a load restriction on these cars, then it would have had to place a star (*) next to the LDLMT to indicate that restriction. There is no evidence that the railroad did that.

of the O&W. Numbered from 901 through 921, these USRA hoppers came equipped with AB brakes and Dalman A.A.R. Standard freight trucks, the only coal cars on the railroad to have these two features. These 21 cars remained in service until the final days.

Not all of the O&W's hoppers ended up at the scrappers. In 1951, the O&W received permission from the court to sell ten of its hoppers to the Northwest Coal Company for $250 each. Five of these hoppers were left stranded at the Northwest Breaker on the Riverside Branch near Eynon, Pennsylvania. The cars were ultimately buried in the culm pile, where they are waiting to be dug up and put back in service.

Later that same year, the O&W sold four of its hoppers, numbers 11065, 11066, 12562, and 19585, to

FIGURE 7.36

**Former O&W car numbers 12562 and 11066 decked out in their new Waddell Coal Company livery.** *[Walter Kierzkowski Collection]*

the Waddell Coal Company. These cars were subsequently repainted into a distinctive orange color that made the Waddell hoppers a favorite of O&W fans. O&W car number 12562 became Waddell 101; O&W 19585 became Waddell 104, and O&W 11065 and 11066 became Waddell 102 and 103.

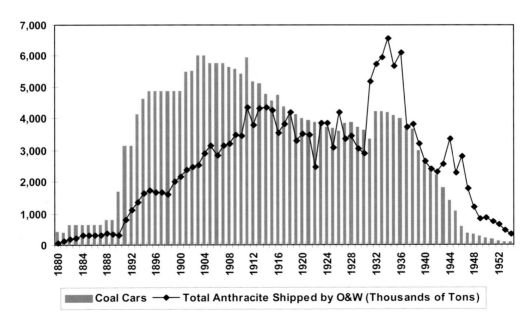

FIGURE 7.37

**Total number of O&W coal cars and tons of anthracite shipped 1880-1954.** *[Multiple Sources]*

| | | | | | | | | Inside | | | Outside | | | | | |
|---|---|---|---|---|---|---|---|---|---|---|---|---|---|---|---|---|
| | Series | | Capacity | | Build Information | | | | | | | Width to: | | | Height to: | |
| Description | From | To | CUB FT | LBS | Dates | Builder | Design | Length | Width | Height | Length | Eaves | Extreme | Ex Width | Eaves | Extreme |
| Hopper, Steel | 303 | 899 | 1880 | 110000 | 1920-2;26 | Camb/Beth STL | USRA | 30' 6" | 9' 6" | 7' 5" | 31' 11" | 10' 2" | 10' 2" | 10' 9" | 10' 9" | 11' 7" |
| Hopper, Steel | 303 | 899 | 1880 | 100000 | 1920-2;26 | Camb/Beth STL | USRA | 30' 6" | 9' 6" | 7' 5" | 31' 11" | 10' 2" | 10' 2" | 10' 9" | 10' 9" | 11' 7" |
| Hopper, Steel | 901 | 921 | 1880 | 110000 | 1929-30 | New Haven | USRA | 30' 6" | 9' 5" | 7' 5" | 31' 11" | 10' 1" | 10' 2" | 10' 5" | 10' 8" | 10' 9" |
| Hopper, Steel | 906 | 935 | 1683 | 100000 | 1906-8 | Unknown | GLa | 30' 5" | 9' 6" | ... | 32' 3" | 10' 2" | 10' 2" | 10' ... | 10' ... | 11' 1" |
| Hopper, Steel | 1203 | 2647 | 1683 | 100000 | 1913-15 | Cambria STL | GLa | 30' 5" | 9' 6" | ... | 32' 3" | 10' 2" | 10' 2" | 10' ... | 10' ... | 11' 1" |
| Hopper, Steel | 3249 | 3466 | 1683 | 100000 | 1913-15 | Cambria STL | GLa | 30' 5" | 9' 6" | ... | 32' 3" | 10' 2" | 10' 2" | 10' ... | 10' ... | 11' 1" |
| Gondola, Drop Bottom AB | 4400 | 4409 | 660 | 40000 | 1895 | Middletown | | 31' 4½" | 8' ... | 2' 8½" | 33' 6" | 9' 5" | ... | ... | 6' 11½" | 8' 2" |
| Gondola, Drop Bottom AB | 4410 | 4563 | 650 | 60000 | 1895-1901 | Middletown | | 31' 10½" | 7' 10½" | 2' 6" | 34' ... | 9' 2" | ... | ... | 6' 3" | 8' 2" |
| Gondola, Drop Bottom AB | 4600 | 4704 | 902 | 60000 | 1900; 1908 | Middletown | | 34' ... | 8' ... | 3' 6" | 34' ... | 9' 2½" | ... | ... | 7' 8" | 7' 10" |
| Gondola, Low Side | 4951 | 4952 | 853 | 80000 | 1910; 1915 | Norwich | | 36' 8½" | 7' 10½" | 3' ... | 38' 8" | 9' 6" | ... | ... | 6' 6" | 6' 6" |
| Gondola, Drop Bottom | 4501 | 5100 | 332 | 24-28000 | pre-1880 | Midland | | 26' 7" | 7' 10" | 1' 7" | 28' 4" | 9' 0" | ... | ... | 5' 8" | 7' 0" |
| Gondola, Hopper Bottom | 5101 | 5399 | 578 | 40000 | 1882 | Middletown | | 23' 5½" | 7' 7" | 3' 3" | 25' 8½" | 9' 0" | ... | ... | 7' 5" | 7' 10" |
| Gondola, Hopper Bottom | 5400 | 5550 | 717 | 40000 | 1887 | Terre Haute | | 23' 7" | 7' 7" | 4' ... | 25' 8½" | 9' 0" | ... | ... | 8' 2" | 7' 10" |
| Gondola, Channel Steel | 5601 | 5625 | 1275 | 85000 | 1901 | Sterlingworth | Rolled STL | 34' ... | 9' 4½" | 4' ... | 35' 11" | 10' ... | ... | ... | 7' 8" | 8' 3" |
| Gondola, Pressed Steel | 5701 | 5725 | 1190 | 85000 | 1901 | Pressed STL | Pressed STL | 34' ... | 9' 2" | 3' 9½" | 35' 4" | 9' 7" | ... | ... | 7' 3½" | 8' ... |
| Gondola, Drop Bottom | 6201 | 6400 | 818 | 80000 | 1911; 1916 | AC&F | | 38' ... | 8' 7" | 2' 6" | 39' 10" | 9' 9" | ... | ... | 6' 3¼" | 6' 10" |
| Gondola, Twin Hopper | 6600 | 7700 | 1460 | 85000 | 1901-02 | AC&F/Mdltown | | 36' ... | 8' 6" | 4' 4" | 37' 11½" | 9' 9½" | ... | ... | 8' 6½" | 9' 1½" |
| Coal, Twin Hopper | 7518 | 7518 | 1460 | 85000 | 1901 | AC&F | | 36' 8" | 8' 6" | 4' 4" | 38' 9" | 9' 0" | 9' 9" | 8' 7" | 8' 6" | 9' 4" |
| Coal, Hopper Bottom | 10001 | 10500 | 867 | 50000 | 1890 | Michigan Car | | 25' 6" | 7' 6½" | 4' ... | 27' 8" | 9' 0" | ... | ... | 8' 1" | 8' 7" |
| Coal, Hopper Bottom | 10501 | 11500 | 867 | 50000 | 1890-91 | Lafayette Car | | 25' 6" | 7' 6½" | 4' ... | 27' 8" | 9' 0" | ... | ... | 8' 1" | 8' 7" |
| Coal, Hopper Bottom | 11501 | 12350 | 973 | 60000 | 1891 | Lafayette Car | | 27' 3" | 8' ... | 4' ... | 29' 1" | 9' 5" | ... | ... | 8' 4¼" | 8' 7" |
| Coal, Hopper Bottom | 12351 | 12850 | 973 | 60000 | 1892 | Peninsular Car | | 27' 3" | 8' ... | 4' ... | 29' 1" | 9' 5" | ... | ... | 8' 4¼" | 8' 7" |
| Coal, Hopper Bottom | 12851 | 13350 | 973 | 60000 | 1893 | Mich-Peninsular | | 27' 3" | 8' ... | 4' ... | 29' 1" | 9' 5" | ... | ... | 8' 4¼" | 8' 7" |
| Coal, Hopper Bottom | 13351 | 13850 | 973 | 60000 | 1894 | Mich-Peninsular | | 27' 3" | 8' ... | 4' ... | 29' 1" | 9' 5" | ... | ... | 8' 4¼" | 8' 7" |
| Coal, Hopper Bottom | 13851 | 14120 | 973 | 60000 | 1895 | Mich-Peninsular | | 27' 3" | 8' ... | 4' ... | 29' 1" | 9' 5" | ... | ... | 8' 4¼" | 8' 7" |
| Hopper, Steel | 10500 | 10799 | 1970 | 110000 | 1939 | Middletown | OVRSZ 3244 | 30' 5" | 9' 6" | ... | 32' 3" | 10' 2" | 10' 2" | 11' ... | 11' ... | 11' 10" |
| Hopper, Steel | 11000 | 11399 | 1952 | 110000 | 1939-1940 | Middletown | OVRSZ 18000 | 30' ... | 9' 5½" | ... | 31' 6" | 10' ... | 10' 1" | 11' ... | 11' ... | 11' 8" |
| Hopper, Steel | 12500 | 12600 | 1952 | 110000 | 1939-1940 | Middletown | OVRSZ 19000 | 30' ... | 9' 5½" | ... | 31' 6" | 10' ... | 10' ... | 11' ... | 11' ... | 11' 10" |
| Hopper, Steel | 15001 | 15500 | 1385 | 80000 | 1910 | Middletown | Seley | 33' ... | 8' 11½" | 5' ... | 34' 6½" | 9' 8½" | 10' 2" | 8' 6" | 8' 10" | 9' 4½" |
| Hopper, Steel | 15501 | 16350 | 1385 | 80000 | 1910-11 | AC&F | Seley | 33' ... | 8' 11½" | 5' ... | 34' 6½" | 9' 8½" | 10' 2" | 8' 6" | 8' 10" | 9' 4½" |
| Hopper, Steel | 17000 | 17039 | 1960 | 110000 | 1920 | Pressed STL | OVRSZ GLa | 30' 5" | 9' 6" | 8' ... | 32' 3" | 10' 2" | 10' 2" | 10' 11" | 10' 11" | 11' 10" |
| Hopper, Steel | 18001 | 18900 | 1670 | 100000 | 1913; 1916 | Cambria STL | "A.R.A." | 30' ... | 9' 5½" | 6' 10" | 31' 6½" | 10' ... | 10' 1" | 9' 8" | 10' ... | 11' ... |
| Hopper, Steel | 19000 | 19399 | 1670 | 100000 | 1916 | Standard STL | "A.R.A." | 30' ... | 9' 5½" | 6' 8" | 31' 6" | 10' ... | 10' ... | 10' ... | 10' ... | 10' 10" |
| Hopper, Steel | 19000 | 19399 | 1800 | 110000 | 1916-17 | AC&F | "A.R.A." | 30' ... | 9' 5½" | 7' 4" | 31' 7" | 10' ... | 10' ... | 10' 6" | 10' 6" | 11' 2" |
| Hopper, Steel | 19400 | 19699 | 1800 | 110000 | 1916-17 | AC&F | "A.R.A." | 30' ... | 9' 5½" | 7' 4" | 31' 7" | 10' ... | 10' ... | 10' 6" | 10' 6" | 11' 2" |
| Hopper, Steel | 20000 | 20499 | 1683 | 100000 | 1923 | AC&F | GLa | 30' 5" | 9' 6" | ... | 32' 3" | 10' 2" | 10' 2" | 10' ... | 10' ... | 11' 1" |

FIGURE 8.1
**Capacities and dimensions of O&W coal cars 1880-1957.** ***[Official Railway Equipment Registers and NYO&W Railway Annual Reports]***

## Chapter 8

*INDEX TO IDENTIFICATION GUIDE*

Note: Cars are generally presented in this chapter in the order in which they entered service on the O&W

## 4501-5100 Series, Wood, Drop-Bottom Gondola

**Nomenclature:** Gondola, Wood,
Drop-Bottom
**Manufacturer:** Unknown
**Dates Mfgd:** Prior to 1880
**Capacity:**
   **Weight:** 24,000-28,000 pounds
   **Volume:** 332 cubic feet
**Cost per Car:** Unknown

**Appliances:**
   **Couplers:** Link and pin
   **Air Brakes:** Not installed
   **Side Trusses:** Installed 1900-1910

**Inside Dimensions:**
   **Length:** 26' 7"
   **Width:** 7' 10"
   **Height:** 1' 7"
**Outside Dimension:**
   **Length:** Unknown
   **Width:** Unknown
   **Height:** Unknown

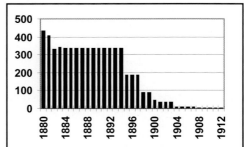

FIGURE 8.2
**Inventory of cars in 4501-5100 series**

**Remarks:** These are the cars that the O&W inherited from the New York & Oswego Midland. Beginning in 1895, the O&W began retiring the cars in this early series and replacing them on a one for two basis with 30-ton cars numbered in the same series. By 1897, all cars in this series from 4501 to 4600 had been retired; by 1900; all cars from 4601 to 5000 had been retired. After 1900, the only cars of the original series that remained were numbered 5000 to 5100.

## 5101-5400 Series, Wood, Hopper-Bottom Gondola

**Nomenclature:** Gondola, Wood,
Hopper-Bottom
**Manufacturer:** Middletown Shops
**Dates Mfgd:** 1882
**Capacity:**
   **Weight:** 40,000 pounds
   **Volume:** 578 cubic feet
**Cost per Car:** Unknown

**Appliances:**
   **Couplers:** Perry automatic (standard); MCBA installed 1895-1904
   **Air Brakes:** Not standard; no record of installation
   **Side Trusses:** Installed 1900-1910

**Inside Dimensions:**
   **Length:** 23' 5½"
   **Width:** 7' 7"
   **Height:** 3' 3"
**Outside Dimension:**
   **Length:** Unknown
   **Width:** Unknown
   **Height:** Unknown

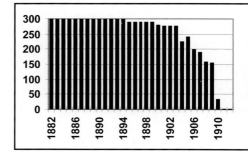

FIGURE 8.3
**Inventory of cars in 5101-5400 series**

**Remarks:** The O&W manufactured the 300 cars in this series in its Middletown shops in 1882 to comply with the agreement that it had signed the year before with the Delaware & Hudson Canal Coal Company to transport anthracite from Sidney Junction to Oswego. Two hundred of these cars were equipped with Perry Automatic Safety Couplers. Drawings for this series are shown on pages 124 and 125.

## 5401-5550 Series, Wood, Hopper-Bottom Gondola

**Nomenclature:** Gondola, Wood,
Hopper-Bottom
**Manufacturer:** Terre Haute
**Dates Mfgd:** 1887
**Capacity:**
   **Weight:** 40,000 pounds
   **Volume:** 717 cubic feet
**Cost per Car:** $411.72

**Appliances:**
   **Couplers:** Smillie automatic (standard); MCBA installed 1895-1904
   **Air Brakes:** Not standard; no record of installation
   **Side Trusses:** Installed 1900-1910

**Inside Dimensions:**
   **Length:** 23' 7"
   **Width:** 7' 7"
   **Height:** 4' 0"
**Outside Dimension:**
   **Length:** Unknown
   **Width:** Unknown
   **Height:** Unknown

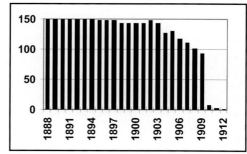

FIGURE 8.4
**Inventory of cars in 5401-5550 series**

**Remarks:** These cars were purchased from Terre Haute in 1887 to provide additional carrying capacity as a result of the O&W's leasing the Rome & Clinton and the Utica, Clinton & Binghamton Railroads from the Delaware & Hudson Canal Company. They were similar in design to the cars in the 5101-5400 series, though slightly larger. These cars were equipped with the Smillie automatic coupler as original equipment.

FIGURE 8.5
One of the original hopper-bottom gondolas built by the O&W in 1882 is seen in Middletown in 1908. The train line for the automatic brakes can be seen running just beneath the side sill. Automatic couplers were installed in this series in the late 1890's and early part of the 20th century. Drawings for the car as built are shown on the next two pages. *[Walter Kierzkowski Collection]*

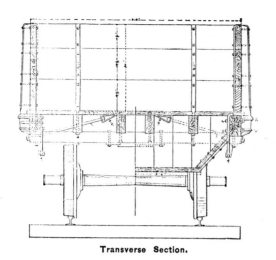

Transverse Section.

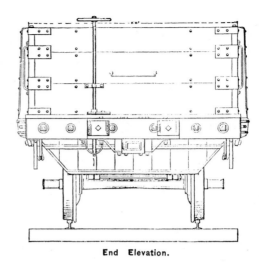

End Elevation.

FIGURE 8.6
**Transverse section and end elevation for 5101 series hopper-bottom gondola built in Middletown shops in 1882.**
*[National Car Builder, December 1882]*

### Body Timbers—Finished Sizes

2 outside sills . . . . . . . . . . . . . . .yellow pine .5¼" x 9⁵⁄₈" x 24' 7"
4 intermediate sills . . . . . . . . . .yellow pine .4" x 8½" x 6' 1"
2 center sills . . . . . . . . . . . . . . .white oak ..4" x 8½" x 24' 7"
2 end sills . . . . . . . . . . . . . . . . .white oak ..8" x 9⁵⁄₈" x 8' 3"
2 body bolsters . . . . . . . . . . . . .white oak ..5" x 12" x 8' 1"
2 cross pieces . . . . . . . . . . . . . .white oak ..4" x 8½" x 7' 0"
4 side planks . . . . . . . . . . . . . . .yellow pine .2¾" x 14³⁄₈" x 24' 0"
2 side planks . . . . . . . . . . . . . . .yellow pine .2¾" x 11" x 24' 0"
4 end planks . . . . . . . . . . . . . . .yellow pine .2¾" x 14³⁄₈" x 7' 6½"
2 end planks . . . . . . . . . . . . . . .yellow pine .2¾" x 11" x 7' 6½"
2 buffer timbers . . . . . . . . . . . .white oak ..4" x 9½" x 3' 6"
4 draw timbers . . . . . . . . . . . . .white oak ..4" x 7" x 5' 1"
12 stakes . . . . . . . . . . . . . . . . . .white oak ..3⁷⁄₈" x 4½" x 4' 3"
8 keys in sides . . . . . . . . . . . . . .white oak ..2¾" x 3" x 0' 8"
2 blocks between draw timbers white oak ..8½" x 9" x 1' 6"
2 body bolster truss blocks . . . .white oak ..8" x 9" x 1' 0"
2 doors of hopper . . . . . . . . . . .white oak ..2" x 15" x 5' 0"
2 sides of hopper . . . . . . . . . . . .white oak ..1¾" x 12" x 8' 8"
2 sides of hopper . . . . . . . . . . . .white oak ..1¾" x 12" x 5' 10"
2 ends in body . . . . . . . . . . . . . .white oak ..1¾" x 12" x 7' 6½"
2 planks on side sills . . . . . . . . .white oak ..1¾" x 6¾" x 11' 7"
Flooring . . . . . . . . . . . . . . . . . . .white oak ..1¾" x 6"- 8" x 8' 3"
Hopper ends . . . . . . . . . . . . . . .white oak ..1¾" x 10"-12" x 5' 8"
[End sills tapered at ends to 7" x 9⁵⁄₈". Stakes tapered at top
to 3 ¾" x 3⁷⁄₈".]

### Materials in Car Body

Yellow pine . . . . . . . . . . . . . . . . . . . . . . . . . . . . . . . . . . . .986 pounds
White oak . . . . . . . . . . . . . . . . . . . . . . . . . . . . . . . . . . . . .1,302 pounds
Bolts . . . . . . . . . . . . . . . . . . . . . . . . . . . . . . . . . . . . . . . . . .419 pounds
Rods . . . . . . . . . . . . . . . . . . . . . . . . . . . . . . . . . . . . . . . . . .478 pounds
Wrought Iron . . . . . . . . . . . . . . . . . . . . . . . . . . . . . . . . . . .1,488 pounds
Castings . . . . . . . . . . . . . . . . . . . . . . . . . . . . . . . . . . . . . .1,451 pounds
Nuts . . . . . . . . . . . . . . . . . . . . . . . . . . . . . . . . . . . . . . . . . .116 pounds

### Construction

Side and intermediate sills framed to end sills by double tenons, secured to end sill and cross-pieces, and cross-pieces secured to center and side sills by ⁷⁄₈" rods.

Body bolster housed out to receive sills and secured by ¾" bolts; bolster trussed by 1" rods, with ³⁄₈" x 3 ½" center bearing straps.

Hopper supported by 3" x 1" wrought-iron straps, with ends turned outward 2", resting on side sills.

Side plank secured to frame by eight ¾" bolts and four ⁷⁄₈" strap bolts on each side.

Ends secured to frame by two ⁷⁄₈" strap bolts each end, and to sides with angle plates of ¼" x 6" and ¼" x 3" wrought iron, four inside and four outside.

Angle plates, stakes and strap bolts secured to side plank with ½" carriage bolts the required length.

Sides protected from wear by ¼" x 2½" iron, extending full length of top of sides.

Doors of hopper fitted with wrought-iron hinges of ⁵⁄₈" x 2½" iron, connected by ³⁄₈" and ½" chains to wrought-iron winding shaft of 1¾" diameter.

Buffer timbers fastened to end sills by two ⁷⁄₈" bolts and two ⁷⁄₈" rods through body bolster, end sill and buffer timbers.

Body truss rods, two in number, of 1¹⁄₈" round iron, with 1¼" upset ends, located immediately inside of side sill, resting on cast-iron saddles on top of body bolsters and on saddle castings under side sill.

Rods to be bent warm to a templet, and made to fit in their place.

Body bolster capped across ends with ⁵⁄₈" x 3 ½" wrought-iron plates, bent over at the end, forming a lip on the side.

Draw-head and dead blocks of cast iron, N.Y., O. & W. Railway standard pattern.

Draw-bar springs to be 5½" diameter, 6" rise, with ultimate capacity of 18,000 pounds.

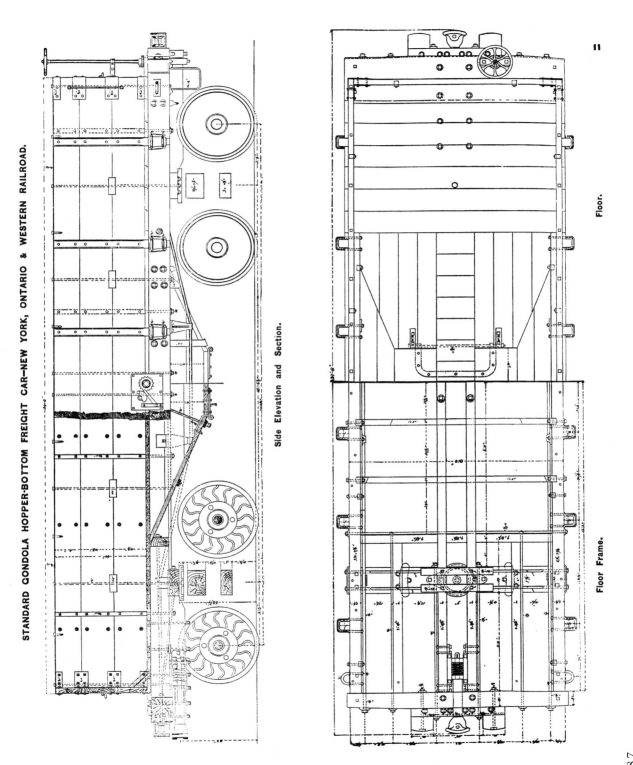

STANDARD GONDOLA HOPPER-BOTTOM FREIGHT CAR—NEW YORK, ONTARIO & WESTERN RAILROAD.

Side Elevation and Section.

Floor.

Floor Frame.

FIGURE 8.7
Side elevation and top section for 5101 series hopper-bottom gondola built in Middletown shops in 1882. [*National Car Builder, December 1882*]

## 10001-14120 Series, Wood, Hopper-Bottom Gondola

### Car Numbers 10001-10500

**Nomenclature:**
  Gondola, Wood, Hopper-Bottom
**Manufacturer:**
  Michigan Car Company
**Dates Mfgd:** 1890
**Capacity:**
  **Weight:** 50,000 pounds
  **Volume:** 867 cubic feet
**Cost per Car:** $378.08

**Inside Dimensions:**
  **Length:** 25' 6"
  **Width:** 7' 6½"
  **Height:** 4' 0"
**Outside Dimension:**
  **Length:** 27' 8"
  **Width:** 9' 0"
  **Height:** 8' 1"

**Appliances:**
  **Couplers:** MCBA (standard)
  **Air Brakes:** Installed 1896-1909
  **Side Trusses:** Installed 1899-1907

### Car Numbers 10501-11500

**Nomenclature:**
  Gondola, Wood, Hopper-Bottom
**Manufacturer:**
  Lafayette Car Works
**Dates Mfgd:** 1890-91
**Capacity:**
  **Weight:** 50,000 pounds
  **Volume:** 867 cubic feet
**Cost per Car:** $419.00

**Inside Dimensions:**
  **Length:** 25' 6"
  **Width:** 7' 6½"
  **Height:** 4' 0"
**Outside Dimension:**
  **Length:** 27' 8"
  **Width:** 9' 0"
  **Height:** 8' 1"

**Appliances:**
  **Couplers:** MCBA (standard)
  **Air Brakes:** Installed 1896-1909
  **Side Trusses:** Installed 1899-1907

### Car Numbers 11501-12350

**Nomenclature:**
  Gondola, Wood, Hopper-Bottom
**Manufacturer:**
  Lafayette Car Works
**Dates Mfgd:** 1890-91
**Capacity:**
  **Weight:** 60,000 pounds
  **Volume:** 973 cubic feet
**Cost per Car:** $440.00

**Inside Dimensions:**
  **Length:** 27' 3"
  **Width:** 8' 0"
  **Height:** 4' 0"
**Outside Dimension:**
  **Length:** 29' 1"
  **Width:** 9' 5"
  **Height:** 8' 4¼"

**Appliances:**
  **Couplers:** MCBA (standard)
  **Air Brakes:** Installed 1896-1909
  **Side Trusses:** Installed 1899-1907

### Car Numbers 12351-12850

**Nomenclature:**
  Gondola, Wood, Hopper-Bottom
**Manufacturer:**
  Peninsular Car Company
**Dates Mfgd:** 1892
**Capacity:**
  **Weight:** 60,000 pounds
  **Volume:** 973 cubic feet
**Cost per Car:** $431.50

**Inside Dimensions:**
  **Length:** 27' 3"
  **Width:** 8' 0"
  **Height:** 4' 0"
**Outside Dimension:**
  **Length:** 29' 1"
  **Width:** 9' 5"
  **Height:** 8' 4¼"

**Appliances:**
  **Couplers:** MCBA (standard)
  **Air Brakes:** Installed 1896-1909
  **Side Trusses:** Installed 1899-1907

### Car Numbers 12851-13350

**Nomenclature:**
  Gondola, Wood, Hopper-Bottom
**Manufacturer:**
  Michigan-Peninsular Car Company
**Dates Mfgd:** 1893
**Capacity:**
  **Weight:** 60,000 pounds
  **Volume:** 973 cubic feet
**Cost per Car:** $436.25

**Inside Dimensions:**
  **Length:** 27' 3"
  **Width:** 8' 0"
  **Height:** 4' 0"
**Outside Dimension:**
  **Length:** 29' 1"
  **Width:** 9' 5"
  **Height:** 8' 4¼"

**Appliances:**
  **Couplers:** MCBA (standard)
  **Air Brakes:** Installed 1896-1909
  **Side Trusses:** Installed 1899-1907

| Nomenclature: | Inside Dimensions: | | Appliances: |
|---|---|---|---|
| Gondola, Wood, Hopper-Bottom | **Length:** | 27' 3" | **Couplers:** MCBA (standard) |
| **Manufacturer:** | **Width:** | 8' 0" | **Air Brakes:** Installed 1896-1909 |
| Michigan-Peninsular Car Company | **Height:** | 4' 0" | **Side Trusses:** Installed 1899-1907 |
| **Dates Mfgd:** 1894 | **Outside Dimension:** | | |
| **Capacity:** | **Length:** | 29' 1" | |
| **Weight:** 60,000 pounds | **Width:** | 9' 5" | |
| **Volume:** 973 cubic feet | **Height:** | 8' 4¼" | |
| **Cost per Car:** $415.00 | | | |

| Nomenclature: | Inside Dimensions: | | Appliances: |
|---|---|---|---|
| Gondola, Wood, Hopper-Bottom | **Length:** | 27' 3" | **Couplers:** MCBA (standard) |
| **Manufacturer:** | **Width:** | 8' 0" | **Air Brakes:** Standard |
| Michigan-Peninsular Car Company | **Height:** | 4' 0" | **Side Trusses:** Installed 1899-1907 |
| **Dates Mfgd:** 1895 | **Outside Dimension:** | | |
| **Capacity:** | **Length:** | 29' 1" | |
| **Weight:** 60,000 pounds | **Width:** | 9' 5" | |
| **Volume:** 973 cubic feet | **Height:** | 8' 4¼" | |
| **Cost per Car:** $450.00 | | | |

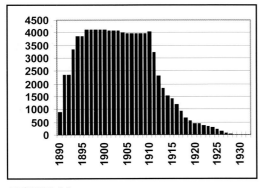

FIGURE 8.8
**Inventory of cars in 10001-14120 series**

FIGURE 8.9
**A pair of hopper-bottom gondolas from the 10001 to 14120 series stand shivering in the yard at Mayfield on a cold winter day in December 1910. On the right is car number 11329, one of the first cars bought in this series, still in its 25-ton configuration. On the left is one of the larger 30-ton cars, its car number worn by age. [O&WRHS Archives]**

**Remarks:** The 10001-14120 series was used by the O&W to open up the Scranton Division. It was the largest series of coal cars or freight cars ever purchased by the O&W. The first 1500 cars were rated at a capacity of 867 cubic feet and 50,000 pounds. All cars purchased, built, or rebuilt thereafter had a capacity of 973 cubic feet and 60,000 pounds. After the initial purchases, the O&W bought more cars in this series as the railroad gained access to more mines and traffic increased. This accounts for the multiple purchases of these cars from 1889 through 1895. Even though the cars in this series were of two different sizes, the O&W tended to account for them as a single series. All cars in this series came equipped with MCBA standard automatic couplers. Cars built on or after 1895 were also equipped with air brakes. At the turn of the 20th century, the railroad began a series of modifications to these cars to extend their lives, including the addition of air brakes, side trusses to keep the sides from bulging, and steel truck and body bolsters. In 1902, it experimented with steel underframes by putting them under three of these cars. In that same year, it began rebuilding cars in this series with wood underframes, gradually rebuilding a total of 606 cars from 1903 to 1909. In 1908 alone, it rebuilt a total of 423 of these cars with wood underframes. In that same year, it also began rebuilding cars in this series with Martin steel underframes (see Figure 3.21) and K-series air brakes. From 1908 through 1911, it modified 265 cars in this way. Shortly thereafter, as the composite cars hoppers in the 15000 series and the all-steel hoppers in the 18000 series entered service, the O&W began a wholesale retirement of those cars that had not been recently rebuilt. By 1920, fewer than 600 of these cars were left, and by 1933, they were gone.

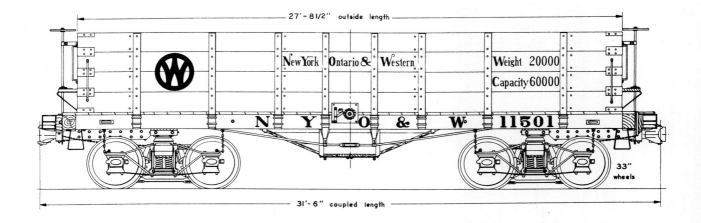

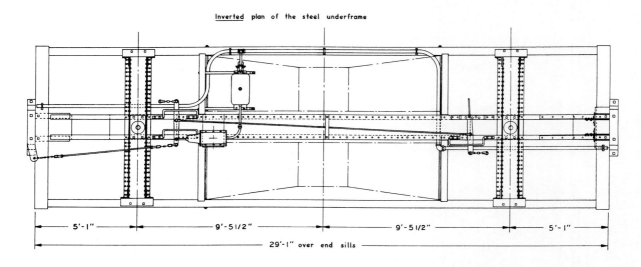

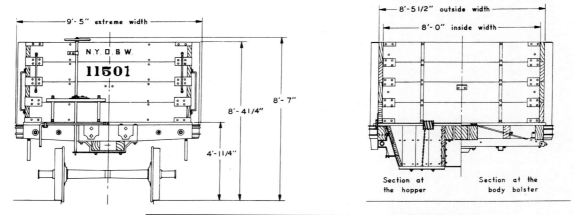

FIGURE 8.10

**These elevation drawings of the 30-ton cars in the 10001-14120 series were published in the O&WRHS *Observer* entitled *New York, Ontario & Western Railway Scranton Division*. They show the general layout of the 30-ton hopper, including the brake piping. Complete drawings are in the *Scranton Division Observer*. Car number 11501 was the first coal car on the O&W with a capacity of 30 tons. [*Courtesy: Edward J. Crist*]**

FIGURE 8.11

This photo taken in Hancock in 1911 provides almost a complete history of the 10001-14120 series. From front to rear, car number 12786 is an original, all-wood, 30-ton car purchased from Peninsular Car Company in 1892. It has never been rebuilt, although it has been equipped with K-series air brakes. With its hopper doors open, it provides a glimpse of their operation. Interestingly, the car is equipped with a mix of truck bolsters on its arch bar trucks. Car number 12245 directly behind it is also an original 30-ton gondola from the same series as 12786. Behind it is car number 10316, one of the original, all-wood, 25-ton cars purchased from Lafayette Car Works in 1890 still in service 20 years later. The difference between the 25-ton cars and the 30-ton cars can clearly be seen when comparing this car with those in front of it. The last car in the series is car number 10365. This car number was originally assigned to one of the five hundred, 25-ton cars purchased from Michigan Car Company in 1889. However, that car was retired and the car seen here was built new in the Middletown shops in 1908, reusing the original car's number. This car has both a wood body and wood underframe. In 1908, the O&W was building and/or rebuilding cars in this series with both wood and steel underframes. The cast steel trucks under this car are unidentified. [O&WRHS Archives]

## 4400-4563 Series, Wood, Drop-Bottom Gondola

**Nomenclature:** Gondola, Wood, Drop-Bottom
**Manufacturer:** Middletown & Norwich Shops
**Dates Mfgd:** 1895-1901
**Capacity:**
    **Weight:** 60,000 pounds
    **Volume:** 650 cubic feet
**Cost per Car:** $450 (average)

**Inside Dimensions:**
    **Length:** 31' 10½"
    **Width:** 7' 10½"
    **Height:** 2' 6"
**Outside Dimension:**
    **Length:** 34' 0"
    **Width:** 9' 2"
    **Height:** 6' 3"

**Appliances:**
    **Couplers:** MCBA (standard)
    **Air Brakes:** Standard on cars 4410-4563
    **Bolster:** Simplex Steel
    **Draft Gear:** Miner

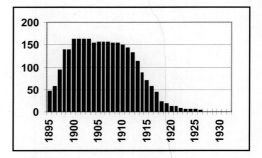

FIGURE 8.12
**Inventory of cars in 4600-4704 series**

**Remarks:** The O&W began retiring its old Midland cars in 1895 and replacing them on a one for two basis with these 30-ton, drop-bottom gondolas built in its company shops. The first ten of the cars in this series were six inches shorter than the rest and had a capacity of 660 cubic feet and 40,000 pounds. Cars 4410 through 4563, however, carried the dimensions and capacity listed above, with the exception of car number 4414, which had the same dimensions as cars 4400-4409. Cars 4400-4409 were not originally equipped with air brakes, but they were added later. Cars 4410-4563 were built with air brakes. They are listed in the 1916 ICC inventory as all-wood construction with steel bolsters.

## 4600-4704 Series, Wood, Drop-Bottom Gondola

**Nomenclature:** Gondola, Wood, Drop-Bottom
**Manufacturer:** Middletown & Norwich Shops
**Dates Mfgd:** 1900, 1908
**Capacity:**
    **Weight:** 60,000 pounds
    **Volume:** 902 cubic feet
**Cost per Car:** $520 (average)

**Inside Dimensions:**
    **Length:** 34' 0"
    **Width:** 8' 0"
    **Height:** 3' 6"
**Outside Dimension:**
    **Length:** 32' 2½"
    **Width:** 9' 2½"
    **Height:** 7' 8"

**Appliances:**
    **Couplers:** MCBA (standard)
    **Air Brakes:** Standard
    **Bolsters:** Simplex Steel
    **Draft Gear:** Miner

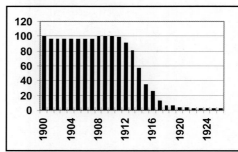

FIGURE 8.13
**Inventory of cars in 4600-4704 series**

**Remarks:** The O&W built 100 of these drop-bottom gondolas in 1900 as replacements for the Midland cars being retired, and it built four more in this series in 1908. They are dimensionally similar to the cars in the 6600-7700 series but can be distinguished by the lack of hopper bottoms and by the spacing of the side stakes. These cars are still listed as all-wood construction during the 1916 ICC inventory but equipped with Simplex steel bolsters and Miner draft gear.

## 4951-4952 Series, Composite Wood and Steel, Low-Side Gondola

**Nomenclature:** Gondola, Composite, Solid-Bottom, Low-Side
**Manufacturer:** Norwich shops
**Dates Mfgd:** 1910, 1914
**Capacity:**
    **Weight:** 80,000 pounds
    **Volume:** 853 cubic feet
**Cost per Car:** $653.30 (1910), $524.46 (1914)

**Inside Dimensions:**
    **Length:** 36' 8½"
    **Width:** 7' 10½"
    **Height:** 3' 0"
**Outside Dimension:**
    **Length:** 38' 8"
    **Width:** 9' 6"
    **Height:** 6' 6"

**Appliances:**
    **Couplers:** MCBA (standard)
    **Air Brakes:** Standard
    **Bolsters:** Steel
    **Draft Gear:** Westinghouse friction

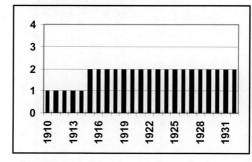

FIGURE 8.14
**Inventory of cars in 4951-4952 series**

**Remarks:** Little is known about these two cars, but they may have been an experiment in composite construction in the company's own shops. These solid bottom, composite construction gondolas were listed as "low-side coal cars" during the ICC inventory. They were built in the company's Norwich shops and equipped with Westinghouse friction draft gear, steel bolsters, and cast-steel side frames.

Hard Coal and Coal Cars

FIGURE 8.15
Drop-bottom gondola number 4608 watches a new turntable being installed in Utica in August 1910. The first one hundred cars in this series were built in the Middletown shops in 1900 to replace cars inherited from the Midland on a one-for-two basis. Four additional cars in this series were built in 1908. *[Walter Kierzkowski Collection]*

## 5601-5700 Series, Rolled-Steel, Hopper-Bottom Gondola

**Nomenclature:** Gondola, Rolled-Steel,
   Hopper-Bottom
**Manufacturer:** Sterlingworth
**Dates Mfgd:** 1901
**Capacity:**
   **Weight:** 85,000 pounds
   **Volume:** 1275 cubic feet
**Cost per Car:** $902.23 (from 1916 report
   to ICC)

**Appliances:**
   **Trucks:** Sterlingworth-Joughins Rolled Steel

**Inside Dimensions:**
   **Length:** 34' 0"
   **Width:** 9' 4½"
   **Height:** 4' 0"
**Outside Dimension:**
   **Length:** 35' 11"
   **Width:** 10' 0"
   **Height:** 7' 8"
**Weight Empty:** 35,000 pounds

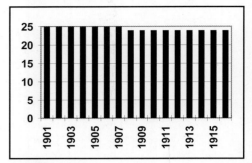

**FIGURE 8.16**
**Inventory of cars in 5601-5700 series**

**Remarks:** The Sterlingworth rolled-steel car was part of the great debate taking place at the turn of the 19th century as to whether rolled, structural steel shapes or pressed-steel shapes would dominate in the construction of freight cars. The Sterlingworth car, manufactured in Easton, Pennsylvania, was virtually 100% rolled-steel shapes including sides, brake beams, and Joughins style (later called Sterlingworth) trucks. The sides were constructed of 12 inch channels bolted together at 12" intervals. This car was rated in trade publications at 80,000 pounds capacity but it entered service on the O&W at 85,000 pound capacity. These cars were all transferred from interchange service to maintenance of way service in August 1916, and twelve of them were still listed in that service as late as 1932. Although the Sterlingworth car was featured in a number of trade journals of the period, records indicate that fewer than 100 of these cars were ever produced. Other users included the Delaware, Lackawanna & Western and Mexican International Railways. Note that this car is equipped with Ajax automatic couplers.

## 5701-5800 Series, Pressed-Steel, Hopper-Bottom Gondola

**Nomenclature:** Gondola, Pressed-Steel,
   Hopper-Bottom
**Manufacturer:** Pressed Steel Car Co.
**Dates Mfgd:** 1901
**Capacity:**
   **Weight:** 85,000 pounds
   **Volume:** 1190 cubic feet
**Cost per Car:** $928.00 (from 1916 report
   to ICC)

**Appliances:**
   **Trucks:** Vogt-Style Pressed Steel

**Inside Dimensions:**
   **Length:** 34' 0"
   **Width:** 9' 2"
   **Height:** 3' 9½"
**Outside Dimensions:**
   **Length:** 35' 4"
   **Width:** 9' 7"
   **Height:** 7' 3½"
**Weight Empty:** 33,300 pounds

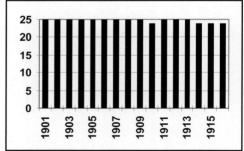

**FIGURE 8.17**
**Inventory of cars in 5701-5800 series**

**Remarks:** Charles Schoen was the leading advocate for pressed-steel shapes in the construction of freight cars, and his Pressed Steel Car Company produced the first production runs of pressed-steel hoppers, as well as the first production run of cars manufactured from structural-steel shapes for the Bessemer & Lake Erie Railroad in 1898. The Schoen pressed-steel gondola was first produced for B&LE that same year and was featured in a number of trade journals of the period. It enjoyed considerable popularity and was employed on several major railroads including the Pennsylvania. Like the Sterlingworth, every feature of this car employed the shapes for which it was named, that is, this car had pressed-steel sides, brake beams, bolsters, and side frames. Despite the fact that the Sterlingworth and the Schoen car had similar cubic capacities, the O&W carried the pressed-steel car at only 80,000 pounds capacity until 1906, when it was finally upgraded to 85,000 pounds capacity. These cars were also transferred to maintenance of way service in August 1916, and twelve are still listed in MOW service in 1932. A 1902 pressed-steel gondola is on display at the Railroad Museum of Pennsylvania in Strasburg, PA. It is worth noting the light weight of this gondola. One of Schoen's claims was that pressed-steel cars would weigh less than their structural steel counterparts. Indeed, this car weights almost a ton less than the Sterlingworth car or an equivalent capacity wood car.

**FIGURE 8.18**
A Sterlingworth hopper-bottom gondola and a wood, hopper-bottom gondola from the 6600 series stand side-by-side on the trestle at Oswego in 1912. Although the rolled-steel cars were removed from interchange service in 1916, they remained in maintenance of way service well into the 1930's. In the foreground, the slots through which the anthracite fell into the coaling pockets are clearly visible. *[Walter Kierzkowski Collection]*

**FIGURE 8.19**
This undated photo provides what some believe is the only close-up view of the side of a Pressed Steel gondola in O&W service. *[O&WRHS Archives]*

**FIGURE 8.20**
The condition of this Sterlingworth hopper at Weehawken in 1911 may indicate why the O&W never ordered any more of these cars. This photo also provides an excellent view of the interior of a car from the 10000-14120 series. *[Walter Kierzkowski Collection]*

**Identification Guide for O&W Coal Cars**

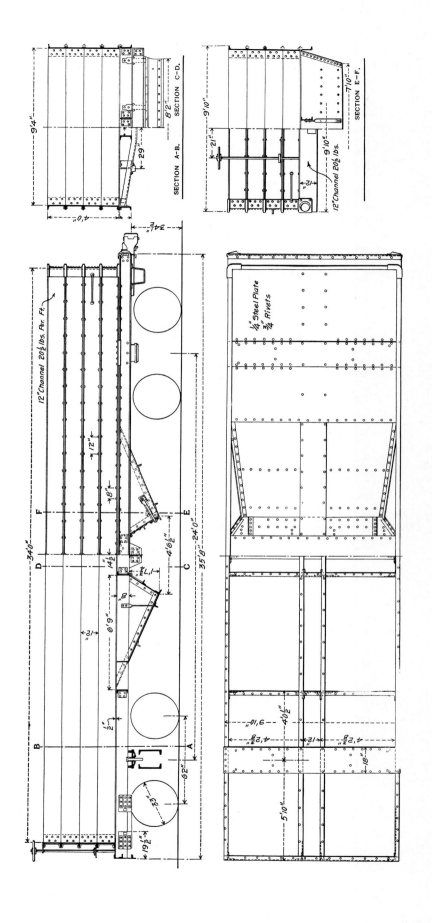

FIGURE 8.21

Elevation drawings for the Sterlingworth rolled beam, hopper-bottom gondola were presented in the *1903 Car Builders' Dictionary*. The car depicted here is dimensionally identical to the car produced for the O&W. The Sterlingworth Car Company was also marketing a rolled beam hopper of similar construction during this period, though it appears that neither car gained much favor. Records indicate that fewer than 100 of these gondolas were ever produced. [*Car Builders' Dictionary, 1903; Courtesy: Simmons-Boardman Publishing Corp.*]

**Hard Coal and Coal Cars**

FIGURE 8.22

The features of the Sterlingworth rolled beam hopper-bottom gondola can be seen in this early builder's photo. Sterlingworth displayed one of the O&W's rolled beam cars at the Master Car Builder's Association annual meeting in Saratoga, New York in 1901. The O&W purchased 25 of these cars and 25 pressed steel cars during the debate about which construction technique would prevail in steel car construction. The Delaware, Lackawanna & Western Railroad and the Mexican International Railway also used these cars. *[O&WRHS Archives]*

**Identification Guide for O&W Coal Cars**

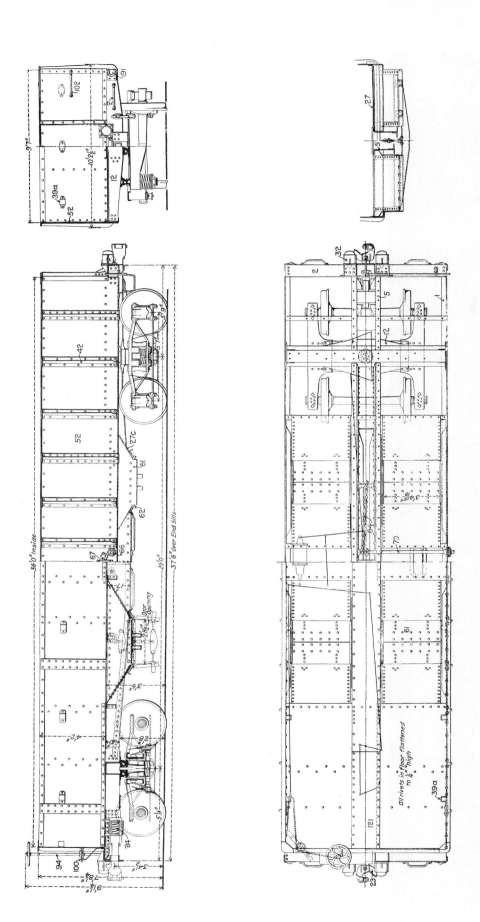

FIGURE 8.23

The 1903 *Car Builders' Dictionary* also provided these drawings of a Schoen Pressed Steel Hopper-Bottom Gondola as produced for the Bessemer & Lake Erie Railroad. No plans have been located for the car built by Pressed Steel Car Company for the O&W, but these plans do show the general construction techniques that would have been used in their construction. The O&W's car had an inside length of 34' 0" whereas the B&LE car shown here had an inside length of 36' 0." [*Car Builders' Dictionary, 1903; Courtesy: Simmons-Boardman Publishing Corp.*]

FIGURE 8.24
This is the only known picture of a pressed steel, hopper-bottom gondola in service on the O&W. It was taken in the Middletown yard in 1909, and it shows that car number 5712 has already been relegated to cinder service. The Vogt-style pressed steel arch bar trucks can be seen beneath the car. *[John Stellwagen collection; O&WRHS Archives, Enhanced by Carl A. Ohlson]*

## *6600-7700 Series, Wood, Hopper-Bottom Gondola*

**Nomenclature:** Gondola, Wood, Hopper-Bottom
**Manufacturers:**
Middletown shops (1900-1906)
AC&F (1901, 1902)
**Capacity:**
**Weight:** 85,000 pounds
**Volume:** 1275 cubic feet
**Cost per Car:** $804.35 (1901), $795.00 (1902)

**Inside Dimensions:**
**Length:** 34′ 0″
**Width:** 9′ 4½″
**Height:** 4′ 0″
**Outside Dimension:**
**Length:** 35′ 11″
**Width:** 10′ 0″
**Height:** 7′ 8″
**Weight Empty:** 35,000 pounds

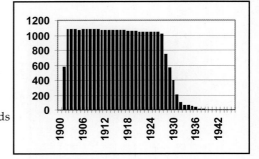

FIGURE 8.25
**Inventory of cars in 6600-7700 series**

**Modifications:** Steel underframes, 1000 cars, 1911-16

**Remarks:** The O&W built the first of this series, car number 7000, in its Middletown shops in 1900 similar to a design used by the Delaware & Hudson. A period comparison of the two cars is shown below. The O&W went on to built two more of these cars in its shops with a capacity of 85,000 pounds, and based upon their success, the O&W ordered 575 from American Car & Foundry in December 1900. In February 1902, it ordered another 500 cars from AC&F. It numbered the first purchase from AC&F 7101 to 7675, and the second purchase 6601-7100. The O&W numbered the cars it built in its company shops 7676 to 7689. The evidence is that car number 7000 became car number 7688 and the second car produced in 1900 became 7689. The balance of the cars built in the company shops were apparently replacements for other cars damaged or destroyed. This series was equipped with arch bar trucks, metal brake beams, and Miner draft gear. They were equipped with a door operating mechanism patented by George H. Lawrence, who worked in the Middletown shops. Beginning in 1912 and extending through 1915, the O&W added steel underframes to 1000 of these cars at a cost of $127.00 per car plus the cost of the steel underframe it purchased from American Car & Foundry for $145.25 each. Some of these cars with wood underframes served well into the 1920's, when they were retired.

| D&H. Car 17583. | Ny O&W Car 7000 |
|---|---|
| Weight 38,900 lbs. | 36,900 lbs |
| Capacity, 80,000 " | 80,000 " |
| 37′ 11½″ long over end sills | 38′ |
| 9′ wide — 4′ 3″ high floor to top of side. | 8′ 11½″ wide 4′ 4″ high from floor to top of side |
| American Steel Foundry Co. bolsters & transoms | Cloud Steel |
| Central brake beam, | Marden |
| Diamond S brake shoes, | Lappin |
| Westinghouse brakes | Wellington |
| Trojan couplers | Gould |
| Butler tandem draft rigging. | Thornburgh |
| McCord journal boxes & lids | McCord |
| Johnson hopper doors | Lawrence |
| Average load 42.6 tons | 43 1/10 tons |
| Maximum load 44.3 " | 45 4/10 " |
| 1750 in use on D&H R.R. | Sample Car |

(Copied Mch. 28/00)

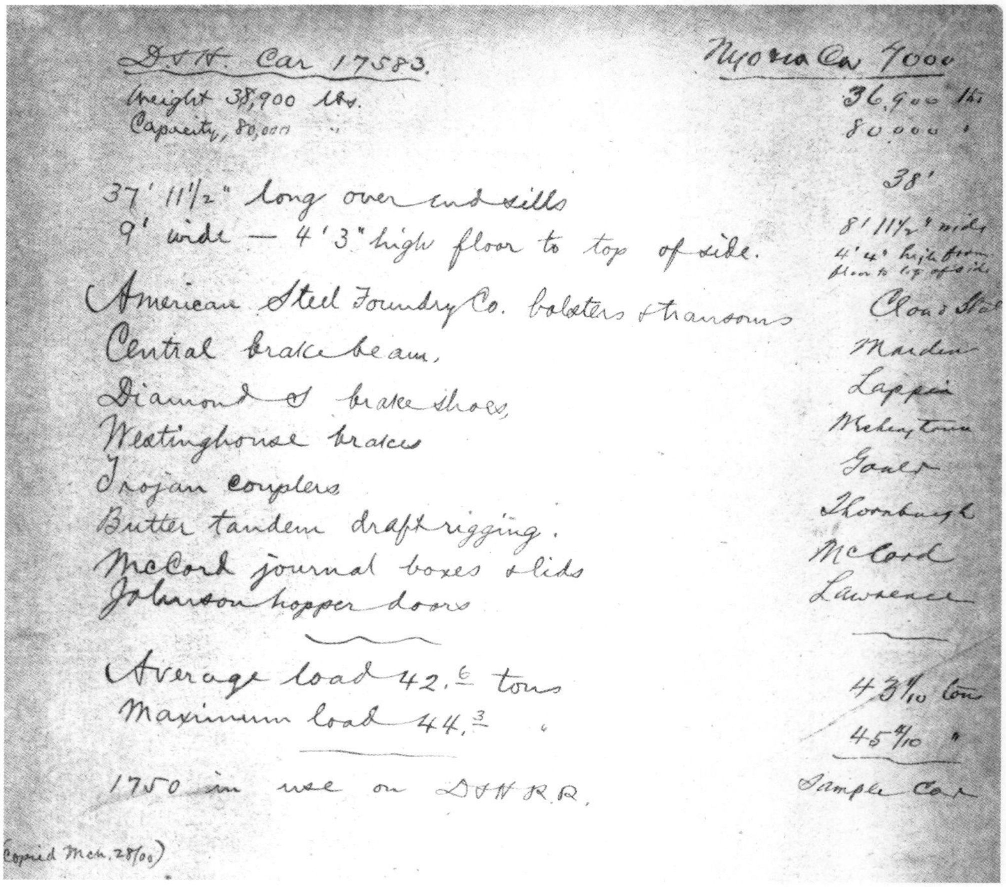

FIGURE 8.26
**This memo, dated March 28, 1900, compares the O&W's car number 7000 with D&H car number 17583.** ***[O&WRHS Archives]***

FIGURE 8.27

The first cars in the 6600-7700 series were built in the Middletown shops in 1900. In December 1900, the O&W purchased 575 cars in this series, numbered 7101-7675, from American Car & Foundry. In February 1902, it purchased 500 more, numbered 6601-7100. Car number 7495, shown above, was part of the first lot, and car number 6625 was part of the second. The O&W built a total of 39 of these cars in its Middletown shops. It numbered fourteen of those cars 7676-7689. The remainder were used as replacements for other cars. From 1911-1914, the Middletown shops added steel underframes to 1000 of these cars because the wood underframes could not withstand the handling in mixed trains with the heavier cars that were being introduced during this period. [Andrew Merrillees Collection; National Archives of Canada/PA-205900; PA-205901]

## 15000-16350 Series, Composite Wood and Steel, 40-Ton Hopper

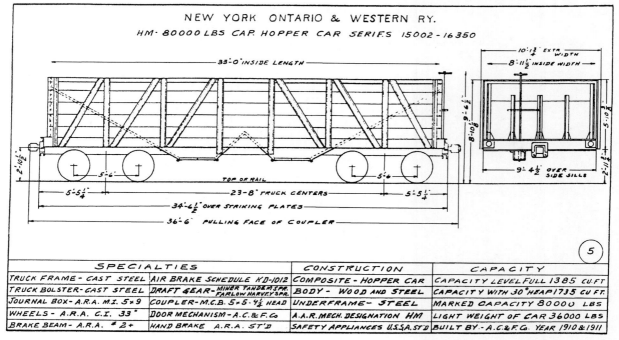

**FIGURE 8.28**
**Shop drawing of 15000 series, composite, 40-ton hopper** *[Walter Kierzkowski Collection]*

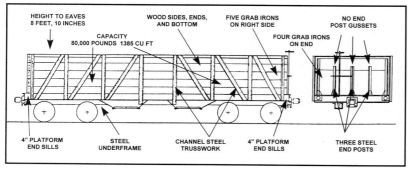

**FIGURE 8.29**
**Spotter's Guide to the 15000-16350 series**

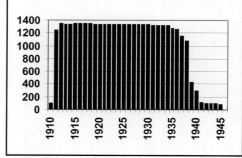

**FIGURE 8.30**
**Inventory of 15000-16350 series**

### Key Facts

**Nomenclature:** Hopper, Composite, 40-Ton
**O&W Procurement**
    **Date(s) Procured:** 1910-1911
    **Source:** Middletown Shops/AC&F
    **Quantity:** 500/850
    **Cost per Car:** $933 (Middletown Shops average),
      $965 (AC&F average)

**Modifications:** None.

**Remarks:** These were the first true hoppers owned by the O&W. They were based upon the design introduced by C.A. Seley of the Norfolk & Western Railway in 1898 and came to be known as "Seley hoppers." Cars 15001 to 15500 were built in the Middletown shops in 1910-11. Cars 15501 to 16000 were purchased from American Car & Foundry in 1910 and delivered in 1911. Cars 16001 to 16350 were purchased from AC&F in 1911. The cars built in the Middletown shops were equipped with Andrews "L-Section" trucks. The cars purchased from AC&F were equipped with Gould trucks. All cars were equipped with spring draft gear with Harvey friction springs to dampen the action. Cars 15001 to 15900 were equipped with Miner draft gear; cars 15901 to 16350 were equipped with Farlow draft gear. All cars were also equipped with Barber roller side bearings. Records show that these cars were so badly beaten up by the end of the 1930's that the O&W started a wholesale retirement of the fleet. The last car was retired in 1946.

FIGURE 8.31

Car number 15029 was one of the first "Seley hoppers" put into service on the O&W. Car numbers 15001-15500 were built in the Middletown shops in 1910 and 1911. They came equipped with Miner spring draft gear with Harvey friction springs and Andrews L-section cast-steel truck side frames. Note the weight of this car built in Middletown versus the two cars in the next succeeding pages built by American Car & Foundry. [Courtesy: Bob's Photo]

FIGURE 8.32

This is an American Car & Foundry builder's photo of car number 15500 as it was released from that company's Berwick, Pennsylvania, plant as part of the first lot of these cars that the O&W purchased from that company. Car numbers 15501-15900 came equipped with Miner draft gear with Harvey friction springs and Gould cast-steel truck side frames. Car numbers 15901-16000 were equipped with Farlow spring draft gear with Harvey friction springs. This photo of the left side of the car shows the details of the door operating mechanism. The car number on this photo seems to be an anomaly. O&W archival records show that car numbers 15001-15500 were built in Middletown, and car numbers 15501-16350 were built by American Car & Foundry. *[American Car & Foundry photo; from the John W. Barriger III National Railroad Library at the University of Missouri-St. Louis]*

Hard Coal and Coal Cars

FIGURE 8.33
This AC&F builder's photo shows car number 16055, which was part of the O&W's second purchase of "Seley hoppers" from that company in 1911. These cars were numbered 16001-16350 and came equipped with Farlow spring draft gear with Harvey friction springs and Gould cast truck side frames. It was also built to comply with the 1911 ICC safety appliance standards. Note the difference in the grab irons between this and the earlier versions of these cars. "NYO&W" is clearly visible on the inside of the cast iron wheels. [American Car & Foundry photo; from the John W. Barriger III National Railroad Library at the University of Missouri-St. Louis]

### 6200-6399 Series, Composite Wood and Steel, 40-Ton Gondola

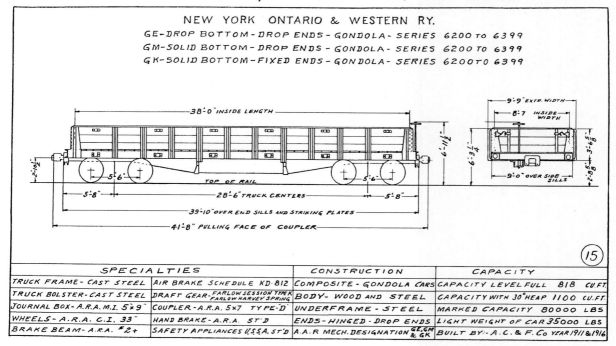

**FIGURE 8.34**
**Shop drawing of 6200-6399 series, composite, 40-ton gondola** *[Walter Kierzkowski Collection]*

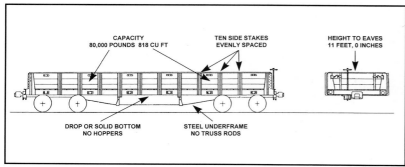

FIGURE 8.35
**Spotter's Guide to the 6200-6399 series**

FIGURE 8.36
**Inventory of 6200-6399 series**

### *Key Facts*

**Nomenclature:** Gondola, Composite, 40-Ton
**O&W Procurement**
    **Date(s) Procured:** 1911, 1916
    **Source:** American Car & Foundry (New)
    **Quantity:** 100, 100
    **Cost per Car:** $868.66 (1911), $1092.75 (1916)

**Modifications:** As built, these cars had drop bottoms and drop ends. Over time, the O&W modified some of these cars to eliminate the drop bottoms and/or the drop ends. By the 1940's, it was converting them all to fixed bottoms.

**Remarks:** The O&W purchased the first 100 of these composite gondolas from American Car & Foundry in 1911. As built, they had drop bottoms and drop ends. In 1916, the railroad purchased 100 more from AC&F. The first 100 cars purchased were equipped with Farlow spring draft gear with Harvey friction springs to dampen the spring action. They were also equipped with Gould cast-steel side frames, Barber roller side bearings and metal brake beams. The second purchase came equipped with Andrews "T-Section" cast-steel side frames, Barber rollers, Sessions friction draft gear with Farlow attaching mechanism, and metal brake beams. These proved to be versatile cars indeed, seeing service in a wide variety of roles right up until 1957.

FIGURE 8.37
(Top to Bottom)—At the top is car number 6262 as she leaves the Berwyck Works of American Car & Foundry in 1911. At the bottom, car number 6347 as she leaves the factory in 1916. Note the differences between these two cars in the same series produced five years apart, including the new paint scheme mandated by the M.C.B.A. The earlier car is riding on Gould trucks; the later, Andrews "T-Section trucks." The drop door operating mechanisms are clearly visible on the sides of the cars. These cars were originally equipped with drop bottoms and drop ends, but during their lives, many would have their drop bottoms replaced with solid bottoms, and others would have their drop ends replaced with solid ends, as well. These cars would do yeoman's service right up until the final days of the O&W. [American Car & Foundry photo; from the John W. Barriger III National Railroad Library at the University of Missouri-St. Louis]

**Identification Guide for O&W Coal Cars**

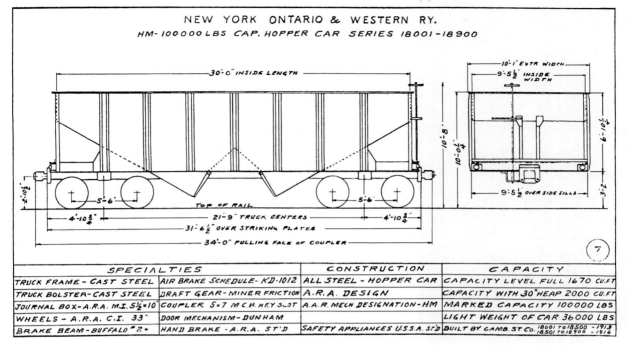

**FIGURE 8.38**
**Shop drawing of 18000-18900 series, 50-ton steel hopper** *[Walter Kierzkowski Collection]*

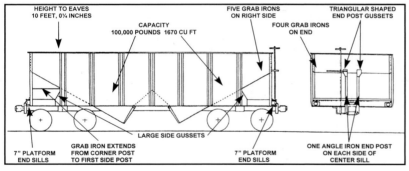

**FIGURE 8.39**
**Spotter's Guide to the 18000-18900 series**

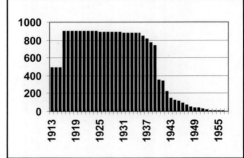

**FIGURE 8.40**
**Inventory of cars in 18000-18900 series**

### Key Facts

**Nomenclature:** Hopper, Steel, 50-Ton
**O&W Procurement**
    **Date(s) Procured:** 1913, 1916
    **Source:** Cambria Steel Company (New)
    **Quantity:** 500 (1913); 400 (1916)
    **Cost per Car:** $1012 (1913); $1135/$1150 (1916)

**Modifications:** In 1939-40, the O&W modified 399 of these cars to increase their capacity by raising their sides and ends one foot. The modified cars were renumbered into the 11000 series, causing the sharp drop in inventory seen in the chart above. Some of the remaining cars in the 18000 series received power hand brakes and Wine door locks in the 1940's.

**Remarks:** These were the first all-steel hoppers bought by the O&W, and they were the only all-steel hoppers that the O&W ever purchased new. As such, they were also some of the most enduring hoppers on the railroad. They were purchased from Cambria Steel Company in two separate buys in 1913 and 1916. All were equipped with Andrews "T-Section" cast steel side frames and Barber roller side bearings. Cars 18001-18500 were equipped with Miner A-24-A friction draft gear. One hundred of the cars in the second buy were equipped with the same draft gear, and three hundred were equipped with the more expensive Sessions draft gear with Farlow attaching mechanism. This accounts for the two different prices in the 1916 buy.

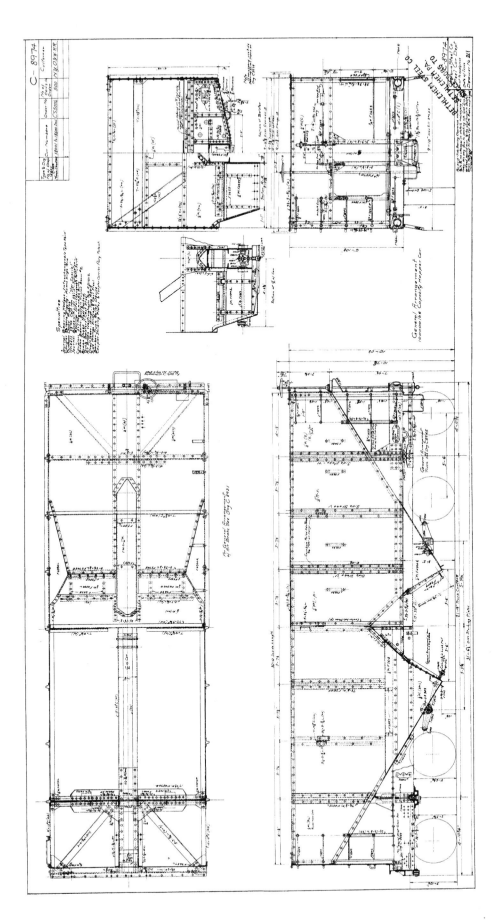

FIGURE 8.41
Original elevation drawings for the 18000 series, all-steel hopper produced by Cambria Steel Company in 1913. [Courtesy: Johnstown American Corporation]

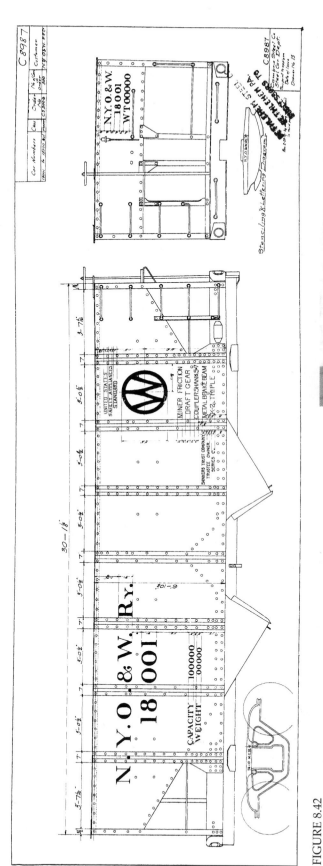

FIGURE 8.42
Original stenciling scheme for the 18000 series, all-steel hoppers purchased from
Cambria Steel in 1913. [Courtesy: Johnstown America Corporation]

FIGURE 8.43
This is the only known photograph of an 18000 series hop-
per in its original stenciling scheme as shown in Figure 8.42.
[Allan F. Seebach, Jr. Collection]

FIGURE 8.44

Car 18134 was produced in 1913 by the Cambria Steel Company in the first of the O&W's two purchases of new, all-steel hoppers from that company. She's seen here on a siding in the late 1940's, still wearing her original, Andrews "T-section" trucks and Dunham door operating mechanisms, though she has been upgraded with an Ajax power hand brake. She also shows one of the variations of the O&W's lettering and stenciling preferences during this period, in this case placing a period after the "O" and the "W." [Sterling Kimball Collection; O&WRHS Archives]

## 17000-17039 Series, 55-Ton Steel Hopper

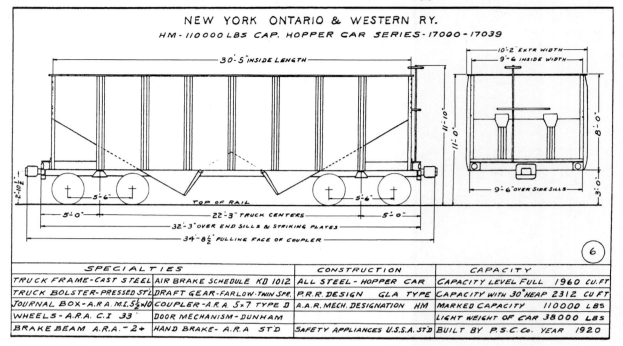

**FIGURE 8.45**
**Shop drawing of 17000-17039 series, 55-ton steel hopper** [*Walter Kierzkowski Collection*]

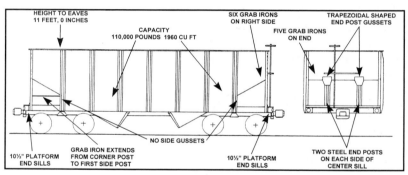

**FIGURE 8.46**
**Spotter's Guide to the 17000-17039 series**

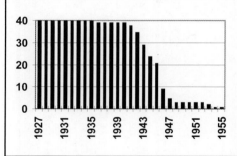

**FIGURE 8.47**
**Inventory of cars in 17000-17039 series**

### Key Facts

| | |
|---|---|
| **Nomenclature:** Hopper, Steel, 55-Ton | **Modifications:** None |
| **O&W Procurement** | |
|    **Date(s) Procured:** 1926 | |
|    **Source:** Struthers Furnace Company (Second-hand) | |
|    **Quantity:** 40 | |
|    **Cost per Car:** $1067.25 | |

**Remarks:** The O&W purchased these cars from the receiver for the Struthers Furnace Company in 1926. Struthers had purchased 60 of these cars new from the Pressed Steel Car Company in 1920. Remarks by railroad officials indicate that they were very pleased with the performance of these cars, which were essentially GLa cars with their sides raised by eleven inches to increase their capacity. It appears that these may have provided the pattern for the 10500 series.

FIGURE 8.48

The O&W's 17000 series consisted of 40 all-steel hoppers that it purchased second-hand from the receiver for Struthers Furnace Company in 1926. This builder's photo shows those cars as they were built by the Pressed Steel Car Company in 1920. Note that this is a GLa-type car with higher sides to allow greater capacity. This car was eleven inches taller than a standard GLa and had a capacity of 1960 cubic feet versus the 1683 cubic feet of a standard GLa. [Pressed Steel Car Company photo; D. K. Retterer Collection]

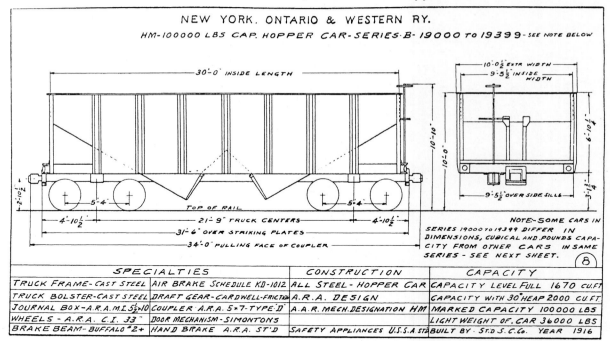

**FIGURE 8.49**
**Shop drawing of 19000 series, 50-ton steel hopper** *[Walter Kierzkowski Collection]*

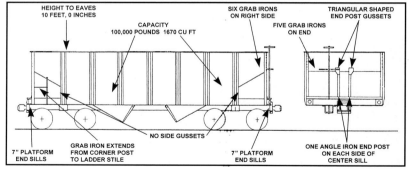

**FIGURE 8.50**
**Spotter's Guide to the 19000-19399 series 50-ton hopper**

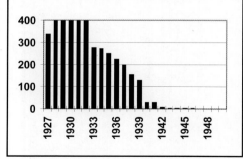

**FIGURE 8.51**
**Inventory of 50-ton cars in 19000-19399 series**

## Key Facts

**Nomenclature:** Hopper, Steel, 50-Ton
**O&W Procurement**
    **Date(s) Procured:** 1928
    **Source:** Bethlehem Steel Company (Second-Hand)
    **Quantity:** 233
    **Cost per Car:** $743.48 (average)

**Modifications:** In 1939-40, the O&W modified 101 of these cars by raising their sides and ends one foot to increase their capacity. These increased capacity cars were renumbered into the 12500 series.

**Remarks:** In 1928, the O&W purchased 400 second-hand hoppers from Bethlehem Steel. This purchase included hoppers of two different dimensions built for Lackawanna Steel in 1916-17. The smaller cars were built by Standard Steel and had a capacity of 1670 cubic feet. The larger cars were built by AC&F and had a capacity of 1800 cubic feet. When these cars arrived on the O&W, the railroad rated them both at a capacity of 100,000 pounds and accounted for them as a single block. Beginning in 1932 the O&W began a process of identifying the larger AC&F cars in this series as a separate block, rated at a capacity of 110,000 pounds. By 1938, it had identified 167 cars as having that higher capacity. The conversion of these cars is reflected in the lower quantities of the inventory of 50-ton cars in the figure above. The remaining 233 cars, which are described on this page, were the 100,000 pound capacity hoppers built by Standard Steel Company in 1916.

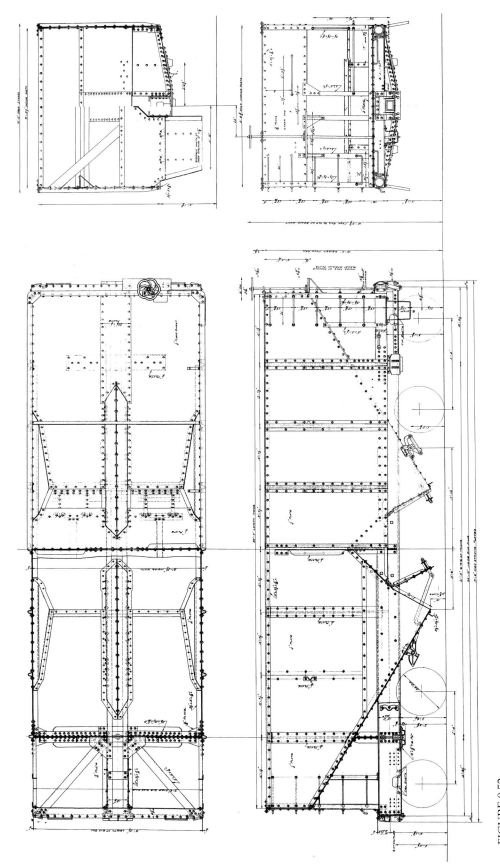

FIGURE 8.52
Standard Steel Company built 700 of these 100,000 pound, all-steel hopper for the Lackawanna Steel Company in 1916. In 1928, the O&W bought 233 of these second-hand hoppers from Bethlehem Steel, which had absorbed Lackawanna Steel in the early 1920's. A builder's photo of this car is shown in Figure 7.25 on page 111. [Pennsylvania State Archives]

## 19000-19399 Series, 55-Ton Steel Hopper

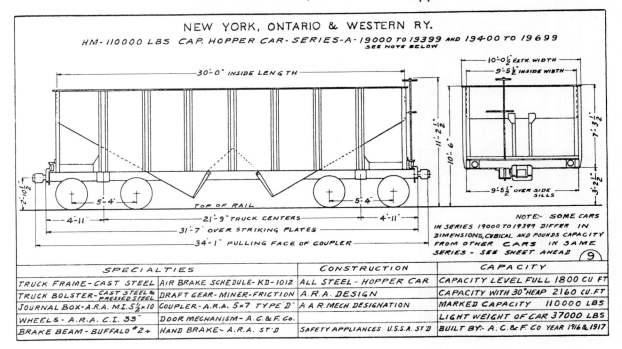

**FIGURE 8.53**
**Shop drawing of 19000 series, 55-ton steel hopper** *[Walter Kierzkowski Collection]*

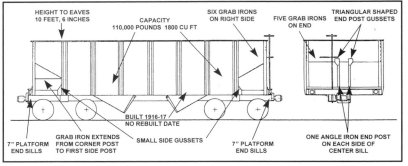

**FIGURE 8.54**
**Spotter's Guide to the 19000-19399 series 55-ton hopper**

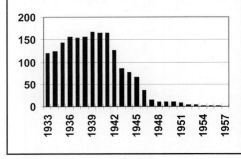

**FIGURE 8.55**
**Inventory of 55-ton cars in 19000-19399 series**

### Key Facts

**Nomenclature:** Hopper, Steel, 55-Ton
**O&W Procurement**
    **Date(s) Procured:** 1928
    **Source:** Bethlehem Steel Company (Second-Hand)
    **Quantity:** 167
    **Cost per Car:** $743.48

**Modifications:** Uncertain; see remarks

**Remarks:** In January 1928, the O&W purchased 400 second-hand hoppers from Bethlehem Steel. This purchase included hoppers of two different dimensions built for Lackawanna Steel in 1916-17. The smaller cars were built by Standard Steel and had a capacity of 1670 cubic feet. The larger cars were built by AC&F and had a capacity of 1800 cubic feet. When these cars arrived on the O&W, the railroad rated them all at a nominal capacity of 100,000 pounds. Beginning in 1932 the O&W began a process of rating the larger AC&F cars at a nominal capacity of 110,000 pounds, and by 1938, it had identified 167 of them as having that higher capacity. It is uncertain what the O&W was doing to raise the capacity of these cars. It may have been nothing more than restenciling the cars to the higher capacity, since their cubic volume and journal size would have permitted this weight. However, the rate at which these cars were recategorized to the higher capacity suggests that the O&W was doing something more substantial before raising these cars' nominal capacity.

FIGURE 8.56

The 19000–19399 series was a mix of cars produced by Standard Steel and American Car & Foundry for Lackawanna Steel in 1916 and 1917. Shown here is a builder's photo of the cars produced by American Car & Foundry, which had a higher cubic capacity than those produced by the Standard Steel Car Company. The car here is riding on Andrews T-Section cast steel sideframe trucks, which the O&W had installed on its 18000 series. The car numbers of the higher capacity cars included: 19002, 19007, 19008, 19010, 19013, 19014, 19015, 19019, 19021, 19024, 19025, 19026, 19027, 19038, 19041, 19053, 19055, 19056, 19057, 19059, 19063, 19069, 19071, 19075, 19076, 19083, 19088, 19090, 19097, 19099, 19100, 19104, 19105, 19108, 19110, 19114, 19115, 19120, 19121, 19122, 19123, 19124, 19125, 19127, 19128, 19129, 19131, 19132, 19133, 19135, 19136, 19142, 19147, 19149, 19153, 19156, 19159, 19165, 19166, 19167, 19169, 19170, 19173, 19174, 19190, 19192, 19194, 19197, 19206, 19207, 19208, 19216, 19217, 19218, 19219, 19221, 19223, 19224, 19225, 19226, 19228, 19229, 19230, 19232, 19235, 19236, 19238, 19240, 19241, 19245, 19250, 19254, 19259, 19262, 19264, 19265, 19267, 19269, 19273, 19274, 19275, 19276, 19278, 19282, 19283, 19291, 19292, 19296, 19297, 19309, 19312, 19317, 19318, 19319, 19321, 19324, 19329, 19331, 19333, 19335, 19337, 19339, 19341, 19343, 19344, 19345, 19350, 19352, 19356, 19357, 19358, 19359, 19360, 19363, 19369, 19371, 19375, 19377, 19379, 19380, 19381, 19385, 19388, 19391, 19394, 19395. Source: *The Official Railway Equipment Register, April 1938, p. 314. [American Car & Foundry photo; from the John W. Barriger III National Railroad Library at the University of Missouri–St. Louis]*

## 19400-19699 Series, 55-Ton Steel Hopper

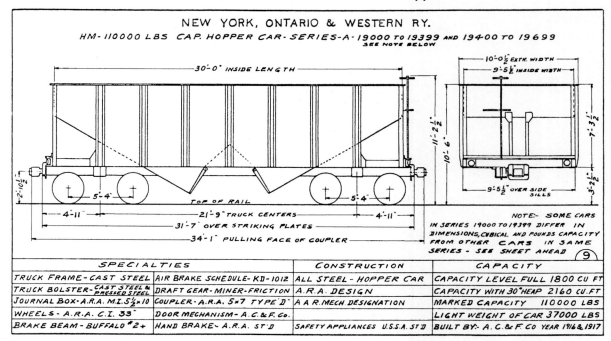

**FIGURE 8.57**
**Shop drawing of 19000 series, 55-ton steel hopper** [*Walter Kierzkowski Collection*]

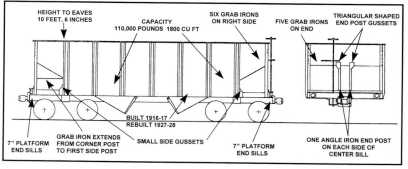

**FIGURE 8.58**
**Spotter's Guide to the 19400-19699 series 55-ton hopper**

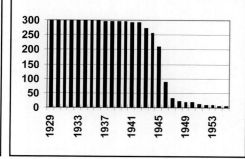

**FIGURE 8.59**
**Inventory of cars in 19400-19699 series**

### Key Facts

**Nomenclature:** Hopper, Steel, 55-Ton
**O&W Procurement**
    **Date(s) Procured:** 1928
    **Source:** Bethlehem Steel Company (Rebuilt)
    **Quantity:** 300
    **Cost per Car:** $827.00

**Modifications:** None

**Remarks:** In December 1928, the O&W purchased another 300 second-hand hoppers from Bethlehem Steel. This series was built by American Car & Foundry for Lackawanna Steel in 1916-17, and they were all rebuilt by Bethlehem Steel before being shipped to the O&W. As a result, the O&W paid about $100 more per car for this purchase than it did for the cars it purchased from Bethlehem Steel earlier in the year. However, that money may have been well spent, because these cars entered service immediately at their full nominal capacity of 110,000 pounds. All cars came equipped with cast-steel side frames. The builder's photo and the picture of 19553 in Figure 8.60 suggest that these were probably Andrews "T-Section" side frames.

FIGURE 8.60
O&W hopper 19553 awaits weighing outside the Middletown shops in 1934 after being outshopped and freshly painted. This series was built by American Car & Foundry in 1916-1917 and was rebuilt by Bethlehem Steel before being purchased by the O&W at the end of 1928. The built and rebuilt dates can be seen in the sixth panel from the left on the car. The car is equipped with Andrews T-section trucks. The O&W paid $827.75 apiece for the cars in this series, 19400-19699. *[Jeff Otto Collection]*

**Identification Guide for O&W Coal Cars**

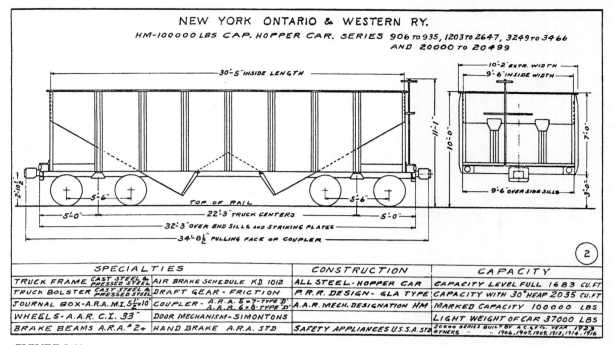

**FIGURE 8.61**
**Shop drawing of GLa-type, 50-ton steel hopper** *[Walter Kierzkowski Collection]*

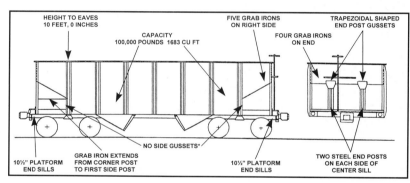

**FIGURE 8.62**
**Spotter's Guide to GLa-type hopper**

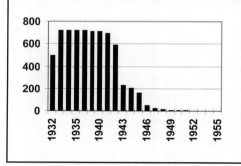

**FIGURE 8.63**
**Inventory of GLa-type cars**

*Key Facts*

**Nomenclature:** Hopper, Steel, 50-Ton
**O&W Procurement**
   **Date(s) Procured:** 1932/1933
   **Source:** PCC/Westmoreland Coal (Second-Hand)
   **Quantity:** 500/220
   **Cost per Car:** $625/$550

**Modifications:** In 1939, the O&W modified one of these cars to increase its capacity by raising the sides and ends by one foot. The modified car was renumbered as O&W 10500.

**Remarks:** In a desperate need for capacity, the O&W turned to two coal companies for second-hand hoppers. In 1932, it assumed the remaining lease payments for 500 used hoppers from the Pennsylvania Coal & Coke Company that were built by AC&F in 1923 based upon the PRR's Gla design. These cars were delivered in January 1933. In April 1933, it purchased 500 second-hand hoppers that it had been leasing from the Westmoreland Coal Company, 220 of which were of the GLa design. The O&W was so anxious to put the Westmoreland cars into service that it did not repaint or renumber those hoppers. It simply painted over the Westmoreland reporting marks, painted in its own, and continued to use the Westmoreland numbers. These cars had been built over a ten year period from 1906-1916, mostly by Cambria Steel Car Company. The shop drawing states that some of these cars were equipped with pressed steel side frames. This is probably a reference to the Symington side frames with which some of the PCC cars were equipped and are shown in the accompanying builder's photo.

FIGURE 8.64
Former Westmoreland Coal GLa number 1250 is seen on Long Island in this 1939 photo. The car has been repainted in O&W livery, and a second grab iron has been added on the left end of the car in compliance with safety appliance standards. *[Ron Ziel Collection; Courtesy Richard Burg]*

FIGURE 8.65
This photo of car number 2045 in cinder service provides a good view of the B end of a GLa hopper. *[Walter Kierzkowski Collection]*

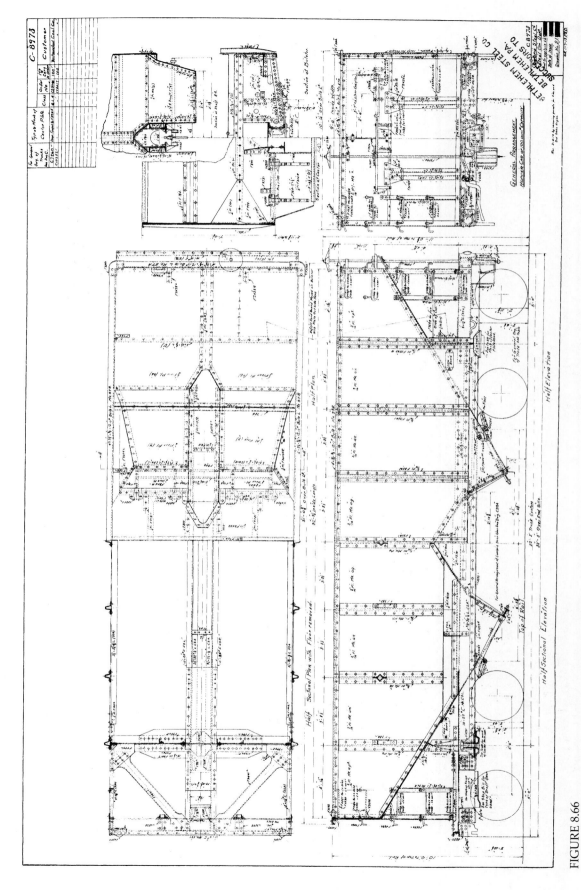

FIGURE 8.66

Original elevation drawing for GLa-type car produced by Cambria Steel for the Westmoreland Coal Company in 1913-1915. Cambria Steel produced two separate lots of 100 GLa-type cars each for Westmoreland using this drawing. The O&W purchased a number of these cars second-hand from Westmoreland in 1933. [Courtesy: Johnstown America Corporation]

Hard Coal and Coal Cars

FIGURE 8.67

In 1923, American Car & Foundry produced 1000 GLa-type cars for the Pennsylvania Coal & Coke Company. In 1933, the Lehigh Valley and the O&W each bought 500 of those cars second hand from PCC for $625 each. This is the AC&F builder's photo for those cars. Of special interest are the Symington wrought steel trucks seen on the car in this photo. It is not certain whether all of these cars were equipped with these trucks, and if so, whether any of these trucks made it to the O&W. The presence of these trucks, though, may explain the remark in the shop drawing of some of the GLa's being equipped with pressed steel trucks, since it's unlikely that any pressed steel trucks from the turn of the century survived through the 1940's when the shop drawings were made. *[Andrew Merrillees Collection; National Archives of Canada/PA-188065]*

**Identification Guide for O&W Coal Cars**

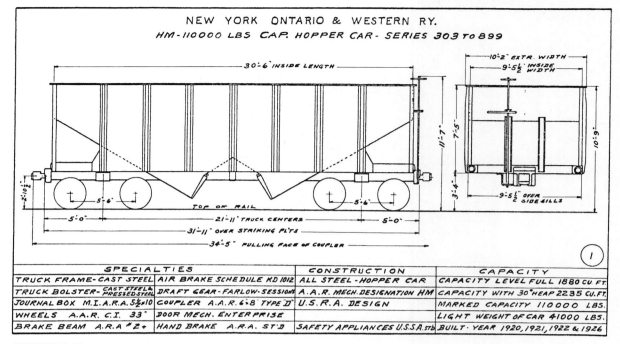

**FIGURE 8.68**
**Shop drawing of USRA-type, 55-ton steel hopper** *[Walter Kierzkowski Collection]*

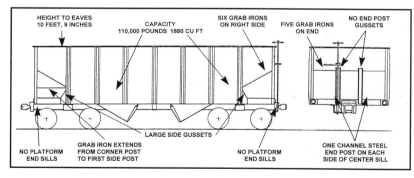

**FIGURE 8.69**
**Spotter's Guide to USRA-type hoppers**

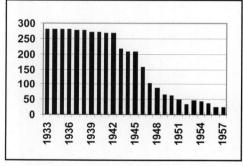

**FIGURE 8.70**
**Inventory of USRA-type cars**

## Key Facts

**Nomenclature:** Hopper, Steel, 55-Ton
**O&W Procurement**
    **Date(s) Procured:** 1933/1951
    **Source:** Westmoreland Coal/New Haven RR
    **Quantity:** 280/21
    **Cost per Car:** $550/$1000

**Modifications:** In 1933, when the O&W received the 280 USRA hoppers from Westmoreland Coal, it rated 124 as having 110,000 pound capacity and 156 as having only 100,000 pound capacity. Over the next six years, it gradually upgraded them all to the higher capacity. It is uncertain what, if any, modifications the O&W was making to achieve this increase, though Figure 7.31 may provide a clue.

**Remarks:** In April 1933, the O&W purchased 500 second-hand hoppers it had been leasing from the Westmoreland Coal Company—220 GLa-type hoppers and 280 USRA-type hoppers. The O&W was so anxious to put these cars into service that it simply painted over the Westmoreland reporting marks and painted in its own, keeping the Westmoreland car numbers as seen in the photo at Figure 7.30. Most of these cars were probably equipped with USRA Andrews "U-Section" cast-steelside frames. In 1953, the O&W found it necessary to purchase 21 USRA-type hoppers equipped with "AB" brakes and Dalman trucks from the New Haven, because none of its other hoppers were fit for interchange service.

**FIGURE 8.71**

These photos show the variety of stenciling schemes that the O&W used on the twenty-one USRA hoppers that it bought from the New Haven Railroad in 1953. The O&W purchased these cars because none of its other hoppers were fit for interchange service because they lacked AB brake systems. These cars came equipped with AB brakes, power hand brakes, Dalman AAR standard trucks, and Wine door locks. The evidence indicates that these cars were built in the New Haven's own shops in 1929 and 1930. *[Sterling Kimball Collection; O&WRHS Archives]*

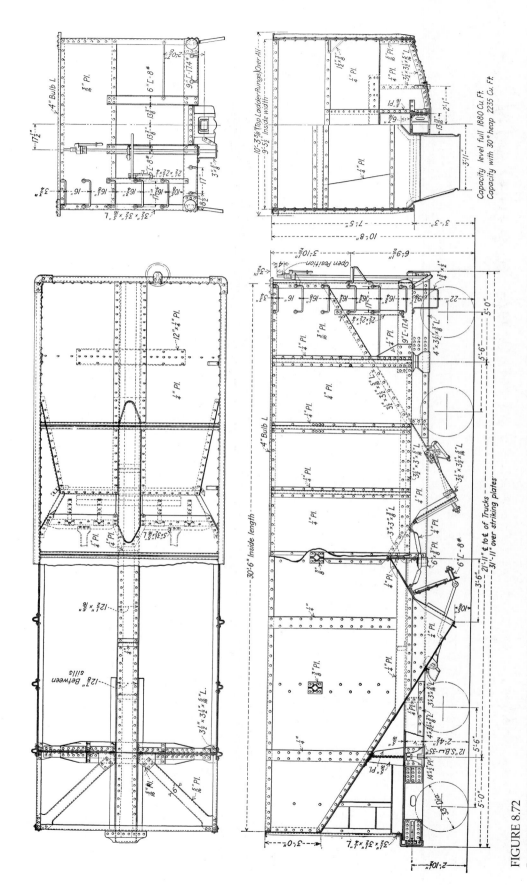

FIGURE 8.72

In 1918, within months of its being established, the United States Railroad Administration (USRA) adopted standard designs for freight cars to facilitate production and repairs during World War I. Included among these designs was the 55-ton, all-steel hopper car shown here. The O&W purchased 280 of these USRA hoppers second-hand from the Westmoreland Coal Company in 1933. In 1953, the O&W purchased another 21 cars of this design from the New Haven Railroad. [*Car Builders' Dictionary and Cyclopedia, 1919; Courtesy: Simmons-Boardman Publishing Corp.*]

Hard Coal and Coal Cars

FIGURE 8.73

This photo, taken in the early 1950's, shows one of the few remaining USRA Hoppers that the O&W purchased from Westmoreland Coal in 1933. It's still equipped with her Enterprise door operating mechanisms, K-style brakes, and vertical hand brake shaft. Note the way the car number is stenciled. [*Sterling Kimball Collection; O&WRHS Archives*]

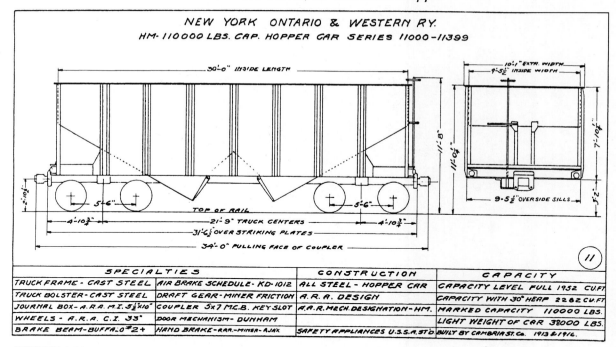

FIGURE 8.74
**Shop drawing of 11000-11399 series, 55-ton steel hopper** *[Walter Kierzkowski Collection]*

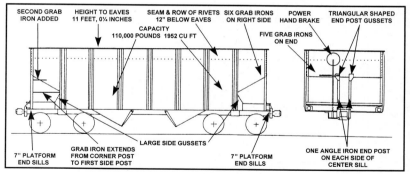

FIGURE 8.75
**Spotter's Guide to the 11000-11399 series**

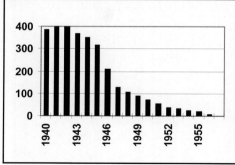

FIGURE 8.76
**Inventory of 11000-11399 series**

## *Key Facts*

**Nomenclature:** Hopper, Steel, 55-Ton
**O&W Procurement**
    **Date(s) Procured:** 1939-40
    **Source:** Cambria Steel Company (new)
    **Quantity:** 399
    **Cost per Car:** $1071.67 (average, when new)

**Modifications:** The 11000 series consists of cars from the 18000 series that were modified in the Middletown shops to increase their capacity by raising their sides and ends by one foot. The cars also received power hand brakes. The cost per car for these modifications was $115.

**Remarks:** The 11100 series was produced by raising the sides and ends of the 18000 series, 100,000 pound cars by one foot to increase their capacity to 1952 cubic feet and 110,000 pounds. In 1939, the O&W petitioned the bankruptcy court to increase the capacity of 500 of its existing steel hoppers to reduce the per diem charges it was paying to other railroads. In the petition, the O&W estimated that raising the sides and ends of 500 cars by one foot would produce additional capacity equivalent to 100 hoppers. It estimated the total cost not to exceed $40,000, and it would recover that cost in reduced per diem charges within two years. The O&W subsequently filed a petition to add power hand brakes and regulators because of the additional weight of the cars. In the process of upgrading these cars, some were equipped with Wine door locks. Similar modifications were made to 101 of the cars in the 19000 series to produce the 12500 series.

FIGURE 8.77
This undated photo shows an 11000 Series Hopper as it would have appeared in the mid to late 1940's. Note that the car still has Andrews "T-Section" trucks with cast iron wheels. This car is not equipped with Wine door locks, so it is probably still equipped with its original Dunham door operating mechanism. [Al Patterson Collection; Courtesy: Keith Sirman]

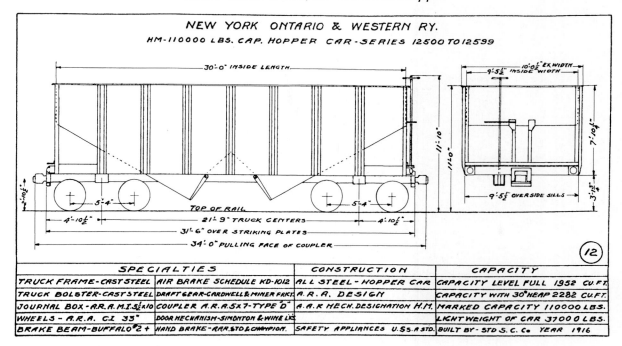

**FIGURE 8.78**
**Shop drawing of 12500-12599 series, 55-ton steel hopper** *[Walter Kierzkowski Collection]*

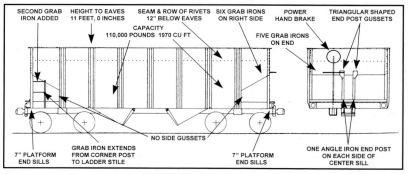

**FIGURE 8.79**
**Spotter's Guide to the 12500-12599 series**

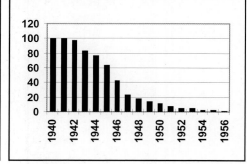

**FIGURE 8.80**
**Inventory of 12500-12599 series**

## Key Facts

**Nomenclature:** Hopper, Steel, 55-Ton
**O&W Procurement**
    **Date(s) Procured:** 1939-40
    **Source:** Bethlehem Steel (Second-Hand)
    **Quantity:** 101
    **Cost per Car:** $743.48 (average, when purchased)

**Modifications:** The 12500 series consists of the Standard Steel Car Company, 50-ton cars from the 19000 series that were modified in the Middletown shops to increase their capacity by raising their sides and ends by one foot. The cars also received power hand brakes. The cost per car for these modifications was $115.

**Remarks:** The 12500 series was produced by raising the sides and ends of the 19000 series, 100,000 pound cars that had been purchased second-hand from Bethlehem Steel in 1928 by one foot to increase their capacity to 1952 cubic feet and 110,000 pounds. In 1939, the O&W petitioned the bankruptcy court to increase the capacity of 500 of its existing steel hoppers to reduce the per diem charges it was paying to other railroads. In the petition, the O&W estimated that raising the sides and ends of 500 cars by one foot would produce additional capacity equivalent to 100 hoppers. It estimated the total cost not to exceed $40,000, and it would recover that cost in reduced per diem charges within two years. The O&W subsequently filed a petition to add power hand brakes and regulators because of the additional weight of the cars. In the process of upgrading these cars, some were equipped with Wine door locks. Similar modifications were made to 399 of the cars in the 18000 series to produce the 11000 series.

FIGURE 8.81
A car in the 12500 series is seen here in this undated photo. Note the Wine door locks and Ajax power hand brakes. It's still riding on Andrews T-Section trucks. [Sterling Kimball Collection; O&WRHS Archives]

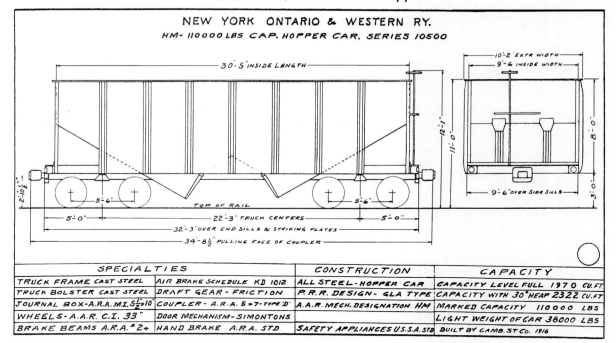

FIGURE 8.82
**Shop drawing of 10500 series, 55-ton steel hopper** *[Created by author]*

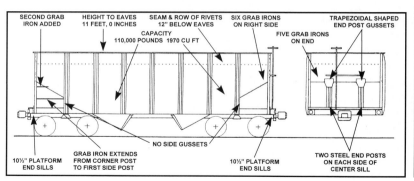

FIGURE 8.83
**Spotter's Guide to the 10500 series**

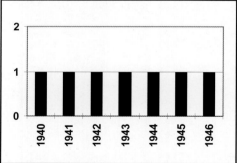

FIGURE 8.84
**Inventory of 10500 series**

## Key Facts

**Nomenclature:** Hopper, Steel, 55-Ton
**O&W Procurement**
  **Date(s) Procured:** 1939
  **Source:** Westmoreland Coal (Second-Hand)
  **Quantity:** 1
  **Cost per Car:** $550 (average)

**Modifications:** Car number 10500 is a GLa-type car that was modified in the Middletown Shops to increase its capacity by raising its sides and ends by one foot. It provided the pattern for the 11000 and 12500 series.

**Remarks:** The 10500 series is a standard GLa car with its sides raised one foot. It appears that the O&W's intention was to raise the sides on 300 of its GLa cars when it received permission from the bankruptcy court to increase the capacity of its coal car fleet. This choice was probably based upon the better condition of these cars and the success that it had with its 17000 series, high-capacity GLa cars. The first car that the O&W modified with raised sides was one of the GLa cars that it purchased from Westmoreland Coal, probably out of its 3249 series. The O&W must not have liked the results, because car number 10500 was the only GLa so modified, and thus it had the distinction of becoming a series of one until it was retired in 1946. No photo of this car has been found.

One of the important tasks facing the railroads as they began interchanging freight cars was developing a common set of terms with which they could identify the parts and the locations of component parts. This was an important undertaking not only for the railroads but also their suppliers. Two efforts grew out of this need. In 1879, The *Railroad Gazette* published *The Car Builder's Dictionary* with the cooperation of the Master Car Builders' Association to establish common terms for the parts of railroad cars. *The Car Builder's Dictionary* succeeded by *The*

*Car Builder's Cyclopedia* has been published every few years since. The M.C.B.A. also participated in this effort with entries in its *Code of Rules Governing the Condition of, and Repairs to, Freight Cars for the Interchange of Traffic.* Using common terms is essential in the productive discussion of freight cars, and this appendix is designed to assist the railroad historian and railroad buff in that endeavor. While not as extensive as either of the two works cited, it should assist the reader in general discussions of the freight cars and their construction.

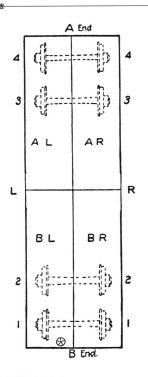

FIGURE A.1

This drawing answers the simple question of which is left and which is right, and it provides a way of identifying each axle by number. As you look at a freight car, if the brake wheel is on your right, you are looking at the left side of the car. *[Courtesy: American Association of Railroads]*

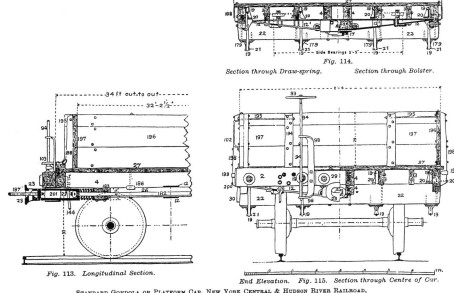

*Fig. 113. Longitudinal Section.*

*Fig. 114.*
*Section through Draw-spring.    Section through Bolster.*

*End Elevation. Fig. 115. Section through Centre of Car.*

STANDARD GONDOLA OR PLATFORM CAR, NEW YORK CENTRAL & HUDSON RIVER RAILROAD, with HOIT DRAW-GEAR (shown separately in Figs. 426–427.)

NAMES OF PARTS OF GONDOLA CAR; *Figs.* 113–115.

| | | |
|---|---|---|
| 1. *Side-sill.* | 21. *Body Truss-rod Bearing on Queen-post.* | 93. *Brake-wheel.* |
| 2. *End-sill.* | | 94. *Brake-shaft.* |
| 3. *Intermediate-sill.* | 22. *Needle-beam or Cross-frame Tie-timber.* | 98. *Brake-shaft Step.* |
| 4. *Centre-sill.* | | 103. *Brake Ratchet-wheel.* |
| 12. *Body-bolster.* | 23. *Drawbar.* | 144. *Brake-hanger.* |
| 12'. *Body - bolster Spacing-block.* | 24. *Draw-spring.* | 179. *Queen-post.* |
| | 26. *Draw-timbers.* | 182. *Draw-rod.* |
| 19. *Body Truss-rod.* | 27. *Floor.* | 183. *Follower-plate Block.* |
| 20. *Body Truss-rod Saddle.* | 29. *Buffer-block.* | 186. *Packing-blocks.* |
| | 30. *Sill-step.* | |

| |
|---|
| 187. *Link.* |
| 194. *Side-straps.* |
| 195. *Side-strap Tie-rod.* |
| 196. *Side-plank.* |
| 197. *End-plank.* |
| 198. *Stake.* |
| 199. *Stake-pocket Strap.* |
| 200. *Stake-bolt.* |
| 201. *Drawbar Carry-iron.* |

FIGURE A.2

**The parts of a wood gondola.** *[The Car Builder's Dictionary, 1888]*

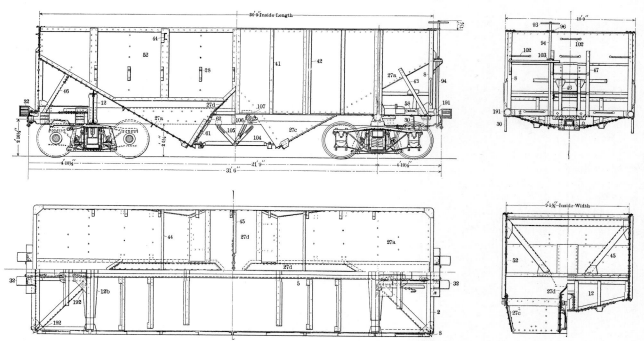

Figs. 409-412. Plan, Elevations and Sections of 30-ft. Hopper Car, Pressed Steel. Capacity, 100,000 lbs.

## Names of Parts of Hopper and Ore Cars. Figs. 409-412

| | |
|---|---|
| 1 Side Sill | 41 Side Plate Stiffening Angle |
| 2 End Sill | 42 Stake |
| 5 Center Sill | 44 Side Strut Angle Tie |
| 8 Corner Post | 45 Hopper Support |
| 10 Sill Tie Rod | 46 Center Strut for Hopper Floor |
| 10a End Sill Tie Rod | 47 End Post |
| 11 End Sill Diagonal Brace | 52 Side Plank or Sheet |
| 12 Body Bolster | 61 Drop Door |
| 12b Bottom Plate of Body Bolster | 62 Drop Door Hinge |
| 16 Body Side Bearing | 63 Drop Door Eye Bolt |
| 17 Body Center Plate | 64 Drop Door Chain |
| 19 Body Truss Rod | 65 Drop Door Chain Ring |
| 20 Body Truss Rod Saddle | 70 Winding Shaft |
| 21 Body Truss Rod Bearing | 74 Door Pin |
| 22 Cross Tie or Needle Beam | 93 Brake Wheel |
| 23 Drawbar | 94 Brake Shaft |
| 26 Draft Timbers | 96 Upper Brake Shaft Bearing |
| 27a End Slope | 100 Brake Shaft Bracket |
| 27b Side Slope or Hopper Slope | 102 Hand Hold |
| 27c Same as 27b | 103 Brake Ratchet Wheel |
| 27d Same as 27b | 104 Hopper Door Toggle Arm |
| 28 Bracket Steps | 105 Hopper Door Toggle Link |
| 30 Sill Steps | 106 Hopper Door Locking Pawl |
| 32 Buffer Blocks | 191 Push Pole Corner Iron |
| 39 Stake Pocket | 192 Gusset Plates |

FIGURE A.3

As all-steel hopper cars were introduced, *The Car Builder's Dictionary* began publishing diagrams such as this one to enable railroads to use a common language in referring to their parts. This diagram is taken from the 1906 edition of *The Car Builder's Dictionary*, but it appeared as early as the 1903 edition. It shows the component parts of a Pressed Steel Car Company's structural steel hopper. Over time, some of the construction techniques and terminology has changed. For example, part 27a, labeled here as "End Slope," will later be referred to as the "Slope Floor Sheet" or just "Slope Sheet." Similarly, part 42, labeled as "Stake," will eventually become "Side Post" to differentiate it from replaceable stakes that can fit into and can be removed from stake pockets. Also, part 45, labeled as "Hopper Support," will be replaced on later hopper cars with the "Body Cross Tie," which runs from side to side across the entire width of the car. The O&W was forced to modify a number of coal cars in this period with body cross ties to prevent their sides from bulging. Finally, part 191, the "Push Pole Corner Iron" will become the "Push Pole Pocket."
*[The Car Builders' Dictionary, 1906; Courtesy: Simmons-Boardman Publishing Corp.]*

Several terms have been used throughout this book that may require further explanation or clarification. These are discussed below. To assist in this effort, numbers have been inserted to identify the part in Figure 3. In addition, the diagram in Figure 3 has been prepared.

**Corner Posts** (#8)—The corner posts support the top corners of the slope sheets and tie in the end sheets.

**End Posts** (#47)—The end posts provide one of the most distinctive identifying features of the hopper car. They are mounted vertically on either side of the coupler to support the center, top end of the slope sheet and end sheet. These have sometimes been referred to as "verticals," but "end post" is the preferred term in the industry.

**End Sill** (#2)—The American Association of Railroads distinguishes between two types of end sills. The first is the end sill that is flush with the end of the hopper end (USRA-type hopper). The second is the end sill which projects beyond the end of the hopper (GLa-type hopper). The latter is known as a "platform end sill." This distinction is drawn because it affects the safety appliances required on the car. Most of the O&W's all-steel hoppers had platform end sills.

**Gussets or Gusset Plates** (#192)—The term "gusset" is a generic term that means a flat plate used to join together two pieces of steel and strengthen a joint. There are several on a hopper car. Gussets are used to strengthen the intersection of the end and side sheets. The triangular extension of the side sheets into the open area on some hoppers is referred to as the "side gusset" in this book. You will note that the junction of the end post and the end sheet is also reinforced. This is referred to as the "end post gusset" in this book.

**Side Panels** (not called out in Figure A.3)—The space between two vertical posts (side posts or corner posts). Thus, the sides of the hopper in Figure 3 would have eight panels.. All O&W all-steel hoppers were of the eight panel design.

**Side Rail** (not called out in Figure A.3)—The topmost edge of the hopper.

**Side Sheets** (#52)—The enclosing sides of the hopper are referred to as the side sheets. Each side sheet is made up of a series of sheets of steel that are riveted together at the side post. The number of sheets varies by car. The junction of two sheets is marked by the rivets on each side of the side post being adjacent to each other. Where a side post is not at the junction of two side sheets, the rivet pattern alternates up the post.

**Side Stakes** (#42)—More commonly referred to today as "side posts" because stakes are posts that fit into a stake pocket. The number and type of side posts become an important identifying feature of hopper cars. These are sometimes referred to as "ribs" by hobbyists, but this is not an industry term.

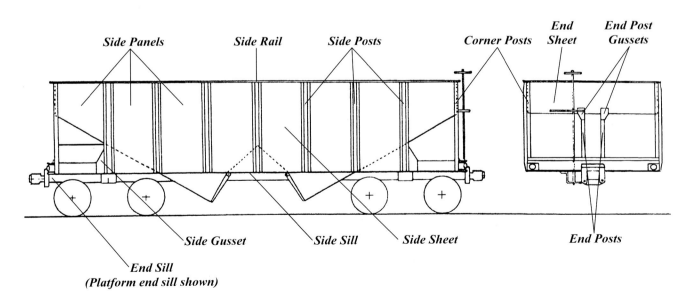

FIGURE A.4
**Common hopper terminology used in this book. The accompanying text provides further explanation of these terms.**

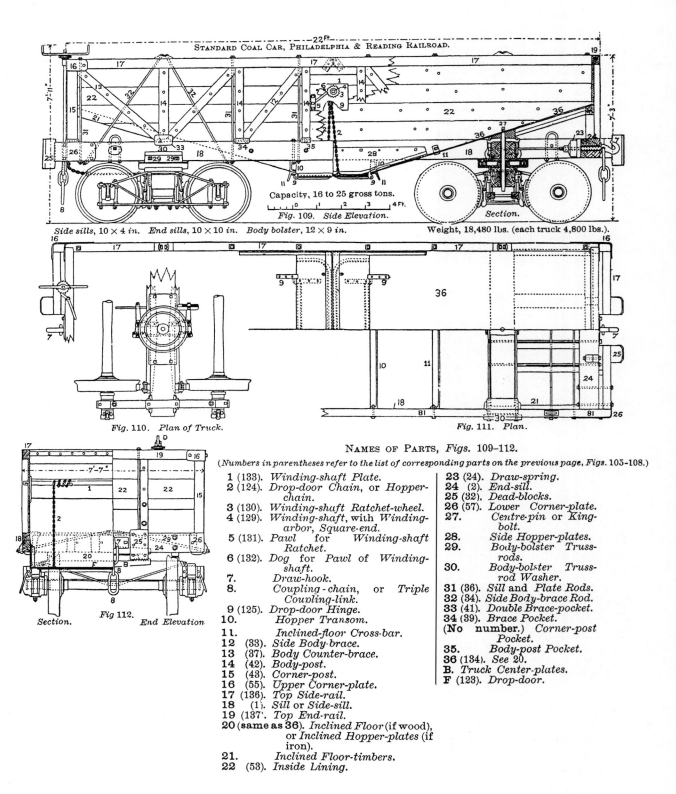

STANDARD COAL CAR, PHILADELPHIA & READING RAILROAD.

Capacity, 16 to 25 gross tons.

*Fig. 109. Side Elevation.*

Side sills, 10 × 4 in.   End sills, 10 × 10 in.   Body bolster, 12 × 9 in.   Weight, 18,480 lbs. (each truck 4,800 lbs.).

*Fig. 110. Plan of Truck.*

*Fig. 111. Plan.*

Section.   *Fig 112*   End Elevation.

NAMES OF PARTS, *Figs.* 109–112.

(*Numbers in parentheses refer to the list of corresponding parts on the previous page, Figs. 105–108.*)

1 (133). *Winding-shaft Plate.*
2 (124). *Drop-door Chain,* or *Hopper-chain.*
3 (130). *Winding-shaft Ratchet-wheel.*
4 (129). *Winding-shaft,* with *Winding-arbor, Square-end.*
5 (131). *Pawl* for *Winding-shaft Ratchet.*
6 (132). *Dog* for *Pawl* of *Winding-shaft.*
7.       *Draw-hook.*
8.       *Coupling-chain,* or *Triple Coupling-link.*
9 (125). *Drop-door Hinge.*
10.      *Hopper Transom.*
11.      *Inclined-floor Cross-bar.*
12 (33). *Side Body-brace.*
13 (37). *Body Counter-brace.*
14 (42). *Body-post.*
15 (43). *Corner-post.*
16 (55). *Upper Corner-plate.*
17 (136). *Top Side-rail.*
18 (1). *Sill* or *Side-sill.*
19 (137). *Top End-rail.*
20 (same as 36). *Inclined Floor* (if wood), or *Inclined Hopper-plates* (if iron).
21.      *Inclined Floor-timbers.*
22 (53). *Inside Lining.*

23 (24). *Draw-spring.*
24 (2). *End-sill.*
25 (32). *Dead-blocks.*
26 (57). *Lower Corner-plate.*
27.      *Centre-pin* or *King-bolt.*
28.      *Side Hopper-plates.*
29.      *Body-bolster Truss-rods.*
30.      *Body-bolster Truss-rod Washer.*
31 (36). *Sill* and *Plate Rods.*
32 (34). *Side Body-brace Rod.*
33 (41). *Double Brace-pocket.*
34 (39). *Brace Pocket.*
(**No number.**) *Corner-post Pocket.*
35.      *Body-post Pocket.*
36 (134). *See 20.*
B. *Truck Center-plates.*
F (123). *Drop-door.*

FIGURE A.5

**The parts of a wood hopper car**  [*Car Builder's Dictionary, 1888*]

This glossary is prepared to assist the reader with terms used throughout this book. The freight car definitions spanning the life of the O&W are drawn principally, and often verbatim, from the pages of the *Car Builders' Dictionary* and the *Car Builders' Cyclopedia* with the permission of Simmons-Boardman Books. Definitions pertaining to anthracite and coal mining are drawn from study books prepared by the International Textbook Company with permission of Education Direct.

This glossary is by no means intended to be a complete list of terms used in the freight car or anthracite industry but rather as a guide to assist the reader in understanding the discussions in this book. For a complete listing, the reader is invited to visit the sources described above.

**"A" End of Cars:** The opposite end to that on which the brake shaft is located, that end being called the "B" end.

**"AB" Brake Equipment:** The name by which is designated the type of brake equipment made standard for new freight cars built after September 1, 1933, rebuilt cars after August 1, 1937, and compulsory in interchange after July 1, 1952. Replaces Type "K." Desirable characteristics of the "AB" brake include the following: preliminary quick service; effective throughout entire length of long trains in level service; automatically compensated to conform with operating conditions in grade service; accelerated service application; service release insured; quick recharge following service operation; emergency at any time; protection against undesired emergency application; accelerated emergency transmission; controlled development of brake-cylinder pressure; higher brake-cylinder pressure in emergency; positive release following emergency; improved means of brake-cylinder lubrication; effective protection against leakage and dirt. The essential parts of this equipment are the "AB" valvular device; a double compartment reservoir—auxiliary and emergency; and a brake cylinder having several distinctive improvements.

**Air Brake:** Any brake operated by air pressure, but usually restricted to systems of power brakes operated by compressed air, in distinction from vacuum brakes, which are operated by creating a vacuum. The air is compressed by some form of pump on the locomotive and is conveyed by pipes and flexible hose between the cars to cylinders and pistons under each car, by which the pressure is transmitted to the brake levers, and thence to the brake shoes. This system is termed the straight-air brake. It is now obsolete, having been replaced by the automatic air brake.

**Air Brake Hose:** The flexible hose at each end of a car which is fastened to the brake pipe angle cock on one end, and has a fitting on the other end which engages with a similar coupling on an adjoining car.

**Angle Cock:** A special type of valve located at both ends of the brake pipe on locomotive and cars used to control admission of air to the brake pipe on individual cars.

**Angle Iron or Angle:** A general term applied by makers to rolled steel having an L-shaped cross section.

**Anthracite (Hard Coal):** The type of coal found principally in Northeastern Pennsylvania with a very high carbon content. While it is difficult to ignite, anthracite burns longer and cleaner than other types of coal.

**Arch Bars:** The wrought iron or steel bars which form the top and bottom members of a diamond arch bar truck side frame. They are attached to the bolster guides or truck columns by column bolts and to the journal boxes by the journal box bolts. This type of construction was prohibited after December 31, 1939.

**Arch Bar Truck:** Shortened name for Diamond Arch Bar Truck.

**Automatic Air Brake:** Any brake system with which the brake will be applied automatically in case of an accident which permits air to escape from the system.

**Automatic Car Coupler:** A device for automatically coupling cars without the necessity of a person going in between the cars. The Master Car Builders' standard type of coupler which is in universal use in the United States is any coupler of the vertical plane type which conforms to the contour adopted by the M.C.B.A. in 1887. In 1903, the solid knuckle was adopted as standard.

**Auxiliary Reservoir:** A reservoir for storage of a supply of compressed air to operate the brakes of each individual car, and supplied from the main reservoir on the engine through the brake pipe.

**Axle:** The cylindrical steel shaft on which the car wheels are mounted. The axle not only holds the wheels to gauge, but also transmits the load from the journal boxes to the wheels. An axle without collars is called a "Muley" axle.

**Axle Collar:** A rim or enlargement on the end of a car axle, which takes the end thrust of the journal bearing.

**"B" End of Car:** The end on which the brake shaft is located, or the end toward which the brake cylinder travels.

**Babbitt Metal:** An alloy, consisting of tin, copper and antimony, used for journal bearings; so called from its inventor, Isaac Babbitt of Boston. The term is commonly applied to any white alloy for bearings, as distinguished from the box metals or brasses in which copper predominates, but is usually limited to alloys containing over 50% tin. Genuine Babbitt is limited to alloys containing from 80% to 90% tin.

**Babbitt Metal Bearings:** A style of bearing of which a great variety of forms exist, which in effect substitutes Babbitt metal in some of its many forms for brass as a bearing surface. Lead-lined bearings are different in that they merely use a thin sheet of lead over the brass to correct slight irregularities and give an even bearing surface.

**Body (of a car):** The main or principal part in or on which the load is placed.

**Body Bolster:** The transverse members of the underframe over the trucks which transmit the load carried by the longitudinal sills to the trucks through the center plates.

**Body Brace:** An inclined member of the body side or end framing of the car. In the construction of freight cars the braces are inserted in the panels between the bolster and the center of the car, inclining toward the transverse center line of the car, which the counter braces are framed in the panel between the bolster and the end of the car, inclining toward the end of the car.

**Body Cross Tie:** A metal bar extending across a hopper or other form of open-top freight car and fastened the sides to prevent their bulging.

**Body End Plate:** A transverse member in the end of the car connecting the side plates.

**Body Post (Freight Car Bodies):** An upright piece which is fastened to the sill and plate of a freight car. The body posts and corner posts from the vertical members of the side frame of a car body.

**Bolster:** A cross member on the underside of a car and in the center of a truck through which the weight is transmitted. The bolsters carry the body and truck center plates, the body bolster resting on the truck bolster.

**Brace:** An inclined piece which unites two or more of the points of a frame or truss, where other members of the structure are connected together, and which prevents them from turning about their joints.

**Brake or Brake Gear:** The whole combination of parts by which the motion of a car or train is retarded or arrested. The foundation brake gear includes all the parts by which the pressure of the air in the brake cylinder is transmitted to the wheels.

**Brake Beam:** The immediate supporting structure for the two brake heads and two brake shoes acting upon any given pair of wheels. In freight service the practically universal type is of truss construction consisting primarily of tension and compression members fastened at the ends and separated at the middle by a strut or fulcrum to which the truck brake lever is attached. Brake beams are said to be inside hung or outside hung, according to whether they are in the space between the axles or outside the axles.

**Brake Cylinder:** A cast-iron cylinder attached to the body frame or truck frame of a car containing a piston which is forced outwardly by the compressed air to apply the brakes, and when the air pressure is released is returned to its normal position by a release spring coiled about the piston rod inside the cylinder. For freight cars the brake cylinder and the auxiliary reservoir are usually combined, the reservoir being bolted to one end of the cylinder and forming one of the cylinder heads. The piston rod of the freight brake cylinder is hollow and loosely encloses a push rod, which is attached to the cylinder lever.

**Brake Pawl:** A small specially shaped iron or steel piece, pivoted to engage the teeth of a brake ratchet wheel to prevent the wheel turning backward, and thus releasing the brakes.

**Brake Pipe:** An iron pipe extending from one end of the car to the other and connected to the pipes on adjoining cars by a flexible brake hose. The air from the air pump or motor compressor is conveyed through the brake pipe to the auxiliary reservoir under each car. The brake pipe is normally filled with compressed air at 70 lbs. pressure and the auxiliary reservoirs with air at the same pressure. A reduction of this pressure in the brake pipe of from 5 to 20 pounds causes the triple valves to open communication between the auxiliary reservoir and the brake cylinder so that compressed air stored in the reservoir acts on the piston and brake levers and applies the brakes.

**Brake Shaft:** A shaft on which a chain is wound and by which the power of a hand brake is applied to the wheels.

**Brake Step:** A small shelf or ledge on the end of a freight car near the top on which the brakeman stands when applying the hand brake.

**Brass:** An alloy of copper and zinc. Also a term commonly used to designate a journal bearing.

**Breaker:** The building used in anthracite operations to break the coal into marketable sizes, separate the coal from the waste rock, and load the coal in railroad cars.

**Bronze:** An alloy composed of copper and tin, sometimes with addition of small quantities of other metals silicon, nickel, and phosphorus.

**Buffer:** An elastic apparatus or cushion attached to the end of a car to receive and absorb the shocks caused by other cars running against it.

**Buffer Beam:** A short timber bolted to the face of the end sill, usually protected with a striking plate against which the shoulder on the head of the drawbar strikes when the draft gear springs are closed solid. Its function is to protect the end sill from damage and to act as a distance block to keep the cars a sufficient distance apart to allow a man to step between them. Frequently called a deadwood or dead block

**Buffer Blocks:** Two block of wood or iron attached to the end sill or buffer beam of a freight car, in contradistinction to buffer beam, which is a single block in the middle of the end sill, although the latter is sometimes designated as a single dead block. Buffer blocks are sometime call dead blocks.

**Capacity:** The nominal load in pounds or gallons which the car is designed to carry. Stenciled on the car "CAPY."

**Carline:** Framing members which extend across the top of a car from one side to the other and support the roof.

**Center Bearing:** The place in the center of a truck where the weight of the body rests. A body center plate attached to the car body rests on a truck center plate attached to the truck. The general term center bearing is used to designate the whole arrangement and the functions it performs in distinction from the side bearing.

**Center Pin:** A large bolt which passes through the center plates on the body bolster and truck bolster. The truck turns about the bolt but the stress is taken up by the center plates. Sometimes referred to as the "king bolt."

**Center Plate:** One of a pair of plates made of cast or malleable iron or pressed or cast steel which fit one onto the other and which support the car body on the trucks, allowing them to turn freely under the car. The center pin or king bolt passes through both, but does not really serve as a pivot.

**Center Sill:** The central longitudinal member of the underframe of a car, which forms, as it were, the backbone of the underframe and transmits most of the buffing shocks from one end of the car to the other.

**Channel or Channel Bar:** More commonly merely channel. A general term applied by makers to iron or steel with the following cross section: [

**Colliery:** The entire mining operation including all the buildings, the rail plant, and the loading equipment.

**Corner Brace or Corner Plate:** A pressed steel angle plate or knee on the outside corner to strengthen and protect the frame. There are three types of corner plates—upper, lower, and middle. Very commonly a push pole pocket is combined with lower corner plate.

**Corner Post:** The vertical member which forms the corner of the frame of a car body.

**Coupler:** The device by which the connection of one car to another is maintained and conversely by which cars can be disconnected.

**Coupler Horn:** The projecting lug cast on top of the coupler head which bears on the striker plate when the draft gear is fully compressed.

**Coupler Shank:** That part of a coupler behind the head which connects to the yoke and draft system.

**Culm:** The waste product from anthracite mining including slate, shale, and low grade coal.

**Dead Block:** A single wooden block or stick of timber attached to the end sill of freight cars to protect persons between the cars from injury, by preventing the cars from coming together in case the drawbar or its attachment should give way.

**Diamond Arch Bar Truck:** The type of freight car truck which was in practically universal use from the time of the first attempts at standardization until the end of the 19th century. Known first as the Diamond Truck, then the Diamond Arch Bar Truck, and finally the Arch Bar Truck.

**Draft Gear:** The mechanism that connects the coupler with the car sills. The energy absorbing component of the draft system.

**Draft Gear Pocket:** The space in the draft sill that contains the energy absorbing components of the draft system.

**Draft System:** The term used to describe the arrangement on a car for transmitting coupler forces to the center sill. On standard cars, the draft system includes the coupler, yoke, draft gear, follower, draft key, draft lugs and draft sill.

**Drop Bottom Car:** A gondola car with a level floor or bottom equipped with a number of drop doors for discharging the load.

**Drop Door:** A door at the bottom of a drop bottom or hopper bottom car for unloading it quickly by allowing the load to fall through the opening. Drop doors are usually in pairs and are supported by a chain wound around a winding shaft; or by a lever arrangement. Frequently a drop door beam extends across the car above the winding shaft to assist in supporting it and to stiffen the car.

**Drop Door Chain:** A chain attached to a drop door, and usually connecting it with a winding shaft for the purpose of controlling the door.

**Eaves:** The edge of the roof projecting over the side of the car.

**End Plate:** A member across the end and connecting the tops of the end posts of a car body and fastened at the ends to the tow side plates. It is usually made of the proper form to serve as an end carline.

**End Play (Axle):** The movement or the place left for movement endwise. Usually called lateral motion.

**End Post:** The vertical members in the end body framing between the corner post. With reference to hopper cars, a vertical support for the overhand of the hopper floor, resting on the end sill.

**End Sill:** The transverse member of the underframe of a car, extending across the ends of all the longitudinal sills.

**End Slope:** The sloping floor from the end of a hopper to the hopper door.

**Fillet:** A small light molding more generally called a bead. A rounded corner left on the inside of the angle where two surfaces join as in a casting or a machined part such as an axle journal.

**Grab Iron:** Also termed corner handles, or ladder handles, or hand holds. The handles attached to freight cars for the use of trainmen in boarding the cars.

**Gondola Car:** The common gondola car is a freight car with low side and ends, a solid floor, and no roof.

**Gusset Plate:** A flat plate used to fasten two parts of a metal frame together by riveting through each member and the plate, or to stiffen a joint between two pieces which are fastened together by angle plates, in which the gusset plate is riveted to the flanges of the adjoining pieces. The term gusset is most often applied specifically to plates with a triangular or diamond shape.

**"H-Type" Brake:** Original quick-action brake developed by George Westinghouse in 1887 for trains with up to 50 cars.

**Hand Brake:** The name applied to the brake apparatus with which all cars are equipped, which permits the brakes being applied by hand.

**Hand Brake Chain:** The chain which forms part of the connection between the hand brake shaft and the system of brake levers.

**Hopper Bottom Gondola Car:** A gondola car having a level floor or bottom and one or more hopper equipped with drop doors for discharging the load.

**Hopper Car:** A car with the floor sloping from the ends and sides to one or more hoppers, which will discharge its entire load by gravity through the hopper doors. Modern hopper cars are of the self-clearing type.

**Hopper Door:** A door at the bottom of the slope or hopper of a hopper car which when opened permits the load to discharge.

**Hopper Door Locking Pawl:** In a hopper door gear, the catch which, when thrown into engagement with the toggle arms, prevents the arms from moving from the closed position and opening the hopper doors.

**Hopper Plates:** The metal sheets constituting the bottom of a hopper car. Also termed inclined floor or hopper slope. The term hopper plate is generally confined to the metal lining plate used in wooden hopper cars.

**Hopper Slope Sheet:** A metal sheet used in the sloped floor of a hopper car.

**Hopper Support:** An angle riveted to the ridge of the hopper car at the center and the top of the side sheet, forming a support for the hopper.

**Hot Box:** Railroad slang for an overheated journal bearing.

**House Car:** An enclosed freight car like a box, automobile, or refrigerator car.

**I-Beam:** A general term applied by makers to iron or steel with the following cross section: I

**Journal:** The part of an axle or shaft on which the journal bearing rests.

**Journal Bearing:** A combination of rollers and races or a block of metal, usually brass or bronze, in contact with a journal on which the load rests. In car construction the term when unqualified means a car axle journal bearing. A standard shape for brass bearings has been adopted by the A.A.R. and a recommended practice for its composition specified.

**Journal Bearing Key or Wedge:** A device used to hold the journal bearing in place; to distribute the load evenly over the bearing; and to allow it to be removed easily.

**Journal Box:** The metal housing which encloses the journal of a car axle, the journal bearing and wedge, and which hold the oil and packing for lubricating the journal. Also called an axle box, car box, grease box, housing box, oil box, and pedestal box.

**Journal Box Cover or Lid:** A door or lid covering an opening in the end of the journal box, by means of which oil and packing are supplied and journal bearing are inserted or removed.

**"K-Type" Brake:** An improved quick-action brake developed by Westinghouse in 1908 for trains of 50 to 100 cars.

**Knuckle:** The pivoting hook-like casting that fits into the head of a coupler and rotates about a vertical pin to either the open position (to engage a mating coupler) or to the closed position (when fully engaged).

**"L" or Ell:** A general term applied by makers to iron or steel with the following cross section: L

**Ladder:** Bars of wood or iron attached to the side or end of a box car so as to form steps by which persons may climb to and from the top of the car. The individual bars, whether of wood or iron, and whether round or square, are termed ladder rounds. They are sometimes made with Ladder Side Rails. The handles alongside the ladder are termed grab irons or hand holds or sometimes corner handles.

**Load Limit:** The maximum weight of lading that can be loaded in a car. Stenciled on the car "LDLMT."

**Panel:** The space between two vertical posts or braces.

**Pedestal:** A casting of somewhat the form of an inverted letter U, bolted to the wheel piece of a truck frame to hold the journal box in its place, while permitting vertical movement.

**Pedestal Truck:** Trucks so called because the journal boxes are held in jaws or pedestals which are an integral part of the truck frame as distinguished from trucks using pedestals bolted to the truck frame.

**Plate:** A horizontal member on top of the posts of a car body supporting the roof carlines. Also called side plate, in distinction from an end plate, which is a similar member across the end of the car.

**Queen Posts:** One of a pair of vertical posts against which the truss rods bear.

**Recommended Practice:** A specification, design, product or device which is accepted by the A.A.R. for use on rolling stock. A recommended practice shall not substitute for a Standard or Alternate Standard.

**Safety Appliance:** Any one of several specific components required on railway cars, the functions of which are directly related to the safety of train crew members and other persons whose duties require being on or around the equipment. Safety appliances include hand brakes, handholds, ladders, uncoupling levers, sill steps and safety railings.

**Shank:** That portion of a coupler between the head and rear surface of the butt.

**Side Bearings:** Bearings attached to the bolsters of a car body, or truck, 2 feet or more on each side of the center plate to steady the car and prevent excess motion while passing curves.

**Side Brace:** Commonly designated as body brace or brace, except when the end braces are to be distinguished from them.

**Side Frame:** The frame which forms the side of a body or a truck. It includes the posts, braces, plate, bet rail, etc. for the car body and the side member of a truck frame.

**Side Plate:** More properly, simply plate. The longitudinal member connecting the tops of the side posts of the car body. So called as distinguished from the end plate. See Plate.

**Side Post:** Vertical member used in the side framing of freight and passenger cars.

**Side Rail:** A longitudinal member extending along the top of the side frame of a coal or ore car. It rests upon the posts and braces and connects with end rails, which go across the end of the car. It corresponds to the plate of a box car, but does not carry any carlines, as does a plate.

**Side Sheet:** A plate used for closing in the sides of a steel car.

**Side Sill:** The outside longitudinal members of the underframe. In some designs of steel cars, the side sills are dispensed with and the entire side of the car is designed as a deep plate girder to carry most of the load to the bolster.

**Side Slope:** That part of the floor which slopes from the side of a hopper to the hopper door.

**Side Stake:** A piece of timber or metal bar inserted into the sides of flat cars to hold the load in place. The sides of gondola cars are sometimes held in a similar manner. The side stiffening pieces on hopper and gondola cars are frequently called stakes.

**Side Strut for Hopper Floor:** An inclined strut or support for the hopper floor between the bolster and the end of the car, fastened to the corner of the end sill.

**Slack-Water:** Any stretch of water having little or no current.

**Spring Plank:** A transverse member underneath a truck bolster and on which the bolster springs rest. In rigid bolster trucks the spring plank is bolted to the lower arch bar of the truck frame.

**Spring Seat:** A cup-shaped piece of cast steel or cast or wrought iron, on which the bottom of a spring rests. Also called a spring plate.

**Stake:** A piece of timber or metal bar inserted into the sides and ends of flat cars to hold the load in place. The sides of gondola cars are sometimes held in a similar manner. The side stiffening pieces on hopper and gondola cars are frequently called stakes.

**Standard:** A specification, procedure, practice, definition, design, product or device which is approved by the A.A.R. to serve as the requirement for use in unrestricted interchange service.

**Stenciling:** A term used to describe all forms of lettering on cars regardless of the actual method of application.

**Striking Plate:** A steel casting placed on the ends of the center sills of freight cars against which the horn of the coupler strikes, preventing damage to the draft gear and center sills. The length of a freight car is usually measured from the striking plates.

**"T" or Tee:** A general term applied by makers to iron or steel with the following cross section: **T**

**Tidewater:** Those waterways affected by the earth's tides. In the anthracite industry, generally those ports serving the Atlantic seaboard.

**Train Line:** The complete line of air brake, air signal, or steam pipes in a railroad train.

**Transom:** A truck cross member which performs the function of tying together the side frames and providing support for the bolster. Used on early freight trucks but practically extinct by 1940.

**Triple Valve:** A valve device consisting of a body or case, called the triple valve body, which has connections to the brake pipe, the auxiliary reservoir and the brake cylinder, in which a slide valve is operated by a piston, so that when the pressure of the air in the brake pipe is increased the auxiliary reservoir is charged and the air in the brake cylinder is released to the atmosphere; and so that when the air pressure in the brake pipe is reduced, air from the auxiliary reservoir is discharged in the brake cylinder for applying the brakes. The quick-acting triple valve has all the features and performs all the functions of the plain triple valve, and has the additional function of causing a discharge of air from the brake pipe to the brake cylinder, when, in emergencies, the maximum force of the brakes is instantly required.

**Truck:** The general term covering the assembly of parts comprising the structures which support a car body at each end and also provide for attachment of wheels and axles.

**Truck Bolster:** A cross member in the center of a truck, on which the car body rests. The truck bolster is connected to the body bolster by a center pin, which passes through both.

**Truck Center Frame:** A frame cross member made in one piece, riveted to the side frames or wheel pieces of steel passenger equipment trucks and taking the place of the transoms of older types.

**Truck Frame:** A structure made of cast steel in one piece to which the journal boxes or pedestals, springs and other parts are attached, and which forms the skeleton of a truck.

**Truck Side Bearing:** A device attached to the top of the truck bolster and having an upper bearing surface which comes in contact with a similar bearing surface attached to the underside of the body bolster.

**Truck Side Frame:** The longitudinal portion of a truck structure, on the outside of the wheels, which extends from one axle to the other, and to which the journal boxes and bolsters or transoms are attached or form a part.

**Truss:** An engineering term applied to certain types of built-up load-carrying structures so designed that the individual members comprising together the complete unit are subject only to compression or tension loads. A well known type of truss is called the Pratt Type. This resembles in outline a series of letter N's, those on one side of the middle facing to the right and those on the other facing to the right with the bottoms and tops joined by straight lines.

**Truss Rod:** An inclined rod used in connection with a king or queen post truss, or trussed beam, to resist deflection. It is attached to the ends of the beam, and is supported in the middle by a king post, truss block, or two queen posts between the beam and the rod.

**Underframe:** A stout framework, which receives the buffing and pulling stresses and carries the weight of the floor and body of the vehicle.

**Winding Shaft:** A round iron bar supported by the winding shaft plates or bearings, around which the drop door chain or hopper chain is wound.

# Appendix C M.C.B.A. Safety Appliance Standards for Open Top Cars (1893-1911)*

## Brake Shafts

(1) The brake shaft to be located on the end of car, preferably to the left of the centre thereof, when facing the end of car.

(3) The ratchet wheel to be secured from turning on the brake shaft.

(4) The brake pawl to be fastened to a suitable casting or plate attached to the car body or brake step.

## Sill Steps

(1) One substantial sill step to be secured to each side of car at the lower right-hand corner, this being the corner on the right, when facing the side of car. The side of the sill step next to the corner to be as near as practicable to the end of the car.

(2) Sill steps to be made of wrought iron or steel about ½ by 1½ inches cross sectional area or equivalent.

(3) Sill steps to be about 12 inches long between the sides, measured horizontally at the tread.

(4) The lower treads of sill steps to be about 24 inches and not more than 32 inches above the rail, the clear depth of sill steps to be not less than 6 inches.

(5) Sill steps exceeding 18 inches in depth to have an additional tread above the lower tread, and such sill steps to be laterally braced.

(6) Each side of sill steps on cars to be securely fastened by means of lag screws, bolts and rivets.

## Ladders

(1) Box and other house cars, and all cars the top of which cannot be reached from sill steps or platform end sills, shall have two wrought iron wooden ladders.

(2) Ladders to be located at diagonal corners, on right-hand end of sides of cars or left-hand side of ends of cars. When cars have platform end sills, ladders may be located near center of ends of car. High side gondola cars with fixed ends having brake staff platform at one end of car should have ladders and sill step on both side at same end of car.

(3) Ladder treads of wrought iron or steel, to be 5/8 inch nominal diameter or of hardwood, to be nominally

1½ by 2 inches, about 16 inches clear length.

(4) The spacing of treads of ladders to be about 18 inches.

(5) All ladder treads shall have a minimum clearance around them of 2 inches, nominal clearance 2½ inches.

(6) When wrought iron or steel ladders without sides are placed on ends of cars with non-projecting end sills, the bottom treads to have a guard or upward projection at inside ends.

## Handholds

(14) Gondola cars with fixed ends to be provided with a horizontal or vertical handhold, on each side of car over sill steps, with as much clear length as car construction will permit, provided handholds net not exceed 16 inches in length; and

(15) If horizontal handholds are used they shall be located not more than 30 inches above center line of coupler.

(16) Gondola cars without projecting end sills, having ladders located on sides, to have one vertical or horizontal handhold at upper corner of left-hand side of brake end of car.

(17) Vertical handhold to extend downward from about 4 inches from top of car; horizontal handhold located about 6 inches from top of car.

(18) Each side of each car to be provided with two horizontal handholds not less than 12 inches, and preferably 16 inches in the clear, or longer, located not over 30 inches above the center line of coupler or placed under the end sill as near the face as will insure a good, safe fastening, or if preferred, may be placed on the face of the end sill. The coupler unlocking rod, when properly located, and having proper clearance around it, is a suitable end handhold.

(19) Exception to be made when the car is provided with a brake step, in which case the bracket of the brake step, if of suitable height, may be used as a handhold on that side of the end of the car, as shown.

(20) The arrangement without brake step is shown.

(21) High cars with vertical end handholds are shown.

(22) High cars with horizontal side handholds are shown.

(36) Hopper cars to be provided with horizontal or vertical handholds on each side of each car over sill steps, with as much clear length as the car constructions will

---

* These standards have been adapted and consolidated from the Master Car Builder's Association Safety-Appliance Standards to reflect only those standards that apply to gondolas and hopper cars.

permit, provided handholds need not exceed 16 inches in length.

(37) If horizontal handholds are used, they shall be located not more than 30 inches above center line of coupler.

(38) Hopper cars without platform end sills, having ladders located on sides, to have one vertical or horizontal handhold at upper corner of left-hand side of brake end of car;

(39) Vertical handhold to extend downward from about 4 inches from top of car; horizontal handhold located about 6 inches from top of car.

(40) Each end of hopper cars to be provided with two horizontal handholds not less than 12 inches, and preferably 16 inches in the clear, or longer, located not over 30 inches above center line of coupler, or placed under the end sill as near the face as will insure a good safe fastening, or, if preferred, may be placed on the face of end sill. The coupler unlocking rod, or a tread of ladder, when properly located and having proper clearance around it is a suitable end handhold.

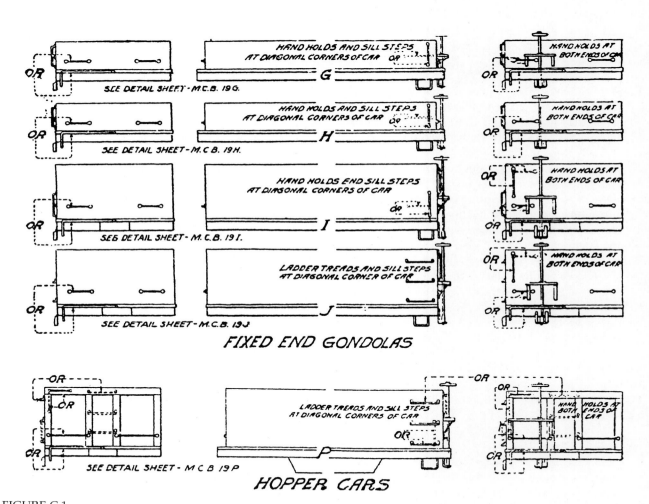

FIGURE C.1

**M.C.B.A. Safety Appliance Standards for Open-Top Cars 1893-1911** *[The Car Builders' Dictionary, 1909; Courtesy: Simmons-Boardman Publishing Corp.]*

Hard Coal and Coal Cars

**HOPPER CARS AND HIGH SIDE GONDOLAS WITH FIXED ENDS** [Cars with sides more than thirty-six (36) inches above the floor are high-side cars.]

**HAND BRAKES:**

**Number**-Each hopper car shall be equipped with an efficient hand-brake which shall operate in harmony with the power brake thereon. The hand-brake may be of any efficient design, but must provide the same degree of safety as the design shown on Plate A.

**Dimensions**-The brake shaft shall not be less than one and one-fourth (1¼) inches in diameter, of wrought iron or steel without weld. The brake wheel may be flat or dished, not less than fifteen (15) preferably sixteen (16), inches in diameter, of malleable iron, wrought iron or steel.

**Location**-Each hand-brake shall be so located that it can be safely operated while car is in motion. The brake shaft shall be located on end of car to the left of, and not more than twenty-two (22) inches from, center.

**Manner of application**-There shall be not less than four (4) inches clearance around rim of brake wheel. Outside edge of brake wheel shall be not less than four (4) inches from a vertical plane parallel with end of car and passing through the inside face of knuckle when closed with coupler-horn against the buffer block or end sill.

Top brake-shaft support shall be fastened with not less than one-half (½) inch bolt or rivets. (See Plate A.) A brake-shaft step shall support the lower end of brake shaft.

A brake-shaft step which will permit the brake chain to drop under the brake shaft shall not be used. U-shaped form of brake-shaft step is preferred. (See Plate A.)

Brake shaft shall be arranged with a square fit at its upper end to secure the hand-brake wheel; said square fit shall be not less than seven-eighths (⅞) of an inch square. Square-fit taper; nominally two (2) in twelve (12) inches. (See Plate A.)

Brake chain shall be of not less than three-eighths (³/₈), preferably seven-sixteenths (⁷/₁₆) inch, wrought iron or steel, with a link on the brake-rod end of not less than seven-sixteenths (⁷/₁₆), preferably one-half (½) inch, wrought iron or steel, and shall be secured to brake-shaft drum by not less than one-half (½) inch hexagon or square-headed bolt. Nut on said bolt shall be secured by riveting end of bolt over nut. (See Plate A.)

Lower end of brake shaft shall be provided with a trunnion of not less than three-fourths (¾), preferably one (1), inch in diameter, extending through brake-shaft step and held in operating position by a suitable cotter or ring. (See Plate A.)

Brake-shaft drum shall be not less than one and one-half (1½) inches in diameter. (See Plate A.)

Brake ratchet wheel shall be secured to brake shaft by a key or square fit; said square fit shall be not less than one and five-sixteenths (1⁵/₁₆) inches square. When ratchet wheel with square fit is used, provision shall be made to prevent ratchet wheel from rising in shaft to disengage brake pawl. (See Plate A.)

Brake ratchet wheel shall be not less than five and one-fourth (5¼), preferably five and one-half (5½) inches in diameter and shall have not less than fourteen (14), preferably sixteen (16), teeth. (See Plate A.)

If brake ratchet wheel is more than thirty-six (36) inches from brake wheel, a brake-shaft support shall be provided to support this extended upper portion of brake shaft; said brake-shaft support shall be fastened with not less than one-half (½) inch bolts or rivets.

The brake pawl shall be pivoted upon a bolt or rivet not less than five-eighths (⁵/₈) of an inch in diameter, or upon a trunnion secured by not less than one-half (½) inch bolt or rivet, and there shall be a rigid metal connection between brake shaft and pivot of pawl.

Brake wheel shall be held in position on brake shaft by a nut on a threaded extended end of brake shaft; said threaded portion shall be not less than three-fourths (¾) of an inch in diameter; said nut shall be secured by riveting over or by the use of a lock-nut or suitable cotter.

Brake wheel shall be arranged with a square fit for brake shaft in hub of said wheel; taper of said fit, nominally two (2) in twelve (12) inches. (See Plate A.)

**BRAKE STEPS**-If brake step is used, it shall be not less than twenty-eight (28) inches in length. Outside edge shall be not less than eight (8) inches from face of car and not less than four (4) inches from a vertical plane

---

[*] These standards have been adapted and consolidated from the *United States Safety Appliance Standards, Order of Commission of March 13, 1911*[1] to reflect only those standards that apply to gondolas and hopper cars.

parallel with end of car and passing through the inside face of knuckle when closed with coupler horn against the buffer block or end sill.

**Manner of application**-Brake step shall be supported by not less than two metal braces having a minimum cross-sectional area three-eighths (³/8) by one and one-half (1½) inches or equivalent, which shall be securely fastened to body of car with not less than one-half (½) inch bolts or rivets.

**SILL STEPS:** Number-Four (4).

**Dimensions**-Minimum cross-sectional area one-half (½) by one and one-half (1½) inches, or equivalent, of wrought iron or steel. Minimum length of tread, 10 preferably 12 inches. Minimum clear depth, eight (8) inches.

**Location**-One (1) near each end on each side of car, so that there shall be not more than eighteen (18) inches from end of car to center of tread of sill step. Outside edge of tread of step shall be not more than four (4) inches inside of face of side of car, preferably flush with side of car. Tread shall be not more than twenty-four (24), preferably not more than twenty-two (22), inches above the top of rail.

**Manner of application**-Sill steps exceeding twenty-one (21) inches in depth shall have an additional tread. Sill steps shall be securely fastened with not less than one-half (½) inch bolts with nuts outside (when possible) and riveted over, or with not less than ½ inch rivets.

**LADDERS:** Number-Four (4).

**Dimensions**-Minimum clear length of tread: Side ladders, sixteen (16) inches ; end ladders, 14 inches. Maximum spacing between ladder treads, 19 inches. Top ladder tread shall be located not more than four (4) inches from top of car. Spacing of side ladder treads shall be uniform, within a limit of two (2) inches from top ladder tread to bottom tread of ladder. Maximum distance from bottom tread of side ladder to top tread of sill step, twenty-one (21) inches. End ladder treads shall be spaced to coincide with treads of side ladders, a variation of two (2) inches being allowed. Where construction of car will not permit the application of a tread of end ladder to coincide with bottom tread of side ladder, the bottom tread of end ladder must coincide with second tread from bottom of side ladder. Hardwood treads, minimum dimensions one and one-half (1½) by two (2) inches. Iron or steel treads, minimum diameter five-eighths (⁵/8) of an inch. Minimum clearance of treads, two (2), preferably two and one-half (2½), inches.

**Location**-One (1) on each side, not more than eight (8) inches from right end of car; one (1) on each end, not more than eight (8) inches from left side of car; meas-

ured from inside edge of ladder stile or clearance of ladder treads to corner of car.

**Manner of application**-Metal ladders without stiles near corners of cars shall have foot guards or upward projections not less than two (2) inches in height near inside end of bottom treads. Stiles of ladders will serve as foot guards. Ladders shall be securely fastened with not less than one-half (½) inch bolts with nuts outside (when possible) and riveted over, or with not less than one-half (½) inch rivets. Three-eighths (³/8) inch bolts may be used for wooden treads which are gained into stiles.

**SIDE HANDHOLDS:** Number-Four (4). [Tread of side ladder is a side handhold.]

**Dimensions**-Minimum diameter, five-eighths (⁵/8) of an inch, wrought iron or steel. Minimum clear length, sixteen (16) inches, preferably twenty-four (24) inches. Minimum clearance, two (2), preferably two and one-half (2½), inches.

**Location**-Horizontal: One (1) near each end of each side of car. Side handholds shall be not less than twenty-four (24) nor more than thirty (30) inches above center line of coupler, except as provided above, where tread of ladder is a handhold. Clearance of outer end of handhold shall be not more than eight (8) inches from end of car.

**Manner of Application**-Side handholds shall be securely fastened with not less than one-half (½) inch bolts with nuts outside (when possible) and riveted over, or with not less than one-half (½) inch rivets.

**Specifications covering additional Grab Irons for Hopper Cars and High Side Gondola Cars** (Including alternate arrangement for Hopper Cars)-Adopted as standard by the American Railway Association in 1932.

**Side Handholds:** Number eight (8). Two (2) treads of side ladder are considered as side handholds.

**Dimensions:** Minimum diameter five-eighths (⁵/8) of an inch, wrought iron or steel. Minimum clear length, sixteen (16) inches, preferably twenty four (24) inches. Minimum clearance two (2) inches, preferably two and one-half (2½) inches.

**Alternate for Hopper Cars:** Same as above, except extending from corner post to slope sheet or stake in which case the lower handhold is to have minimum diameter of three-quarters (¾) of an inch.

**Location**-Horizontal: Two (2) near each end on each side of car. Lower side handhold shall be not less than twenty-four (24) nor more than thirty (30) inches above center line of coupler, except as provided above, where tread of ladder is a handhold. Upper side handhold shall be not less than twenty (20), nor more than twenty-six (26) inches above lower side handhold, except as provided above, where tread of ladder is a handhold. On cars with sides too low to permit locating upper side handhold, a minimum of twenty (20) inches above lower side handhold, the former shall be located not more than four (4) inches from top of car. Clearance of outer end of handhold shall be not more than eight (8) inches from end of car.

**Manner of Application**: Side handholds shall be securely fastened with not less than one-half (½) inch bolts, with nuts outside (when possible), and riveted over, or with not less than one-half (½) inch rivets.

**HORIZONTAL END HANDHOLDS**: Number-Eight (8) or more. (Four (4) on each end of car.) [Tread of end ladder is an end handhold.]

**Dimensions**-Minimum diameter, five-eighths (⅝) of an inch, wrought iron or steel. Minimum clear length, sixteen (16) inches, preferably twenty-four (24) inches. A handhold fourteen (14) inches in length may be used where it is impossible to use one sixteen (16) inches in length. Minimum clearance, two (2), preferably two and one-half (2½), inches.

**Location**-One (1) near each side on each end of car, not less than twenty-four (24) nor more than thirty (30) inches above center line of coupler except as provided above, when tread of end ladder is an end handhold. Clearance of outer end of handhold shall be not more than eight (8) inches from side of car. One (1) near each side of each end of car on face of end sill or sheathing over end sill, projecting outward or downward. Clearance of outer end of handhold shall be not more than sixteen (16) inches from side of car. On each end of cars with platform end sills six (6) or more inches in width, measured from end post or siding and extending entirely across end of car, there shall be one additional end handhold not less than twenty-four (24) inches in length, located near center of car, nor less than thirty (30) nor more than sixty (60) inches above platform end sill.

**Manner of application**-Horizontal end handholds shall be securely fastened with not less than one-half (½) inch bolts with nuts outside (when possible) and riveted over, or with not less than one-half (½) inch rivets.

**VERTICAL END HANDHOLDS**: Number-Two (2) on full-width platform end-sill cars, as here-to-fore described.

**Dimension**-Minimum diameter, five-eighths (⅝) of an inch, wrought iron or steel. Minimum clear length, eighteen (18), preferably twenty-four (24), inches.

Minimum clearance, two (2), preferably two and one-half (2½), inches.

**Location**-One (1) on each end of car opposite ladder, not more than eight (8) inches from side of car; clearance of bottom end of handhold shall be not less than twenty-four (24) nor more than thirty (30) inches above center line of coupler.

**Manner of Application**-Vertical end-handholds shall be securely fastened with not less than one-half (½) inch bolts with nuts outside (when possible) and riveted over, or with not less than one-half (½) inch rivets.

**UNCOUPLING-LEVERS**: Number-Two (2).

**Dimensions**-Uncoupling levers may be either single or double, and of any efficient design.

Handles of uncoupling levers, except those shown on Plate B-or of similar designs, shall be not more than six (6) inches from sides of car.

Uncoupling levers of design shown on Plate B and of similar designs shall conform to the following prescribed limits:

Handles shall be not more than twelve (12), preferably nine (9), inches from sides of cars. Center lift arms shall be not less than seven (7) inches long.

Center of eye at end of center lift arm shall be not more than three and one-half (3½) inches beyond center of eye of uncoupling pin of coupler when horn of coupler is against the buffer block or end sill.
Ends of handles shall extend not less than four (4) inches below bottom of end sill, or shall be so constructed as to give a minimum clearance of two (2) inches around handle. Minimum drop of handles shall be twelve (12) inches; maximum, fifteen (15) inches over all. (See Plate B.)

Handles of uncoupling levers of the "rocking" or "push-down" type shall be not less than eighteen (18) inches from top of rail when lock block has released knuckle, and a suitable stop shall be provided to prevent inside arm from flying up in case of breakage.

**Location**-One (1) on each end of car. When single lever is used it shall be placed on left side of end of car.

**END-LADDER CLEARANCE**: No part of car above end-sills within thirty (30) inches from side of car, except buffer block, brake shaft, brake wheel, brake step, or uncoupling lever shall extend to within twelve (12) inches of a vertical plane parallel with end of car and passing through the inside face of knuckle when closed with coupler horn against the buffer block or end sill, and other part of end of car or fixtures on same above end sills, other than exceptions herein noted, shall extend beyond the outer face of buffer block.

## FIXED-END LOW SIDE GONDOLA AND LOW SIDE HOPPER CARS [Cars with sides thirty-six (36) inches or less above the floor are low-side cars.]

**HAND BRAKES**: Number-Each hopper car shall he equipped with an efficient hand-brake which shall operate in harmony with the power brake thereon. The hand-brake may be of any efficient design, but must provide the same degree of safety as the design shown on Plate A.

**Dimensions**-The brake shaft shall not be less than one and one-fourth (1¼) inches in diameter, of wrought iron or steel without weld. The brake wheel may be flat or dished, not less than fifteen (15), preferably sixteen (16), inches in diameter, of malleable iron, wrought iron or steel.

**Location**-Each hand-brake shall be so located that it can be safely operated while car is in motion. The brake shaft shall be located on end of car to the left of, and not more than twenty-two (22) inches from, center.

**Manner of application**-There shall he not less than four (4) inches clearance around rim of brake wheel. Outside edge of brake wheel shall be not less than four (4) inches from a vertical plane parallel with end of car and passing through the inside face of knuckle when closed with coupler-horn against the buffer block or end sill.

**Top brake**-Shaft support shall be fastened with not less than one-half (½) inch bolt or rivets. (See Plate A.)

A brake-shaft step shall support the lower end of brake shaft. A brake-shaft step which will permit the brake chain to drop under the brake shaft shall not be used. U-shaped form of brake-shaft step is preferred. (See Plate A.)

Brake shaft shall be arranged with a square fit at its upper end to secure the hand-brake wheel; said square fit shall be not less than seven-eighths (7/8) of an inch square. Square-fit taper; nominally two (2) in twelve (12) inches. (See Plate A.)

Brake chain shall be of not less than three-eighths (3/8), preferably seven-sixteenths (7/16) inch, wrought iron or steel, with a link on the brake-rod end of not less than seven-sixteenths (7/16), preferably one-half (½) inch, wrought iron or steel, and shall be secured to brake-shaft drum by not less than one-half (½) inch hexagon or square-headed bolt. Nut on said bolt shall be secured by riveting end of bolt over nut. (See Plate A.)

Lower end of brake shaft shall be provided with a trunnion of not less than three-fourths (¾), preferably one (1), inch in diameter, extending through brake-shaft step and held in operating position by a suitable cotter or ring. (See Plate A.)

Brake-shaft drum shall be not less than one and one-half (1½) inches in diameter. (See Plate A.)

Brake ratchet wheel shall be secured to brake shaft by a key or square fit; said square fit shall be not less than one and five-sixteenths (1⁵/16) inches square. When ratchet wheel with square fit is used, provision shall be made to prevent ratchet wheel from rising in shaft to disengage brake pawl. (See Plate A.)

Brake ratchet wheel shall be not less than five and one-fourth (5¼), preferably five and one-half (5½), inches in diameter and shall have not less than fourteen (14), preferably sixteen (16), teeth. (See Plate A.)

If brake ratchet wheel is more than thirty-six (36) inches from brake wheel, a brake-shaft support shall be provided to support this extended upper portion of brake shaft; said brake-shaft support shall be fastened with not less than one-half (½) inch bolts or rivets.

The brake pawl shall be pivoted upon a bolt or rivet not less than five-eighths (5/8) of an inch in diameter, or upon a trunnion secured by not less than one-half (½) inch bolt or rivet, and there shall be a rigid metal connection between brake shaft and pivot of pawl.

Brake wheel shall be held in position on brake shaft by a nut on a threaded extended end of brake shaft; said threaded portion shall be not less than three-fourths (¾) of an inch in diameter; said nut shall be secured by riveting over or by the use of a lock-nut or suitable cotter.

Brake wheel shall be arranged with a square fit for brake shaft in hub of said wheel; taper of said fit, nominally two (2) in twelve (12) inches. (See Plate A.)

**BRAKE STEP**-If brake step is used, it shall be not less than twenty-eight (28) inches in length. Outside edge shall be not less than eight (8) inches from face of car and not less than four (4) inches from a vertical plane parallel with end of car and passing through the inside face of knuckle when closed with coupler horn against the buffer block or end sill.

**Manner of application**-Brake step shall be supported by not less than two metal braces having a minimum cross-sectional area three-eighths (3/8) by one and one-half (1½) inches or equivalent, which shall be securely fastened to body of car with not less than one-half (½) inch bolts or rivets.

**SILL STEPS**: Number-Four (4).

**Dimensions**-Minimum cross-sectional area one-half (½) by one and one-half (1½) inches, or equivalent, of wrought iron or steel. Minimum length of tread, 10 preferably 12 inches. Minimum clear depth, eight (8) inches.

**Location**-One (1) near each end on each side of car, so that there shall be not more than eighteen (18) inches from end of car to center of tread of sill step. Outside edge of tread of step shall be not more than four (4) inches inside of face of side of car, preferably flush with side of car. Tread shall be not more than twenty-four (24), preferably not more than twenty-two (22), inches above the top of rail.

**Manner of application**-Sill steps exceeding twenty-one (21) inches in depth shall have an additional tread. Sill steps shall be securely fastened with not less than one-half (½) inch bolts with nuts outside (when possible) and riveted over, or with not less than ½ inch rivets.

**SIDE HANDHOLDS**:  Number-Four (4). [Tread of side ladder is a side handhold.]

**Dimensions**-Minimum diameter, five-eighths (⁵/₈) of an inch, wrought iron or steel.  Minimum clear length, sixteen (16) inches, preferably twenty-four (24) inches.  Minimum clearance, two (2), preferably two and one-half (2½), inches.

**Location**-Horizontal: One (1) near each end of each side of car,  not less than twenty-four (24) nor more than thirty (30) inches above center line of coupler, if car construction will permit, but hand hold shall not project above top of side.  Clearance of outer end of handhold shall be not more than eight (8) inches from end of car.

**Manner of Application**-Side handholds shall be securely fastened with not less than one-half (½) inch bolts with nuts outside (when possible) and riveted over, or with not less than one-half (½) inch rivets.

**HORIZONTAL END HANDHOLDS**:  Number-Eight (8) or more.  (Four (4) on each end of car.) [Tread of end ladder is an end handhold.]

**Dimensions**-Minimum diameter, five-eighths (⁵/₈) of an inch, wrought iron or steel.  Minimum clear length, sixteen (16) inches, preferably twenty-four (24), inches.  A handhold fourteen (14) inches in length may be used where it is impossible to use one sixteen (16) inches in length.  Minimum clearance, two (2), preferably two and one-half (2½), inches.

**Location**-One (1) near each side on each end of car, not less than twenty-four (24) nor more than thirty (30) inches above center line of coupler, if car construction will permit. Clearance of outer end of handhold shall be not more than eight (8) inches from side of car. One (1) near each side of each end of car on face of end sill, projecting outward or downward.  Clearance of outer end of handhold shall be not more than six-

teen (16) inches from side of car.

**Manner of application**-Horizontal end handholds shall be securely fastened with not less than one-half (½) inch bolts with nuts outside (when possible) and riveted over, or with not less than one-half (½) inch rivets.

**UNCOUPLING-LEVERS**:  Number-Two (2).

**Dimensions**-Uncoupling levers may be either single or double, and of any efficient design.

Handles of uncoupling levers, except those shown on Plate B-or of similar designs, shall be not more than six (6) inches from sides of car.

Uncoupling levers of design shown on Plate B and of similar designs shall conform to the following prescribed limits:

Handles shall be not more than twelve (12), preferably nine (9), inches from sides of cars.  Center lift arms shall be not less than seven (7) inches long.

Center of eye at end of center lift arm shall be not more than three and one-half (3½) inches beyond center of eye of uncoupling pin of coupler when horn of coupler is against the buffer block or end sill.

Ends of handles shall extend not less than four (4) inches below bottom of end sill, or shall be so constructed as to give a minimum clearance of two (2) inches around handle.  Minimum drop of handles shall be twelve (12) inches; maximum, fifteen (15) inches over all.  (See Plate B.)

Handles of uncoupling levers of the "rocking" or "push-down" type shall be not less than eighteen (18) inches from top of rail when lock block has released knuckle, and a suitable stop shall be provided to prevent inside arm from flying up in case of breakage.

**Location**-One (1) on each end of car.  When single lever is used it shall be placed on left side of end of car.

**END-LADDER CLEARANCE**:  No part of car above end-sills, within thirty (30) inches from side of car, except buffer block, brake shaft, brake wheel, brake step, or uncoupling lever shall extend to within twelve (12) inches of a vertical plane parallel with end of car and passing through the inside face of knuckle when closed with coupler horn against the buffer block or end sill, and other part of end of car or fixtures on same above end sills, other than exceptions herein noted, shall extend beyond the outer face of buffer-block.

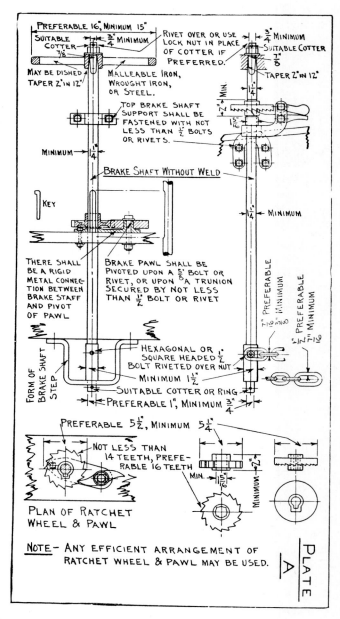

FIGURE D.1

United States Safety Appliance Standards only specify that cars have an "efficient" hand-brake which operates in harmony with the power brake and complies with the minimum standards displayed in Plate A above. In 1924, the American Railway Association adopted minimum standards for the force required to set the hand brakes on freight cars.[2] In 1936, the American Association of Railroads established requirements for geared handbrakes and required that all cars built new or rebuilt on or after January 1, 1937, be so equipped.[3] In 1942, the A.A.R. revised its specifications for hand brakes and required that all cars built or rebuilt after January 1, 1946, comply with this new standard.[4] *[Courtesy: American Association of Railroads]*

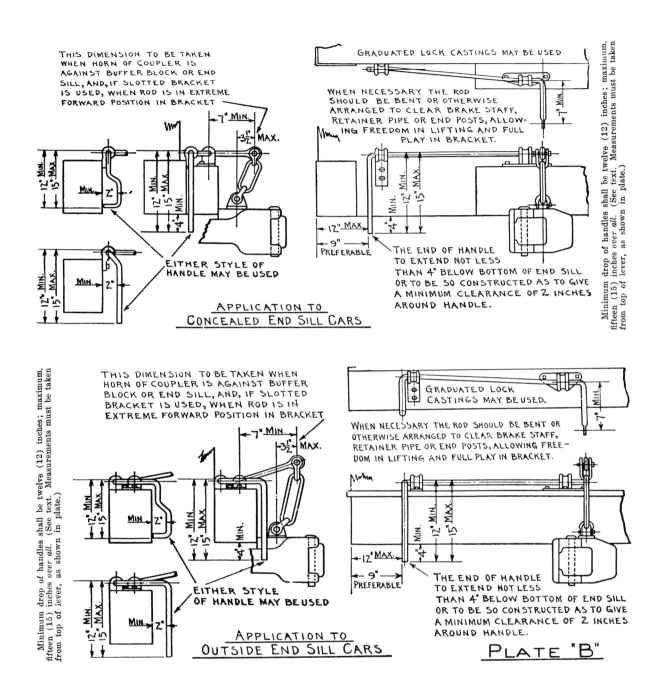

FIGURE D.2
**United States Safety Appliances; Plate B, Uncoupling Levers** *[Courtesy: American Association of Railroads]*

**United States Safety Appliance Standards for Hoppers and Gondolas** 189

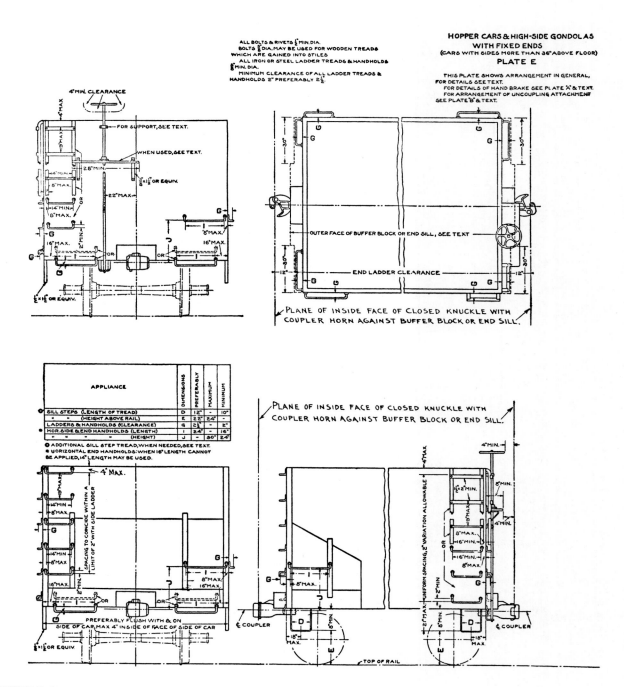

FIGURE D.3

**United States Safety Appliances; Plate E, Hopper Cars & High-Side Gondolas with Fixed Ends** *[Courtesy: American Association of Railroads]*

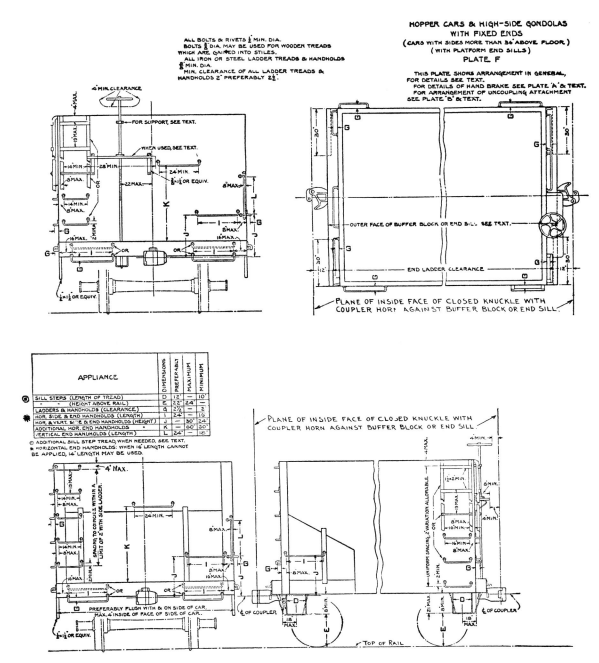

**FIGURE D.4**

United States Safety Appliances; Plate F, Hopper Cars & High-Side Gondolas with Fixed Ends & with Platform End Sills *[Courtesy: American Association of Railroads]*

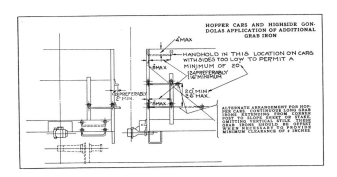

**FIGURE D.5**

United States Safety Appliances; Application of Additional Grab Irons on Hopper Cars and High Side Gondolas, American Railway Association (1932). A.A.R. Rules required that all "house cars, hopper cars and high side gondola cars built new or rebuilt on or after August 1, 1933" be equipped with this additional grab iron. Additionally, it recommended that all other such cars be so equipped when undergoing general maintenance.[5] *[Courtesy: American Association of Railroads]*

**United States Safety Appliance Standards for Hoppers and Gondolas**

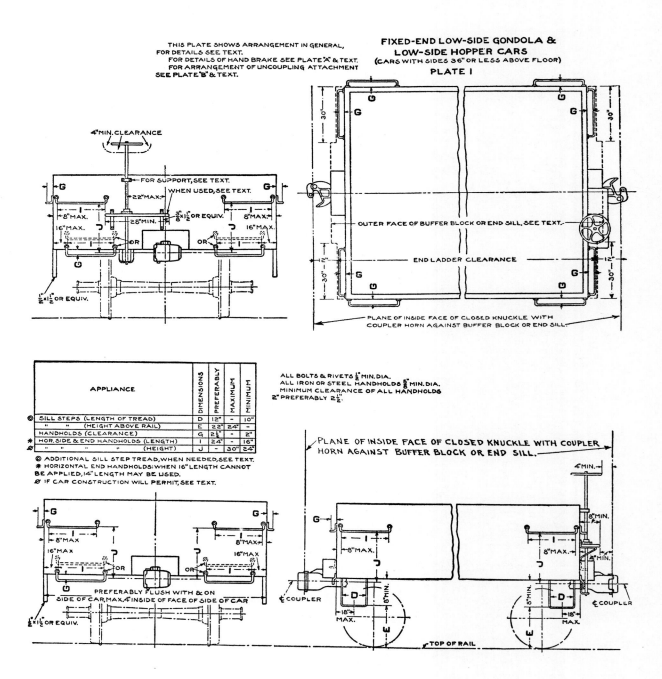

FIGURE D.6
**United States Safety Appliances; Plate I, Fixed-End Low-Side Gondola & Low-Side Hopper Cars.** *[Courtesy: American Association of Railroads]*

Hard Coal and Coal Cars

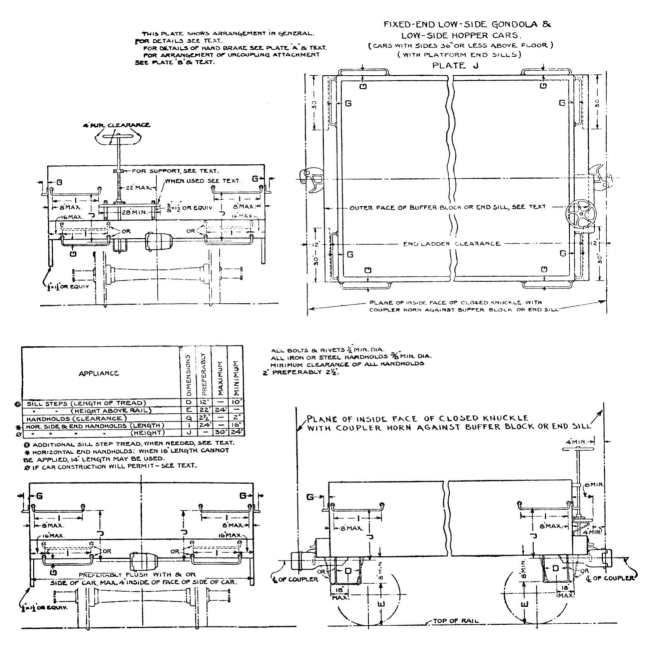

**FIGURE D.7**
United States Safety Appliances; Plate J, Fixed-End Low-Side Gondola & Low-Side Hopper Cars with Platform End Sills. *[Courtesy: American Association of Railroads]*

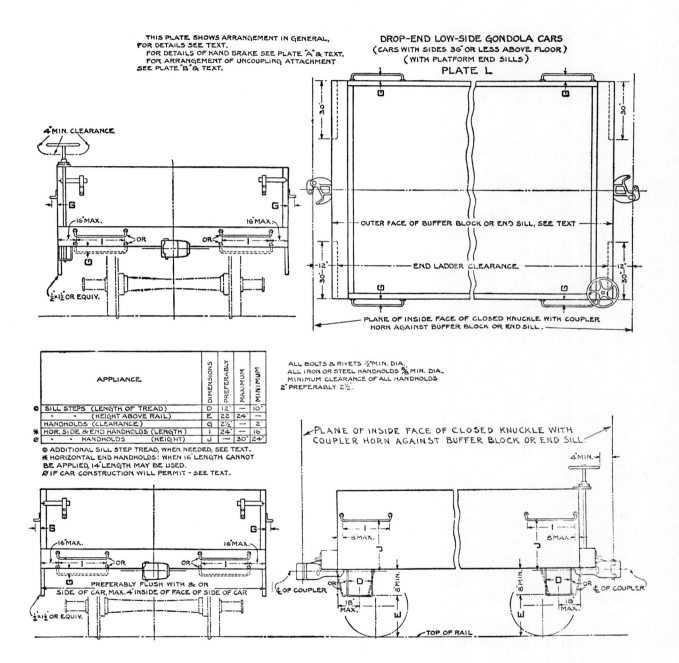

FIGURE D.8

**United States Safety Appliances; Plate L, Drop-End Low-Side Gondola with Platform End Sills.** *[Courtesy: American Association of Railroads]*

## Chapter 1

1. The Hudson Coal Company, *The Story of Anthracite*, International Textbook Press (Scranton, Pennsylvania, 1932), p. 24.
2. *Ibid.*, p. 38.
3. *Ibid.*, p. 37.
4. *Ibid.*, p. 50.
5. Philip Ruth, *Of Pulleys and Ropes and Gear; The Gravity Railroads of The Delaware and Hudson Canal Company and the Pennsylvania Coal Company*, The Wayne County Historical Society (Honesdale, Pennsylvania, 1997), pp. 6-7.
6. The Hudson Coal Company, *The Story of Anthracite*, p. 58.
7. *Ibid.*, pp. 84-87.
8. *Ibid.*, p. 78.
9. J. L. Ringwalt, *Development of Transportation Systems in the United States*, Railway World Office (Philadelphia, 1888), p. 71.
10. Jules I. Bogen, *The Anthracite Railroads: A Study in American Railroad Enterprise*, The Ronald Press Company (New York, 1927), p. 10.
11. Ruth, *Of Pulleys and Ropes and Gear*, p. 18.
12. *Ibid.*, p. 21.
13. The Hudson Coal Company, *The Story of Anthracite*, p. 97.
14. Ruth, *Of Pulleys and Ropes and Gear*, p. 40.
15. Bogen, *The Anthracite Railroads*, p. 27.
16. *Ibid.*, p. 29.
17. Ringwalt, *Development of Transportation Systems in the United States*, p. 133.
18. Bogen, *The Anthracite Railroads*, pp. 82-85, 95.
19. *Ibid.*, p. 111.
20. *Ibid.*, p. 91.
21. *Ibid.*, pp. 158-161.
22. *Ibid.*, pp. 123-124.
23. Ruth, *Of Pulleys and Ropes and Gear*, p. 45.
24. Bogen, *The Anthracite Railroads*, p. 186.
25. Ruth, *Of Pulleys and Ropes and Gear*, p. 59.
26. *Ibid*, p. 62.
27. Manville B. Wakefield, *Coal Boats to Tidewater: The Story of the Delaware & Hudson Canal*, Wakefair Press (Grahamsville, New York, 1981), p. 19.
28. Roger B. Saylor, *The Railroads of Pennsylvania*, Bureau of Business Research, College of Business Administration (The Pennsylvania State University, 1964), pp. 48-49.
29. The Hudson Coal Company, *The Story of Anthracite*, p. 91.
30. The Delaware and Hudson Company, *A Century of Progress: History of The Delaware and Hudson Company, 1823-1923*, J. B. Lyon Company (Albany, 1925), pp. 265-266.
31. *Minutes of the Board of Directors of the New York, Ontario & Western Railway*, May 29, 1908.
32. Wakefield, *Coal Boats to Tidewater*, p. 197.
33. Anthracite Coal Strike Commission, *Report to the President on the Anthracite Coal Strike of May-October 1902 by the Anthracite Coal Strike Commission*, Government Printing Office (Washington, 1903), pp. 23-24.
34. International Library of Technology, *Surface Arrangements at Anthracite Mines*, International Textbook Company (Scranton, Pennsylvania, 1906), p. 73-24.
35. The Hudson Coal Company, *The Story of Anthracite*, pp. 207-208.
36. Anthracite Coal Strike Commission, *Report to the President on the Anthracite Coal Strike of May-October 1902*, p. 25.
37. Ringwalt, *Development of Transportation Systems in the United States*, p. 196.
38. Bogen, *The Anthracite Railroads*, p. 214.
39. Ringwalt, *Development of Transportation Systems in the United States*, p. 196.
40. Saylor, *The Railroads of Pennsylvania*, p. 163.
41. Ringwalt, *Development of Transportation Systems in the United States*, p. 273.
42. William Griffith, "Anthracite Coal," *The Bond Record*, The Bond Record Publishing Company (New York, June 1896), p. 502.
43. Bogen, *The Anthracite Railroads*, p. 227.
44. *Ibid.*, p. 264.

## Chapter 2

1. The Delaware and Hudson Company, *History of the Delaware and Hudson Company 1823-1923*, J. B. Lyon Company (Albany, 1925), p. 226.
2. *Ibid.*, p. 265.
3. *Minutes of the Board of Directors of the New York, Ontario & Western Railway*, 18 October 1881.
4. *Minutes of the Board of Directors of the New York, Ontario & Western Railway*, 26 May 1886.
5. *Seventh Annual Report of the President and Officers of the New York, Ontario and Western Railway Company with Statements of Account for the Fiscal Year ending 30th September 1886* (New York, 1887), p. 23.
6. *Ninth Annual Report of the President and Officers of the New York, Ontario and Western Railway Company with Statements of Account for the Fiscal Year ending 30th September 1888* (New York, 1889), p. 24.
7. *Tenth Annual Report of the President and Officers of the New York, Ontario and Western Railway Company with Statements of Account for the Fiscal Year ending 30th September 1889* (New York, 1890), p. 9.
8. *Eleventh Annual Report of the President and Officers of the New York, Ontario & Western Railway Company with Statement of Accounts for the Fiscal Year ending June 30th, 1890* (New York, 1890), p. 23.
9. *Tenth Annual Report*, p. 14.
10. *Ibid.*, p. 12.
11. *Twelfth Annual Report of the President and Officers of the New York, Ontario & Western Railway Company with Statement of Accounts for the Fiscal Year ending June 30th, 1891* (New York, 1891), p. 5.
12. *Ibid.*, pp. 20-21.
13. *Ibid.*, p. 25.
14. *Fifteenth Annual Report of the President and Officers of the New York, Ontario & Western Railway Company with Statement of Accounts for the Fiscal Year ending June 30th, 1894* (New York, 1894), p. 8.

15. *Marine Line Equipment*, The Ontario & Western Railway Historical Society, Inc. (Middletown, New York, January-September 1992), p. 33.

16. *Sixteenth Annual Report of the President and Officers of the New York, Ontario & Western Railway Company with Statement of Accounts for the Fiscal Year ending June 30th, 1895* (New York, 1895), p. 22.

17. *Ibid.*, p. 5.

18. *Seventeenth Annual Report of the President and Officers of the New York, Ontario & Western Railway Company with Statement of Accounts for the Fiscal Year ending June 30th, 1896* (New York, 1896), p. 19.

19. *Eleventh Annual Report*, p. 20.

20. *Eighteenth Annual Report of the President and Officers of the New York, Ontario & Western Railway Company with Statement of Accounts for the Fiscal Year ending June 30th, 1897* (New York, 1897), p. 23.

21. *Twenty-Second Annual Report of the President and Officers of the New York, Ontario & Western Railway Company with Statement of Accounts for the Fiscal Year ending June 30th, 1901* (New York, 1901), p. 7.

22. *Minutes of the Board of Directors of the New York, Ontario & Western Railway*, 10 February 1899.

23. *Minutes of the Board of Directors of the New York, Ontario & Western Railway*, 15 December 1900.

24. *Minutes of the Board of Directors of the New York, Ontario & Western Railway*, 21 February 1905.

25. Rosamond D. Rhone, "Anthracite Coal Mines and Mining," *The American Monthly Review of Reviews* (New York, July 1902), p. 54.

26. *Twenty-Third Annual Report of the President and Officers of the New York, Ontario & Western Railway Company with Statement of Accounts for the Fiscal Year ending June 30th, 1902* (New York, 1902), p. 11.

27. *Ibid.*, p. 11.

28. *Eleventh Annual Report*, p. 23.

29. *Twenty-Second Annual Report*, p. 11.

30. *Ibid.*, p. 11.

31. *Ibid.*, p. 11.

32. William F. Helmer, O. & W., *The long life and slow death of the New York, Ontario & Western Ry.*, Howell-North (Berkeley, California), 1959, pp. 186-190.

33. *Twenty-Third Annual Report*, p. 26.

34. *Thirtieth Annual Report of the President and Officers of the New York, Ontario & Western Railway Company with Statement of Accounts for the Fiscal Year ending June 30th, 1909* (New York, 1909), p. 27.

35. *Thirty-Fourth Annual Report of the President and Officers of the New York, Ontario & Western Railway Company with Statement of Accounts for the Fiscal Year ending June 30th, 1913* (New York, 1913), p. 11.

36. *Twenty-First Annual Report of the President and Officers of the New York, Ontario & Western Railway Company with Statement of Accounts for the Fiscal Year ending June 30th, 1900* (New York, 1900), p. 5.

37. Manville B. Wakefield, *Coal Boats to Tidewater: The Story of the Delaware & Hudson Canal*, Wakefair Press (Grahamsville, New York, 1981), p. 200.

38. *36th Annual Report of the President and Officers of the New York, Ontario & Western Railway Company with Statement of Accounts for the Fiscal Year ending June 30th, 1915* (New York, 1915), p. 7.

39. *Thirty-First Annual Report of the President and Officers of the New York, Ontario & Western Railway Company with Statement of Accounts for the Fiscal Year ending June 30th, 1910* (New York, 1910), p. 5.

40. *Annual Report of the New York, Ontario & Western Railway Company with Statement of Accounts for the Year Ended December 31st 1917* (New York, 1918), p. 6.

41. *Thirty-Third Annual Report of the New York, Ontario & Western Railway Company with Statement of Accounts for the Year Ended December 31st 1912* (New York, 1923), p. 5.

42. The Hudson Coal Company, *The Story of Anthracite*, International Textbook Press (Scranton, Pennsylvania), 1932, p. 294.

43. *Annual Report of the New York, Ontario & Western Railway Company with Statement of Accounts for the Year Ended December 31st 1921* (New York, 1922), p. 5.

44. *Annual Report of the New York, Ontario & Western Railway Company with Statement of Accounts for the Year Ended December 31st 1923* (New York, 1924), p. 3.

45. *Annual Report of the New York, Ontario & Western Railway Company with Statement of Accounts for the Year Ended December 31st 1914* (New York, 1925), p. 6.

46. *Annual Report...for the Year Ended December 31st 1923*, p. 6.

47. *Annual Report of the New York, Ontario & Western Railway Company with Statement of Accounts for the Year Ended December 31st 1928* (New York, 1929), p. 29.

48. *Annual Report of the New York, Ontario & Western Railway Company with Statement of Accounts for the Year Ended December 31st 1925* (New York, 1926), p. 6.

49. *Moody's Manual of Investments*, Moody's Investment Service (New York, 1931), p. 1104.

50. *Minutes of the Board of Directors of the New York, Ontario & Western Railway*, 25 November 1930.

51. Root, Clark, Buckner & Ballantine, *Legal Analysis of Penn Anthracite Collieries Company* (New York, undated).

52. *Annual Report of the New York, Ontario & Western Railway Company with Statement of Accounts for the Year Ended December 31st 1933* (New York, 1934), p. 5.

53. *Minutes of the Board of Directors of the New York, Ontario & Western Railway*, 19 April 1935.

54. *Moody's Manual of Investments*, Moody's Investment Service (New York, 1938), p. 676.

55. Root, Clark, Buckner & Ballantine, *Legal Analysis of Penn Anthracite Collieries Company*, np.

56. *Annual Report of the New York, Ontario & Western Railway Company with Statement of Accounts for the Year Ended December 31st 1937* (New York, 1938), p. 5.

57. *Poor's Steam Railroads*, Poor's Railroad Manual Co. (New York, 1938), p. 605.

58. *Moody's Manual of Investments 1939*, Moody's Investment Service (New York, 1939), p. 2110.

59. *Moody's Manual of Investments 1943*, Moody's Investment Service (New York, 1943), p. 1049.

60. Alan Kennedy, "Crew of 30-Year Veterans Bring in Last O&W Train; Torpedoes Sound Requiem," *Middletown Times Herald* (Middletown, New York, March 30, 1957), p. 1.

## Chapter 3

1. "Coal Hopper Car, Baltimore & Ohio Railroad," *The National Car Builder*, R. M. Van Arsdale (New York, May 1884), p. 89.

2. C. H. Caruthers, "The Evolution of the Coal Car," *The Railroad Gazette* (New York, October 20, 1905), pp. 372-374.

3. William H. Brown, *The History of the First Locomotives in America*, D. Appleton and Company (New York, 1871), p. 21.

4. J. B. Calvert, *Tramway Engineering*, http://www.du.edu/~jcalvert/railway/woodtred.htm, 13 February 2000.

5. Brown, *The History of the First Locomotives in America*, p. 41.

6. *Ibid.*, p. 50.
7. J. L. Ringwalt, *Development of Transportation Systems in the United States*, Railway World Office (Philadelphia, 1888), p. 71.
8. *Ibid.*, p. 68.
9. Horace Porter, "Railway Passenger Travel," *The American Railway*, Charles Scribner's Sons (New York, 1889), p. 228.
10. Brown, *The History of the First Locomotives in America*, p. 56.
11. B. J. Eck, "Cast Steel Freight Car Development," *Railway Mechanical Engineering, A Century of Progress, Car and Locomotive Design*, The American Society of Mechanical Engineers (New York, 1979), p. 301.
12. Oliver Jensen, *American Heritage History of Railroads in America*, American Heritage Wings Books (New York, 1993), p. 17.
13. John H. White, Jr., *The American Railroad Freight Car: From the Wood-Car Era to the Coming of Steel*, The Johns Hopkins University Press (Baltimore, 1993), p. 156.
14. Ringwalt, *Development of Transportation Systems in the United States*, p. 69.
15. *Ibid.*, p. 71.
16. The Hudson Coal Company, *The Story of Anthracite*, International Textbook Press (Scranton, Pa, 1932), pp. 93-95.
17. White, *The American Railroad Freight Car*, p. 306.
18. Ruth, Phillip, *Of Pulleys and Ropes and Gear; The Gravity Railroads of the Delaware and Hudson Canal Company and the Pennsylvania Coal Company*, The Wayne County Historical Society (Honesdale, Pennsylvania, 1997), pp. 12 & 17.
19. Ringwalt, *Development of Transportation Systems in the United States*, p. 101.
20. White, *The American Railroad Freight Car*, p. 19.
21. Jules I. Bogen, *The Anthracite Railroads; A Study in American Railroad Enterprise*, The Ronald Press Company (New York, 1927), pp. 27-28.
22. White, *The American Railroad Freight Car*, p. 305.
23. "Four-Wheeled Gondola Car, Delaware & Hudson Canal Company," *Railroad Car Journal* (New York, November 1898), p. 341.
24. International Library of Technology, "Haulage," *Hoisting, Haulage, Mine Drainage*, International Textbook Company (Scranton, Pennsylvania, 1906), Section 54, p. 2.
25. The Hudson Coal Company, *The Story of Anthracite*, p. 185.
26. *Ibid.*, p. 185.
27. "Thirty-ton Freight Cars," *National Car Builder*, R.M. Van Arsdale, New York, May 1882, p. 57.
28. *Ibid.*, p. 57.
29. White, *The American Railroad Freight Car*, p. 55.
30. *Ibid.*, p. 185.
31. "Twenty-Ton Coal Car, Philadelphia & Reading Railroad," *National Car Builder*, R.M. Van Arsdale (New York, March 1884), p. 31.
32. William T. Faricy, *"A.A.R." The Story behind a Symbol*, The Newcomen Society of North America (New York, 1951), p. 7.
33. F. W. Brazier, "Founders of Master Car Builders' Association," *Railway Age* (June 23, 1923), p. 1543.
34. "Twenty-Ton Coal Car, Philadelphia & Reading Railroad," p. 31.
35. *Ibid.*, p. 31.
36. White, *The American Railroad Freight Car*, p. 337.
37. *Ibid.*, p. 582.
38. "Self-Clearing Coal Cars Profitable," *The American Engineer and Railroad Journal*, R.M. Van Arsdale (New York, May 1907), p. 196.
39. Arthur M. Waitt, "The Era of Steel in Car Construction," *American Engineer and Railroad Journal*, R. M. Van Arsdale (New York, March 1908), pp. 104-105.

40. White, *The American Railroad Freight Car*, pp. 593-596.
41. "Steel Cars on the Bessemer & Lake Erie Railroad," *American Engineer and Railroad Journal*, R. M. Van Arsdale (New York, May 1903), pp. 168-169.
42. *Ibid.*, p. 172.
43. *Ibid.*, p. 171.
44. *Ibid.*, p. 172.
45. Marshall M. Kirkman, *Cars, Their Construction, Handling and Supervision: The Science of Railways*, The World Railway Publishing Company (New York, 1906), p. 229.
46. "Pressed Steel Car Co. Catalogue," *Railroad Digest* (New York, July 1901), p. 283.
47. Kirkman, *Cars, Their Construction, Handling and Supervision: The Science of Railways*, The World Railway Publishing Company (New York, 1903), p. 233.
48. "40-Ton Composite Hopper Cars, Norfolk & Western Railway," *American Engineer and Railroad Journal*, R. M. Van Arsdale (New York, June 1902), p. 181.
49. "40-Ton Steel Underframe Hopper Car," *American Engineer and Railroad Journal*, R. M. Van Arsdale (New York, September 1904), p. 343.
50. "40-Ton Composite Hopper Cars, Norfolk & Western Railway," p. 181.
51. "Trade Supply Notes," *Railroad Digest* (New York, December 1901), p. 476.
52. "Maintenance and Repair of Freight Cars," *American Engineer and Railroad Journal*, R.M. Van Arsdale (New York, March 1909), p. 86.
53. *Ibid.*, p. 86.
54. "Steel Car Development, Pennsylvania Railroad," *American Engineer and Railroad Journal*, R.M. Van Arsdale (New York, May 1905), p. 149.
55. "Report of the Committee on Car Construction," *Railway Age* (New York, June 17, 1924), p. 1634.
56. Richard Burg, "Pennsy GLa Hoppers," *Railmodel Journal* (Denver, Colorado, February 2002), p. 22.
57. James E. Lane, "USRA Freight Cars: An Experiment in Standardization," *Railroad History No. 128*, The Railway and Locomotive Historical Society (Boston, Spring 1973), p. 5.
58. "Report of Committee on Car Construction," *Railway Age* (New York, June 12, 1926), p. 1718.
59. "Report of Committee on Car Construction," June 12, 1926, p. 1718.
60. "Report of Committee on Car Construction," *Circular No. D.V.—836*, Association of American Railroads (New York, June 1935), p. 1-2.
61. "Report on Car Construction," *Railway Age* (New York, June 29, 1935), p. 1021.
62. "Report of Committee on Car Construction," *Circular No. D.V.—836*, p. 1-2.

## Chapter 4

1. *United States Safety Appliances For All Classes of Cars and Locomotives (A.A.R. Edition) Fifteenth Edition (1945)*, Gibson, Association of American Railroads, Pribble & Co. (Richmond, VA, 1945), p. 5.
2. "Car Coupling Inventions," *National Car Builder*, R.M. Van Arsdale (New York, October 1882), p. 107.
3. "Automatic Freight Car Couplers," *National Car Builder*, R.M. Van Arsdale (New York, August 1884), p. 97.
4. "The Michigan Selection of Car Couplers," *The Railroad Gazette*, New York, May 7, 1886; "Car Couplers selected by the Massachusetts Railroad Commissioners," *National Car Builder*, R.M. Van Arsdale (New York, January 1885), pp. 151-152; and

"Decision of the New York Railroad Commission on the Car Coupler Tests," *The Railroad Gazette* (New York, July 9, 1886), p. 471.

5. "Car Couplers selected by the Massachusetts Railroad Commissioners," pp. 151-152.

6. "Automatic Freight Car Brakes," *National Car Builder*, R.M. Van Arsdale (New York, August 1884), p. 97.

7. "Freight Train Brakes in the New England Railroad Club," *The Railroad Gazette* (New York, December 23, 1887), p. 823.

8. "Automatic Freight Car Brakes," p. 97.

9. D. J. Albanese, "The History and Development of Standard Railroad Car Couplers," *Railway Mechanical Engineering, A Century of Progress; Car and Locomotive Design, American Society of Mechanical Engineers* (New York, 1979), p 357.

10. *Annual Report of the New York, Ontario & Western Railway Company to the Interstate Commerce Commission of the United States, Year Ending June 30, 1889*, New York, Ontario & Western Railway, (New York 1892, 1893), p. 65.

11. B. B. Adams, "The Every-Day Life of Railroad Men," *The American Railway*, Charles Scribner's Sons (New York, 1889), p. 393.

12. "The Adoption of a Standard Car Coupler," *The Railroad Gazette* (New York, October 3, 1884), p. 716.

13. William D. Wallace, "An Abbreviated History of Draft Gears for American Freight Cars," *Railway Mechanical Engineering, A Century of Progress; Car and Locomotive Design, American Society of Mechanical Engineers* (New York, 1979), p. 372.

14. "Freight Cars & Heavy Locomotives," *National Car Builder*, R.M. Van Arsdale (New York, April 1883), p. 47.

15. Albanese, "The History and Development of Standard Railroad Car Couplers," p 357.

16. *Report on the Operations of the New York, Ontario & Western Railway for the year ending September 30th, 1885*, New York, Ontario & Western Railway (New York, 1886), p. 16.

17. "Passenger and Freight Car Couplers," *The Railroad Gazette* (New York, October 3, 1885), p. 630.

18. John H. White, Jr., *The American Railroad Freight Car: From the Wood-Car Era to the Coming of Steel*, The Johns Hopkins Press (Baltimore, 1993), pp. 510-511.

19. "The Car Coupling Problem," *National Car Builder*, R.M. Van Arsdale (New York, January 1883), p. 11.

20. M. N. Forney, "American Locomotives and Cars," *The American Railway*, Charles Scribner's Sons (New York, 1889), p. 141.

21. Slason Thomson, *A Short History of American Railways*, D. Appleton and Company (New York, 1925), p. 236.

22. "Automatic Freight Car Couplers," p. 97.

23. "Decision of the New York Railroad Commission on the Car Coupler Tests," *The Railroad Gazette* (New York, July 9, 1886), p. 716.

24. *Report on the Operations of the New York, Ontario & Western Railway for the year ending September 30th, 1885*, New York, Ontario & Western Railway (New York, 1886), p. 16.

25. "Car Coupler Tests by the New York Railroad Commissioners," *The Railroad Gazette*, New York, May 7, 1886, p. 716.

26. "Passenger and Freight Car Couplers," *The Railroad Gazette* (New York, October 2, 1885), p. 630.

27. "Uniform Couplers for Freight Service," *The Railroad Gazette* (New York, December 9, 1887), p. 797.

28. "Proceedings of the Committee on Uniform Couplers," *The Railroad Gazette* (New York, August 5, 1887), p. 507.

29. White, *The American Railroad Freight Car*, p. 514.

30. "Diversity of Car Couplers," *Railway and Locomotive Engineering*, Angus Sinclair (New York, January 1901), p. 18.

31. Albanese, "The History and Development of Standard Railroad Car Couplers," pp. 357-359.

32. *Code of Rules (M.C.B.) Governing the Condition of, and Repairs to, Freight and Passenger Car for the Interchange of Traffic, Effective January 1, 1922*, The American Railway Association (New York, 1921), p. 16.

33. *Code of Rules Governing the Condition of, and Repairs to, Freight and Passenger Cars for the Interchange of Traffic, Effective January 1, 1950*, The American Association of Railroads (Chicago, 1949), p. 16.

34. *Code of Rules Governing the Condition of, and Repairs to, Freight and Passenger Cars for the Interchange of Traffic, Effective January 1, 1940*, Association of American Railroads (Chicago, 1939), p. 19.

35. *Code of Rules Governing the Condition of, and Repairs to, Freight and Passenger Cars for the Interchange of Traffic, Effective January 1, 1944*, The American Association of Railroads (Chicago, 1943), p. 19.

36. *Code of Rules Governing the Condition of, and Repairs to, Freight and Passenger Cars for the Interchange of Traffic, Effective January 1, 1969*, The American Association of Railroads (Chicago, 1968), p. 33.

37. H. G. Prout, "Safety in Railroad Travel," *The American Railway*, Charles Scribner's Sons (New York, 1889), p. 192.

38. White, *The American Railroad Freight Car*, p. 608.

39. *75th Anniversary of the Westinghouse Air Brake Company, Commemorating Three-Quarters of a Century of Pioneering*, The Westinghouse Air Brake Company (Wilmerding, Pennsylvania, 1944), p. 17.

40. *The Westinghouse Air-Brake Handbook*, International Textbook Company (Scranton, Pennsylvania, 1926), p. 174.

41. *75th Anniversary of the Westinghouse Air Brake Company, Commemorating Three-Quarters of a Century of Pioneering*, p. 21.

42. David G. Blaine, "Train Braking and Speed Control Systems," *Railway Mechanical Engineering, A Century of Progress; Car and Locomotive Design*, American Society of Mechanical Engineers (New York, 1979), p 23.

43. Prout, "Safety in Rail Travel," p. 201.

44. White, *The American Railroad Freight Car*, p. 543.

45. *Ibid.*, pp. 533-538.

46. *The Westinghouse Air-Brake Handbook*, International Textbook Company, p. 175.

47. White, *The American Railroad Freight Car*, p. 545.

48. Prout, "Safety in Rail Travel," p. 201.

49. "Freight Train Brakes in the New England Railroad Club," *The Railroad Gazette* (New York, December 23, 1887), p. 823.

50. Blaine, "Train Braking and Speed Control Systems," p. 23.

51. Prout, "Safety in Rail Travel," p. 202.

52. *The Westinghouse Air-Brake Handbook*, International Textbook Company, pp. 355-358.

53. *Ibid.*, p. 176.

54. White, *The American Railroad Freight Car*, p. 546.

55. *United States Safety Appliances For All Classes of Cars and Locomotives (A.A.R. Edition) Fifteenth Edition (1945)*, Association of American Railroads, Gibson, Pribble & Co. (Richmond, VA, 1945), p. 7.

56. *Ibid.*, p. 8.

57. J. W. Harding, *Freight-Car Brake Equipment, Type K Freight-Car Brake Equipment*, International Textbook Company (Scranton, Pennsylvania, 1935), p. 1.

58. Roy V. Wright, *Car Builders Cyclopedia*, Simmons-Boardman Publishing Corporation (New York, 1946), p. 982.

59. Blaine, "Train Braking and Speed Control Systems," p 23.

60. "Westinghouse Air Brake Equipment for Freight Cars," *Car Builders Cyclopedia*, Simmons-Boardman Publishing

Corporation (New York, 1946), p. 986.

61. *Code of Rules Governing the Condition of, and Repairs to, Freight and Passenger Car for the Interchange of Traffic, Effective January 1, 1952*, The Association of American Railroads (Chicago, 1951), p. 16.

62. William D. Wallace, "An Abbreviated History of Draft Gears for American Freight Cars," p. 372.

63. *Ibid.*, p. 372.

64. "To Investigate Draft Gear," *Railway and Locomotive Engineering*, Angus Sinclair (New York, January 1901), p. 17.

65. Wallace, "An Abbreviated History of Draft Gears for American Freight Cars," pp. 372-3.

66. *Code of Rules Governing the Condition of, and Repairs to, Freight and Passenger Cars for the Interchange of Traffic, Effective January 1, 1938*, American Association of Railroads (Chicago, December 1937), p. 19.

67. G. V. Williamson, "Draft Gears," *Draft Gears and Box Cars*, International Textbook Press, Scranton, Pennsylvania, 1945, p. 4.

68. C. H. Caruthers, "The Evolution of the Coal Car," *The Railroad Gazette* (New York, October 20, 1905), p. 372.

69. "O&W's Large Contract for Cars," *Orange County Times* (Middletown, New York, November 14, 1900), p. 3.

70. Mattias N. Forney, *The Car-Builder's Dictionary*, The Railroad Gazette (New York, 1888), p. E 167.

71. Francis E. Lister, *The Car Builders' Dictionary, 1909 Edition*, The Railway Age Gazette (New York, 1909), p. 137.

72. *United States Safety Appliances For All Classes of Cars and Locomotives (A.A.R. Edition) Fifteenth Edition (1945)*, p. 8.

73. *Code of Rules Governing the Condition of, and Repairs to, Freight and Passenger Cars for the Interchange of Traffic, Effective January 1, 1940*, Association of American Railroads (Chicago, 1939), p. 21.

74. "Report on Brakes and Brake Equipment," *Railway Age* (New York, June 19, 1924), p. 1729.

75. *Code of Rules...Effective January 1, 1940*, p. 19.

76. *Ibid.*, pp. 19-20.

## Chapter 5

1. M. N. Forney, "American Locomotives and Cars," *The American Railway*, Charles Scribner's Sons (New York, 1889), p. 108.

2. Carl E. Tack and Robert B. Love, "History of the Railway Freight Car Truck in the United States," *Railway Mechanical Engineering, A Century of Progress, Car and Locomotive Design*, The American Society of Mechanical Engineers (New York, 1979), p. 338.

3. William Voss, *Railway Car Construction*, R. M. Van Arsdale (New York, 1892), p. 75.

4. John Zupez, "Technological History of Plain Journal Bearing Development," *Railway Mechanical Engineering, A Century of Progress, Car and Locomotive Design*, The American Society of Mechanical Engineers (New York, 1979), pp. 307-309.

5. *Ibid.*, p. 309.

6. *Code of Rules Governing the Condition of, and Repairs to, Freight and Passenger Cars for the Interchange of Traffic as revised and adopted by the Master Car Builders' Association at Atlantic City, N.J.*, Master Car Builders' Association (Chicago, 1914), p. 6; (Chicago, 1916), pp. iv & 12.

7. *Code of Rules Governing the Condition of, and Repairs to, Freight and Passenger Cars for the Interchange of Traffic adopted by the Master Car Builders' Association revised at Atlantic City, N.J., June, 1912*, Master Car Builders' Association (Chicago, 1912) p. 51.

8. Marshall M. Kirkman, *Supervision of Cars, Supplement to The Science of Railways*, The World Railway Publishing Company (New York and Chicago, 1904), p. 24.

9. *Code of Rules Governing the Condition of, and Repairs to, Freight Cars for the Interchange of Traffic revised at Saratoga, N. Y., June, 1900*, Master Car Builders' Association (Chicago, 1900), p. 12.

10. Roy V. Wright, *Car Builders' Cyclopedia of American Practice, Tenth Edition—1922*, Simmons-Boardman Publishing Company (New York, 1922), p. 601.

11. Tack and Love, "History of the Railway Freight Car Truck in the United States," p. 341.

12. "The Passing of the Wooden Freight Car," *American Engineer, Car Builder and Railroad Journal*, R. M. Van Arsdale (New York, December 1897), p. 419.

13. D. C. Royce, "Arch-Bar Trucks," *Car Trucks*, International Textbook Company (Scranton, Pennsylvania, 1930), p. 7.

14. John H. White, *The American Railroad Freight Car, From the Wood-Car Era to the Coming of Steel*, The Johns Hopkins University Press (Baltimore, 1993), pp. 469-471.

15. *Twentieth Annual Report for the Year Ending 1899*, New York, Ontario & Western Railway (New York, 1900), p. 19.

16. White, *The American Railroad Freight Car*, pp. 471-473.

17. O. H. Reynolds, "The Joughins Steel Truck," *Locomotive Engineering* (New York, March 1898), p. 145.

18. *Twenty-Seventh Annual Report for the Year Ending 1906*, New York, Ontario & Western Railway (New York, 1907), p. 18.

19. *Code of Rules Governing the Condition of. and Repairs to, Freight and Passenger Cars for the Interchange of Traffic, Effective January 1, 1956*, Association of American Railroads (Chicago, 1956), p. 26.

20. Tack and Love, "History of the Railway Freight Car Truck in the United States," p. 352.

21. *Ibid.*, p. 352.

22. *Code of Rules (M.C.B.) Governing the Condition of, and Repairs to, Freight and Passenger Cars for the Interchange of Traffic, Effective January 1, 1929*, The American Railway Association (New York, 1928), p. 17.

23. *Code of Rules (M.C.B.) Governing the Condition of, and Repairs to, Freight and Passenger Cars for the Interchange of Traffic, Effective January 1, 1932*, The American Railway Association (New York, 1931), p. 19.

24. *Code of Rules Governing the Condition of, and Repairs to, Freight and Passenger Cars for the Interchange of Traffic, Effective January 1, 1940*, Association of American Railroads (Chicago, 1939), p. 22.

25. *Code of Rules Governing the Condition of, and Repairs to, Freight and Passenger Cars for the Interchange of Traffic, Effective January 1, 1938*, Association of American Railroads (Chicago, 1937), p. 20.

26. *Code of Rules Governing the Condition of, and Repairs to, Freight and Passenger Cars for the Interchange of Traffic, Effective January 1, 1947*, Association of American Railroads (Chicago, 1946), p. 24.

27. *Code of Rules...Effective January 1, 1956*, p. 26.

28. *Code of Rules Governing the Condition of, and Repairs to, Freight and Passenger Cars for the Interchange of Traffic, Effective January 1, 1950*, Association of American Railroads (Chicago, 1949), p. 27.

29. G. V. Williamson, *Freight-Car Trucks, Part I*, International Textbook Press (Scranton, Pennsylvania), p. 37.

30. Roy V. Wright, *Car Builders' Cyclopedia of American Practice*, Simmons-Boardman Publishing Company, (New York, 1931), p. 777.

31. Harry M. Jones, "Railroad Roller Bearing Development," *Railway Mechanical Engineering, A Century of Progress, Car and*

*Locomotive Design*, The American Society of Mechanical Engineers (New York, 1979), p. 317.

32. Zupez, "Technological History of Plain Journal Bearing Development," p. 310.

33. *Ibid.*, p. 310.

34. *Ibid.*, p. 311.

35. *The Use of Roller Bearings on Freight Cars*, The Timken Roller Bearing Company (Canton, Ohio), 1956, p. 1.

36. Jones, "Railroad Roller Bearing Development," p. 320.


## Chapter 6

1. Rodney Hitt, *The Car Builders' Dictionary, 1906 Edition*, The Railway Gazette (New York, 1906), p. 141.

2. *Ibid.*, p. 141.

3. *Ibid.*, p. 142.

4. *American Engineer, Car Builder and Railroad Journal*, R. M. Van Arsdale (New York, August 1898), p. 272.

5. Marshall M. Kirkman, *Cars Their Construction, Handling and Supervision, The Science of Railways*, The World Railway Publishing Company (New York and Chicago, 1906), p. 266.

6. *Report of the Proceedings of the Master Car Builders' Association held at Manhattan Beach, N.Y., June 19, 20 and 21, 1905*, The Henry O. Shepard Company (Chicago, 1905), p. 225.

7. *Ibid.*, p. 226.

8. Roy V. Wright, *Car Builders' Dictionary, 1916 (Eighth) Edition*, Simmons-Boardman Publishing Company (New York, 1916), p. 114.

9. *Report of the Proceedings of the Master Car Builders' Association held at Manhattan Beach, N.Y., June 19, 20 and 21, 1905*, p. 225-6.

10. "Standard Marking of Freight Equipment Cars, *American Engineer and Railroad Journal*, R. M. Van Arsdale, New York (August 1908), p. 326.

11. Roy V. Wright, *Car Builders' Dictionary and Cyclopedia, Ninth Edition, 1919*, Simmons-Boardman Publishing Company (New York, 1919), p. 131-132.

12. H. S. Brautigam, *United States Safety Appliances*, Simmons-Boardman Publishing Company (New York, 1924), p. 30-31.

13. *Code of Rules Governing the Condition of, and Repairs to, Freight Cars for the Interchange of Traffic, Master Car Builders' Association revised at Atlantic City, N.J., June 1914*, (Chicago, 1914), p. 6.

14. Marshall M. Kirkman, *Cars, Their Construction and Handling: Kirkman's Science of Railways*, Cropley Phillips Company (Chicago, 1921), p. 596.

15. Wright, *Car Builders' Dictionary and Cyclopedia, Ninth Edition 1919*, p. 96.

16. *Code of Rules (M.C.B.) Governing the Condition of, and Repairs to, Freight and Passenger Cars for the Interchange of Traffic Effective January 1, 1926*, American Railway Association (New York, 1925), p. 68.

17. *Code of Rules (M.C.B.) Governing the Condition of, and Repairs to, Freight and Passenger Cars for the Interchange of Traffic Effective January 1, 1934*, American Railway Association (New York, 1933), p. 18.

18. *Code of Rules (M.C.B.) Governing the Condition of, and Repairs to, Freight and Passenger Cars for the Interchange of Traffic effective January 1, 1924*, American Railway Association (New York, 1923), p. 16.

19. *Code of Rules...Effective January 1, 1934*, p. 18.

20. *Code of Rules Governing the Condition of, and Repairs to, Freight and Passenger Cars for the Interchange of Traffic*, Association of American Railroads (Chicago, 1968), p. 150.

21. *Kirkman, Cars Their Construction, Handling and Supervision, The Science of Railways*, 1906, p. 266.

22. *Code of Rules Governing the Condition of, and Repairs to, Freight Cars for the Interchange of Traffic revised at Atlantic City, N.J., June 1912*, Master Car Builders' Association (Chicago, 1912), pp. 27-28.

23. *Code of Rules Governing the Condition of, and Repairs to, Freight Cars for the Interchange of Traffic Effective October 1, 1916*, Master Car Builders' Association (Chicago, 1915), p. 54.

24. *Code of Rules Governing the Condition of, and Repairs to, Freight Cars for the Interchange of Traffic, American Railway Association Effective January 1, 1929* (New York, 1928), p. 65-67.

25. *Code of Rules Governing the Condition of, and Repairs to, Freight Cars for the Interchange of Traffic, American Railway Association Effective January 1, 1935* (Chicago, 1934), p. 83.

26. *Code of Rules Governing the Condition of, and Repairs to, Freight Cars for the Interchange of Traffic, American Railway Association Effective January 1, 1932* (New York, 1932), p. 69.

27. *Code of Rules Governing the Condition of, and Repairs to, Freight Cars for the Interchange of Traffic, American Association of Railroads, Effective January 1, 1950* (Chicago, 1949), p. 112.

28. *Code of Rules...Effective January 1, 1924*, American Railway Association, p. 76.

29. *Code of Rules...Effective January 1, 1929*, American Railway Association, p. 85.

30. *Code of Rules...Effective January 1, 1934*, American Railway Association, p. 99.

31. *Code of Rules Governing the Condition of, and Repairs to, Freight and Passenger Cars for the Interchange of Traffic Effective January 1, 1956*, Association of American Railroads (Chicago, 1955), p. 152.


## Chapter 7

1. The Delaware and Hudson Company, *History of the Delaware and Hudson Company*, J. B. Lyon Company (Albany, 1925), p. 265.

2. William F. Helmer, *O&W: The Long Life and Slow Death of the New York, Ontario & Western Ry.*, Howell-North (Berkeley, California, 1959), p. 27.

3. "Jottings," *Middletown Daily Press* (Middletown, New York, August 18,1881), p. 3.

4. *Fifth Annual Report of the President of the New York, Ontario and Western Railway Co. to the Stockholders for the Fiscal Year ending September 30th, 1884* (Cambridge, Massachusetts, 1885), p. 16.

5. *Seventh Annual Report of the President and Officers of the New York, Ontario and Western Railway Company with Statements of Account for the Fiscal Year ending 30th September 1886* (New York, 1887), p. 19.

6. *Ninth Annual Report of the President and Officers of the New York, Ontario and Western Railway Company with Statements of Account for the Fiscal Year ending 30th September 1888* (New York, 1889), p. 33.

7. *Eleventh Annual Report of the President and Officers of the New York, Ontario & Western Railway Company with Statement of Accounts for the Fiscal Year ending June 30th, 1890* (New York, 1890), p. 22.

8. *Minutes of the Board of Directors of the New York, Ontario & Western Railway*, 26 February 1891.

9. "Railroad Notes," *The Middletown Daily Press* (Middletown, New York, December 12, 1889), p. 2.

10. *Minutes of the Board of Directors of the New York, Ontario & Western Railway*, 26 February 1890.

11. "Railroad Notes," *The Middletown Daily Press* (Middletown, New York, July 9, 1890), p. 3.

12. *Minutes of the Board of Directors*, 22 October 1890.

13. *Minutes of the Board of Directors*, 20 December 1893.

14. *Minutes of the Board of Directors*, 25 March 1891.

15. *Fifteenth Annual Report of the President and Officers of the New York, Ontario & Western Railway Company with Statement of Accounts for the Fiscal Year ending June 30th, 1894* (New York, 1894), p. 10.

16. *Minutes of the Board of Directors*, 6 November 1895.

17. *Twentieth Annual Report of the President and Officers of the New York, Ontario & Western Railway Company with Statement of Accounts for the Fiscal Year ending June 30th, 1899* (New York, 1899), p. 18.

18. *Fifteenth Annual Report*, p. 24.

19. *Annual Report to the Interstate Commerce Commission*, New York, Ontario & Western Railway (New York, 1904), p. 64.

20. *Annual Report to the Interstate Commerce Commission*, New York, Ontario & Western Railway (New York, 1913), p. 65.

21. *Twentieth Annual Report*, p. 18.

22. *Capital Expenditure Accounts*, New York, Ontario & Western Railway, year ending 1901.

23. *Capital Expenditure Accounts*, year ending 1902.

24. Richard H. Hendrickson, "Arch Bars to Roller Bearings; Freight Car Trucks 1900-1960," *Railroad Prototype Cyclopedia; RPC 4* (Chesterfield, Missouri, 2000), p. 36.

25. *Authorization for Expenditure AFE 047EQ*, New York, Ontario & Western Railway, August 1916.

26. *Capital Expenditure Accounts, 1909.*

27. *Capital Expenditure Accounts*, years ending 1910-1913.

28. *Engineering Report upon the New York, Ontario & Western Railway Company Showing Cost of Reproduction New and Cost of Reproduction Less Depreciation*, Interstate Commerce Commission Bureau of Valuation, 1916, pp. 179-183.

29. John Nehrich, "Seley Hoppers, Beyond the D&H," *The Mainline Modeler* (Mukilteo, Washington, March 1988), p.73.

30. *Minutes of the Board of Directors*, 23 October 1917.

31. *Internal Memorandum Regarding Valuation of O&W Coal Cars*, New York, Ontario & Western Railway (1917).

32. *Minutes of the Board of Directors*, 25 January 1916.

33. *Capital Expenditure Accounts*, year ending June 1909.

34. J. E. Childs, Letter to R.D. Rickard, American Car and Foundry Company, February 17, 1912.

35. *Minutes of the Board of Directors*, 21 November 1912.

36. *Minutes of the Board of Directors*, 14 December 1915.

37. *Minutes of the Board of Directors*, 25 January 1916.

38. *Internal Memorandum regarding valuation of O&W Coal Cars* (1917).

39. *Code of Rules Governing the Condition of, and Repairs to, Freight and Passenger Cars for the Interchange of Traffic*, American Railway Association (Chicago, Illinois, 1928), p. 19.

40. *Authorization for Expenditure AFE 576Q*, December 21, 1926.

41. *Authorization for Expenditure AFE 643Q*, January 18, 1928.

42. *Authorization for Expenditure AFE 702Q*, December 10, 1928.

43. "New York, Ontario & Western Railway Company," *Moody's Manual of Investments*, Moody's Investor Services (New York, 1933), p. 1514.

44. *Minutes of the Board of Directors*, 27 September 1932.

45. *Authorization for Expenditure AFE 877EQ*, January 7, 1933.

46. *Minutes of the Board of Directors*, 28 February 1933.

47. *Authorization for Expenditure AFE 886EQ*, April 10, 1933.

48. *Authorization for Expenditure AFE 886EQ*, April 10, 1933.

49. *Internal Memo*, New York, Ontario & Western Railway, dated April 13, 1937.

50. "In Proceedings for the Reorganization of a Railroad, No. 68,276, Trustee's Petition for Authority to Expend Not to Exceed $40,000 to Enlarge the Capacity of Certain Cars of the Debtor," *Petition for Order No. 132 in the District Court of the United States for the Southern District of New York in the Matter of New York, Ontario and Western Railway Company, Debtor*, Dated April 10, 1939.

51. "In Proceedings for the Reorganization of a Railroad, No. 68276, Order Authorizing Trustee to Expend Not to Exceed $40,000 to Enlarge the Capacity of Certain Cars of the Debtor," *Order No. 132 in the District Court of the United States for the Southern District of New York in the Matter of New York, Ontario and Western Railway Company, Debtor*, Dated May 1, 1939.

52. "In Proceedings for the Reorganization of a Railroad, No. 68276, Trustee's Petition for Leave to Install Power Hand Brakes and Brake Regulators on 500 Coal Cars," *Petition for Order No. 153 in the District Court of the United States for the Southern District of New York in the Matter of New York, Ontario and Western Railway Company, Debtor*, Dated July 21, 1939.

53. "In Proceedings for the Reorganization of a Railroad, No. 68276, Order Authorizing Trustee to Expend Not to Exceed $17,500 to Apply Power Hand Brakes and Brake Regulators on 500 Coal Cars," *Order No. 153 in the District Court of the United States for the Southern District of New York in the Matter of New York, Ontario and Western Railway Company, Debtor*, Dated August 3, 1939.

54. "In Proceedings for the Reorganization of a Railroad, No. 68276, Trustee's Petition in re: Purchase of Fifteen Steel Hopper Cars," *Petition for Order No. 963 in the District Court of the United States for the Southern District of New York in the Matter of New York, Ontario and Western Railway Company, Debtor*, Dated April 9, 1953; and "In Proceedings for the Reorganization of a Railroad, No. 68276, Trustee's Petition in re Purchase of Six Steel Hopper Cars," *Petition for Order No. 963-A in the District Court of the United States for the Southern District of New York in the Matter of New York, Ontario and Western Railway Company, Debtor*, Dated June 12, 1953.

55. "In Proceedings for the Reorganization of a Railroad, No. 68276, Order re: Purchase of Fifteen Steel Hopper Cars," *Order No. 963 in the District Court of the United States for the Southern District of New York in the Matter of New York, Ontario and Western Railway Company, Debtor*, Dated April 29, 1953; and "In Proceedings for the Reorganization of a Railroad, No. 68276, Order re Purchase of Six Steel Hopper Cars," *Order No. 963-A in the District Court of the United States for the Southern District of New York in the Matter of New York, Ontario and Western Railway Company, Debtor*, Dated June 29, 1953.

56. *Code of Rules Governing the Condition of, and Repairs to, Freight and Passenger Cars for the Interchange of Traffic (M.C.B.) in Effect January 1, 1922*, American Railway Association (Chicago, Illinois, 1921), p. 93.

57. *Anthracite Mining Manual*, Wilmot Engineering Company (Hazleton, Pennsylvania, 1950), p. 61.

## Appendix D

1. *United States Safety Appliances For All Classes of Cars and Locomotives (A.A.R. Edition) Fifteenth Edition (1945)*, Association of American Railroads, Gibson, Pribble & Co., Richmond, VA, 1945, pp. 12-41

2. "Report on Brakes and Brake Equipment," Railway Age, New York, June 19, 1924, p. 1729.

3. *Code of Rules Governing the Condition of, and Repairs to, Freight and Passenger Cars for the Interchange of Traffic, Effective January 1, 1940*, Association of American Railroads, New York, 1937, p. 19.

4. *Ibid.*, p. 19-20.

5. *Ibid.*, p. 21.

*5th Anniversary of the Westinghouse Air Brake Company*, The Westinghouse Air Brake Company, Wilmerding, Pennsylvania, 1944.

Abbot, Lyman, "The American Railroad," *Harper's New Monthly Magazine*, Harper & Brothers Publishers, New York, August 1874, p. 375-394.

*The "AB" Freight Brake Equipment*, Westinghouse Air Brake Company, Wilmerding, PA, 1945.

*American Engineer and Railroad Journal*, R. M. Van Arsdale, New York, (Monthly), 1899-1910.

*American Engineer, Car Builder and Railroad Journal*, R. M. Van Arsdale, New York, (Monthly), 1897-1898

*American Railroad Journal*, American Railroad Journal Co., New York, (Monthly) 1879-1883

*Annual Report to the Interstate Commerce Commission*, New York, Ontario & Western Railway, New York, 1889-1955.

"Anthracite Coal Statistical Summaries 1870 to 2000," *Annual Report on Mining Activities*, Commonwealth of Pennsylvania, 2000.

*Anthracite Mining Manual*, Wilmot Engineering Co., Hazleton, Pennsylvania, 1950.

*Appletons' Railway and Steam Navigation Guide*, D. Appleton & Co., New York, July, 1864 - July 1871.

*ASME Rail Transportation Division, Railway Mechanical Engineering, A Century of Progress, Car and Locomotive Design*, The American Society of Mechanical Engineers, New York, 1979.

Baer, Christopher, *Canals and Railroads of the Mid-Atlantic States, 1800-1860*, Regional Economic History Research Center, Wilmington, Delaware, 1981.

Bogen, Jules I., *The Anthracite Railroads: A Study in American Railroad Enterprise*, The Ronald Press Company, New York, 1927.

Brown, William H., *The History of the First Locomotives in America*, D. Appleton and Company, 1874, reprinted by The Astragal Press, Mendham, New Jersey, 2003.

Burg, Richard, "Pennsy GLa Hoppers," *Railmodel Journal*, February 2002, pp. 20-30.

Bux, Joe and Crist, Ed, *New York, Ontario & Western Railway, Scranton Division*, The New York, Ontario & Western Railway Historical Society, Middletown, New York, 1984.

Clouse, Shirley, *Steel-Car Repairs (Parts 1 & 2)*, International Textbook Press, Scranton, Pennsylvania, 1948.

*Coal Washing*, International Textbook Press, Scranton, Pennsylvania, 1906.

*Code of Rules Governing the Condition of, and Repairs to, Freight Cars for the Interchange of Traffic, Master Car Builders Association*, Chicago, Illinois, 1900-1918; American Railway Association, Chicago, Illinois, 1921-1934; Association of American Railroads, Chicago, Illinois, 1935-1969.

Cooley, Thomas M., *The American Railway: Its Construction, Development, Management, and Appliances*, Charles Scribner's Sons, New York, New York, 1889.

Corliss, Carlton J., *Development of Railroad Transportation in the United States*, Association of American Railroads, Washington, D.C., 1945.

Diver, DeForest Douglas Collection Railroad Photographs, Division of Rare and Manuscript Collections, Cornell University Library, Cornell, NY.

*Engineering Report upon the New York, Ontario & Western Railway Company showing Cost of Production New and Cost of Reproduction Less Depreciation*, Interstate Commerce Commission Bureau of Valuation, 1916, 1929.

Faricy, William T., *"A.A.R.," The Story Behind A Symbol*, The Newcomen Society in North America, New York, 1951.

Forney, Matthias H., *The Car-Builder's Dictionary*, The Railroad Gazette, New York, 1879, 1884, 1888.

Helmer, William F., *O. & W.: The Long Life and Slow Death of the New York, Ontario & Western Ry.*, Howell-North, Berkeley, California, 1959.

Griffith, William, "Anthracite Coal," *The Bond Record*, The Bond Record Publishing Company, New York, New York, February, March, May, June 1896.

*History of The Delaware and Hudson Company 1823-1923*, The Delaware and Hudson Company, Albany, New York, 1925.

Hale, Sydney, *1937 Keystone Coal Buyers Manual including Directory of Mines*, McGraw-Hill Publishing Co, Inc, New York, New York, 1937

Harding, J. W., *Freight Car Brake Equipment, The "AB" Freight Brake Equipment, Type K Freight-Car Brake Equipment*, International Textbook Press, Scranton, Pennsylvania, 1946, 1935.

"Haulage," International Library of Technology, International Textbook Company, Scranton, Pennsylvania, 1906.

Hendrickson, Richard H., "Arch Bars to Roller Bearings, Freight Car Trucks 1900-1960," *Railway Prototype Cyclopedia*, RP CYC Publishing Co, Chesterfield, MO, 2000, pp. 35-51.

Hitt, Rodney, *The Car Builders' Dictionary*, The Railroad Gazette, New York, 1903, 1906, 1909.

Holbrook, Stewart H., *The Story of American Railroads*, Crown Publishers, New York, 1947.

The Hudson Coal Company, *The Story of Anthracite*, International Textbook Press, Scranton, Pennsylvania, 1932.

Jensen, Oliver, *American Heritage History of Railroads in America*, American Heritage Wings Books, New York, New York, 1993.

Johnson, Emory R., *American Railway Transportation*, D. Appleton and Company, New York, 1903.

Kaminski, Edward S., *American Car & Foundry*, A Centennial History 1899-1999, Signature Press, Wilton, California, 1999.

Kennedy, William Sloan, *Wonders and Curiosities of the Railway*, S. C. Griggs and Company, Chicago, Illinois, 1884.

Kirkman, Marshall M., *Kirkman's Science of Railways*, Cropley Phillips Company, Chicago, Illinois, 1921.

Kirkman, Marshall M., *Cars, Their Construction, Handling and Supervision: The Science of Railways*, The World Railway Publishing Company, New York, New York and Chicago, Illinois, 1906.

Kirkman, Marshall M., *The Science of Railways*, The World Railway Publishing Company, New York, New York and Chicago, Illinois, 1902.

Kirkman, Marshall M., *Supervision of Cars—The Science of Railways*, The World Railway Publishing Company, New York, New York and Chicago, Illinois, 1904.

Kolko, Gabriel, *Railroads and Regulation 1877-1916*, W. W. Norton & Company, Inc., New York, New York, 1965.

Krause, John & Crist, Ed, *The Final Years, New York, Ontario & Western Ry*, Carstens Publications, Inc., Fredon, New Jersey, 1977.

Lane, James E., "USRA Freight Cars: An Experiment in Standardization," *Railroad History No. 128*, The Railway and Locomotive Historical Society, Boston, Massachussetts, Spring 1973.

Lewis, Robert G., *Handbook of American Railroads*, Simmons-Boardman Publishing Corporation, New York, New York, 1951.

Lewis, Robert G., *Railway Age's Comprehensive Railroad Dictionary*, Simmons-Boardman Books, Inc., Omaha, Nebraska, 1984.

*Locomotive Engineering, A Practical Journal of Railway Motive Power and Rolling Stock*, Locomotive Engineering, New York, New York, (Monthly) 1888-1892.

*Locomotive Engineering, A Practical Journal of Railway Motive Power and Rolling Stock*, Angus Sinclair, New York, New York, (Monthly) 1893-1900.

Marder, Stephen A., *From Scranton to Cadosia along the N.Y.O. & W. Ry. Co.*, New Visions Digital Publishing, Old Forge, Pennsylvania, 1998.

*Marine Line Equipment*, The Ontario & Western Railway Historical Society, Middletown, NY, 1992.

*Mayfield Yard*, The Ontario & Western Railway Historical Society, Middletown, New York, 1990.

*Mining and Preparation of Anthracite*, The Hudson Coal Company, Scranton, Pennsylvania, 1931.

*Manual of Statistical Information The Pennsylvania Anthracite Industry*, Anthracite Institute, Wilkes-Barre, Pennsylvania., January 1953.

*Middletown, Home of the O&W and the O&WRHS*, The Ontario & Western Railway Historical Society, Inc., Middletown, New York, 1991.

*Minutes of the Board of Directors*, The New York, Ontario & Western Railway, New York, 1880-1941.

Mohowski, Robert E., *The New York, Ontario & Western Railway and the Dairy Industry in Central New York State: Milk Cans, Mixed Trains and Motor Cars*, Garrigues House Publishers, Laurys Station, Pennsylvania, 1995.

Mohowski, Robert E., *The New York, Susquehanna & Western Railroad*, The Johns Hopkins University Press, Baltimore, Maryland, 2003.

Mohowski, Robert E., *New York, Ontario & Western in the Diesel Age*, Andover Junction Publications, Andover, New Jersey, 1994.

Moody, John, *Moody's Analyses of Investments, Steam Railroads*, Moody's Investment Service, New York, New York, 1920.

Moody, John, *Moody's Manual of Investments, Railroad Securities [Steam Railroads]*, Moody's Investment Service, New York, New York, 1926-1951.

*Moody's Transportation Manual*, Moody's Investment Service, New York, New York, 1954-1958.

Mundy, Floyd W., *Mundy's Earning Power of Railroads*, Jas. H. Oliphant & Co., New York, New York, 1926, 1936.

Mundy, Floyd W., Editor, *Oliphant's Earning Power of Railroads*, Jas. H. Oliphant & Co., New York, New York, 1945.

*The National Car Builder*, R. M. VanArsdale, New York, New York, (Monthly), 1882-1895.

Nehrich, John, "Seley Hoppers Beyond the D&H," *Mainline Modeler*, March 1988, pp. 72-76.

Newcomb, H.T., "The Anthracite-Carrying Railways," *The American Monthly Review of Reviews*, New York, New York, July 1902, pp. 66-69.

*The Official Railway Equipment Register*, New York, New York, 1888-1957.

Patton, Norman F., "The Economics of the Distribution of Anthracite," The American Institute of Mining and Metallurgical Engineers, Inc, New York, New York, 1935

Peck, C. B., *Car Builders' Cyclopedia of American Practice*, Simmons-Boardman Publishing Company, New York, New York, 1953.

Petrillo, F. Charles, *Anthracite and Slackwater: The North Branch Canal 1828-1901*, Center for Canal History and Technology, Easton, Pennsylvania, 1986.

*Poor's Manual of the Railroads of the United States*, Poors Railroad Manual Company, New York, New York, 1889-1924.

Pratt, George William, "History of the New York, Ontario and Western Railroad," excerpts edited by Thomas B. Girard and Archibald E. Vail, *Fifth Annual Year Book*, The Historical Society of Middletown and the Wallkill Precinct, Inc., Middletown, New York, 1957.

*Pullman Standard Car Manufacturing Company of Butler, PA Records*, Pennsylvania State Archives, Harrisburg, Pennsylvania.

*Preparation of Anthracite*, International Textbook Press, Scranton, Pennsylvania, 1906.

*The Quick Action Automatic Brake, Instruction Book*, The Westinghouse Air Brake Company, Pittsburgh, Pennsylvania, 1897.

*Railroad and Engineering Journal*, M. N. Forney, New York, New York, (Monthly), 1887-1888

*Railway Age*, Simmons-Boardman Publishing Company, New York, New York, (Weekly), 1923-1928.

*Railway and Locomotive Engineering*, Angus Sinclair, New York, New York, (Monthly), 1901-1913.

*Railroad Car Journal*, Car Journal Publishing Company, New York, New York, (Monthly) 1898-1899.

*Railroad Digest*, Car Journal Publishing Company, New York, New York, (Monthly), 1901-1902

*Report to the President on the Anthracite Coal Strike of May-October, 1902*, by the Anthracite Coal Commission, Government Printing Office, Washington, D.C., 1902.

Rhone, Rosamond D., "Anthracite Coal Mines and Mining," *The American Monthly Review of Reviews*, New York, New York, July 1902, pp. 54-63.

Ringwalt, J. L., *Development of Transportation Systems in the United States*, Published by the Author, Railway World Office, Philadelphia, Pennsylvania, 1888.

Roberts, Peter, *The Anthracite Coal Industry*, The Macmillan Company, New York, New York, 1901.

Royce, D. C., *Car Trucks, Arch-Bar Trucks Parts 1-2, Modern Car Trucks*, International Textbook Press, Scranton, Pennsylvania, 1921; 1930.

Royce, D. C., *Draft Gears Parts 1-2*, International Textbook Press, Scranton, Pennsylvania, 1922, 1930.

Royce, D.C., *Steel Gondola and Hopper Cars (Parts 1 &2)*, International Textbook Press, Scranton, Pennsylvania, 1946.

Ruth, Philip, *Of Pulleys and Ropes and Gear: The Gravity Railroads of The Delaware and Hudson Canal Company and The Pennsylvania Coal Company*, The Wayne County Historical Society, Honesdale, PA, 1997.

Saylor, Roger B., *The Railroads of Pennsylvania*, Bureau of Business Research, College of Business Administration, The Pennsylvania State University, State College, Pennsylvania, 1964.

Smallshaw, Earl, "The Sterlingworth Steel Hopper Car," *Model Railroader*, Waukesha, Wisconson, January 1978, pp. 71-79.

Summers, A. Leonard, *All About Anthracite: The World's Premier Coal*, The Technical Publishing Company, London, England, 1914.

*Surface Arrangements at Anthracite Mines*, International Textbook Press, Scranton, Pennsylvania,1906.

Teichmoeller, John, *Pennsylvania Railroad Steel Open Hopper Cars*, Highland Station, Inc., Aurora, Colorado, 2000.

Thompson, Slason, *A Short History of American Railways*, D. Appleton and Company, New York, New York, 1925.

*Travelers' Official Guide of the Railway and Steam Navigation Lines in the United States and Canada*, National Railway Publication Company, Philadelphia, Pennsylvania, June 1879.

*The Use of Roller Bearings on Freight Cars*, The Timken Roller Bearing Company, Canton, Ohio, 1956.

Voss, William, *Railway Car Construction*, R. M. Van Arsdale, New York, New York, 1892.

Wait, John C., *The Car-Builder's Dictionary*, The Railroad Gazette, New York, New York, 1895.

Wakefield, Manville B., *Coal Boats to Tidewater, The Story of the Delaware & Hudson Canal*, Wakefair Press, Grahamsville, New York, 1981.

Wakefield, Manville B., *To The Mountains by Rail*, Wakefair Press, Grahamsville, New York, 1970.

*The Westinghouse Air-Brake Handbook*, International Textbook Press, Scranton, Pennsylvania., 1926.

*The Westinghouse Air Brake Instruction Book*, The Westinghouse Air Brake Co., Pittsburgh, Pennsylvania., 1901.

*Westinghouse Quick-Action Automatic Brake Equipment, Instruction Pamphlet No. 5038*, Westinghouse Air Brake Co., Pittsburgh, Pennsylvania, 1922.

Westwood, John, *World Railways, An Illustrated History of the Iron Horse*, Gramercy Books, New York, New York, 2001.

White, John H., Jr., , *A History of the American Locomotive, Its Development: 1830-1880*, Dover Publications, Inc., New York, New York, 1968.

White, John H., *The American Railroad Freight Car, From the Wood-Car Era to the Coming of Steel*, The Johns Hopkins University Press, Baltimore, Maryland, 1993.

Williamson, G. V., *Draft Gears and Box Cars*, International Textbook Press, Scranton, Pennsylvania., 1945.

Williamson, G. V., *Freight-Car Trucks*, International Textbook Press, Scranton, Pennsylvania, 1944.

Wright, Roy V., *Car Builders' Dictionary*, Simmons-Boardman Publishing Company, New York, New York, 1912, 1916

Wright, Roy V., *Car Builders' Dictionary and Cyclopedia*, Simmons-Boardman Publishing Company, New York, New York, 1919, 1922, 1925, 1928, 1931, 1940, 1946.

Yungkurth, Chuck, "Hard Coal, A Study of the Anthracite Industry," *Railroad Model Craftsman*, Carstens Publications, Inc., Newton, New Jersey, March - June 1982.

Three generations of coal cars are seen in this photo taken at Norwich in September 1915. In the foreground, the corner of a wood hopper-bottom gondola from the 6600 series can be seen, providing a good view of the pressed-steel side posts used in that car's construction. On the coal trestle, one of the O&W's composite wood and steel hoppers is being unloaded. Car number 16266 was built by American Car & Foundry in 1911. Behind it, an all-steel hopper from the Pittsburgh & Shawmut Railroad is dropping its load of Shawmut bituminous coal. Locomotive #105 is an M-Class Mogul purchased from New York in 1899 to accommodate the railroad's increasing passenger traffic. Here it is seen relegated to switching duties. It is noteworthy that the flanges have been removed from the center set of drivers, perhaps to accommodate the sharp radii encountered as part of its new duties. It will be scrapped in January 1929. *[Courtesy: Bob's Photo]*

---

*Page numbers in italics indicate a picture or illustration.*

**Index**

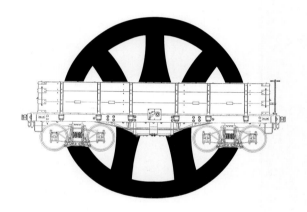

Hard Coal and Coal Cars